Dinner Talk

*Cultural Patterns of Sociability
and Socialization in Family Discourse*

Dinner Talk
Cultural Patterns of Sociability and Socialization in Family Discourse

Shoshana Blum-Kulka
Hebrew University of Jerusalem

LEA LAWRENCE ERLBAUM ASSOCIATES, PUBLISHERS
1997 Mahwah, New Jersey   London

Lawrence Erlbaum Associates, Inc., Publishers
10 Industrial Avenue
Mahwah, New Jersey 07430

Cover design by Ilan Kulka

Library of Congress Cataloging-in-Publication Data

Blum-Kulka, Shoshana.
Dinner talk : Cultural patterns of sociability and socialization in family discourse / Shoshana Blum-Kulka.
p.   cm.
Includes bibliographical references and indexes.
ISBN 0-8058-1775-1 (alk. paper). — ISBN 0-8058-1776-X (pbk. : alk. paper).
1. Discourse analysis. 2. Communication in the family.
3. Socialization. 4. Dinners and dining. 5. Israelis—United States—Language. 6. Communication and culture. I. Title.
P302.B57 1997
306.87—dc21   96-46362
                                                                                                    CIP

Books published by Lawrence Erlbaum Associates are printed on acid-free paper, and their bindings are chosen for strength and durability.

Printed in the United States of America
10 9 8 7 6 5 4 3 2 1

Dedicated to my family—
Dick, Michal, Jonny, and Ilan Kulka,
Rachel and Egon Erdodi

and to the memory of my father

CONTENTS

PREFACE

This book grew out of a cross-cultural Israeli American project on family discourse, carried out in two stages between 1985 to 1988 and 1989 to 1992. The project was funded by two grants from the Israeli-American Binational Science Foundation, and involved many people from both Israel and the United States. Telling the story of the project allows me to thank my collaborators, other members of the research team, friends and colleagues with whom I shared ideas about family discourse and who read earlier parts of the manuscript, as well as the families studied.

My initial interest in family discourse developed from work in cross-cultural pragmatics; I wanted to compare Jewish American and Israeli interactional styles as manifest in a natural setting, through talk at dinner. The first problem in setting up the project was to select the families to be studied in Israel and the United States in a way that would ensure maximum compatibility. The process of selection was coordinated with David Gordon and Susan Ervin-Tripp, the U.S. collaborators in the first stage of the project. David and Susan then went on to supervise observation of the four Jewish American families recruited in Berkeley. With the help of Catherine Snow, who became a consultant to the project, we recruited another eight Jewish American families from Boston, subsequently observed and taped by Yael Zupnik and Susan Kline.

At the first stage of the project, the main focus of the investigation was on adult speech. Continuing my previous work on directives, I was particularly interested in issues of politeness and power in dinner talk. This interest coincided with the research agenda at the time of my U.S. collaborators, and I received much help from both in pursuing these issues. Susan generously shared with me her coding scheme for directives, which, with Esther Ziv from the Israeli research team, we adapted and applied to the family data. Over the years, Susan has been a major source of inspiration for my understanding of issues of power and control in family discourse; her influence is reflected clearly in my discussion of these issues in this book.

On the Israeli scene, much of the organizational work in setting up the project was carried out by Rachel Meisler, who acted as project coordinator. Rachel played an invaluable role in recruiting the 24 Israeli families and in supervising all aspects of data collection, transcription, and storing. She did an admirable organizational job and also played an important role as researcher, carrying out several of the observations and contributing many insightful comments on the families studied. She was helped by Kobi Abelman, Kary Erenberg, Elda Baruch, Sarah Glazer, Marit Moran-Tzameret, and Miriam Tivon, the participant observers who taped the Israeli family dinners, carried out the first interviews, provided careful field notes, and transcribed the data.

The more I read the transcripts of the dinner conversations, listened to the tapes, and watched the videos, the more I became intrigued with the richness of dinner talk as a prime site of pragmatic socialization. My association with Catherine Snow played an important role in pursuing this theme. Catherine has been involved in the project throughout, first as consultant, and then as collaborator during its second stage. She has been an unwavering source of support and inspiration, helping me understand many aspects of American culture and directly influencing my thinking on all matters pertaining to the development of children's pragmatic competencies. Once I realized the full significance of family discourse at dinner for pragmatic development, it became a focal point in the analysis, and subsequently a central theme developed in the book.

One of the many puzzles of the dinner talk we observed was its indeterminacy of goals, its constant wavering between different speech modes and speech genres, sociable talk and socializing talk. On the onset of the second stage, we decided to add another dimension toward solving this puzzle by going back to the families for an interview, seeking the participants' own views about what was going on at dinner, especially with regard to language socialization. Rosalind Davidson, a member of the research team in Boston, helped develop the guidelines for the parents' interview, carried out the Boston family interviews with great care and involvement, and, in later years, was always willing to help.

Most of our energy during the second phase of the project was devoted to exploring empirically discourse genres that emerged as central in dinner talk, such as narratives and metapragmatic discourse. Members of the research team (all graduate students) during this time—Naomi Mazoz, Talya Miron-Shatz, Abigail Neubach, Leslie Polss, Hadas Scheffer, and Sigal Ravina—helped develop the various coding schemes, carried out the empirical analyses, and made many valuable contributions toward the interpretation of our findings. In some cases, work in the project led to independent research undertakings based on the family project data, as in the case of Leslie Polss' study of conversational openings and Talya Miron-Shatz's study of gender differences in narrative support and challenge.

It took me several years to reach an understanding of dinner talk in Jewish American and Israeli families, to feel that I have a coherent story to tell. I was helped in this process of shaping my ideas by several people in different parts of the world. My fellow teachers at the Dubrovnik Inter-University Graduate Seminar on Cross-Cultural Pragmatics during the summer of 1990 all agreed to discuss transcripts of the family dinner conversations during the seminar. Present were Guy Aston, Juliane House, Gabriele Kasper, Tamar Katriel, Susan Paulston, Catherine Snow, and Elda Weizman. All of these people offered valuable comments on the transcripts, and have discussed various aspects of the project with me on numerous other occasions. My association with Tamar Katriel in particular has been extremely fruitful. Our ongoing dialogue has been a major influence in many ways; she has opened up new vistas in my thinking about culture and ethnography in general and in understanding Israeli culture—our common interest—in particular. I am also indebted to her for careful critical reading of large parts of the manuscript.

Much of the conceptualization of this book, and part of its writing, took place during my sabbatical at Harvard in 1991 and 1992: Catherine Snow and her colleagues on the third floor of Larsen Hall were most generous with their hospitality. Lowrie Helphill was a pleasure to talk to on matters of discourse and culture and provided helpful comments on the first version of two of the chapters.

In the preparation of the final version of the manuscript, Talya Habib commented on one of the chapters, Sherna Kissilevitz provided invaluable editorial help, and Naomi Mazoz helped to bring the manuscript to completion in a large variety of technical ways.

The summer that this manuscript was submitted to the publisher, Haim Rabin, my teacher and PhD supervisor in the early 1970s, died. In a way this book could have never come into being without his formative influence on my thinking as a sociolinguist; his enthusiasm for modern Hebrew, as actually used, and his deep and broad understanding of sociolinguistic issues in general have been a major source of inspiration for me throughout the years.

Finally, I would like to express my special thanks to all of the American and Israeli families involved in the family discourse project, for letting us into their homes and sharing their lives with us for a few moments. This book is, after all, about them, and I thank them deeply.

1

CULTURAL PATTERNS OF COMMUNICATION

This book is about cultural patterns of communication in family discourse. More precisely, it juxtaposes the dinner table conversations of Israeli and Jewish American families, exploring the relations between linguistic use and cultural codes and the role of discourse in shaping and invoking familial, social, and cultural identities. The relationship between language, society, and culture—seen as a set of ideas, values, or symbolic codes—has challenged linguists and social scientists for more than a century. My approach shares the assumptions of those traditions in sociolinguistics, conceived in terms of the ethnography of communication formulated by Gumperz and Hymes in the early 1960s, which view the patterns of language usage as intimately linked with the social and cultural lives of the communities studied (cf. Hymes, 1974). It is an approach that insists on the need for detailed analysis of discursive practices in particular settings and events to show how language in itself is a form of cultural behavior and how patterning of communicative behavior constitutes one of the systems of culture. In exploring the culture-specific systematicity of the discursive patterns studied I follow micro-sociolinguistic discourse analytical methods, enriched by insights from pragmatics, and draw upon several traditions in the study of face-to-face interaction.[1]

---

[1]The specific approaches drawn upon for the analyses undertaken here vary with the issues investigated. Insights from both discourse-analytical and conversational analysis approaches to coherence in discourse were helpful in unveiling the dynamics of topical control at dinnertime (Brown & Yule, 1983; Bublitz, 1988; Craig & Tracy, 1983; Keenan & Schieffelin, 1976; Maynard, 1980). Narrative events at dinner are approached by combining a social interactionalist position

The perspective developed here for the study of situated communicative practices is further enriched by two insights from phenomenological approaches to human communication such as Garfinkel's and Sacks' ethnomethodology and Goffman's interactional approach and conversational analysis: Even the most mundane instances of face-to-face interaction are complex social performances and social meanings are jointly and dynamically negotiated rather than static and individual. Hence, their process of formation is located in the context of face-to-face interaction. I follow a culture-sensitive reading of these ideas, searching for the cultural meanings embedded and negotiated in mundane instances of interaction at the family dinner table, in some ways an undertaking similar to Varenne's (1992) exploration of cultural patterns in familial talk. The ideas of the phenomenologists have a close affinity to those of the social theorists such as Berger and Luckman (1966), Ricoeur (1983), and Foucault (1972), who strongly argued for the primary role of language in the social construction of reality, and the cultural theorists who view culture as a web of interconnected symbolic meanings, continually in the process of being recreated and renegotiated by its members (Geertz, 1973; Schneider, 1976).

This book is based on a comparative case study of family discourse in middle-class Jewish American, native Israeli, and American-born Israeli families of European origin. The database for the study comprises natural conversations at dinnertime and extensive interviews. Three analytical concerns motivated the study. The first concern is cultural variation in ways of speaking as manifested in the dynamics of dinner talk. This concern is motivated by the quest for the degree of diversity in interactional styles between present-day Jewish communities sharing a common past. As Hymes (1974) proposed, the general problem for "socially constituted linguistics" is

> to identify the means of speech and ways of speaking of communities; to find, indeed, where are the real communities, for language boundaries do not give them, and a person or a group may belong to more than one—to characterize communities in terms of their repertoires of these; and through ethnography, comparative ethnology, historical and evolutionary considerations, become able to explain something of the origin, development, maintenance, obsolescence, and loss of ways of speaking and types of speech communities. (p. 203)

---

to oral storytelling (Jefferson, 1978; Polanyi, 1989; Sacks, 1974; Schiffrin, 1984a) with insights from the study of verbal performance (Bauman, 1986; Briggs, 1988; Hymes, 1981; Kirshenblatt-Gimblett, 1975). The analysis of the language of control and metapragmatic discourse in the family is grounded in pragmatics, particularly speech act theory (Austin, 1962; Searle, 1969, 1979) and developmental pragmatics (Becker, 1988; Ervin-Tripp & Gordon, 1986). Patterns of code switching in the bilingual families are investigated from a functional perspective (Gumperz, 1982; Scotton, 1988, 1990), considering the literature on native language maintenance in Israel (Ben Rafael, 1994).

The problem of characterizing communities in terms of their ways of speaking is particularly intriguing due to the specific history of the communities involved. It is my goal to demonstrate that the Jewish Americans, native Israelis, and Israeli Americans diverge in their ways of speaking to an extent that warrants considering their styles as culturally distinct.

A second, related concern is enculturation. The third group studied comprises of American-born old-time immigrants to Israel. Processes of immigration necessarily bring different cultures into contact on an unequal footing, requiring linguistic and sociocultural accommodation on the part of the immigrants to the cultural patterns of the host country. The social imbalance associated with immigration may be somewhat compensated for by the high prestige associated with English, the immigrants' native tongue. Indeed, the families studied strive to maintain English in the home.

Against the background of cultural diversity found between Jewish Americans and Israelis, the issue investigated in the case of the immigrant families is the degree of congruity between the interactional style of this group and that of its two contact cultures. An additional issue is the nature of bilingual usage in the family. The findings demonstrate a particularly rich case of intercultural style: These American immigrants to Israel, fully competent in two languages (English and Hebrew), create an intercultural way of speaking that is both related to and distinct from the styles prevalent in the two substrata, a style on which they rely regardless of the language being used. From the point of view of bilingual practices, of particular interest is the finding that these families represent a successful case of mother tongue maintenance, the children cooperating with the parents to keep English as the main language of the home.

A third concern is the role of dinner talk in pragmatic socialization. By *pragmatic socialization* I mean the ways in which children are socialized to use language in context in socially and culturally approriate ways. Cultures differ to a great extent in their beliefs about and practices of language socialization (e.g., Ochs & Schieffelin, 1984), particularly with regard to the pragmatic aspects of language use. To become competent conversationalists, children have to learn how to choose and introduce topics for talk, respond appropriately, tell a story, or develop an argument. Cultural variation in opportunities provided for children to participate in dinner talk, or in the ways children's participation is monitored, may result in different pathways to access to adult discourse, may reflect variation in perceptions of the relations between power and language, and may result in different socialization agendas for children. The study explores the ways in which dinnertime serves a culturally distinctive role in pragmatic socialization by juxtaposing the three groups studied with regard to children's modes of participation in dinner talk and parental beliefs and attitudes toward pragmatic socialization.

THE CROSS-CULTURAL PERSPECTIVE

The cross-cultural angle of the study is pursued foremost by comparing Jewish families from two communities, Israeli and American.[2] This comparison does not assume a priori that these two communities represent two different cultures but rather attempts to discover whether observed differences between them in interactional styles link up with broader parameters of culture in the respective societies. The comparison is complicated by the fact that the communities studied intersect with each other in a multiplicity of ways, both diachronically and synchronically.

On the one hand, all the families in the study come from an Eastern and Central European Jewish background. Whereas the parent generation of the families studied are native Israelis or Americans who speak Hebrew or English as their first language, the parents or grandparents of our subjects were born and educated in Europe, and many spoke Yiddish in the home. The two communities are thus tied to a common Jewish heritage; furthermore, they share the belief in a common ancestry, common history, and a sense of shared peoplehood. This Judaic heritage meets Geertz's (1973) definition of a culture as a "historically transmitted pattern of meanings embedded in symbols, a system of inherited conceptions expressed in symbolic forms by means of which men communicate, perpetuate and develop their knowledge about attitudes towards life" (p. 89).

On the other hand, sociologists of Jewish culture, such as Liebman and Cohen (1990), claim that these two societies have developed sharply distinct conceptualizations of Judaism, warranting their recognition as two distinct cultures.[3] This claim is based on the assumption that Judaism is indeed a culture but that the originally shared transmitted patterns of meanings and symbolic forms were reinterpreted and reconceptualized to a degree that by now sharply differentiates the two societies. Divergent impacts of modernity and statehood have brought about radical reformulations of shared myths as well as of moral values and beliefs. Consider, for example, the meanings attached to the shared myths of the Jewish holiday of Hannukah. Liebman and Cohen noted that American Jews relate the story of Hannukah as the account of a successful fight by courageous Jews against the forces

---

[2]The following discussion juxtaposes the group of American Jewish families with both native and non-native (immigrant) Israelis. The unique intercultural position held by the group of American Israelis is discussed in Chapter 7.

[3]For a comparative discussion of Jewish identity in the United States and Israel see Cohen (1989), Herman (1977), and Liebman and Cohen (1990). For the problematics of Israeli identity, see Ben Rafael (1982), Bruner and Gorfain (1984), Dominguez (1989), Kahane and Kopstein (1980), Liebman and Don-Yehiya (1981), Rubinstein (1977), and Shavit (1987). The case of American Israelis is discussed by Avruch (1981).

of Hellenization (assimilation), and the holiday is celebrated as an alternative to Christmas, symbolizing the ongoing struggle against cultural and religious assimilation. To Israelis, Hannukah recalls a successful military struggle of national liberation from foreign domination; in Handelman's (1990) formulation, it symbolizes "the struggle of the Jewish people to create a unified national homeland" (p. 170).

The focus of this study is on language; by following patterns of communication in the family in these two communities I show how observed differences in interactional style reflect and shape cultural identities. From a synchronic point of view, the study lends support to Liebman and Cohen's (1990) claims with regard to cultural diversity between these two communities. The findings of this study reveal that the two groups have developed unique interactional styles, styles that are deeply grounded in cultural patterns of the respective societies at large. From a diachronic point of view, the issue is which of the two communities shows more affinity in style to what might be considered as the premodern, Eastern European Jewish way of speaking. The search for continuity in this regard is complicated by the impossibility of a truly systematic diachronic comparison; what we know about traditional ways of speaking can be inferred indirectly either from anthropological (but nostalgic) attempts to reconstruct the life in the Shtetl, based on recollection and historical research (e.g., Zborowski & Herzog, 1952), or from discussion of the speech patterns of elderly Jews of Eastern European origin (Myerhoff, 1978), sociolinguistic studies of current American Jewish ways of speaking (Schiffrin, 1984b; Tannen, 1981a, 1981b, 1984), and sociolinguistic studies of interactional patterns in the Ashkenazi synagogue and Yeshiva (Spolsky & Walters, 1985). Both Tannen and Schiffrin have identified distinctive features of style that they attribute to the Jewish identity of the speakers. In the context of Tannen's and Schiffrin's studies, this "Jewish" style distinguishes its speakers from other Americans, presumably indexing their Jewish, Eastern European personal or family origins. In the Israeli American comparative context developed here, the characteristics of this style, as well as those identified by Spolsky and Walters for the interactional style of Ashkenazi synagogues, become a yardstick for comparing American and Israeli ways of speaking and their degree of affinity with traditional ways of speaking.

Surprisingly, the findings suggest that the features of the Jewish style are more prominent in the Israeli than the Jewish American ways of speaking. It seems to be the case then that the Israeli discursive practices, rather than the Jewish American, more clearly carry on a dialogic relationship (in Bakhtin's, 1981, sense of dialogue) with practices embedded in the historic past. The family histories of the families involved provide a crucial background against which these issues need to be considered.

Family Origins: A Microcosm of Historical and Cultural Divergence

Three groups of families participated in the study: native-born Jewish Americans ($n = 12$), native-born Israelis ($n = 11$), and American Israeli (Jewish) immigrants to Israel ($n = 11$). All adult participants were university-educated, middle- to upper-middle-class, from an Ashkenazi (European) background and non-observant (see the Method section for further details).

The search for diversity in cultural patterns that is aimed at in this study has been carried out against a considerable level of shared historical and linguistic background common to all families. To assess the degree of commonality, we asked the adults in the families to provide us with demographic information about their families, going back two generations (see section on Method). The responses confirmed the common roots: Between 67% to 82% of our subjects' parents came from families that originated in Russia and Poland. However, there is an interesting difference between the groups in the historical distancing from this common past. In the Israeli sample, the vast majority (93%) of individuals in the subjects' parent generation immigrated to Palestine as young adults; in both the American and American Israeli groups, about half of the parents (45% to 53%) were born and raised in the United States as sons and daughters of Jewish immigrants from Eastern Europe. This means that the Israelis are all first generation, whereas in the other two groups half of the adults are second or even third generation born to immigrant parents.

The proximity of the Israeli families to their Eastern European origins is also apparent in the distribution of languages in the subjects' parent generation. In response to the question, "what languages did your parents speak at home when you were a child?" Yiddish was mentioned as one language by 59% of the Israeli adults, 65% of the American Israelis,[4] and only 37% of the American households. This divergence in family histories means that about half of the American-born parents come from families that have been part of American society for at least one generation.

Although the community of American Jews is far from homogeneous, all its members have enjoyed in America the freedom and equality consistent with basic values of American culture and share a sense of common history with other Americans (Liebman & Cohen, 1990). It is to be expected that cultural patterns of communication in the Jewish American families studied reflect (to a certain degree) the adaptation of this community to what are perceived as "American" values (e.g., Bellah, Madsen, Sullivan, Swidler, & Tipton, 1985) and

---

[4]It might be that the families of the American immigrants to Israel were more traditionally oriented than the American Jews living in the United States; hence the higher incidence of Yiddish in the family background of the former group. (For the distribution of languages spoken in the two past generations of our subjects, see Appendix B).

ways of speaking (Carbaugh, 1988; Katriel & Philipsen, 1981/1990; Kochman, 1981; Tannen, 1984; Varenne, 1977). On the other hand, it is also a community that defines its ethnic identity in terms of its relation to a shared Jewish history and tradition, regardless of how radically reformulated are its concepts of Judaism, especially among its non-observant members.

Many of the Israeli adults, on the other hand, descend from parents who came to Palestine as pioneers, consciously abandoning tradition and motivated by the secular ideology of Zionist Socialism (cf. Eisenstadt, 1985). An integral part of this process was the breaking away from ways of speaking that were associated with the old world. As demonstrated by Katriel (1986), the *dugri* (straightforward) way of speaking that emerged in the subculture of the native *sabras* in this society celebrated ideals of simplicity, naturalness, and sincerity in interpersonal relationships as a symbol of rebellion against the world of the Diaspora. Indeed, empirical sociolinguistic studies of speech act performance in Israeli society at large indicate a high prevalence of the direct mode, expressed both in levels of directness chosen for the realization of specific speech acts (Blum-Kulka, Danet, & Gerson, 1985; Olshtain & Weinbach, 1987) and in folk notions of politeness (Blum-Kulka, 1992). Yet a close look at patterns of communication in Ashkanezi, secular, sabra families, like the one undertaken here, suggests that simultaneously an undercurrent of continuity is constantly at work. A meshing of influences can be detected with regard to several dimensions of discourse. For instance, in issuing directives, Israeli parents opt for high levels of directness, in the spirit of the *dugri* mode, yet they simultaneously tend to embed the direct forms in a web of mitigating devices including nicknames, the suffixes of which often echoing Slavic and Yiddish sound patterns. Thus, patterns of mitigation in general and forms for indexing affect in particular seem to echo ways of speaking associated with the diaspora of Eastern Europe. Traces of such continuity have been depicted both in Modern Hebrew and in the rhetoric of ceremonial practices in Israel. Harshav (1990) claimed that the process of the revival of Hebrew is characterized by a double coding. It is a process typified by a drastic imposition and ideological acceptance of a new pattern of behavior, radically different from that of the diaspora past and coexistent with an undercurrent subtext of old ways of behavior that are becoming more and more apparent with time (pp. 18–20).[5] Katriel (1991) argued for such continuity within an ideology of change with regard to several current Israeli cultural practices. For instance, she noted that in the creation of youth movement ceremonies, "traditional Jewish as well as European cultural forms were selectively—though not always consciously—

---

[5]Harshav (1990) claimed that the influence of Yiddish on Modern Hebrew is recognizable in syllabic stress for first names and foreign words, emotional and idiomatic expressions, and slang.

drawn upon" (p. 54). The novelty of the present study is its exploration of this dialectic of continuity and change from a cross-cultural angle, in order to demonstrate, through fine-grained discourse analysis of natural talk in the family, the different paths followed by the Jewish communities studied.

CULTURAL PATTERNS OF PRAGMATIC SOCIALIZATION AT DINNER

Dinnertime as a Communicative Event

Family dinnertime, in the families we studied, is a communicative event bounded in time and space, delimited in its participants and governed by its own rules of interaction. It occupies a particular place on a continuum between mundane, day-to-day informal encounters and formal public events (such as ceremonies of Remembrance Day and Independence Day in Israel). Following Goffman (1961), Handelman (1990) argued that "any occasion of face-to-face interaction comes into existence through the selection and re-organization of phenomenal elements, together with a degree of closure, however fragile, that sets the occasion apart from other activities" (p. 16).

Handelman contrasted the "fragile closure" of such casual encounters with the high degree of formalization in space, time, and behavior of public events, "occasions that people undertake in concert to make more, less or other of themselves, than they usually do" (p. 3). In his analysis, public events have four distinctive features: replicability, intentionality, symbolic formation (i.e., "a connectivity that extends beyond itself," p. 13), and for-mality. Replicability is encoded through organizational structure, partici-pants, and sequence. Any specific enactment of a specific public event contains roughly the same organizational components, appearing in a pre-set sequence, with more or less the same participants. Such events are goal directed (e.g., have intentionality), with "a fairly well-defined outset that points in the direction of a particular ending or outcome" (p. 13). By pointing beyond themselves, such events are symbolic of something outside them-selves and have the dense presence and the high production of symbols. Finally, public events are highly formalized.

Considering family dinners through Handelman's grid for public events highlights their uniqueness, as compared to both casual conversations and public events. For the purposes of the present analysis, it is the features of dinners as speech events that need to be specifically highlighted. In casual encounters, replicability is limited to the phatic components of the talk, which tend to be placed at openings and closings (Schegloff, 1968; Schegloff & Sacks, 1973). There is no pre-set organizational structure, nor can the participants be predicted. Family dinners, on the other hand, have an ele-ment of replicability: Provided the family adheres to a familial convention of family dinners (with all the cultural, social, and individual variation in this domain), then these dinners have certain organizational principles and will be enacted with more or less the same participants. The organizational principles in this instance relate to the way the nature of the activity affects certain layers of the talk. At all dinners, food has to be brought to the table and accessed by the participants. This activity in turn generates minimally the instrumental business talk of having dinner. In the families studied, the instrumental layer of dinner talk is replicated at all dinners, but it is also superimposed by other, more open-ended, conversational layers of talk.

Ordinary conversations are, at least ostensibly, not goal oriented (Goffman, 1981; Lakoff, 1990). They satisfy, in Simmel's (1961) terms, our human instinct for "sociability," achieved in social gatherings where "talking is an end in itself" (p. 161). Family dinners are also familial *we* events shared with children; as such, they may carry important intentional socialization functions, ranging from table manners to socialization of family values. This built-in tension between sociability and socialization further sets dinners apart from both ordinary conversations and public events and has important consequences for the thematic organization of dinner talk. Dinners, like ordinary conversation, allow members to engage in conversation for social enjoyment only, with no visible outcome; simultaneously, they may have crucial outcomes, especially with regard to socialization.

For Handelman (1990), the symbolic nature of public events is most apparent with relation to culture: "It is in various public occasions that cultural codes—usually diffused, attentuated and submerged in the mundane order of things—lie closest to the behavioral surface" (p. 9). In studying dinner table conversations, we are indeed dealing with cultural codes submerged in the mundane order of things, in unveiling cultural meanings, which, in Garfinkel's (1984) terms, are usually "seen but unnoticed" (p. 9). The task is then to demonstrate how discourse at dinner is dialogically related, in the Bakhtinian sense of the term (Bakhtin, 1981), to discourse drawn from and invoked in broader linguistic, social, and cultural environments.

On a continuum of formality (Irvine, 1979), family dinners occupy an interim position: Compared to public events, they are "backstage" (Goffman, 1959) events. Even when no guests are present, the presence of children may set formal criteria for what is acceptable and what is mentionable at dinner. In the families we recorded, almost no mention was made of three topics: money, sex, and politics. These unmentionables thus appear as a covert formal rule for topic selection that is shared by all families, regardless of cultural background, although the interpretations attached to these avoidance practices may still vary by culture. Perceptions of formality for family dinners may and do vary overtly by culture; one interesting finding that emerged from comparing Israeli and Jewish American dinners relates to this dimension. As witnessed by spatial arrangements, physical proximity at the dinner table, the presence or absence of a tablecloth on the table, and especially in the mutual relationships developed with the observer from the research team, Jewish American families enacted dinners in a comparatively more formal manner than Israeli families, and this difference, in turn, affected many dimensions of the talk.

Sociocultural Conventions

It is important to note that the study of pragmatic socialization in middle-class family meals undertaken here is contingent on the sociocultural convention of treating children at shared meals as ratified participants. The construct of family dinner as necessarily an intergenerationally shared social conversational event is a sociocultural construct, one that seems empirically valid at least for many urban middle-class families throughout the Western world, but one that is not necessarily found in other sociocultural contexts. When dinner is construed as an intergenerationally shared social speech event, it can serve as a pragmatic socialization context in which children learn how to become competent conversational partners in intergenerational multiparty talk. Bruner (1986), adopting a Vygotskian perspective, viewed language acquisition as embedded in a matrix of social activity; he postulated a Language Acquisition Support System, provided by the social world, which "helps the child navigate across the Zone of Proximal Development to full and conscious control of language use" (p. 86). The crucial pragmatic socialization role of family dinners thus lies in their potential to serve as a social support system that eases a child's passage into adult discourse.[6]

Consider, though, the strength of sociocultural conventions. At the onset of the research project, we approached potential families and asked them to allow us to tape family meals. None of the families questioned the underlying assumptions of this request—namely, that the family normally partakes of meals together and that such events contain conversation that can be taped. As members of a Western middle-class culture, both the researchers and the adults in the families regarded the task from a shared set of background expectancies typically "seen but unnoticed" (Garfinkel, 1967/1984, p. 9) in everyday life. We all took for granted that children are present at the dinner table, that the event occasions conversation, and that the children, in one form or another, participate in the talk.

Of course, not one of these assumptions is universally true. In some cultures, and even within other social groups in Israeli and American societies, meals may not even be shared intergenerationally. It may even be the case that families who report having regular family meals are like the rural French

---

[6]For a discussion of Vygotsky's ideas see Bruner (1986), Vygotsky (1978), and Wertsch (1985).

family depicted by Margaret Mead (1959) in her film *Four Families*, where the meal is completely task oriented, generating only occasional remarks associated with the business of having dinner but containing no extended conversation. Our Israeli and Jewish American middle-class urban families contrast sharply with the French example. In listening to the tapes, our difficulty is not to hear the voices of family members but to distinguish among them. Talk is the unmarked state, silence the marked one. All those present participate in the talk, young children included. Participation, however, is no simple matter; not all have the same rights nor do they use them in similar ways. Dinnertime, for these families is talking time; families in all three groups frame and enact it as both a sociable and a socializing speech event.

In comparing patterns of pragmatic socialization across the groups, we are thus looking for variation within a fairly established, shared frame of sociocultural conventions. The study indeed reveals variation on many dimensions of discourse.

Dinners as Opportunity Space for Pragmatic Socialization

Dinner in the families we studied is a natural, daily occurrence in which all members regularly participate and hence is uniquely suited to the analysis of spontaneous family discourse. Ochs, Smith, and Taylor (1989) aptly referred to dinnertime as "an opportunity space":

> Dinnertime is a time when adults and children often come together after being apart throughout the day, a somewhat unique time period for many families wherein there is some assurance of a relatively captive audience for sounding things out. Dinnertime is thus an opportunity space—a temporal, spatial and social moment which provides for the possibility of joint activity among family members. (p. 238)

However, we still know relatively little about how families use this opportunity space and how they vary by culture in doing so. Although there is a rich research tradition that shows how cultures and ethnic groups vary substantially in practices and beliefs of language socialization (Heath, 1983; LeVine, 1990; Ochs, 1988; Schieffelbush & Pickar, 1984; Schieffelin, 1990; Schieffelin & Eisenberg, 1984; Scollon & Scollon, 1981),[7] there are relatively few studies that

---

[7]Studies in language socialization across cultures come mainly from observing dyadic mother–child interactions of young children. The present research focuses on interaction of school-age children in the presence of several adults. The findings from language socialization studies provide an important background for the present research in showing the multiplicity of dimensions on which cultures differ in their attitudes and practices in helping children to acquire communicative competence. Middle-class and working-class White American mothers talk to their infants directly, address questions to them as potential conversational partners

consider such variation from the perspective of the socialization role of one given speech event. One of my goals is to show that when the mealtime is shared physically and conversationally with children, it serves as a critical social context in which children become socialized to local cultural rules regulating conversation, such as the choice of topics, rules of turn taking, modes of storytelling, and rules of politeness. Such cultural rules may be quite distinct, creating culturally defined discourse environments for all members. Findings that point in these directions come from psychological studies in pragmatic development (Ninio & Snow, 1996), sociolinguistic, discourse analysis (Erickson, 1990; Tannen, 1984; Watts, 1989, 1991) or conversation analysis based studies of adult conversation (Goodwin, 1981), and anthropological studies of family discourse (e.g., Ochs et al., 1989; Ochs, Taylor, Rudolph, & Smith, 1992)—some with a focus on family meals and others with data from family meals in their database. Three issues investigated in these traditions are of particular relevance here: the development of conversational skills, cultural variation in socialization for politeness, and the use and meaning of extended discourse at dinner.

Conversational Skills

Participation in family discourse may be a particularly important determinant of the development of conversational skills. Whereas young children learn turn-taking aspects of conversation quite early, as evidenced by their ability to sustain well-timed turn alterations with adults by the time they are producing their first words (Snow, 1977) and with peers by at least age 3 (Ervin-Tripp, 1979), more subtle conversational skills such as entering a conversation, maintaining one's turn and, most important perhaps, linking coherently with previous talk, develop much more slowly (Corsaro, 1979; Dorval & Eckerman, 1984; Sacks, 1982). Once such skills develop, children are recognized by adults as good conversationalists: Schley and Snow (1992) found that among second to fifth graders the children who produced more topic continuations and more sophisticated topic continuations, topic initiations, and responses were the ones identified as good conversationalists.

(Heath, 1982; LeVine, 1990; Snow, 1984), and create predictable responses and contexts for learning politeness formulae (Gleason & Weintraub, 1976). Romany-speaking Gypsy mothers expose infants to lengthy and dramatic narratives (Reger & Gleason, 1991); in contrast, Kaluli mothers in New Guinea (Schieffelin, 1990), Gusii mothers in Kenya (LeVine, 1990), and Black working adults in America rarely address talk (including questions) specifically to very young children, as they do not see infants as suitable partners for conversation. Cultures also emphasize different speech functions, such as teasing challenges in New Guinea and among American working-class Blacks (Heath, 1983; Schieffelin, 1990) and information-giving in White America (Heath, 1983). American middle-class caretakers package their messages structurally and content-wise to accommodate children and help make children's contributions appear timely and relevant (Snow, 1977, 1984).

Perlman's (1984) study of family meals is one of the few studies that focused particularly on dinner talk. Perlman studied variation in socialization styles among White middle-class American families and found individual variation in the degree of participation by family members and in the degree of child-centeredness in choice of topics; sex differences were depicted in verbal responsiveness to the child (i.e., mothers talked significantly more than fathers). From a different perspective, Vuchinich (1984, 1990) analyzed the sequential organization of family conflict, and Feiring and Lewis (1987) looked at the effects of family size on the amount of interaction among family members and the predominant function of the interaction, whether for nurturance, control, or information exchange. The amount and mode of participation of the child in dinner talk, as well as the topics and genres of talk he or she is exposed to at dinner, may play a crucial role in the development of notions of discourse and of skills in applying them. The present research addresses these issues by analyzing the relation between social roles (e.g., being an adult or a child) and discourse roles (i.e., the degree of participation and topical control) at dinner, with special emphasis on children's modes of participation. Although not framed developmentally, the study may have important implications for pragmatic development because it shows how the families foster children's conversational skills through social interaction within the complex network of multigenerational talk, providing culturally distinct patterns for children's passages to adult discourse.

Politeness

Family discourse at dinner offers a rich source for the study of politeness in the broadest sense. Since the publication of Brown and Levinson's (1987) theory of politeness, it is becoming apparent that politeness encompasses all aspects of human social interaction: It means knowing the culturally complex rules for what is said and how it it said relative to goals, interactants, context and culture. Most empirical research on adult politeness to date has focused on the cross-cultural study of politeness as the strategic accomplishment of single speech acts (e.g., Blum-Kulka, House, & Kasper, 1989) and on cultural differences in the underlying notions of *face* that motivate such choices (e.g., Ide, 1989; Matsumoto, 1989; see Kasper, 1990, for a comprehensive review). In child language, the emphasis in politeness research has been, on the one hand, on the acquisition of politeness formulae (Bates, 1976; Gleason, 1987; Gleason, Perlman, & Grief, 1984) and parental input to such acquisition (Becker, 1990; Snow, Perlman, Gleason, & Hooshyar, 1990) and, on the other hand, on the ways children develop sensitivity to distance and power in realizing speech acts (Becker, 1990; Corsaro, 1979; Ervin-Tripp 1982; Ervin-Tripp & Gordon, 1986).

Dinner table conversations are rarely taken into account in politeness research. One exception is Watts' (1989) study of dinner table conversations between adult British and Swiss German participants at a family dinner. Watts found different conversational styles, which he linked to different politeness orientations with regard to several dimensions of discourse. For instance, whereas the British participants predominantly highlighted the maintenance of interpersonal harmony through cooperative conversational activity, the Swiss conversationalists displayed competitiveness by placing more emphasis on displaying positions and counterpositions on the topic. Tannen's (1984) study of a Thanksgiving dinner among friends demonstrates that interactional styles may also vary ethnically and geographically within the same language community.

Developmental studies of politeness that incorporate mealtime data among home interactions (Becker 1988, 1990; Snow et al., 1990) show how parents use modeling and metapragmatic comments to teach children to use politeness formulae, apologize, avoid rude behavior and interruptions, and generally provide information about the rules governing both positive and negative politeness strategies.

Within the broad definition of politeness endorsed here, all aspects of the present research are relevant to issues of politeness: The quest for the uniqueness of culturally defined interactional styles is the quest for a culture's notions about the appropriate, polite ways of jointly accomplishing social interaction at dinner. In this respect, one specific contribution of the study to politeness theory is the shifting of emphasis from speech acts to discourse. Politeness is equated here with the cultural group's notions of the appropriate ways for the joint accomplishment of dinner talk, as manifested in choice of themes, topical control, and narratives, as well as with the realization of the speech act of requests and metapragmatic discourse. A second contribution lies in showing that the nature of the given speech event, namely family dinners, has a determining role in shaping the politeness systems at work. In all the dimensions of discourse studied, cross-cultural variation, though highly marked, is subsumed under overall organizational patterns of dinner talk shared by all the families we studied.

From the perspective of language socialization, again all aspects of discourse at dinner are relevant to politeness. The ways children learn to become effective members of their cultures involve learning appropriate ways for the use of all dimensions of discourse; at dinner they are provided with opportunities for learning how to select topics for conversation with adults, how to take turns in multiparty talk, how to tell about one's day, how to choose the level of directness appropriate in realizing speech acts, and how males and females differ in ways of talking. We found, for instance, that Israeli and Jewish American participants at dinner differ in their preferences for styles of control. Although the nature of the speech event seems to allow for high levels of directness, which predominate in all groups, as their second choice, Americans opt for strategies of conventional indirectness whereas Israelis prefer strategies of mitigated directness. Culturally different notions of how to make polite requests may thus be one of the socialization products of dinner talk.

Extended Discourse

Mealtime conversations may well serve as social facilitators (cf. Snow, 1989) for the development of monolog skills as well: Whereas there is ample evidence to show how the ability to tell stories develops through mother–child interactions (McCabe & Peterson, 1991; Schieffelin & Eisenberg, 1984; Wells, 1981), the present research suggests that children's participation in such multiparty talk is conducive to learning not only how to construct autonomous narrative texts but also how to choose tellable topics and tell stories in culturally appropriate styles.

A prime example of the use of extended discourse at dinner is co-narration. Ochs and her colleagues have demonstrated how dinnertime is used to sort out problematic events in the lives of family members through co-narration at dinner (Ochs et al., 1989), and co-narration simultaneously serves as a theory-building activity, drawing on "cognitive and linguistic skills that underlie scientific and other scholarly discourse as they [family members] jointly construct and deconstruct theories of everyday events" (Ochs et al., 1992, p. 37). This work shows that many intellectual skills that have been viewed as the outcome of formal schooling are in fact—in American homes from a variety of social backgrounds with younger than school-aged children—fostered through everyday practices such as storytelling at dinnertime. Similarly, in a study of narratives at family meals in American and Israeli homes, undertaken to compare middle-class with working-class practices, Blum-Kulka and Snow (1992) demonstrated how in both groups competencies for the construction of autonomous, decontextualized texts are fostered through co-narration with children. In the present study the analysis of co-narration at dinner serves to show how the groups differ in their attitudes to narrative performance and content and how such differences are reflected in roles assigned to children within the narrative event.

DINNERS AS SITUATED ACTIVITY

The choice of dinners as the studied event follows the major shift in studies of language use from linguistic units to speech events. As Hymes (1974) argued, it is necessary in sociolinguistic description "to deal with activities which are in some recognizable way bounded or integral" (p. 56). In his grid for research in the ethnography of communication, Hymes proposed two levels of such activities: *speech situations,* like fights, hunts, or meals, which are not necessarily governed by a single set of rules for the use of speech and *speech events,* which are directly governed by rules or norms. In this tradition, speech events are considered the basic unit for the analysis of verbal interaction (Gumperz, 1972/1986: "The speech event is to the analysis of verbal interaction what the sentence is to grammar," p. 17). One goal of the present research is to demonstrate that family dinners are indeed speech events and not merely speech situations. They represent, in Goffman's (1961) terms, a "situated activity," a "circuit of interdependent actions" (p. 96) within which the nature of the event plays a major role in shaping patterns of interaction.[8]

There are several methodological reasons for the choice of dinners as the specific speech event studied. The first relates to the issue of boundaries: Any collection of speech in natural settings necessarily imposes criteria of selection. By focusing on a certain situation or segment we are necessarily, in Cicourel's (1992) formulation, creating "a contextual frame that limits what is to be identified as relevant data, their organization, and the kinds of analysis and inferences to which these data will be subjected" (p. 293). Mead (1973) argued that one solution is to collect "large, sequential, simultaneous natural lumps on which no analytical devices of selection have operated" (p. 43). Family dinners represent such a large, sequential, natural lump. Dinners are naturally bounded spatiotemporally regardless of our observation of them, creating an activity-type defined context (cf. Duranti & Goodwin, 1992). This means that no analytic criteria is applied a priori for the selection of segments of talk that will occur at dinner. Talk is framed externally by the nature of the activity type, and the framing is not imposed by the researcher.

Another important reason for focusing on dinners is their high ecological validity: At least for the families studied, getting together with the children for dinner is a daily occurrence, a natural part of everyday life. During the years the data were collected (1985–1987), family meals in Israel were found to be a viable institution for the population at large as well. A survey conducted in 1986 shows family meals as central in Israeli family life: 35% reported regularly having two shared meals a day, 27% at least one meal a day with all members present, and 18% at least one family meal over the weekend.[9]

---

[8]The importance of activities as a locus for the study of human interaction is stressed in several traditions (see Duranti & Goodwin, 1992, for a thorough overview of different approaches to the more general concept of context). Particularly relevant to my purposes are the anthropological approaches that argue for the need to ground the study of culture in situated activities rather than societies (Goodenough, 1981; M. Goodwin, 1990) and the social interactionist, Vygotskian approaches that demonstrate how language development starts as part of a social activity system (Wertsch, 1985).

[9]The survey was conducted by the Smart Institute of Communication at the Hebrew University and included a representative sample of the Jewish population in Israel.

Third, consider cultural variation. In the families studied, children share the meal with the parents and participate in the talk. Thus, these dinners create, at least theoretically, equal opportunity for all family members, including children, to participate in the talk—as speakers, as addressees, and as overhearers (Clark, 1987). Yet the three groups differ in the way they construe participation in dinner talk. This variation within a shared framework makes dinners a particularly rich site for observing how culture is being created, negotiated, and renegotiated through talk in these families and how it serves, in terms used by Ochs (1986), for socialization *through* language as well as for socialization *to use* language.

PARTICIPANT OBSERVATION AT DINNER: THE DOUBLE ROLE OF OBSERVERS

A member of the research team was present at all meals. The presence of a participant-observer enabled us to enrich the information gathered in many ways (e.g., researchers made notes to accompany each recording session, including lists of the menu at each dinner, and later helped with interpretation). On the other hand, the presence of an outsider obviously changed the participation structure (Goffman, 1981)[10] of the family meals and might have had an effect on the nature of the talk. As a rule, all participant-observers were invited to share the meal. In Israel, during the video recordings a video technician was also present and more often than not was invited to join. Video recordings in the United States were carried out by the researchers themselves. A discussion of the merits and drawbacks of the approach inevitably touches on some of the fundamental issues in social science research, such as the possibility of objective observation and the relation of observer to observed.

It was probably Labov (1972a, 1972b), more than anybody else, who convinced sociolinguists to collect natural data yet simultaneously warned them of the impossibility of collecting data that are truly natural (the famous "observer's paradox"). Consequently, in describing their methods of data collection, many investigators of natural talk highlight the techniques used for minimizing their own or the recording equipment's presence (e.g., Goodwin, 1981) or argue that people get used to tape recorders and tend to forget them (Tannen, 1984). These arguments seem to miss the real issue. If we assume, on ethical grounds, that we are not willing to record people without

---

[10]The complexities of participant structures (also referred to as participant frameworks) are elaborated by Goffman (1981, pp. 124–160). For further discussions of participant frameworks, see Clark (1987), Erickson and Mohatt (1982), C. Goodwin (1981, 1984), M. Goodwin (1990), and Levinson (1988).

their knowledge, then truly natural, systematic collection of extended seg-ments of language data become off-limits to social research. The choice is among different modes of intrusion into the lives of people studied, through the presence of researchers, and/or the use of tape recorders and video cameras.

Procedures actually used include asking families to record themselves (Becker, 1988, 1990; Snow et al., 1990; Vuchinich, 1990), setting up the video equipment and then leaving the scene (Ochs et al., 1989), setting up the video equipment and minimizing one's own presence (Goodwin, 1981) and active participant observation plus recording (Tannen, 1984). In the present research we combined participant observation and recording: The observer was present to audiotape two meals and videotaped a third for each family.

The presence of an observer and a tape recorder represent two very different types of intrusion. Though tape recorders are by now widely em-ployed in sociolinguistic research, their possible effects need to be recon-sidered every time they are used. I agree with Goodwin (1981), who viewed recording as one type of observation. He argued that being observed is part of natural conversation. Participants know that they are being observed during any interaction and have techniques for dealing with this knowledge. The issue thus is not

> what the participants do when they are not being observed, but whether the techniques they use to deal with observation by a camera (or a tape recorder) are different from those used to deal with observation by co-participants. (p. 44)

Because the present study involved only those interactions where par-ticipants were observed by a camera or tape recorder, no comparison is possible. Our only indicators for detecting participants' techniques for deal-ing with such observation are through moments of awareness, points in the talk when the presence of the tape recorder or the fact of being recorded are openly discussed during dinner. Typically, such moments tended to appear during the opening phase of the dinner as the researcher set up the equipment and involved the children, who wanted to examine the equip-ment or hear their own voices. Occasionally the topic was brought up again, most often by children: At one point a child refused to respond to a question "because we're on camera" and at another a child referred to the tape recorder as "the evil eye." As mentioned earlier, certain topics never arose at these dinners. The presence of the tape recorder (or the observer) might have had a role to play in censoring conversation, for it seems reasonable to expect that people may avoid certain issues when being recorded, just as they may in the presence of certain participants. Hence, the presence of the tape recorder cannot be completely ignored in considering the contex-tual grid defining the situation.

On the other hand, as Goodwin (1981) and Tannen (1984) argued, the presence of such a mechanical observer does not invalidate the data. In our case, validation is through the type of experiential knowledge argued for in grounded theory research (Strauss, 1987): The fact that members of the research team belonged to the same cultures as the families[11] gave the team the advantage of being able to judge the conversations in light of their own family experience and resulted in what Tannen (1981b) called the "aha" effect of the instant recognition of highly familiar patterns.

Note that the arguments for and against tape recorders (see, for instance, Wolfson, 1976) are voiced within the paradigm of objectivity in the social sciences. Tape recorders become symbols of minimal interference, of the researchers' way for obtaining the "facts" by supposedly nondisruptive means. Along with the general unease with the metaphor of objectivity in the social sciences (Polkinghorne, 1983), voiced most clearly by anthropologists, comes the realization that objective observation is unattainable and should not be sought. Instead, investigators are called upon to study the social realities they help to create, replacing the language of objectivity with that of reflexivity, the language of reports with that of narratives (Clifford, 1988). Wittgenstein (1968) argued that all language meanings are relative to the "grammars" of the *language games* in which they are a part. Having an observer at dinner thus represents a deliberate interference with a specific language game, meant to deepen our understanding of the grammar of that game by having the event shared with a cultural informant. As a member of the same culture as the observed group, this person may play the double roles of a cultural insider—a participant as observer—and, conversely, of an outside researcher participating—an observer as participant. In the latter role, the observer shared the meal with the family and thus became part of the social reality constructed on each occasion; in the former role, the observer played the role of the culturally informed ethnographer, took field notes and participated in the process of transcription, analysis (coding), and overall interpretation of the transcripts. The approach adopted thus combines ethnographic methods of participant observation with micro-sociolinguistic methods of fine-grained text analysis.

METHOD

The initial design of the study was motivated by considerations of group comparability, situational comparability, and the search for large samples of consecutive natural discourse indicative of cultural patterns and proc-

---

[11]As collaborative research, the team included both Israelis and Americans; the observers were native and non-native Israelis in Israel and Jewish Americans in the States (see also footnote 16).

esses of pragmatic socialization. To achieve our initial goal of comparing Jewish American and Israeli interactional styles, we needed to select from a population that is otherwise fairly homogeneous. This consideration led to the focus, in both communities, on middle-class, professional families of European origin. It should be borne in mind that the sample is not representative in any sense. As in Inbar and Adler's (1977) study of Moroccan brothers who settled in France and in Israel, ours too is a case study aimed to allow as meaningful as possible a comparison of discourse patterns in two Jewish communities, other things being equal. Family meals met the criterion of situational comparability, allowing for the collection of natural speech in a situation that has ecological validity for both communities.

Our interest in pragmatic socialization led to a search for families with school-age children. Most of the research in adult–child verbal interaction focuses on preschool children; thus, attempts to develop a comprehensive account of language development, including the development of pragmatic skills (Wells 1981, 1985), are based typically on children between the ages of 2 and 5. An unstated assumption is that the role of home is central only until children reach school age: Studies that focus on older children typically shift the emphasis to verbal interactions of children at school (Cazden, John, & Hymes, 1972; Romaine, 1984; Sinclair & Coulthard, 1975). Hence, there was a strong need to study school-age children interacting in the home in order to explore the degree of cultural variation in styles of pragmatic socialization.

Other major considerations had to do with the search for the optimal balance between text and context, such as Fairclaugh (1993) called for all studies of discourse, and between evidence derived from talk as such and evidence derived from talk *about* talk. The first issue concerns the scope of contextual information needed to understand the texts of the dinner conversations collected in the study. In contrast to the stand taken by conversational analysts that only information made available by the participants in the talk itself is relevant for the analysis (e.g., Schegloff, 1992), the stand taken here is that, as demonstrated by Cicourel (1992) for medical encounters, awareness of various elements of the ethnographic context are essential for understanding the interaction. In the case of the present research, more than basic demographic information on the participants was needed; a broader context also needed to be established, including information about the family origins of the participants, family histories, patterns of immigration, and languages spoken in parents' and grandparents' homes. To this end, the adults in the study were interviewed at length about family background.

The second issue concerns the reasons for our decision to conduct extensive interviews with the families on topics of pragmatic socialization. The issue can be framed in two ways. From a broad methodological perspective, the interview data supplement the data collected through observations, allowing us to combine two types of information for the same research ends, as often called for in methodological discussions of social research (Briggs, 1988; Spradley, 1979). From a more narrow perspective, attuned to the specific aims of the study, the interviews were purposely designed to elicit metacommunication, namely talk about ways of talking. The decision to conduct the interviews evolved after the first phase of the investigation in response to the need to obtain information about the beliefs and attitudes regarding communicative patterns discerned from analysis of actual conversations. As argued by Schieffelin and Eisenberg (1984), underlying most activites in any culture is a set of cultural assumptions. Variation across cultures in styles of pragmatic socialization may reflect important differences with regard to beliefs, views, and norms, and the understanding of variability in styles of pragmatic socialization cannot be complete without an attempt to probe the determinants of such variability. The interviews on pragmatic socialization were designed to probe such determinants.

In explicating the implications of the study of discourse in one family, Varenne (1992) claimed that in "examining local patterns, such as one family, the analyst can discern echoes of patterns which are far from local" (p. 127). For Varenne, these are patterns of American culture at large. Similarly, I demonstrate that the comparative case study of talk in three small groups of families, as undertaken here, allows us to discern echoes of Israeli and American global cultural patterns.

The research was undertaken as a collaborative enterprise, with David Gordon, Susan Ervin-Tripp, and Catherine Snow as the American collaborators. My own Israeli perspective on the data has been greatly enriched by insights offered by the American collaborators as well as by those offered by members of the research team at various stages of the study. However, as single author of the book, responsibility for all interpretations is ultimately mine, and it is important to note the imbalance in my position vis-à-vis the two cultures investigated. My view on Israeli cultural ways of speaking is that of a cultural member,[12] whereas my position with regard to American or specifically Jewish American ways of speaking is that of a participant observer. This imbalance in perspectives might have colored my comparative interpretations to some extent; it probably heightened my awareness of formal and performative aspects of the (to me) relatively experience-distant Jewish American communicative patterns, and it might have introduced a note of empathy to my interpretations of the experience-near phenomena of Israeli cultural patterns.

---

[12]However, I retain a certain sense of distancing vis-à-vis Israeli culture, due to the fact that I was not born in Israel (I arrived at the age of 9) and was raised in the home of immigrant parents of European origin (see Katriel, 1986, for an insightful discussion of a similar ambivalence in the position of an Israeli researcher in her own culture).

Selection of Families

The research was conducted in two stages: 1985 to 1988 and 1989 to 1992.[13] The selection of the families took place during the first year of the project with the help of my American collaborators, who also supervised all data collection in the States. All families were taped and interviewed in their homes in Israel or in the United States.

Given the richness of social and personal variables that may affect language use, such as social class (Bernstein, 1990; Labov, 1972a), ethnicity (Giles, 1979), age (Helfrich, 1979), sex (Gal, 1989; Swacker, 1976; Tannen, 1990), and religiosity (Spolsky & Walters, 1985), the focal population was delimited to middle- and upper-middle-class, white collar, professional, nonobservant Jewish families from a European background. The level of education was set at minimally a B.A. for both parents, both parents were expected to be occupied professionally outside the home, families had to have at least two children, at least one of school age, and for both the Israeli and Jewish American families, both parents had to be native-born Israeli or American and educated in the country of their origin at least to the completion of high school. Parents in the immigrant families were expected to be born and educated in the United States. A length of stay of 9 years in the target community was shown in previous studies to be the critical period needed both for mastering the target language and for approximating pragmatic norms of the target community (Olshtain & Blum-Kulka, 1985). Accordingly, we required 9 years as the minimal period of stay for the immigrant families included in the study. We selected Ashkenazi (i.e., European families) for comparability across the three groups, and because of the great variaton in religious practices in the Jewish population, we decided to search for families who viewed themselves as secular in orientation. This criterion proved easier to apply for Israeli than for American and immigrant families: In the last two groups a certain level of observance of religious practices is quite common (Liebman & Cohen, 1990). The solution was to apply the criterion flexibly, excluding American Jewish families who defined themselves as "observant" or "dati" (i.e., "religious," in Hebrew) but accepting families who reported adherence to some traditions.

Included in the study were 34 college-educated, middle- to upper-middle-class Ashkenazi, nonobservant Jewish families: 12 Jewish American (4 from Berkeley and 8 from Boston), 11 American Israeli (living in Israel between 9 to 19 years), and 11 Israeli born,[14] all residents of Jerusalem.

---

[13]The research was funded at both stages by the Israeli-American Binational Science Foundation—in stage one, by Grant No. 82-3422 to Shoshana Blum-Kulka and David Gordon, with Susan Ervin-Tripp and Catherine Snow as consultants, and in stage 2 by Grant No. 87-00167/1 to Shoshana Blum-Kulka and Catherine Snow.

[14]Two families, one Israeli (family number 5) and one Israeli American (family number 12), dropped out of the project after part of the data had been collected and were subsequently excluded.

Adults

Most parents in all three groups were at the time of data collection in their late 30s or early 40s (mean age 41, range 34 to 54). All parents were at least college educated: Among the Israelis, four held master's degrees and two held doctorates, whereas among the immigrants and Jewish Americans eight (in each group) held a master's degree, and four in the immigrant group and five among the Jewish Americans held doctorates. In all families, both parents were occupied professionally outside the home, mainly as school teachers (14), psychologists and social workers (8), university professors of history or biology (7), civil servants (4), T.V. directors and producers (3), and lawyers (2).[15]

Children

Information on family constellations in the three groups is presented in Table 1.1. Families have two, three, or four children; and the school-age children (the target group) range from 6.1 to 17.2 years, with most children (59 out of 86) between 6.1 and 13.5 years.

Recruiting the Families and Data Collection

The families were selected through the snowball technique—the candidate families contacted helped us to find others. The process of selection was carried out simultaneously in Israel and the United States. Following initial contacts by phone, a member of the research team, in the case of native Israelis and Jewish Americans of the same cultural background as the family,[16] visited the home, became acquainted with the family and explained the research plan. The families were told that we were interested in comparing Israeli and Jewish American family dinners but were not told of our interest in language. As specified in a release letter signed by one of the principal investigators and the parents, families gave us permission to tape, provided the data would be used only for professional purposes and privacy would be guarded. Accordingly, all names in this book, including first names, are pseudonyms. A small contribution to the meal (e.g., ice cream or chocolate) was made by the observer on each occasion, and the families were given a copy of the video as a token of gratitude for their participation.

---

[15]Other professions are represented by one parent each, including an archaeologist, an economist, a graphic artist, a tax advisor, a museum director, and an interior decorator.

[16]The observers for the Israeli families (all women) were three native Israelis and for the American Jewish families were four native (Jewish) Americans. From among the five observers for the American Israelis (one man and four women), three were American born, two were Israeli born, and all were competent English–Hebrew bilinguals (see Chapter 7 for discussion of the effect of the observer's dominant language on patterns of language use at dinner in the immigrant families).

TABLE 1.1
Family Constellations in Three Groups*

	Israeli Families			American Israeli Families			Jewish American Families	
Family no.**	School-age children 6.2–16.1	Preschool siblings 0.5–5.6	Family no.***	School-age children 6.1–17.3	Preschool siblings 0.5–5.8	Family no.	School-age children 6.5–12.5	Preschool siblings 3–6.5
1	10.5 M 12.0 M		1*	7.2 M 11.4 F		1*	13.2 M 15.5 F	
2	11.4 M 13.2 M	5.2 M	2*	6.1 F 8.0 M		2*	6.1 M 8.5 M	4.4 M
3	8.5 F 9.5 F		3*	6.3 M 9.0 M		3*	10.0 M	5.11 M
4	8.6 M 12.2 F 16.1 M		4*	7.5 F 9.4 F 13.4 F 17.2 M		4*	7.5 M	4.3 F
5*	10.8 M 13.1 M	4.0 F	***			5*	9.5 F 11.3 F	
6*	6.2 F 6.2 F	[0.5 M]	6*	13.11 F 15.10 M	5.5 F	6	12.4 M 16.10 F	

Group 1

Family	Children (age, sex)	Later-born
7	11.3 M, 12.7 F, 16.2 F	
8	14.2 M, 15.6 F	
9*	7.3 F, 9.5 M	
10*	8.2 F, 10.4 M	3.1 M
11*	9.6 F, 11.7 M	
12*	10.1 F, 13.4 F	4.1 M
TOTAL	23	5

Group 2

Family	Children (age, sex)	Later-born
7*	9.0 F, 12.4 F, 13.11 F	
8*	9.5 F, 12.9 F	5.8 M
9*	6.4 M, 10.2 M, 13.7 M	
10	8.0 M, 10.9 M	5.0 M
11	10.5 F, 14.0 F	
12*	8.4 F, 12.2 M	[0.5 F]
TOTAL	26	4

Group 3

Family	Children (age, sex)	Later-born
7*	11.0 M, 13.5 M, 16.0 F	
8*	8.7 M, 10.5 F	
9*	8.8 M	5.6 M
10*	8.3 F, 11.5 F	3.2 M
11	6.7 F, 8.0 M, 9.9 M	4.3 F
**		
TOTAL	24	5

*Marks here and on subsequent tables the eight families per group included in the sample at Stage 2.

**Israeli Family 12 dropped out of the project.

***American Israeli Family 5 dropped out of the project.

Taping

We participated in three family meals over a period of 2 to 3 months. Two of these meals were audio recorded and one was videotaped. The same observer stayed with the family throughout the data collection period. To minimize disruption caused by handling the equipment, a small external microphone attached to a Sony portable tape recorder was placed in the center of table (usually attached to a glass or to the lamp) for the duration of the meal. For videotaping, the camera was placed at an angle that showed the dinner table for the duration of the meal. Recording started when the family began to gather around the table and stopped when they left the table. Meals lasted on average from 1 to 1½ hours. Information on the physical setting of the dinner (including menus and seating arrangements) was recorded in field notes taken immediately after the meal. For the Israeli groups, the observers also transcribed the data and added comments; observers in the United States took field notes and transcribed the first 5 minutes of the data. The rest of the Jewish American data were transcribed by native English speakers in Israel.

Interviews

Demographic Questionnaire. This questionnare was completed during the observer's first visit to the family. Its purpose was to collect demographic information. For parents, the information included the country of origin, education, languages spoken at home, and present occupation. Parents in the immigrant families were also asked for the age and year of their immigration and their background in learning Hebrew as a second language. Information gathered on children included date of birth, grade in school, country of birth, extracurricular activities, hobbies, and reading habits.

Family Origin Questionnaire. Following the first meal, the observer interviewed the families about their backgrounds. The purpose of this interview was to gather demographic information on family origins. Each parent was asked to specify for each of his or her parents and grandparents the country of origin; year, date, and country of immigration, if relevant; occupation; and languages spoken at home.[17] See Appendices A, B, and C for a summary of this information.

---

[17]In the Appendices that summarize the demographic information, the exact number of subjects in the subjects' parent and grandparent generation for whom information is available in each case differs slightly. First, four of the Jewish American families did not fill out the family origin questionnaire at the start of the project. However, we know from the demographic interview that these four families are of European origin. Also, in some families our subjects did not have all the information we asked for, especially regarding grandparents who did not immigrate to either Israel or the United States.

Pragmatic Socialization Interview. The goal of this interview was to tap familial attitudes and beliefs toward pragmatic socialization, especially with regard to issues that emerged from the transcripts.[18] To allow for multigenerational perspectives on the same issues, we asked that both parents and one of the children participate. The interview focused on four content areas: social control (e.g., types of verbal and nonverbal behavior prohibited, reacted to negatively, or expected from children at the dinner table); address terms and nicknames used among members of the family; children's speech (i.e., expectations from children in terms of grammaticality, conversational norms, and politeness); and literacy (i.e., the reading habits of all family members). The immigrant families were also asked a series of open-ended questions on their and their children's bilingual speech and reading practices (i.e., the use of English and Hebrew). Each topic area included a structured part followed by open-ended questions. The interview concluded by asking the parents to compare their parenting styles with that of their own parents.

Database

The database for the study at stage one included broadly transcribed conversations from three meals for each of 34 families and of the demographic and family origin questionnaires. This set of mealtime data served as the basis for the analysis of the language of control and metapragmatic comments presented in Chapters 5 and 6. For stage two, 24 families (eight per group) were selected for further investigation.[19] During this second stage, transcription and text analysis were carried out within the Child Language Data Exchange Program (CHILDES; MacWhinney, 1991). One family meal per family was retranscribed using the CHILDES standard transcription system (CHAT), and the CHILDES computer programs (CLAN) were used for the analyses of transcript data. Data collected from these 24 families also included full transcripts of the pragmatic socialization interview. Transcripts of mealtime conversations from these families served as the basis for the

---

[18]This interview was conducted in the winter of 1989 (2 to 3 years after data collection, depending on family) with the 24 families selected for inclusion at stage two (but see note 19). In Israel, most interviews were conducted by me and one of the members of the research team. The interviews in the United States were closely coordinated with Catherine Snow and (except one, in which I participated) were carried out by Rosalind Davidson, a member of the Harvard Home and School research project.

[19]Because we planned to go back to families for further interviews, we decided to focus on the eight families from Boston who were accessible to us through our collaboration with Catherine Snow. The size of the Israeli samples was reduced accordingly. Eventually the plan did not quite work out because by the time we were ready to interview, four of the Bostonian families had moved out of town and could not be reached. Four new families, matched for background and family constellation with the four families from the original sample, were recruited and interviewed by Rosalind Davidson. All other (18) interviews on pragmatic socialization were conducted with the families from the original sample; all analyses of dinner table conversations are derived from data from the original sample.

analyses of topical control, narrative events, and bilingual practices presented in Chapters 2, 3, 4, and 7.

The distribution of children by age in the two stages is presented in Table 1.2, and the number of participants at one dinner at both stages is presented in Table 1.3.

Transcription

All examples presented in the book follow the CHAT format, with some modifications introduced to ease readability. Hebrew data are presented in the original, with English translations. Hebrew is transcribed following the

TABLE 1.2
Children's Age Constellation in Three Groups

	Preschool 1.5–5.8		School-Age Early Grades 6.1–13.5		Teens 13.5–17.2		Total	
	S1	S2	S1	S2	S1	S2	S1	S2
Israelis	5	5	21	14	3	2	29	21
Jewish Americans	4	3	20	15	6	3	30	21
American Israelis	5	5	18	13	4	2	27	20
Total	14	13	59	42	13	7	86	62

TABLE 1.3
Participants at Dinner

	Israelis		Jewish Americans		American Israelis	
	S1	S2	S1	S2	S1	S2
Parents*	21	15	23	16	21	16
Observer**	3	2	4	3	6	5
Other adults***	6	3	6	2	4	4
Adults total	30	20	32	21	31	25
Children of the family	29	20	28	19	29	21
Guest children	3	2	2	2	3	3
Children total	32	22	30	21	32	24
Total	61	42	62	42	63	49

S1—stage one. Includes all families (11 Israelis, 11 American-Israelis, 12 Jewish-Americans).
S2—stage two. Includes only 8 families of each group.
*Each group includes one single-parent family.
**Two observers for the group of the immigrants were Israeli born and three were American born.
***Other adults include family friends, grandparents, and the technician operating the video.

rules developed by Berman and her colleagues for adapting Hebrew transcriptions for CHILDES.[20] The transcripts follow CHAT for the following conventions:

< >	= overlap; [>] = overlap follows; [<] = overlap precedes.
#	= noticeable pause (other than following utterance terminators and longer than one second; each subsequent second is marked by additional # signs).
[/]	= retracing without correction.
[//]	= retracing with correction.
+/.	= interrupted utterance.
+...	= trailing off (incompletion).
+^	= quick uptake (latching).
+,	= self completion.
++	= other completion.
&	= an incomplete word.
[text]	= paralinguistic material.
%comment:	= contextual information.
xxx	= inaudible utterance(s); number of xs stands for length of inaudible utterance in seconds.

Several deviations from CHAT were introduced. First, punctuation symbols were used to indicate intonation contours, as used by Schiffrin (1994):[21]

.	= utterance final falling intonation followed by noticeable pause (as at the end of a declarative sentence).
?	= utterance final rising intonation followed by noticeable pause (as at the end of an interrogative sentence).
,	= continuing intonation (as—but not only—at the end of a clause, may be followed by a short pause and/or a slight rise or fall in contour).

---

[20]The transcription follows the guidelines for the Hebrew transcription as laid out by Berman and Armon-Lotem (1990), with some minor modifications. The text line is kept close to the way it was uttered, except for some corrections of pronounciation to make the text comprehensible. The vowels used are a, e (including schwa at the beginning of the word, when pronounced); *yeladim* = children), o, i, and u. The consonants used, in order of the Hebrew alphabet are ', b~v, g, d, h, v, z, x (as in loch), t, y, k, l, m, n, s, p~f, c (as in German, "zeit"), k, r, sh, t, j (as in joke), ch (as in child), zh (as in genre). The glottal stop (alef or ayin) is used only between two identical vowels (e.g., *ra'a* = saw) or between a consonant and a vowel (e.g., *tir'e* = will see). It is not used in initial position of the word nor between two nonidentical vowels. To facilitate automatic CLAN searches, certain bound morphemes (such as prepositions) are transcribed as prefixes (e.g., *ba-maxberet* = in the notebook).

[21]In CHAT, the period, the question mark, and exclamation mark are considered utterance terminators; they are further qualified (by "-") when used to mark intonational contours.

:   = colon following vowel indicates elongated vowel sound.
!   = exclamatory intonation.

Second, capitals and quotation marks (for reported speech) were used to ease reading. Third, the text was segmented by turns (the relevant units here), rather than by utterances. Fourth, additional symbols were added:

italics   = emphatic stress.
CAPS   = very emphatic stress.
{text}   = language mix (units smaller than a clause inserted in the host language, e.g., "I have a {*maxma'a*} [compliment] for Naomi."
>   = used at left-hand margin of the transcript to point to a feature of interest.
@End   = marks end of topical segment.

In all examples, families are identified by group and number, and participants are identified by role (for adults) and by name (for children). The age and sex of a child is given in parentheses, in the following order: Andrew (8m) = Andrew, age 8 years, male. Main conversational features (e.g., interruptions and overlaps) are marked approximatively on English translations. The following transcript segment from Israeli data illustrates several of the markings used:

Israeli family 10; the children are Ruti (11.5f), Naomi (8.3f) and Yaron (3.2.m). Present at the meal are also the parents, Rachel, the observer, Markus, the cameraman, and Tamy, a neighbor.

1 Mother: Yaron, tesaper lanu ma <asita ha-yom ba-gan.>[>] — Yaron, tell us what <you did today in school>.[>]
2 Ruti: <ma [//] ex haya ba-gan?> [<] — <What [//] how was school?> [<]
3 Yaron: naim. — Nice.
4 Mother: +^ naim? *ma* haya naim? tesaper lanu ex haya naim. — Nice? *What* was nice? Tell us how it was nice.
5 Yaron: sixaknu. — We played.
6 Mother: be-ma sixaktem? — What did you play?
7 Yaron: be-misxakim. — Games.
8 Mother: eze? ba-xuc? ba-xacer? — What kind? Outside? In the yard?

In this example, Ruti's utterance in turn 2 overlaps with the second half of the mother's utterance in turn 1. Ruti rephrases her question as a "how" rather than a "what" question within the same turn. Yaron's laconic response is followed by a quick uptake in the next question (turn 4), with an emphatic stress on the word *ma* ("what").

PLAN OF THE BOOK

The main body of the book is organized around two themes, each represented by one section: cultural styles of sociability and patterns of pragmatic socialization. Individual chapters present these themes from the point of view of one discourse dimension: thematic frames and topical actions (Chapters 2 & 3), narratives (Chapter 4), control acts (Chapter 5), metapragmatic discourse (Chapter 6), and bilingual practices (Chapter 7). A comparative stance is adopted throughout, exploring cultural variation across the groups with regard to the discourse dimension analyzed.

Part I, entitled "Cultural Styles of Sociability," is concerned with cultural variation with regard to overall organizational principles of dinner talk and the relations between social roles and discourse roles. In Chapter 2 I trace the shared thematic framework of dinner talk in these families, developing the notion of thematic frame as a topical genre and arguing that the shared thematic framework emerges from a tension between sociability and socialization goals. In Chapter 3, the relations between social and discourse roles are considered by analyzing how being a parent or child, a man or a woman, a family member or guest is related to participation in the talk in the form of performing topical actions such as introducing, changing, and elaborating topics during the conversation. Observed differences by social role in partaking in the discourse of topical action raises the issue of the relation between language and power in this context. I argue that observed imbalances in the distribution of topical actions by social role do not index power relations in a simple way and that the social meanings participants attach to the performance of topical action vary with social role, thematic frame, and culture. Within this framework, I discuss the way children's rights and modes of participation vary with thematic frame and how this variation is further subject to cultural constructions of the discursive role of children at dinner, shaping culturally different pathways for children's passage into adult discourse. I argue that cultural diversity in participation roles enacted by men and women (i.e., dominance of men over women in the American families but of women over men in the Israeli families) does not necessarily reflect power relations by gender in the respective societies but is rather a reflection of culturally different perceptions of the situation at hand.

Chapter 4 includes stories told around the dinner table, approached from a theoretical position that considers family storytelling as being an event, a social action unfolding in real time, and simultaneously a text about other events. In this chapter I explore the unique nature of dinner table narrative events as culturally interpreted, three-way intersections between the act of narration (i.e., *telling*), the textual content and form of the narrative (i.e., *tale*), and the persons responsible for the first two (*tellers*). The chapter explores cultural diversity in interactions among the realms of telling, tales, and tellers in family narrative events. The first issue discussed is whether family narrative events of these Jewish, urban, middle-class families constitute a unique genre of oral storytelling. Another concern of this chapter is the degree of cultural diversity with regard to each realm and their interrelations.

Dinnertime provides opportunities for many negotiations of cultural conventions for appropriate verbal and nonverbal behavior. Part II is concerned with three facets of such pragmatic socialization: the discourse of social control acts, metapragmatic discourse, and the social practice of bilingualism. Social control acts (e.g., different types of directives) have been singled out because of the complexity of the relation between their modes of performance and contextual and cultural factors. All types of social control acts constitute a threat to face and impinge on the recipient's freedom of action; hence, they involve social control. Comments made in response to perceived violations of conversational norms (i.e., *metapragmatic comments*) exercise a different type of social control. Whereas for social control acts pragmatic socialization is realized through modeling, by exposing children to the culturally conventional ways of performing directives, in metapragmatic discourse pragmatic socialization takes on a semi-explicit form and is expressed by comments on perceived violations of speech behavior.

Chapter 5 is a discussion of parents' directives and children's patterns of compliance in the framework of politeness theories. A central issue is how to interpret from a politeness perspective the relatively high (compared to other speech events) direct style prevailing in all groups. I argue that this style is essentially polite, enacting its politeness in domain and culturally specific ways. This argument is developed through a consideration of three aspects of family dinner discourse: the negotiation of power relations between parents and children, the degree of formality of the event, and the interaction between the language of affect and the language of control in parent–child discourse. Another issue explored here is cultural variation in styles of control: Examining cultural preferences for directive strategies and patterns of compliance allows us to trace such cultural styles. These styles are then discussed in the wider context of request behavior in the respective societies and in terms of the particular face needs satisfied at family dinners. The argument is that the cultural styles of control depicted reflect culturally varied perceptions of children's face needs.

Chapter 6 is concerned with metapragmatic discourse, defined as comments made to sanction a perceived violation of a conversational norm and, especially in the case of children, to prompt "proper" conversational behavior. The issue investigated is whether the groups differ in their attitudes to performative and expressive aspects of talk, thereby setting a different conversational–pragmatic socialization agenda for their children. We found, for example, that whereas Jewish American parents explicitly attend to rules of conversational management, this aspect is absent from Israeli parents' discourse. This foregrounding of the performative aspects of the talk in the Jewish American families through metapragmatic discourse ties in with performative aspects of Jewish American narratives, discussed in Chapter 4.

Chapter 7 focuses on the group of American-born immigrants to Israel, discussing the bilingual pratices and intercultural style of this group in the context of pragmatic socialization. Both parents and children in the families studied are English–Hebrew bilinguals, with English being the dominant but not sole language in the home. The patterns of language use in these families are examined from two standpoints: first with a focus on practices of bilingualism, through an examination of patterns of language choice, language maintenance, and code switching; and second, in terms of the interactional style used, through a comparison of the discursive patterns of the bilingual families with those of their two contact cultures. I argue that the findings demonstrate a successful case of *bilingual socialization,* namely both bilingual practices in the process of language socialization and socialization toward balanced bilingualism. Simultaneously, I argue that examining the disourse patterns of the immigrant families against the background of cross-cultural variation between Israeli and Jewish American families reveals a unique *pragmatic interlanguage* that does not conform to the interactional style of either one of its contact cultures.

The concluding chapter (Chapter 8) moves away once again from a discourse-specific focus, returning to the issues raised in the Introduction. Commonalities and differences between the groups—in cultural patterns of communication and pragmatic socialization—are examined in light of the wider sociocultural history of Jewish speech communities in Israel and the United States. I argue that the commonalities between the groups need to be traced to the impact of modernity, translated in this context to certain shared features of socialization and sociability. On the other hand, the observed diversity in discursive practices between the groups bears witness to historically shaped, culturally unique interpretations of both costructs and the tensions between them.

A final word is in order about alternations in the choice of first person pronouns throughout the book. "We" stands for the research team that carried out the observations, coding, and analysis and is hence used to report empirical findings. "I" stands for my stance in interpreting the findings, as brought to bear on both text and context.

CULTURAL STYLES
OF SOCIABILITY

2

THE DYNAMICS OF
DINNER TALK

This and the next chapter focus on the dynamics of dinner talk, examining the effects of tensions between sociability and socialization goals at dinner. Dinner talk is considered from two standpoints: first, through a consideration of the overall thematic organization of talk at dinner, and second, in the next chapter, through an examination of the verbal moves that affect the development of the talk agenda.

My first concern is with teasing out the overall organizational principles by which dinners are construed as familial speech events in all the families. I show that despite cultural differences in styles of discourse, dinner talk in all the families encompasses the same tensions between sociability and socialization, realized by constant shifts among different thematic frames of talk. Each of these frames, in turn, evokes its own specific topics and is realized through different genres of talk and participation structures.

My second concern is with cultural variation in the relations between social roles and discourse roles, with a special emphasis on children's voices a dinner. In all the families studied, dinners serve as critical contexts for the passage of children into adult discourse. Cultural differences emerge with regard to the opportunities provided for children to participate in different thematic frames, as well as in the ways the families index gender and construe the role of outsiders. These differences result in different socialization agendas for children and lead to culturally colored interpretations of the relations between power and language for all participants.

SOCIABILITY AND SOCIALIZATION GOALS

Imagine two families sitting down at the dinner table. In the first, all members of the family come to the table, including young children, yet the meal passes in silence, broken only by the moving of cutlery and dishes around the table and the instrumental business talk of having dinner. In the second, all participate, but participation is speech oriented: The necessary dinner talk is just one layer in the talk, superimposed by many other conversational layers. The two examples illustrate the built-in tension between dinner as an activity and dinner as a social, conversational event. Families may vary individually, by social class or by culture, in the ways they balance the two components. In some cultures, or even within other social groups in Israeli and American societies, meals may not even be shared intergenerationally. It may even be the case that families who report having regular family meals are like the French family depicted by Margaret Mead (1959) in her film *Four Families,* where the meal is completely activity-focused, generating little or no conversation. The film shows a French rural family—a husband, a wife, two school-age children, a 4-year-old, and a baby—sitting down for lunch. Margaret Mead's voice-over asks us to focus on the differential treatment given to the boy and the girl, on the strict obedience required of both older children, and on the pleasure these people seem to take in the food itself. The film shows a clear male—female division of labor: It is the woman's task to cook and serve while the man and the children eat. If we try to listen to the voices of the family, we notice there is not that much to hear. The meal passes in silence, broken only by a short sequence triggered by instrumental needs and occasioning a series of social control acts: The father complains that there isn't anything to drink, the mother promptly reprimands the boy for not bringing the pitcher of cider to the table, the boy passes the blame to his sister but is silenced and prompted to act by the father. We have no way of knowing if a meal without the children would yield more conversation, but we know that this is an instance of a sociocultural context in which family mealtime is not conceived as a speech event, an event occasioning sociability through conversation. Nor does it serve to socialize children in ways of speaking.

As noted, the case of our Israeli and American middle-class urban families contrasts sharply with the French rural family. In the middle-class meals we taped, dinner conversations tend to be lively and complex speech events, encompassing a wide range of topics. Furthermore, everyone present participates, including young children. Yet participation is no simple matter. Children's degree and mode of participation is affected by the contextual frame of the talk at any given moment. Children's participation in middle-class family meals is contingent on the sociocultural convention of treating children at shared meals as ratified participants and on the uniqueness of the family meal in these communities as both a sociable and socializing speech event.

Conversations among friends are a prime example of sociable events. They are, at least ostensibly, not goal-oriented and are egalitarian and collaborative (Lakoff, 1990). On the other hand, many institutionalized events, such as trials, therapy sessions, or specifically socializing events (e.g., classroom interactions; Cazden, 1988), are nonegalitarian, are clearly goal-oriented, and are not necessarily collaborative. We asked parents at the interviews whether they had any agenda in mind for family meals. Did they try to achieve certain educational goals? Did they raise certain topics purposely? Their responses reveal a double perception of family meals as both sociable and socializing, at least as far as goal orientation is concerned.

> Mother: It's a social time I mean it's a [time] we talk and you know just and not uh it isn't any kind of directed conversation it's not as if we sit down and everybody reports on their activities for the day or anything like it but we do talk uh about whatever happens to be on anybody's mind. (Jewish Americans, Family 5. The children are 13 and 10.)

The quotation depicts dinner table talk as belonging to the genre of ordinary conversation; it is a "social time" set aside for talk that is not directed (as a lesson, an interview, a service encounter, or courtroom discourse would be). On the contrary, it is a time when "we talk about whatever is on anybody's mind." The focus of such a conversation seems to be on the building of rapport rather than on the transmission of information or the achievement of instrumental goals. In the terms used by Brown and Yule (1983), the overall goal of the talk is framed as interactional rather than transactional. The actual enactment of dinner table conversation does not quite match the idealized construct of dinner as purely social that is presented in the example. Yet the dinners are geared, in Simmel's (1961) terms, to satisfy our human instinct of *sociability*, a "union with others" achieved in social gatherings where "talking is an end in itself" (p. 161).

However, dinners are a very special type of social event; they are familial "we" events shared with children and, as such, carry important *socializing* functions, ranging from the concern with table manners to language socialization in the broadest sense and the enhancement of familial cohesiveness. Some parents' comments in interviews echo these themes as well, framing dinners as quite goal-directed:

> Mother: Dinners are important; they [the children] learned how to eat properly. (Jewish Americans, Family 6. The children are 16 and 12.)

> Mother: We talk, we talk about what happened what everybody did during the day since we're all going in separate directions. *I like to know what they did in school* (my emphasis). (Jewish Americans, Family 7. The children are 10 and 7.)

> Father: I guess like I view this as as uh one of the few times when we are all together ... (Jewish Americans, Family 4. The children are 8 and 4.)

The double function of dinner table conversations as both sociable and socializing events derives as well from parental attitudes toward children's participation. By definition, dinner table conversations represent encounters between unequal intimates. They bring together persons (children and parents) who, in Bateson's (1972) terms, are in a complementary nurturance-dependence relationship. Hence they are structurally nonegalitarian. The families may still practice egalitarian attitudes, if, as in Goffman's (1981) idealized description of ordinary conversation, "everyone is accorded the right to talk as well as to listen" and "everyone is accorded the status of someone whose overall evaluation of the subject matter at hand—whose editorial comments, as it were—is to be encouraged and treated with respect" (p. 14, note 8). Children's participation at dinner talk is universally professed by the parents during interviews to be a very important socializing goal. Asked what is expected of children in terms of conversation during mealtimes, parents said, for example:

Father: If they are at the table they are part of the conversation. (Jewish American, Family 4. The children are 8 and 4.)

Mother: We expect them to be uh an active participant in the mealtime activities. (Jewish Americans, Family 5. The children are 11 and 9.)

Father: And I think I approve of their being communicative about what they are doing ... (Jewish Americans, Family 3. The children are 10 and 6.)

Although the comments depict the status of children as ratified participants (i.e., "they are part of the conversation"), thereby expressing egalitarian attitudes, it is constantly stressed that the status carries with it both rights and obligations. Children are expected to be "active participants" and to gain approval by "being communicative." As expressed by one mother, one of the things she would object to is for a child to "just sit there and kind of pout or really take no interest at all [in the talk]." So children are invited to participate, yet parents reserve the right to accept or dismiss contributions and to pass judgment on their timeliness and relevance. Consider the following interview extracts:

Interviewer: What types of conversational behavior would you object to?

Father: I, I would say [unclear] raise something totally irrelevant. So it's not a question of participation. It's a question of irrelevance. (Jewish Americans, Family 6. The children are 16 and 12.)

Interviewer: What do you think of children joining in the conversation at dinner?

Mother: I think it's important for children to join in a conversation when it's appropriate. But I think they have to wait until it's their turn.

Interviewer: Do you expect children to be quiet during certain conversational occasions?

Mother: Yes. When it's something they don't know anything about, I'd prefer them to be quiet. I try, first of all, not to discuss something that I don't want my kids to hear, you know. But if they don't know anything about the subject, then I expect them to be quiet unless they have a specific question. (Jewish Americans, Family 3. The children are 10 and 6.)

Criteria of relevance, conversational appropriateness, and knowledge are among those mentioned by the parents as crucial for controlling children's contributions to the talk; cumulatively, the interview quotations express parental checks and balances of egalitarian ideologies expressed elsewhere. Children are granted talking privileges at dinner, but parents reserve the right and power to modify and withhold these privileges. The question then is how children actually participate. Do they raise topics of their own? Do they contribute to all topics raised at dinner? To answer these questions we first need to understand the overall organizational principles that govern dinner talk in these families. Despite many cultural differences in styles of discourse, the families across the three groups share the same organizational principles by which dinners are construed as familial speech events.

THEMATIC FRAMES

Do family dinner conversations, in any sense, resemble Goffman's (1981) idealized construct of conversation as "a period of idling felt to be an end in itself, during which everyone is accorded the right to talk as well as to listen without reference to a fixed schedule" (p. 14)? The answer will depend on how we approach the notions of a "shared conversational end" and a "fixed schedule." Within a philosophical, pragmatic theory framework of conversation the notion of "end" corresponds to *purpose* or *direction*:

> Our talk exchanges are characteristically, to some degree at least, cooperative efforts; and each participant recognizes in them, to some extent, a common purpose or set of purposes, or at least a mutually accepted direction ... at each stage, some possible conversational moves would be excluded as conversationally unsuitable. (Grice, 1975, p. 45)

Searle (1981) and Dascal and Idan (1989) take Grice's principle of cooperativeness, built on the assumption of a mutually accepted direction, a step further: They suggest a view of conversation as *collective action*. As such, conversations involve a "we" level of shared intentionality that is not the sum of individual intentions. In ritualized speech events, we-purposes define desired outcomes, such as establishing a marriage, negotiating social peace, or expressing condolence. In ordinary conversation, we-purposes can range in degree of specificity (from merely general cooperativeness to a specific goal), in sharedness, and in overtness (Dascal & Idan, 1989). Family dinners have one clear collective we-purpose on the level of action, *having dinner*. This collective purpose is also associated with individual socialization goals (like teaching children table manners) and may be verbalized through instrumental and socializing discourse. Individual members may further come to the table with a variety of vaguely or precisely defined goals. For example, during one of the taped dinners one American Israeli family engaged in a speech ritual of reciprocal complaints and compliments (e.g., "I have a *maxma'a* [compliment] for Neta"). We were told that this is a purposeful, weekly activity, believed to be important for enhancing family relations.

The notion of schedule (Goffman, 1981) has to do with the participant's perceptions of *aboutness*: the general theme of the conversation, the semantically congruent set of entities that together determine the conversational world of discourse (van Dijk, 1977, 1981). If such themes are preplanned, as in classrooms, trials, newsbroadcasts, and interviews, we can say that the speech event has a fixed schedule, and participants will be expected to make their contributions with reference to this schedule. Having a fixed schedule normally also entails specific discourse regulatory rights, which allow those in power not only the privilege of discourse management but also that of passing judgment on the degree of topical relevance of the contribution of others. At dinner, most of the talk is not scheduled in either this or other ways. Talk shifts constantly from the realm of the immediate, instrumental task at hand to a variety of other seemingly nonconnected issues. Topics are sometimes initiated with no apparent link to anything that has gone on before at this particular dinner or any other that we taped. Yet the collaboratively established associative links between long chunks of talk are easily retrievable by our commonsense notions of aboutness. Family dinners do not have a prefixed schedule, at least not in the sense that ritualized speech events do, but do they have collective we-agendas? The answer is affirmative, but only if we understand a shared agenda as a principle of familial coherence, arrived at and "trusted" (Garfinkel, 1984) by the participants engaged in the talk and retrieved retrospectively by the outsider discourse analyst on his or her listening to or reading the conversation. It is the unveiling of this agenda and its interaction with processes of pragmatic socialization that concern us in this chapter. What we are looking for are, first, assumptions of underlying coherence. Can we detect the organizing principles by which families select topics for talk? Are such topics shared across cultures to the degree that justifies a claim for a *we-agenda* of middle-class families at dinner? Second, how is the agenda setting at dinner related to pragmatic socialization?

We approached "topics" and "themes" empirically in two ways (Blum-Kulka, 1994). First, we searched for the semantic macrothemes that summarize the content of a talk segment in terms of global aboutness rather than local coreference (Brown & Yule, 1983; van Dijk, 1981; Guiora, 1985). Such macrothemes constitute in effect thematic frames that organize the discourse in two interrelated ways: in terms of familial notions of relevance and in terms of discourse rules, particularly with regard to children's participation. The topics talked about within each frame, as well as those not talked about at all, are for the discourse analyst indicators of familial notions of relevance. We cannot know why these and not an infinite number of other potential topics are raised at dinner, but the repeated occurrence of the same cluster of themes across all dinners does indicate that these are the themes the participants felt were relevant for conversation at family dinners in the middle-class families studied here. Furthermore, each thematic frame constitutes a different discourse genre, with its own discourse rules that, in terms of pragmatic socialization, define the achievable parental goals and the ways in which children's participation will be accepted.

The second approach follows Bublitz (1988) in considering topics as the conversational moves relevant to shaping discourse structure. This approach views topics as actions. Topical actions include the acts of introducing, elaborating, shifting, and digressing from a topic as ways of having an impact on the talk agenda. These two approaches are complementary: The identification of global thematic frames is facilitated by the coding of local topical actions, because segments bounded by two topical actions tend to constitute thematically coherent units. These approaches allow us to clarify two different aspects of the dynamics of family discourse at dinner. In looking at themes, our concern is the nature of the agenda in these conversations according to how the agenda is established and how children's participation may vary with thematic frames. In discussing topical actions, on the other hand, the focus shifts to issues of the relations between talk and power, specifically, the ways in which rights for performing topical actions are distributed among husbands and wives, adults and children. This dimension is taken up in the next chapter.

Themes at dinner arise within a delimited spatiotemporal physical frame, but, in turn, they may further act constitutively to create contextual frames, each "bounding a set of interactive messages" (Bateson, 1972, p. 191). As Bateson's and Goffman's work has shown, interactional frames, like picture frames, draw imaginary lines such that the messages enclosed within "are defined as members of a class by virtue of their sharing common premises or mutual relevance" (Bateson, 1972, p. 188). These common premises,

whether metacommunicated or not, provide the cues necessary for interpretation and serve as indices for familial notions of relevance. The dinner
table conversations we recorded share three major contextual or thematic
frames: the situational, the urgent familial, and the nonimmediate. Each of
these frames occasions its own local themes, assigns discourse roles in
different ways, and evokes its own rules of interpretation.

Situational Concerns

Malinowsky (1923) was perhaps the first scholar to draw our attention to
the embeddedness of talk in what he called "the context of the situation"
and to the function of language in the universe of practical action. Dinners
are a prime example of a case where "language functions act as a link in
concerted human activity" (Malinowsky, 1923, p. 312). The situational frame
at dinner dictates instrumental goals: Minimally, food has to be brought to
the table and accessed by or served to all present. Many of these activities
are underscored by or assisted verbally by directives ("Could you pass the
salt"; "We do not eat lettuce with our fingers"), by offers ("Wouldn't you like
some potatoes?") and by compliments ("This is wonderful"). The business
talk of having dinner runs through all our conversations. It is the most
consistently recurring thematic frame but also the one that needs the least
coherence grounding work. It can always be shifted back to with no marking
work, giving it a kind of privileged status among other frames. Thus, for
example, interjected between talk about the last Whoopi Goldberg show and
about the new VCR bought by the family, the mother attends to dinner
needs: "We have one bread, so eat it slowly, not all at once."

The unfamiliar experience of being taped for research purposes is another topic of the situational frame, though most of the time the tape
recorder is treated as part of an unnoticed background. Depending on the
family, between 5% and 13% of the time in the first 20 minutes of each dinner
members discussed the taping equipment ("I can see the light is on") and
the goals of the research ("Who is going to listen to this") and used meta-
comments of resurgent awareness ("You are on tape"). The presence of the
video equipment (or tape) may trigger the need to exercise control, as in
the following series of directives uttered in the given sequence to 4-year-old
Michael: "Michael, the videotape can't see you there/ Michael, you get back
here/ Mike, come on back. Mike, you won't get dessert."

A subtheme that links the two themes of food and research is the topi-
calization of food as such—its quality, ways of making it, and so on—which
is oftentimes initiated by the observers. Being a guest at dinner, and hosting
one, is in a sense unfamiliar (or at least less familiar than having dinner at
home with one's family only), imposing on all concerned specific rights and
obligations. The host–guest relationship may be expected to trigger domains

of talk such as complimenting the cook or exchanging recipes, which the family would not, or would less, engage in otherwise.

Other themes within the frame of immediate concerns emerge locally, such as when a baby dozing in the far corner of the room becomes restless, when a neighbor comes to the door, when a telephone conversation during dinner requires some further attention, or when a member of the family is late for dinner. Themes of situational concern are anchored spatiotemporally in the here and now. The language is highly contextualized, contains many deictics which are decipherable only by being present on the scene or by viewing the video, and has relatively long pauses. In addition, the choice of specific topics is often motivated by the actors' personal needs and changes noticed in the physical context, marking this realm (in Shutz's, 1970, terms) as a case of topics of "imposed relevance."

Shutz viewed *topical relevance* in general as the thematization of the unordinary against the horizon of the ordinary. Imposed topical relevance occurs when "the articulation of the field into theme and horizon is imposed by the emergence of some unfamiliar experience, by a shift of the accent of reality from one province to another" (p. 33). It is this shift of "the accent of reality" that is constantly at work at dinner. The instrumental talk concerning the business of having dinner is a province to which participants will turn every time that ensuring the smooth flow of the activity requires verbal intervention. The familiar in this case is scripted and nonverbal (e.g., the motions involved in eating get verbalized by adults for young children, not by adults for adults); when the script is disrupted (e.g., food spilled, help needed in getting to a dish, a child seen as lacking in table manners), the disruption constitutes the unfamiliar experience being thematized. The activity of having dinner, and all that is associated with it, serves as the assumed background for all other talk. Thus, when something requires verbalization, it can be accomplished abruptly, with no need for displaying relevance. Such shifts are mostly accomplished in single utterances or in brief one-to-three move exchanges, each exchange consisting of an act sequence like offer–acceptance or request–compliance.

Occasionally, the dinner as business frame suppresses all other conversational frames. In such cases the discourse is typically lacking in content messages but is rich in directive speech acts and is often built on brief, dyadic parent–child, child–parent exchanges:

(1) Jewish Americans 12; Dara (13f); Daniel (4m); Elizabeth (called Beth, 10f). The conversation begins as the recording starts.

1	Mother:	Daniel you want apple juice?
2	Dara:	<Dad xxx.> [>]
3	Beth:	<xxxxxxx.> [<]
4	Mother:	You want to sit over there?

 5 Daniel: Yeah.
 6 Beth: Where am I sitting?
 7 Dara: Daddy put a napkin like that.
 8 Father: <xxx>. [>]
 9 Mother: <xxx>. [<]
10 Dara: xxx apple juice.
11 Daniel: Hi Mom, hi Dad.
12 Mother: [laughs].
13 Daniel: xxx.
14 Mother: Here, do you want some?
15 Daniel: Me salad give me salad me *salad!*
16 Mother: Oh you want salad Daniel?
17 Father: xxx.
18 Daniel: But with mushrooms. Yeah with mushrooms.
              With mushrooms. I like them! Remember?
19 Mother: Uhhm do you want salad?
20 Daniel: With mushrooms I do.
21 Mother: I didn't hear you, did you say xxx?
22 Father: xxx what's this then? I'm all confused. What's
              this?
23 Daniel: This isn't mine!
24 Father: Where's your mother sitting? Where's your
              mother sitting?
25 Daniel: [screaming].
26 Mother: xxx you're sitting here.
27 Father: Give that to your mother then. Give that to your
              mother.
28 Daniel: NO [/] NO Daddy is sitting here!
29 Mother: xxx +/.
30 Father: I'll sit next to you.
31 Xxx: Daniel!
32 Xxx: Daniel!
33 Daniel: xxx.
34 Mother: [laughs].
35 Daniel: xxx.
36 Beth: xxx
37 Daniel: I wanna take *one* [whining]!
38 Mother: xxx.
39 Daniel: Sroom [/] sroom, I want a mushroom.
40 Mother: Okay.
41 Father: Here Danny have this.
42 Daniel: xxx.
43 Daniel: Not that xxx.

44 Father: It's going to be hot.
45 Mother: Take this here <and then I'm going +...> [>]
46 Father: <Beth do wannah get +...> [<]
47 Mother: You want, you want sauce on your spaghetti?
48 Father: xxx.
49 Mother: <You want more?> [>]
50 Daniel: <xxx mushroom!> [<]
51 Father: How many meatballs do you want? How many meat-
            balls?
52 Xxx: Two.
53 Father: Two.
54 Daniel: xxx.
55 Mother: That's enough Daniel.
56 Daniel: Look what I have!
57 Mother: What?
58 Daniel: xxx
59 Father: This is Judy's special spaghetti. It's not your
            typical spaghetti. I've no idea how much you'll
            like # this much # twice as much # half as much?
60 Daniel: That's fine.
61 Daniel: <xxx.> [>]
62 Mother: <xxx.> [<]
63 Beth: *Mummy!*
64 Mother: It's ok I'll get you more just xxx.
65 Father: I think that you'll want to take down in your
            research report that that there weren't enough
            meatballs.

Example 1 is a rather atypical long stretch of talk within the situational frame. It occurred during the very first minutes of the recording, as the family was settling down to dinner. The talk is concerned with seating arrangements (turns 4, 6, 24, and 26), with both parents serving the food to the children while trying hard to control 4-year-old Daniel, whose screams keep interrupting the smooth flow of food distribution. The highly context-embedded nature of the talk is apparent in the frequent use of deictics, some of which remain obscure on reading the written version. Thus, we do not know what "this" refers to in turns 22 and 23 or 41. Most of the parents' utterances are offers of drink and food to each of the three children or attempts to clarify their exact wishes (turns 1, 14, 16, 47, 49, and 51). Other parental utterances are attempts to control Daniel by calling his name (turns 31 and 32) or by telling him off: "That's enough, Daniel" (turn 56). Finally, there are also comments on the food (turn 59) and an attempt to deal humorously, through reference to the research situation, with the shortage of meatballs (turn 65).

It is important to note that children have a privileged position within this frame. The nurturance–dependence link between them and their parents (Bateson, 1972) calls for heightened parental attention to their physical (especially food-related) needs at dinner. Hence, to ask for a second serving, get a drink, reach for a dish, or refuse an offer for food, children do not need to struggle to gain conversational entry, as would be the case for any topic other than instrumental dinner talk. Furthermore, requests from children within this frame are often phrased in a highly abrupt and direct manner that might be considered impolite on other occasions. Daniel demands rather than asks for salad ("Me salad/ give me salad/me salad"), expresses his wish for mushrooms assertively ("I wanna take one/ sroom [/] room I want a mushroom") and justifies his request by his personal preferences ("I like them, remember?"). On this occasion, the child's requesting style meets with no reaction from the parents. On other occasions, children's requests within the situational frame trigger pragmatic socialization for politeness: 3-year-old Sandra's request for more meat ("*Meat!*") is responded to by the mother with, "What do you say, dear?" prompting the required politeness formula ("Meat please"). Nonverbal aspects of politeness also come to the fore within this frame. Through comments such as "Don't eat lettuce with your fingers" or "We haven't finished eating," parents directly teach children the conventional norms of polite behavior at dinner. Thus, although the situational frame does not provide occasions for children to develop their conversational skills, it serves at least one important goal of pragmatic socialization, socialization for both verbal and nonverbal norms of politeness (see Chapter 5).

Across all families, situational concerns consist of one fifth of the talk.[1]

Immediate Family Concerns

The second thematic frame contains themes of *immediate family concern,* "immediate" in the sense that matters talked about within this frame happened or were noticed in the very recent past of the last day and are being recounted or discussed for the first time and may require further action. The unifying feature of this realm is its circle of protagonists and participants. In this news frame, the family attends to the most recent news of its members. Spouses tell each other about work, parents ask children about school, and children volunteer stories about their day. In this type of talk, the scene moves away from the home to the classroom, the office, and the playground. The focus is often on action ("Mom, we went on a school trip today," "What did you do today at school?") rather than on objects, as in instrumental

---

[1]Proportions of themes were calculated by coding the segments bounded by two topical actions as belonging to one of three thematic frames: instrumental, immediate family concerns, and non-immediate.

dinner talk. The child-centered ethos of Jewish middle-class families is also apparent here: Adults in all families question the children about their activities, and all families yield the floor to children's initiations of personal topics. In addition, the adults bring up child-focused topics not addressed to the children.

Relevance in this frame *is gained by membership rights*: As a child or a spouse, a person is entitled to tell or be asked about his or her news. In Sacks' (1971/1978) terms, such news is tellable, and it is "his [or her] involvement that provides for the story's telling" (p. 261). However, the set of rights and obligations is not equally divided. Children do not as a rule question parents about their day, and if they do, it is not perceived as a serious question. Nor do observers receive or initiate "today" exchanges, except with young children (see Chapter 4). We learned from the interviews that this is the thematic frame least influenced by the observer's presence. Parents and children alike report during interviews that they engage regularly in "my/your news" themes at meal times.

The news-telling frame is inclined toward stories of personal experience, assertive and expressive rather than directive speech acts, great variation in length and genre (from short question–answer sequences to lengthy monologic narratives), and, in the case of adult–child interactions, a style that is reminiscent of classroom discourse: Parents, like teachers, tend to regulate turn-taking by children.

Within this news-telling frame, the parent often acts as a discussion leader, summoning the children by name and allocating potentially extended narrative turns by asking open-ended "today" questions (Blum-Kulka & Snow, 1992; see also Chapter 4):

(2) Jewish Americans 10; Andrew (10m); Jessica (8f); Jonathan (3m).

1	Mother:	Tell me about your day.
2	Jessica:	My day?
3	Mother:	Yes.
4	Jessica:	What?

Even in this display mode, when the topic is initiated by the child, children's topic development within the frame of immediate family matters is closely controlled by adults:

(3) Jewish Americans 4; Jordan (8m); Sandra (4f)

1	Jordan:	Mommy you know what?
2	Mother:	Yes dear.
3	Jordan:	As um Snappy Smurf would say "I wish we didn't have to eat the vegetables." I just [/] I just wish we could eat the little good things inside them.

4 Observer: [laughs]. Sounds like that commercial for #
             Nutrasweet in vitamins.
5 Mother: xxx put Nutrasweet in # broccoli?
6 Jordan: Mommy that's what Snappy Smurf said when farmer
             Smurf told him that there are little good things
             in vegetables and that's why you had to *eat* them.
7 Mother: Oh.

Jordan's first turn is interpreted by the mother as a bid for a turn and is responded to as such. Jordan's contribution is then appreciated by the observer for its "cuteness," leading to a brief exchange between her and the mother (turns 4 and 5) before Jordan can continue. The third-party-addressed comment by the observer sets the child's contibution apart, treating its originator not as a direct addressee but rather as an inadvertent, unofficial overhearer (cf. Goffman, 1981). It is only by reestablishing the mother as recipient by a direct summons ("Mommy" in turn 6) that Jordan elicits a direct response to his contribution ("Oh" in turn 7).

We can see that self-inititation in this display mode offers children opportunities to practice their discourse skills in a multiparty setting. However, the presence of several adults endangers children's participation rights because at any given moment adults may talk to each other as if the child were not present, thereby framing him or her, in Goffman's (1981) terms, as an unratified participant. Furthermore, because children's topical initiations tend to be performed within the frame of immediate family matters and about issues of personal experience, they ultimately allow for parental control over both discourse management and content. Thus, children's rights for participation by self-initiation, perceived as power, are qualified by adult gatekeeping rights for controlling conversational entry, which frame the participatory rights of the child and show appreciation (or lack of it) for the content of children's contribution.

The topics adults tend to raise with children in this frame usually concern the children's lives. It is over responsibility for this private space that the negotiation for the meaning of talk takes place. Whereas in the case of the display mode the emphasis in gaining power through talk is on the Gricean maxim of quantity in terms of simple length (i.e., how many words or turns), in the case of elicitation it shifts to the maxim of quantity in terms of informativeness (Grice, 1975). For children, being informative about their lives in frameworks set up by the adults is risky—it may elicit support as well as challenge, invite concern as well as intervention. The next example illustrates that parental support is not granted automatically:

(4) Jewish Americans 4; Jordan (8m); Sandra (4f). The father's question interrupts Jordan's lengthy account of a soccer game.

1	Father:	Jordan would you like to tell us something? Other than soccer what happened today?
2	Jordan:	Well +...
	% comment:	[simultaneously mother and Sandra engaged in negotiating food.]
3	Jordan:	We had a mean xxx for a teacher.
4	Father:	<You what?> [>]
	% comment:	[overlaps with Sandra softly singing to herself]
5	Jordan:	Our teacher got mean.
6	Father:	Your teacher # the substitute got mean?
7	Jordan:	Yes.
8	Father:	Why? What did you do to her today?
9	Jordan:	Nothing, but she [//] Mrs. Yeomans you know we have gym today. Mrs. Yeomans always lets us go out but our <substitute didn't> [>].
	% comment:	[overlaps with Sandra's request for milk]
10	Father:	She didn't let you go out outside for gym?
11	Jordan:	She didn't let us go outside for recess!
12	Father:	Why not?
13	Jordan:	Right!
14	Father:	Why not?
15	Jordan:	Because she said we had gym. And ALL the kids protested and said "but b- b- but Mrs. Yeomans always lets us!" But she said "Mrs. Modden doesn't."
16	Father:	When is Mrs. Yeomans going to be back?
17	Jordan:	Well me and Darren are *praying* that it's going to be tomorrow.
18	Father:	Because you you're tired of the substitute?
19	Jordan:	Yes. Mhmm. Very.
20	Observer:	What's wrong with your teacher?
21	Father:	Well, it's her kids they have the chicken pox.
22	Observer:	Ohuh!

First, in response to the announcement of a "wrong" done by an institutional representative (i.e., the substitute teacher) the parent half-jokingly, by the tone of voice, sets himself up as a prejudiced judge by assuming a causal link between the teacher's "meanness" and the kids' behavior ("Why? What did you do to her today?"). Jordan presents two versions of the event, that of the substitute teacher holding the pupils in the classroom by the power of her authority ("Mrs. Modden doesn't allow kids out") and his own version, which accuses her of breaking the norm established by the regular teacher (turn 15). In this controversy between the institutional version and the child's version, the parent chooses to withhold judgment. At the crucial point, as

Jordan expands the justification for the complaint (turn 15), thereby setting up a request for support, the father changes the focus of the discussion. Although his question, "When is Mrs. Yeomans going to be back?" (turn 16), is an indirect acceptance of Jordan's plight, it is by no means a challenge of institutional authority. Teachers are teachers are teachers, even if ostensibly unjust.

In this elicited mode, the meanings of talk and power may be reversed. As pointed out by Goody (1978), adult questions to children are easily interpretable as impositions. On the involvement–independence complementary continuum suggested by Tannen (1986) (following Bateson, 1972), "How was school?" may be interpreted as signaling positive involvement, but it may also be perceived as a serious invasion of privacy. In the latter case, there is power in not responding cooperatively and thereby challenging the presumption that children are accountabe to parents, which parents seem to take for granted (Varenne, 1992). Thus, the expressed parental wish of "I want to hear what happened to them" may be translated by children as a face threat. It is an instance where one who cooperates may be perceived, in Bateson's (1972) terms, as being cast in the role of the powerless "exhibitionist" and called upon to display himself to the powerful adults. The extreme examples of this phenomenon in the dinner table conversations come from interactions with young preschoolers, for whom the developmental stage in mastering conversational competence combines with a reluctance to provide information when asked for it ("How was school?" "Pleasant." "Did you play?" "Yes." "What else did you do?" "Nothing."). In conversations with older children, the ambivalence associated with responding to "conversational demands" (Dascal, 1983, p. 109) finds expression in more subtle ways:

(5) Jewish Americans 5; Ruth (10f); Dana (13f).

1	Father:	Do you have any projects coming up Dana?
2	Dana:	I have to do a very very very uh don't don't get excited xxx a report on "A Tale of Two Cities" <but it has to xxxxxxxxxxxxxx> [>].
3	Father:	<You already did, you already> [<] read "A Tale of Two Cities."
4	Dana:	I know xxx I have to do another report on it.
5	Father:	What's it about?
7	Dana:	"A Tale of Two Cities" [irritated].
8	Father:	Yeah but what subjects? How long is your <xxx>?
9	Mother:	<xxx>?
10	Dana:	xxxxx.
11	Ruth:	Oh [laughs].
12	Father:	<If you want me to help you +. . .> [>]

13	Dana:	<xxx geometry> [<]
14	Father:	Dana Dana let me know if you want help on any of these projects and I can help you on # Saturday, ok?
15	Dana:	Do you know how long this xxx has to be?
%comment:		[turning to Ruth]
16	Ruth:	Twenty pages?
17	Dana:	Yup. I'm dead serious. It has to be *twenty* pages long.
18	Mother:	For what, a "Tale of Two Cities"?
19	Dana:	A Tale of Two Cities! [laughs]
20	Father:	That's not very helpful Dana.

None of Dana's responses to her father's questions are fully cooperative. She qualifies her informative first response (turn 2) with a warning ("don't get excited"), which seems uncalled for (although there might be a family history behind her comment). Retroactively, her warning proves justified by her father indeed showing excitement. Note the overlap in turns 2 and 3, which leads to an interruption at the point of what might have been the most informative part of Dana's utterance ("but it has to"). In turn 4 Dana provides the required clarification, but the referential misunderstanding in turns 5 and 6 (if "it" refers to the content or subject of the report) restores the challenging, adversial key of the whole exchange. Dana seems to interpret her father's questions as a challenge to her status as a student, in the sense that Labov and Fanshel (1977) define the notion: "If A asserts a proposition that is supported by A's status, and B questions the proposition, then B is heard as challenging the competence of A in that status" (p. 125). The next round of questions (turn 7) is circumvented by Dana turning to her sister (turn 8) with an utterance (unintelligible on tape) that causes laughter.

As the conversation unfolds, Dana continues to circumvent her father's questions and offers for help ("Dana, Dana, let me know if you want help xxxx and I can help you on Saturday, ok?") by addressing her comments to Ruth ("Do you know how long this xxxx has to be? / Twenty pages? / Yup") and accompanying her comments with laughter. A metacomment by the father at this point, "That's not very helpful Dana," confirms that dissatisfaction with the direction of the conversation is mutual. The conversation then goes on in the same adversial key (with both parents joining in), focusing on attempts to advise Dana how to get the project accomplished well and finished on time. On other occasions, or in other families, we may encounter a mutually cooperative, fully supportive key in a similar interaction. Yet the risk of a nonsatisfactory unfolding of such conversations is inherent in their structure.

The frame of immediate family concerns provides important opportunities for discursive socialization. Both by display of self-initiated topics and in response to adult elicitation, children practice adherence to conversational norms, turn-taking as well as narrative skills. It is interesting to note that many of the conversational strategies that adults employ with children in these exchanges echo the supportive devices that middle-class caretakers in the Western world use with infants at the early stages of language acquisition. Such devices were shown, on the one hand, to facilitate language acquisition (see Snow, 1984, for a review) and, on the other, to differentiate between subcultures within the same society (Heath, 1983). When the mother asks 10-year-old Jessica, "Tell me about your day" (Example 2), she is setting up the child, in the terms used by Heath (1983), as an "information giver," a person to be trusted to share with others information known to her only. As Heath demonstrated, such trust typifies adult–child exchanges among the groups she calls townspeople—educated, ethnically mixed American middle-class parents, but it is almost absent from adult–child interactions in both Black and White working-class communities.

Other scaffolding strategies associated with motherese include acknowledgments, expansions, clarification questions, and recastings. For Bruner (1986), such strategies are part of the Language Acquisition Support System (LASS) provided by the social world. Used with infants, they act to give meaning and status to utterances that would be grammatically unacceptable in adult–adult communication, as when a child's mere vocalization is framed as a rightful turn of talk. Because with older children the issue is no longer grammatical acceptability, the support provided by the adults is less manifest on the surface level of discourse, but it is still detectable as unique to adult–child communication. For example, the mother's response ("Yes dear") to 8-year-old Jordan's opening gambit in Example 3 ("Mommy, you know what?") is not the response that would normally be given in adult–adult communication (to an adult one would probably insert "what?" in this slot) but is rather a clear indication to the child that his wish to take the floor has been understood and accepted. In Example 4, Jordan's story emerges in response to a series of clarification questions from the father (including one expansion in turns 5 and 6: "Our teacher got mean"; "Your teacher the substitute got mean?"). Though each question separately might have appeared just as easily in an adult–adult co-construction of a story, their accumulation gives the exchange the dialogic story co-construction format typical of adult–child communication. It is a format that might be a necessary condition for the story to emerge at all with younger children and is still adhered to when older children are involved.

This dialogic framework of many of the exchanges in the frame of immediate family concerns provides children with practice in building coherence through question–answer sequences and in adhering to the demands of turn-taking rules, as well as providing opportunities for the construction of autonomous texts (for the latter, see Blum-Kulka & Snow, 1992). Furthermore, the topical focus on personal experience necessarily involves the negotiation of moral issues as well: Jordan's story of the substitute teacher (Example 4) concerns justice as applied to teachers. These socialization goals are achieved despite the complex structure of multiparty talk at family dinners, in which children are not necessarily always at the center of supportive attention.

Immediate family concerns occupy an important place at dinners, taking up over a third (35%) of talking time.

Non-Immediate Concerns

The third frame is less easily definable by label because it involves all themes of family and personal relevance felt to be shareable in this event. For convenience, I refer to this frame as that of *non-immmediate concerns*, non-immediate designating a degree of distancing from the world of here and now (see also Perlman, 1984). Specific themes vary in their degree of shared information, spatiotemporal distancing, types of protagonist, key, and nar-rativization. Having a guest for dinner may and did result in retellings of personal and family histories. Spatiotemporally this frame encompasses both the recent and nonrecent past as well as the future and moves across many locations outside the home: an Israeli family's recent visit to Egypt, an American father's planned trip to Italy, an American mother's complaints about working conditions at the college where she teaches. The general key of the interaction varies in the degree of seriousness. Though many stories are meant to entertain, jokes are rare and mostly limited to tellers striving hard for floor space. The presence of an adult guest seems to have had a decisive impact on shaping the discourse within this frame. It allowed, for example, for the display of a genre that can be called *family fables*—stories told repeatedly and based on shared memories, occasioned by the presence of a new audience, and for the exchange of adult cultural information (e.g., books, movies, T.V. programs). Conversation within this frame is manifestly sociable and meets several of Goffman's (1981) idealized requirements for ordinary conversations. There is no fixed schedule, and contributions by all participants are "treated with respect" (Goffman, 1981, p. 14, note 8). Thus, despite the built-in asymmetrical relations between parents and children, within this frame children's contributions are treated on par with contributions from adults.

It is only within the third frame of non-immediate topics that children's contributions are freed from power ambivalence. This is the mode whereby children make a successful contribution to an exchange primarily sustained by adults. Participating in this mode carries a special bonus for child participants: Having your contribution seamlessly woven into the ongoing discourse is a powerful signal of being accepted as an equal, full-fledged conversational partner in the adult discourse world. In the following extract, conversational competence is expressed through the ability to collaborate in phatic talk (performing a topical shift) about the weather:

(6) Jewish Americans 9; Andrew (9.5m); Ellen (7f).

1	Mother:	We had no heat at my office today.
2	Observer:	This is the <coldest day of the year> [>] +...
3	Mother:	<That is the reason I cut> [<] it out early. I couldn't stand it there. I was absolutely freezing this morning.
4	Ellen:	Lisa our student teacher is always cold. She's always freezing.
5	Father:	Speaking of Lisa, I think I saw her on the sidewalk today at Harvard Square.

Ellen's contribution ties in seamlessly with that of the others: It's both coherent (i.e., on topic) and cohesive (through lexical reiteration, repeating both "cold" and "freezing" in a new context). The topical change subsequently accomplished by her father (turn 5) is based on her contribution, acknowledging it ("speaking of Lisa") as well as using it as the springboard for the shift in focus.

Older children may make meaningful contributions not only to phatic talk about the weather but also to the negotiation of meaning of topics concerning moral issues and cultural identities. A long stretch of conversation about Whoopi Goldberg includes the following extract:

(7) Jewish Americans 1; Simon (13m); Jennifer (15f).

1	Father:	It's set very good, um she did this thing on Anna Frank and +...
2	Simon:	It wasn't on, it was just a little bit about +/.
3	Father:	Well, *no* # # it was really the central theme about # that thing with the junkie and +...
% comment:		[6 turns omitted: Father is making sure Jennifer has seen the show].
4	Father:	She was this junkie using all this foul language and also telling funny stuff, you know. People laughing and then she visits Anna Frank, the Anna Frank house in Amsterdam and the whole context of it xxx I mean, talk about a subject like that in the context of her performance, you know. I was ready to say "Oh my God, forget it, I'm not gonna watch this," but she does it. I mean she really pulls it off. She discusses, how do you discuss Anne Frank in a humorous context in a &co +/.

>	5	Jennifer:	But it wasn't humorous.
	6	Observer:	I don't think she was trying to be humorous.
	7	Father:	Well no, it's humor really in the best sense.
>	8	Simon:	On all her things she has like a moral for all of them.
	9	Father:	What was the moral of this?
>	10	Simon:	Her, you know, her image # that she should appreciate her things more.
	11	Jennifer:	That anybody could +. . .
	12	Simon:	That her everyday problems are much less than # you know.
	13	Father:	Yeah.
>	14	Jennifer:	And then the thing with the Valley Girls.
	15	Mother:	That was hysterical.
	16	Father:	I think she's a genius, I think she's a genius.

Several cultural and conversational presuppositions form the basis of this conversation. The particular show in question is presumably familiar to all present except the observer. Yet, to understand the father's concern with the show (i.e., Whoopi Goldberg's talking about a visit to the Anna Frank house) one has to be familiar with the story of Anna Frank in the wider context of the Holocaust and be aware that Whoopi Goldberg is not Jewish. Whereas historical knowledge with regard to Anna Frank is assumed to be shared by all, the comedienne's non-Jewish identity is clarified (in response to a question by Simon) earlier in the conversation. Mutual aware- ness of the Jewish identity of all the participants is another precondition that all build on.

From the father's point of view, the issue is that of *entitlement* (Shuman, 1986, pp. 137–141): Is a non-Jewish artist entitled to touch "a subject like that" in a "humorous context"? In other words, can an outsider give a comic twist to "our" tragic story? It is noteworthy that both children challenge systematically the father's tendency to highlight the Jewish angle and his insistence on the comic twist, first, by debating the centrality of Anna Frank in the show (turn 2: "it wasn't on it, it was just a little bit about") and then by contesting that it was humorous at all (Jennifer, backed by the observer, turn 5 and turn 6). Moreover, it is Simon who insists on the need to interpret Whoopi Goldberg in the wider context of her other shows ("On all her things she has like a moral for all of them"), thereby changing the debate's per- spective and minimizing the importance of her dealing with Anna Frank in this specific one. With the father's encouragement and Jennifer's support (turn 11), Simon then formulates for all the moral of the specific Anne Frank incident: It is one illustration of a higher principle ("that her everyday problems are much less, you know") that Whoopi Goldberg is presumably trying to transmit in all her work. This justification of Whoopi Goldberg accepted (turn 13), the talk can move on to discussing yet another Whoopi Goldberg show ("And then the thing with the Valley Girls").

Non-immediate topics take up 45% of the talk at the dinner table. In the realm of the non-immediate, children may talk less than they do (by initiation or elicitation) on topics of more immediate personal experience. Yet the socializing functions achievable are not less important. From the discourse point of view, such exchanges may serve as models for narratives and provide practice in the intricate skills needed for participating in multiparty talk. Simultaneously, there may be important implications for the development of self. Whereas adults maintain control over children's participation in child-centered topics, thereby implicitly enhancing their status as children, the child's contribution to adult topics grants him or her entry to the adult world, thereby implicitly acknowledging his or her maturity. Furthermore, as indicated by the Whoopi Goldberg conversation (Example 7), this frame is rich not only in terms of the diversity of themes overtly discussed but also in terms of its underlying messages. Thus, by partaking in deliberations on the cultural limits of humor (about what can be presented as laughable matter by whom and to whom), as in Example 7, children are becoming partners in the negotiation of their own cultural identities.

Cultural Accents

The presentation of themes talked about constitutes the general topical frames shared by all families. However, as exemplified in several chapters in this book, Jewish family discourse is highly sensitive to cultural variation between Israeli and Jewish American families. This sensitivity is constrained by the shared features in the speech event: the nature of the participants (parents, children, guest(s); all Jewish, all urban middle-class), the ensuing key of the interaction (being sociable) and the activity (having dinner). These common features seem to play a formative role in shaping the boundaries of the topical presuppositional pool for urban, middle-class Jewish families. Even within these shared frames, cultural accents emerge. The American preoccupation with health (i.e., sports, physical fitness, health foods) is absent from the Israeli conversations. Israelis, on the other hand, tend to topicalize food and language more than Jewish Americans do. Not surprisingly, personal histories of cultural transition (e.g., coming to Israel) and their meanings (e.g., comparing "here" and "there") are in the foreground for the immigrant families. On the level of thematic coherence, Jewish Americans and Israelis are alike in the way in which they construe dinner talk. It emerges as a speech event that embodies both a tension between framing the event as an activity and framing it as an occasion for talk and a tension between sociable and socializing talk goals. These tensions are partially resolved by allowing a constant shift between different planes of talk, from the instrumental and socializing frame of having dinner, through the both socializing and sociable frames of urgent family concerns, to the purely sociable frame of non-immediate themes.

Sociability assumes a meeting between equals. As the analysis of topical actions in the next chapter shows, family dinners do not grant equal participation rights to all. The analysis further reveals that Jewish Americans and Israelis differ dramatically in the distribution of participatory roles at dinner.

3

TOPICAL ACTIONS
AT DINNER

The issue considered here is the relation between the individual's role in the family and the level of his or her topical contribution in family discourse. How do adults compare with children, men with women, and visitors with family members in the impact they have on the talk agenda? The word "impact" suggests effectiveness, influence, power. The findings indicate unequal distributions among participants (by role constellation) in levels of topical activity. Yet I argue that there is no one-to-one, simple correspondence between power (indexed or achieved) and level of topical contribution in family discourse.

The analysis of topical contributions considers the degree of contribution made by each speaker to the family agenda and is grounded in a detailed microanalysis of a 20-minute segment from one meal for each family. A "topical action" is defined by Bublitz (1988) as an action used by a participant "to intervene in the development and the course of the [discourse] topic, and thus to contribute to a topical thread being initiated, maintained and completed" (p. 40). Topical actions contribute to the achievement of discourse goals like introducing a new topic, changing the topic currently on the floor, or shifting back to a previous topic after it has been closed or after a digression. The overall goal of this analysis is to map the structure and process of agenda setting in family discourse—to see who introduces, changes, and shifts topics and how these acts are achievable. We consider the roles of age (children versus adults), culture (Americans versus Israelis), gender (mothers versus fathers) and family membership (outsiders versus insiders) in affecting the rate of success and degree of participation in the domain of topical actions. Excluded from this analysis are turns focused on instrumental dinner talk (e.g., "Pass the salt, please"). Such talk is by definition nontopical and hence subject to a different set of discourse norms from those operating for topical talk.

The unit of analysis for topical actions is thus the content-oriented turn that has an impact on the direction of the talk, is noninstrumental, and performs some function other than topic maintenance.[1] This analysis is complemented by computing the distribution of *conversational turns* (namely, turns contributing to the ongoing conversation) among the participants.

The types of topical actions we coded include **initiations**, **elaborations**, **back shifts**, **digressions**, **readaptations** following a digression, and **closings**. For each topical action we further noted whether it was a success or a failure, as determined by manifest verbal or paralinguistic signals of uptake on the part of the participants. Success means that the topic was taken up by at least one coparticipant, and failure means that the topic was not met with an uptake of any kind or was overtly rejected. Examples of each of the different coding categories of topical actions are incorporated in the discussion.

GENERAL TRENDS

The role of the speaker as an adult or a child, mother or father, family member or guest has an effect on levels of topical contribution, but the effects are manifested in different patterns across the three groups. Figure 3.1 presents a general picture of how topical actions are divided in each group between parents, children, observers, and others present at the dinner table. Table 3.1 complements these findings by presenting the level of participation by role in the family for all conversational talk (excluding talk related to dinner activity).

Three main trends emerge from the distributions presented. First, although children in all groups are active topic contributors, in every case children's levels of contribution are lower than those of adults. In the family dinners studied, children are granted participation rights not only to respond to adult topical initiations but also to try to have an impact on the direction of the talk through their own initiatives. These rights are reflected in the overall proportion of children's contribution to topical actions: 25.5% in the Israeli families, 37% in the Jewish American families, and 34% in the Israeli American families. The findings also indicate that to varying degrees,

---

[1]In this approach, turns that contribute to the maintenance of the topic and that constitute the bulk of the conversation (Crow, 1983) are not coded, because the emphasis is on agenda setting rather than on the process of building local coherence. For discussions of topic continuity (e.g., local coherence) see Keenan and Schieffelin (1976), Reichman (1978), and Brown and Yule (1983).

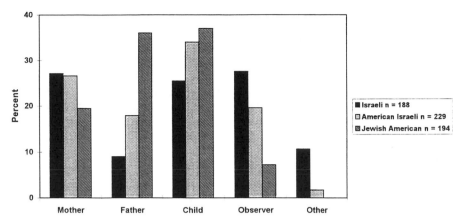

FIG. 3.1. Agenda setting: Percent topical-action turns by role.

it is the adults who dominate the talk agenda, performing in all cases the majority of topical actions (64% to 68%).

Overall participation in the conversation shows similar proportions as contribution to topical action. Children take up between 22% to 38% of talking space, with a considerably higher degree of participation in the Jewish American and American Israeli families. The mean number of utterances for an Israeli child is only 27, whereas for an American Israeli child it is 34; it reaches 48 for a child in the Jewish American families.

The second general trend is that the observers' level of participation differs across the groups. Observers (and guests) play a much greater part in the discourse of the two Israeli groups than in the Jewish American families. In terms of contribution to topical actions, observers in the two Israeli groups reach mean levels of 20% to 28%, whereas in the Jewish American

TABLE 3.1
Level of Participation: Amount of Talk by Role*

	Israelis			Jewish Americans			American Israelis		
	nu**	mnu***	%	nu	mnu	%	nu	mnu	%
Mother	708	88	30	528	66	21.3	566	70	25.5
Father	355	44	15	754	94	31	399	49.8	17.9
Children	536	27	22.2	919	48.3	37.8	745	35.4	33.5
Observer	544	68	25	225	28.1	9.2	466	58.2	21
Others	195	39	8.1	1	0.25	0.04	42	6	1.8
Total	2,406	44.7	100	2,427	57.7	100	2,218	45.2	100

*Including *all turns* contributing to the ongoing conversation, excluding dinner-activity talk and failed attempts.
**nu = number of utterances.
***mnu = mean number of utterances.

families, observers contribute only 7% of topical actions. In the Israeli families, observers also talk more: The mean number of utterances for the Israeli observers ranges from 58 to 68 but is only 28 for the Americans.

The third trend relates to gender differences within the groups. In the native Israeli families, mothers are dramatically more active topic contributors than fathers (by 18%), a trend repeated in the Israeli American families (by 9%). In the Jewish American families, the reverse pattern emerges: Fathers contribute a mean of 36% to the family's topical pool, whereas mothers contribute only 19.5%.

Compared across the three groups, mothers have similar rates of participation in the conversation, their mean number of utterances (mnu) ranging from 66 to 88. The fathers, on the other hand, differ considerably, with the fathers in the Jewish American families talking almost twice as much (mnu = 94) as the fathers in the two Israeli groups (mnu = 44 for native Israelis, 50 for Israeli Americans).[2]

BEING A CHILD AT DINNER

As elaborated in the previous chapter, children's modes of participation in dinner talk shift with thematic frames. Whereas children have a privileged position within the instrumental frame of dinner talk, their participation within the frame of family news is closely controlled by adults. It is only within the frame of non-immediate, adult-initiated topics that their contributions are accepted on par with those of adults. Yet in all three frames, adult–child interactions at dinner are rich in functions of pragmatic socialization, the central one being to provide passages for children into adult discourse. On the one hand, talk with children at dinner serves to enhance the status of children as children, indexing the power imbalance between them and the adults. On the other hand, the same talk serves to mediate between the two worlds of discourse, inviting and encouraging children to develop the discursive skills needed for participation in the adult world. These seemingly conflicting messages are negotiated through the enactment of topical actions by and with children.

---

[2]Naomi Mazoz was the research assistant responsible for the coding and quantitative analysis of topical actions. Statistical analyses of variance of the mean percentage of topical actions by role contrasts yield the following results. The child–adult contrast is significant in the Israeli families, $p < .05$, and the American Israelis, $p < .05$ but not in the Jewish American families. The mother–father contrast (computed originally for 7 families only) is significant in the Israeli families, $p < .05$ and the Jewish American families, $p < .05$ but not in the Israeli American families. The parent–observer contrast is significant only in the Jewish American families, $p < .001$. (Except for the gender analysis, for which the data have been reanalyzed to include eight two parent Israeli families, see Blum-Kulka, 1994, for more details.)

Young children are at an obvious disadvantage in intergenerational gatherings that are not specifically tailored to their needs. Young children in an adult–child multiparty gathering may not be cognitively able to follow the topical development of the talk around them; even if they are, they still may lack the conversational skills needed for topical action, such as recognizing transition-relevant points for turn-taking (Ervin-Tripp, 1979). It is hence not surprising to find that not all the children participated in the traffic of topical actions. In the 20 minutes examined for topical control, only 7 adults (out of 66) abstained from performing topical actions, whereas among the children 2 of 5 Jewish American and 3 of 6 Israeli preschool children did not contribute topical actions at all. In the group of school-age children, all the Jewish American children participated, but 2 of 14 Israeli children and 3 of 16 American Israeli children made no topical contribution. The more difficult time children apparently have in performing topical actions is also witnessed by their rates of topical failure. Not surprisingly, children fail more often than adults in their attempts to initiate: the mean percentage for adults ranges from 7% (Israeli) to 14% (Jewish American), whereas for children it ranges from 18% (Israeli) to 26% (Israeli American). In the two Israeli groups, adults have more than 10% advantage over children in chances for topical success; in the Jewish American families the gap is diminished to 7%. Preschoolers in particular fare poorly in the two Israeli groups: Between 37.5% and 44% of their attempts to initiate topics fail, as compared to only 12.5% in the same age group in the Jewish American families and between 6% to 14% rates of failure for adults in all three groups.

Initiating Topics by and With Children

The power imbalance between adults and children is most apparent in relation to initiation, which we have defined as any attempt to introduce a new topic (Bublitz, 1988). To gain entry to the floor by initiating a new topic, the child needs to work conversationally harder than an adult; whereas an adult can announce a new topic without naming the recipients (e.g., Father: "I took the kids to see 'The Flight of the Navigator' "), a child's entry into the conversation tends to be explicitly targeted to specific recipients:

(1) Jewish Americans 4; Jordan (8m); Sandra (4f).

   1   Jordan: Mommy you know what?
   2   Mother: Yes dear.

The mother interprets Jordan's move as a bid for a turn and responds by granting him the right to speak on the topic of his choice. Subsequently, Jordan raises the topic of why he can be excused from eating vegetables, calling cartoon characters to his aid ("As um Snappy Smurf would say I wish we did not have to eat the vegetables"; see example 3 in Chapter 2).

Targeting potential recipients by direct-address summoning is common practice among both preschoolers and school-age children: "Daddy?" "Yes?" "I've got a math question for you." Preschoolers also use a variety of other attention-getting devices, such as repetitions ("Mommy and Daddy. Mommy and Daddy, Mommy and Daddy, I . . .") and cues that are paralinguistic (e.g., shouting) or nonverbal (e.g., pulling the mother's sleeve or even moving from the lap of an unattentive parent to that of another, more attentive one).

Nomination has a different function when it is used by adults to initiate topics with children. In this case, targeting serves as a subtle form of control, shifting the speaking rights from one child to another:

(2) Jewish Americans 4; Jordan (8m); Sandra (4f).
    The question is raised after Jordan has given a lengthy account of a
    soccer game, and Sandra has reported on her day.

    1 Father: So, are you done telling us about your day?
    2 Sandra: Yes.
    3 Father: Jordan, would you like to tell us something?
                 Other than soccer, what happened today?
    4 Jordan: Well, we had a mean teacher.

The father's question to Jordan (turn 3) summons Jordan to deliver *his* news, and although it establishes coherence with the general frame of the former topic (i.e., one's day), it also narrows Jordan's speaking rights by delegitimizing talk about an aspect of the day that had been discussed earlier ("other than soccer"). Thus the child's participation is doubly controlled, first by being selected to take the floor and second by being told what *not* to speak about. When Jordan complies, giving a lengthy account of the injustices he suffered that day from a substitute teacher (see example 4 in Chapter 2, p. 47), he is given ample opportunity to develop his narrative.

Adult Digressions: Talking Over Children's Heads

In exchanges focused on children, whether adult or child initiated, adult digressions constitute a subtle device of control. We considered as **digressions** cases where, retrospectively, a shift in topics was treated as a bracketed occurrence. Digressions are recognizable on closure by a readaptation of the previous topic (Bublitz, 1988). During a narrative event, a recipient-initiated digression may well be perceived by the main teller, whether child or adult, as challenging his or her telling rights. When the narrator happens to be a child, and the speakers involved in the digression are all adults, the child, however momentarily, is framed as an *unratified participant*[3] (Goffman, 1981). From occupying central stage, he or she is symbolically pushed to the back of the stage. The following dialogue is a good illustration of how a child perceives the adult digression as an infringement on his speaker's rights:

(3) Jewish Americans 2; Marvin (8m); Daniel (6m); Tina (4f); Susan—Observer. The two boys are co-narrating the film "The Flight of the Navigator"; in the extract Daniel acts as the main teller.

	1	Observer:	For an alien he seems like a friendly alien.
	2	Daniel:	No he's actually computerized.
	3	Father:	Ah ha!
	4	Daniel:	He's a computer <living being.> [>]
	5	Observer:	<He's a robot?> [<]
	6	Daniel:	Yeah, robot.
	7	Observer:	Uh huhh
	8	Daniel:	He's called Max.
	9	Observer:	Max?
	11	Daniel:	Because his first name is Maximillian.
>	12	Mother:	Wasn't that the name of the computer in "Two Thousand and One"?
	13	Father:	I can't remember, it might be.
	14	Observer:	Somehow that slips my mind.
>	15	Daniel:	Anyway +/.
	16	Mother:	Really?
>	17	Daniel:	Anyway +/.
	18	Mother:	Susan, such an important fact +...
>	19	Daniel:	Anyway when he goes up xxx just stares at them.

Clearly, the digression is forced on the child—narrator by the adults. The mother's question (turn 12), "Wasn't that the name of the computer in 'Two Thousand and One'?" though not directly addressed to the other adults, is understood as such by them (the wording, "Wasn't that ... ," may serve as signal), and they promptly try to respond (turns 13–14). Sequentially, the question acts as a clarificatory insertion-sequence (cf. Dascal & Katriel, 1979) that shifts attention away from the main storyline. Interactionally, in its

---

[3]Goffman (1981) distinguished between ratified participants (i.e., addressed and unaddressed recipients) and unratified participants (i.e., inadvertent overhearers and engineered eavesdroppers). Clark (1987) divided hearers into participants (i.e., addressees and side participants) and overhearers (i.e., bystanders and eavesdroppers). In my discussion I use Goffman's distinction between ratified and unratified participants, adopting Clark's term *side participant* to designate Goffman's unaddressed recipients. For a discussion of the problematics involved in defining production and recipient roles, see Erickson (1990), C. Goodwin (1981), M. H. Goodwin (1990), and Levinson (1988).

affective function, the adult's digression becomes competitive with the child's story, as the mother adopts an ironic tone clearly targeted for adults only (turns 16 and 18) while the child tries to continue his story. It takes Daniel two futile attempts (turns 15 and 17) to perform a readaptation of the Navigator storyline before he finally succeeds. Note that his attempts (repeating "anyway" three times in turns 15, 17, and 19) completely ignore the adults' comments, treating them as mere disruptions to be overcome. As in the case of initiations, the child at dinner has to work harder than the adult to achieve his or her conversational aim. The adults at least for the duration of the digression create a distanced perspective (on the topic of films favored by children) that the child is not expected to share. Such instances transform stories told collaboratively *with* children to stories told *around* children as "co-present others" (Miller & Byhouwer Moore, 1989, p. 432). Furthermore, treating children as "co-present others" seems a gender-specific practice, found only in the discourse of women.

Controlling by Closing

Another way in which topical control may manifest itself is through topical closure. In classroom discourse (Cazden, 1988), it is the teacher who summarizes, evaluates, paraphrases, and in many other ways signals the closure of the previous topic on the floor, thereby manifestly exercising his or her right to set the agenda. In ordinary conversation, closing a topic is often a component or a by-product of actions such as topical changes, topical shifts, and digressions (Bublitz, 1988). Ending a conversation may also call for closing procedures (Schegloff & Sacks, 1973), but in dinner-table conversation, except for specific cases, the occurrence of explicitly marked closings is relatively infrequent (0.5% of all topical actions for Jewish Americans, 5.8% for Israelis). It is a general feature of this talk that regardless of the general thematic frame, topics as a rule are suspended rather than formally closed.[4] It may well be that many of the topics raised at dinner echo and are related intertextually with topics already raised or to be raised at other family meals and that they thus cohere at the level of an ongoing conversation shaping the family's collective history and identity. Exercising power at dinner through closure hence becomes mainly a matter of negotiating narrative codas and occasionally a matter of simply breaking off a topic. For example,

---

[4]Exceptions are of four kinds. First, closings associated with brief action sequences (e.g., request-compliance, offer-acceptance), as when a request for permission ("Can I leave the table?") is answered with a token of agreement that serves to close the exchange ("okay"). Second, a negotiation of narrative codas may occur, as in the discussion about Whoopi Goldberg (Example 7, Chapter 2). Third, jokes where the punch line is followed only by laughter constitute closure. Fourth, closure can be achieved by metalinguistic moves, as in Example 4.

Jordan's account of his complaints against the substitute teacher (Example 4, Chapter 2) is concluded twice. First, the father formulates the coda for this story and invites Jordan to agree (i.e., he suggests that the children want their home teacher back because they are tired of the substitute). Second, the mother shifts the conversation from a child–adult to an adult–adult interaction by answering a question addressed by the observer to the child: "What's wrong with your teacher?" "Well, it's her kids who have the chicken pox." This allows for the observer's "Uhoh!" response as closure.

Control can be exercised also through closure via explicit, metalinguistic moves called "breaking off a topic" (Bublitz, 1988). Such a closure may be a one-sided or negotiated action, performed as a preventive act against loss of face for self or others that might ensue from continued talk on the same topic. In the family, there must be compelling moral reasons for such a closure to appear. Such reasons surface especially within the frame of immediate family matters, where topics based on personal experience may touch on sensitive issues. At one of the dinners (Jewish American family 11), for example, the topic on the floor at one given moment concerns the "Garbage-pail kid" stickers the children are collecting. Jacky, 9, cannot place her stickers and suspects they were stolen by one of her classmates ("I know someone who stole them"). This accusation occasions a socializing event focused on moral issues, which encompasses parental formulation of the principle involved ("stealing is not right") as well as a discussion of the various alternatives for the morally correct (and practically efficient) ways of getting the stickers back. The suggestion, "Maybe you talk to the teacher then ultimately ask his parents [to get them back]" is interpreted by the child as "telling on" the suspect, a recommendation that clashes with peer-group norms and thereby creates for her a serious moral dilemma. Jacky's response to this suggestion is "Dad, can you talk about this some other time?" However, as Example 4 shows, the child's attempt to close the topic fails (see turn 3), and it is only when the mother intervenes (turn 4) that the closure is achieved. This case shows that adults may exercise topical control by preserving the power to grant the rights to break off a topic:

(4) Jewish Americans 11; Jacky (9f); Gore (11m).

	1	Jacky:	Dad, can you talk about this some other time?
	2	Mother:	Jacky, I want you to eat some string beans. They're good.
	% comment:		[long pause of two seconds]
	3	Father:	Well # when should we talk about it?
>	4	Mother:	Can I change the subject?
	5	Father:	Mm.
	6	Mother:	I want to talk to Gore about his day because he said it was horrible.

Parents as Mediators

Parents at dinner facilitate a child's passage to adult discourse in both direct and indirect ways. By "direct" I mean the wide range of supportive strategies that encourage children to initiate their own topics, that allocate them floor space and that help them with questions and comments to elaborate topics of their choice or topics initiated by adults. As mentioned, many of the supportive strategies manifested with school-age children at the dinner table echo the accommodating style documented as characterizing the interaction of middle-class American caregivers with young children (Ochs & Schieffelin, 1984; Snow, 1984; Snow & Ferguson, 1977). At dinner, these practices usually occur within the frame of immediate family matters and concern topics of personal relevance to the child.

A more subtle but perhaps more important pattern of discursive socialization is provided by indirect means. By "indirect" I mean practices that symbolically signify the acceptance of the child as an equal coparticipant. It is precisely when the child's contribution goes unnoticed metacommunicatively, when it is woven into the normal flow of conversation, that it signals a successful transition to adult discourse. For children to achieve this stage, they need to be exposed to adult topics, to feel comfortable with contributing to these topics, and to be given the chance to direct the talk to topics of their choice that do not necessarily concern their own lives. As we have seen, dinner table conversations provide ample opportunity for children to listen to conversations that concern topics of no immediate concern, such as talk about books, movies, and famous people. The sheer physical presence of the child at the dinner table, however, is of course no guarantee either of the child's attentiveness or of adult acceptance of the child as a ratified participant in this speech event. Therefore, it is particularly illuminating to look at children's brief contributions to conversations that seem at first glance adult-dominated both in terms of participation and choice of topic:

(5) Jewish Americans 1; Jennifer (15f); Simon (13m). Mother and observer are discussing the yearly marathon in Cambridge, Massachusetts.

1	Observer:	I thought it was in the *fall* and I thought it +/.
2	Mother:	I know that's the Bonny Belle. What used to be called the Bonny Belle, now they call it the Bonny xxx.
3	Observer:	Huh.
> 4	Mother:	We had a student once who was in it.
5	Observer:	Oh really.
> 6	Mother:	xxx said she was a secretary ran a um +. . .
7	Jennifer:	Her parents made her train?

8   Mother: She said they interviewed her (be)cause that year
                 she was the youngest runner. So they interviewed
                 her and she said she had just started and her parents
                 xxx.

The conversation is ostensibly between the observer and the mother, with
the mother accomplishing a skillfull *topical shift*[5] in turn 4. Although only
the mother and the observer occupy "center stage" (Varenne, 1992, p. 135)
15-year-old Jennifer is not only a ratified listening participant but also an
active one whose contribution is treated with respect. Children also participate in elaborating and shifting the focus of topics introduced by adults.
Later at the same dinner, the family discusses Woody Allen films, and the
mother mentions to the observer that the family had been to see the film
"Broadway Danny Rose." The adults discuss what it takes to appreciate
Woody Allen (Father: "You have to be from New York and grow up in
Brooklyn to fully appreciate Woody Allen. He's like all the kids I went to
school with"). Simon, Jennifer's brother, contributes to this discussion his
views on another Woody Allen film (" 'Annie Hall' was so funny") and is
interrupted in telling the content of the film by his father saying, "No, don't
talk about it, I'm going to see it." A question by Simon then shifts the talk
from the plane of art appreciation to that of gossip:

(6) Jewish Americans 1; Simon (13m); Jennifer (15f).

> 1   Simon: Is he *Jewish*?
  2   Father: What do you think?
  3   Simon: Yeah.
  4   Jennifer: Yeah.
  5   Mother: His name is Allen Koningsberg.
  6   Observer: Allen what?
  7   Simon: I thought he was Woody Allen.
  8   Mother: Koningsberg.
  9   Observer: Koningsberg?
 10   Mother: Mmhum I taught [//] when I taught in Brooklyn xx
                   with his sister, when he was married to Anita
                   Glacer I was friendly with his sister.
                   [Continued]

---

[5]Topical shifts have been referred to in the literature alternatively as a "topic incorporating
sequence" (Keenan & Schieffelin, 1976, p. 340), "topic shifts" (Bublitz, 1988, p. 125; Maynard,
1980, p. 271), and "shading" (Crow 1983, p. 141). The shading metaphor captures well the subtle
way in which speakers accomplish shifts in topical perspectives. The use of cohesive ties masks
the move in turn 4 as seemingly topic maintaining (in Keenan and Schieffelin's (1976) terms, as
"topic collaborative"), but actually a shift of focus occurs. This shift occasions "a new set of
mentionables" (Maynard, 1980, p. 271), involving the student who was in the race.

Cultural Variation

In all three groups, adults talk more than children and perform more topical actions than children, but the degree of adult domination varies with the culture. Both in terms of participation in dinner talk and in terms of the part played in the traffic of topical actions, the most active are the children in the Jewish American families (see Figure 3.1 and Table 3.1). Although adults still dominate the talk in the Jewish American families, the difference between them and the children is not significant statistically, whereas it reaches statistical significance in the two other groups (see footnote 2).

These findings reflect culturally different perceptions of the role of children in this speech event. In the Jewish American families children play a central role both as participants and as subjects of the talk: The majority of topics raised (63%) are child-focused in the sense that they either concern the children's lives or are addressed to or initiated by children. In the two Israeli groups, these proportions are reversed, with only 41% (Israeli) to 49% (American Israeli) child-focused topics. The underlying cultural norm of treating children as ratified participants at dinner, which is shared by all the families, is thus differently interpreted. For Jewish American families, it means direct focus on the children, often giving them center stage both through the choice of topics and the allocation of talking space, mainly within the frame of immediate family concerns. This practice does not necessarily reflect a striving for discursive equality between adults and children. The adults remain in control through a wide range of strategies, the most important of these perhaps being their unquestioned status as judges of coherence. As Varenne (1992) noted, "coherence is controlled, not by the speaker, but rather by the hearer as he uses institutional means at his disposal to hold the original speaker accountable for (in)coherence—whatever the content of the utterance" (p. 105). At all dinners, it is the adults who exercise power over children by acting as judges of acceptability. Hence, paradoxically, providing more opportunities for children to occupy center stage at dinner allows both more room for children to develop discursive skills under adult guidance and more opportunity for adults to exercise their power. At the Israeli dinner table, children seem to have less of an opportunity to display (and develop) discourse skills through direct practice; hence control over their discourse is less frequently manifest but does not differ in nature.

GENDER OF PARENT

As with all role identities in the family, the relation between language use and the social identity of a parent as mother or father is not a direct one. As argued by Elinor Ochs (Ochs, 1993), speakers have at their disposal in any language sets of linguistic resources for performing social acts and displaying epistemic and affective stances. Thus, for example, all languages seem to have resources for the performance of social acts like requesting, apologizing, summoning, and referencing and naming, as well as linguistic means for signaling knowledgeability, certainty, and affect. Membership in a social and cultural group means that people share the conventions for doing and understanding these acts and stances. It is in this sense that social identities are mediated by the interlocutor's understanding of conventions for how acts and stances are resources for structuring particular social identities. Ochs stated, "Social identity is a complex social meaning that can be distilled into the act and stance meanings that bring it into being" (Ochs, 1993, p. 290). In this constructivist view, which I share, social identity is not directly encoded in the language but rather negotiated at any particular moment of social encounter.

Some acts are more easily associated with particular social identities than others. Thus, a linguistic form like a direct request can be a resource for a wide range of social identities. In Israel at least, not only are the identities of a teacher and a commander in the Army inferrable from such direct style, but with certain modifications that display affect, such forms are also associated with being a parent.

Within the framework of this chapter, the linguistic acts in question are topical actions and conversational contributions. In considering the issue of gender, we are asking whether and how these acts—as performed by fathers and mothers in the family—constitute a resource for structuring gender-linked social identities.

The choice of reference terms ("mother" and "father" rather than "man" and "woman") is meant to provide the proper contextualization for the discussion that follows. In the family context, gendered talk, if it emerges at all, is closely linked to the socialization role of parenting. Though there are several studies comparing the speech of women to the speech of men in various speech events, including semi-official gatherings such as faculty meetings (Swacker, 1976) or intimate talk between couples (Fishman, 1978), gender role is only rarely studied within the famly context (see Gleason, 1987, and Ochs, 1993, for exceptions). On the other hand, the study of language socialization, which focuses mainly on interactions with young children, typically examines interactions between the child and the mother, who is in practice the main caretaker (e.g., Ochs, 1988; Schieffelin, 1990). The following discussion highlights two gender roles, both tied to socialization: the role of fathers in the Jewish American families and the role of mothers in the two groups of Israeli families. This assymmetry is motivated by the quantitative results of our study, which show fathers generally to be more dominant than mothers in the Jewish American families and the reverse in the Israeli families.

Quantitative Findings and General Trends

The quantitative results show a different pattern emerging for each of the groups. Israeli mothers perform significantly more topical actions than Israeli fathers (51 by mothers versus 17 by fathers) and and have a higher rate of overall contribution to dinner talk. This pattern of mothers' higher rate of participation is repeated for both measures in six of the families; in one family (Family 5) the mother and father make equal contributions to the talk, and in another family (Family 9) the father is more dominant.

The American Israeli families show a similar pattern but with a less dramatic gap between mothers and fathers. Mothers perform more successful topical actions than fathers (61 versus 41) and have a higher mean rate of overall contribution to the talk. These trends are consistent for six of the families, with two showing a reverse trend.

The picture is dramatically different in the Jewish American families. Here the fathers make significantly more topical contributions than the mothers (70 for fathers, 38 for mothers), but in terms of overall contribution to dinner talk the gender gap is less noticeable (the mean number of utterances for fathers is 94, vs. 66 for mothers). Again, these trends show some individual variation: In one family (Family 2) the rate of contributions is almost equal, and in another (Family 9) the mother has a slight advantage over the father. No significant gender differences emerge in rates of topical failure.

Considering the small size of the sample and the degree of individual variation within each group, anything said here about gender-linked differences in speech should be considered with caution. Still, the qualitative analysis of the talk yields indications of some culturally different gendered verbal strategies in Jewish American and Israeli families. These strategies tally with the quantitative results in that the two groups of Israelis show very similar patterns. Table 3.2 compares the gender differences among Jewish American and the two Israeli groups.

In the following section, the issue of gendered talk is considered from three perspectives. First I discuss topical choice by mothers and fathers to determine whether the conversations manifest gender-exclusive topical

TABLE 3.2
Gendered Verbal Strategies

	Jewish Americans	*Israelis*
Range of topics	Sports: a male exclusive topic	No gendered topics
Controlling strategies	Fathers: floor-holding; claiming expertise	Mothers: framing children as unratified participants
Degree of topical contribution	Higher for fathers	Higher for mothers

choice. Second, I address the controlling elements in the speech of the quantitatively dominant gender in each group (i.e., fathers in the Jewish American families and mothers in the two Israeli groups). Third, I discuss the differences between the groups in the perception of the situation and the implications of such perceptions for the construction of gender.[6]

Indexing Gender in the Jewish American Families

Are there qualitative differences between the speech of fathers and mothers in the Jewish American families that contribute to different constructions of gender identities? On the macrolevel, topical range does not differentiate mothers from fathers in these families. There is no difference in the choice of thematic frames, and both mothers and fathers are involved in the full spectrum of dinner talk. This means that both parents play a part in discussing family news, in raising topics of general interest, and in the instrumental business of managing dinner, issuing a similar number of directives (see Chapter 5). Yet as we have seen, quantitatively the fathers in these families have a clear advantage, performing more of the functions of family talk, though not necessarily differently.

It is also important to note that most topics raised by both mothers and fathers frame all those present, including the observer, as recipients, with both parents equally active in designing certain topics as prominently adult–child focused and others as adult–adult focused. For example, both mothers and fathers engage in the ritual of asking the children about the day's events, and both tell stories of family history aimed at the observer as primary audience (see Chapter 4).

On the microlevel of specific topical choice and the framing of participant structures, sports is the one clear exception to this general picture. Only male members of the family talk about sports, and such exchanges are framed as male exclusive. A second possibly gendered topic is the domain of topics associated with natural science. Unless the mother is a scientist by profession, children tend to turn to fathers as the knowledgeable adults in this domain.

On the level of controlling strategies, we found attempts to control in individual male styles of floor-holding. The assertive style of topical maintenance exemplified here is not necessarily typical of all the fathers, but it is totally absent from the mothers' talk.

Male-Exclusive Topics

It is only in the Jewish American families that certain topics are framed as exclusively male. Soccer and basketball are two cases in point. When the

---

[6]The gender analysis provided here is confined to issues of topic and is not meant to be an exhaustive description of the speech style of mothers and fathers in the three groups.

topic concerns a boy's soccer or basketball practice, the conversation that ensues remains exclusively male dominated, with none of the female participants (neither children nor adults) making any contribution at all.

(7) Jewish Americans 4; Jordan (8m); Sandra (4f).
     The father's question initiates the first topic at dinner, raised as the recording began.

1	Father:	How was [/] how was [/] how was soccer practice today?
2	Jordan:	Fine.
3	Father:	Wh-what, what did you [/] what did you play today?
4	Jordan:	What?
5	Father:	Did you have a scrimmage? What did you do?
6	Sandra:	Can I have some +/.
7	Jordan:	We had a scrimmage, zero zero [= the score]
8	Sandra:	Can I have some meat [//] meatie?
9	Father:	Yes, I'm getting you some. So what did the <coach have to say?> [>]
10	Sandra:	<xxxxxxxxxxxxxxxxx!> [<] [raised voice]
11	Father:	xxx go ahead, start eating. Don't let it get cold. What did the coach have to say?
12	Sandra:	[xxxxx] [coughing].
13	Jordan:	He said that we're doing really well and there's only one thing I'm not happy about.
14	Father:	What's that?
15	Jordan:	I'm going to have to play halfback.
%	comment:	[said in miserable voice.]
16	Father:	Halfback when on Saturday? Halfback is what? Is that defense?
17	Jordan:	In the game it's defense and offense.
18	Father:	Well what's wrong with *that*? You're, that's probably the most important position in the field.
19	Jordan:	It is! But you know what you're supposed to do?
20	Father:	What's that?
21	Jordan:	Okay # a forward comes down the field. <He really has to think "*I am about to score*"!>[>]
22	Mother:	<xxxxxxxxxxxxxxxxxxxxxxxxxxxxxxxxxxxxxxxxxxxxx.> [<]
23	Jordan:	<He's really happy.> [>]
24	Observer:	<xxxxxxxxxxxxxxxxx.> [<]
25	Jordan:	He's going at top speed. You, you know what you're supposed to do?
26	Father:	What?

27	Jordan:	You're supposed to \<plant a detour> [>] for him.
28	Mother:	\<xxxxxxxxxxxxxx.> [<]
29	Jordan:	I am not strong enough.
30	Father:	What do you mean plant a detour?
31	Mother:	\<Potato xxxxxxxxxxxxxx?> [>]
32	Jordan:	\<Well you're supposed to> [<] throw yourself in front of him and try to knock his, and try to knock the ball away.
33	Father:	You don't throw yourself, you just try to kick and get the ball away from him.
34	Jordan:	You have to run in front of him and charge at him, and I'm +/.
35	Mother:	\<xxxxxxxxxxxxxxxxxxxxxxxxxxxxxx> [>].
36	Father:	\<Is that what he tells you to do> [/] [<] is that what he tells you to do?
37	Jordan:	You don't exactly charge at him, but you +/.
38	Father:	+^ You mean he's dribbling the ball \<down the field> [>] really fast.
39	Sandra:	\<xxxxxxxxxxxxxxxxxxxx.> [<]
40	Jordan:	You come, you have to come from the front and attack the ball!
41	Father:	Jordan, do you want a potato?
42	Mother:	Jordan would you care for some more salad, for instance, some tomatoes? My dear?
43	Jordan:	mm [meaning no].
44	Father:	[chuckles].
45	Mother:	That's all xxx carrots and croutons?
46	Jordan:	No xxx.
47	Father:	Ellen could you help me \<pass xxx> [>] Jordan?
48	Mother:	\<xxxxxxxx> [<].
49	Father:	Yes please.
50	Sandra:	I want some salad! Please some salad bowl.
% comment:		[said in a high-pitched voice.]
51	Mother:	Yes we're going to put some \<salad dressing on it.> [>]
52	Father:	\<Did you want a salad?> [<] Did you want a potato Jordan?
53	Jordan:	Yes.
54	Father:	All right.
55	Father:	Jordan I don't think you *charge* at him. You [/] you he's dribbling down the field, and you just try to take the ball away from him.

56	Jordan:	I know, but! # You have to catch him.
		You know what? Even if you don't *attack* him, you go *at* him, and you stick your foot, and if you miss it [/] miss it and you stay there and go for another chance he'll knock you over.
	% comment:	[Jordan is talking while chewing.]
57	Mother:	Is it okay if we put salad dressing on or is xxx?
58	Jordan:	Yes.
59	Observer:	Yes fine.
60	Father:	Solved.
61	Jordan:	Can I have some butter?
62	Observer:	Yes.
63	Mother:	Yes.
64	Father:	Uh uh.
65	Father:	Did you play xx's team on Saturday? Is that [/] is that when +/.
66	Jordan:	Uhuh [meaning no].
67	Father:	Will you +/.
68	Mother:	A different group.
69	Jordan:	I think I am. # It's the third to last game.
70	Father:	Oh.
71	Sandra:	Mommy, cut this.
72	Mother:	Sandra, put it down and I'll help you. Here, what you do is you take your fork and you scoop it up.
73	Father:	Sa-Sa-Sandra how was your day today?

In the conversation that ensues from the father's inquiry about Jordan's soccer practice, the female participants play no serious speaking role. Except for one brief contribution (in turn 68), which shows that she is attentive throughout the conversation, the mother's comments are focused on offering food to the children and the observer and controlling Sandra (turns 31, 42, 45, 51, 57, 63, and 72). The observer, another woman, also speaks in this segment only in response to queries about food (turns 59 and 62). The father, on the other hand, shows a deep interest in all aspects of the game, encouraging Jordan to feel proud about his role on the team ("That's probably the most important position in the field," turn 18) and going into great detail in clarifying what is meant by the requirement "to plant a detour" (turn 27). The message transmitted systematically is that it is not physical strength that matters but rather skill. When the boy complains that he is not strong enough for the task (turn 29), the father responds by ruling out force (turn 33); when Jordan still insists on describing the task with the metaphor of war ("You have to come from the front and attack the ball!" turn 43) the father instructs him in how to use skill, downplaying the element of force: "I don't think you charge at him. You [/] you he's dribbling down the field, and you just try to take the ball away from him" (turn 55). There is also a covert message that sports for men necessarily involve the risk of getting hurt, expressed by his lack of response to Jordan's fears on that score: When Jordan insists on the danger of getting hurt (turn 56), the father changes the focus of the conversation (turn 65) thereby signaling to the boy that getting hurt is part of the game.

As demonstrated by Erickson (1990) in his analysis of an Italian family's dinner table conversation, a topic framed as an exclusively male topic may carry important messages for the male participants. At the Italian family's dinner table, the youngest boy tells a story of how he has fallen off his bike, and his brothers and father react by telling a series of similar "wipeout" stories that indirectly carry important messages about male behavior, such as the merits of courage, achievement risk taking, and technical skills. All these values are enhanced in the instances of talk about sports between fathers and sons in the family data. It is noteworthy that in these families no parallel sex-linked topic emerged for mothers and daughters, or for mothers and female observers.

There is an interesting parallel between the issue of gender-linked differences in the choice of topics at the family dinner table and gender differences in the interpretation of television news. In an ethnographic study based on interviews with all members of the family following their watching news programs, Liebes and Grissak (1995) found no difference between the sexes in the degree of their involvement in hard, political news items but that—at least in the presence of their husbands—women seemed to acknowledge that politics is a domain of male dominance and therefore displayed a tentative style in talk about politics. The parallel in family talk is represented by talk about science. Science, like politics, may be perceived by one of the sexes, or both, as the province of males only. Even the few examples we have indicate a power struggle between the sexes over the domain of science. In Family 3, most of the talk at one of the dinners is taken up by a discussion, led by the father, of experiments that he and his older son (age 10) have conducted or are planning to conduct following the instructions given in the book accompanying the T.V. show "Mr. Wizard." The mother restricts her participation in this discussion to casual remarks to the observer highlighting the boy's achievements ("He once made a potato clock") and readily declines any claim to the topic ("This is above my head"). In sharp contrast, in Family 9, it is the mother, a chemist who works for a drug company, who raises and develops (in a typical scientific discourse mode) the topic of science, telling her family—primarily the husband, but with the children's queries welcome and responded to in detail—about studies of metholyne chloride: "The two interesting studies that have been done on metholyne chloride have shown a nonsignificant excess of pancreatic cancer, and they have been dismissed xxx studies."

The struggle over hegemony in talk about science is most evident in Family 4. Here the son (age 8) typically presents his father a problem in math ("Daddy, I have a math question for you") that concerns making two squares from six by taking away six sticks. In the long discussion that follows, the father is very reluctant to admit that he is having trouble solving the problem.

(8) Jewish Americans 4; Jordan (8m);

1	Jordan:	Daddy?
2	Father:	Yes.
3	Jordan:	I've a math question for you.
4	Father:	Yes.
5	Jordan:	Not exactly a math question.
		You have sixteen or I mean seventeen # sticks.
		You make a pattern of six squares, right?
		Seventeen sticks make a pattern of six squares, right?
	% comment:	[this utterance overlaps with food talk of mother and Sandra.]
6	Father:	What do you mean a pattern of six squares?
7	Jordan:	Okay you have seventeen sticks. It goes three across and two down, and # no, yeah three across and two down and make it six squares. Each &squa, each square one by one.
	% comment:	[Jordan arranges the sticks on the table.]
8	Father:	Oh! And that takes seventeen sticks? All right.
9	Jordan:	Right. Okay, how are you going to take away six sticks and have only two squares left?
10	Father:	Take away six sticks and have two squares left.
11	Jordan:	Right.
12	Mother:	Stuff like that creativity test xxx +/.
13	Father:	<With no moving of, no moving of any stick?> [>]
14	Observer:	<That's xxxxxxxxxxxxxx creativity [laughs].> [<]
15	Father:	No moving? You just take them away?
16	Jordan:	<You take them away.> [>]
17	Observer:	<Is that xxxxxxxx.> [<]
18	Jordan:	<And everything that's left has to be part of the square.> [>]
19	Observer:	<xxxxxxxxxxxxxxxxxxxxxxxxxx of the course.> [<]
20	Mother:	No, it's one of Torrence's creativity tests for children.
21	Father:	All right. I'll have to +/.
22	Mother:	And I give it to them when I talk about xxx.
23	Father:	I'll have to get a piece of paper and make some drawings.
24	Jordan:	I can't figure it out. I got, I got it where you have to take away five squares to get three.
		I mean um five sticks to get <three squares.> [>]
25	Father:	<that's xxxxxx.> [<]

			Is it really seventeen? Three on the top three

                                            Is it really seventeen? Three on the top three
on the bottom is six two on the sides is ten.
And then you need one two. # Ah <wait a minute[/]
wait a minute wait a minute! No, no, no, NO!> [>]

26	Mother:	<Three four five # six seven.> [<]
27	Father:	You need one two # # three four.
28	Jordan:	Five +/.
29	Mother:	Five six seven.
30	Father:	Oh right, I see.
> 31	Mother:	The squares don't all have to be of equal size.
32	Observer:	That's one of the secrets.
33	Father:	<Oh.> [>]
34	Jordan:	<What> [<] do you mean they don't have oh +/.
35	Father:	When you [/] when you [/] when you take away six to get two squares. The squares should need not be of the same size is what mommy's saying.
> 36	Jordan:	Well, NO!
37	Jordan:	You start out with +/.
38	Father:	Yeah I know you start out when they are all the same size but presumably when you take away the six sticks you get two squares left, right? That's the # supposed to have two squares left?
39	Jordan:	Yeah.
40	Father:	And the squares are not, maybe don't have to be the +... one of them might be a a square that's two by two and the others are squares that one by one. # # Suppose you'd have a one by one here # take away that stick. # # uhm # Can you draw me a piece +... Let, let me get a piece of paper.
> 41	Jordan:	I think they have to be all the same size.
42	Mother:	You sure it isn't three squares?
43	Jordan:	No, *two*!
44	Mother:	Okay. [with doubt].
45	Jordan:	I'm positive. Daddy is having trouble with it. So is there any reason that *I* have to be able to figure it out right off the bat?
46	Father:	I'm not necessarily having trouble, Jordan. It's just that I'm having trouble picturing it in my mind, without drawing a picture.
47	Jordan:	Mm well, I can see that but +... Dad you can't move any sticks around.
48	Father:	No, no I'm not moving them around!

	49	Father:	Okay. # # # Okay. # # # Okay one two <three four five six seven> [>] eight nine ten!
	50	Mother:	<xxxxxxxxxxxxx> [giggles].> [<]
	51	Father:	Eleven twelve thirteen fourteen fifteen sixteen seventeen. Ok, we want to remove two, six sticks so we have a um # two squares left.
	52	Jordan:	All right.
>	53	Mother:	Oh I can do that.
	54	Father:	Oh.
>	55	Mother:	I can do that easily.
	56	Father:	<Maybe one in each corner?> [>]
	57	Mother:	<Want me to tell you what to do?> [<]
	58	Father:	Just a second! # Just a second! We remove one two three +... Oh that's too many. All right, let's have +/.
	59	Mother:	Would you like to know the answer?
	60	Father:	NO!
	61	Mother:	[laugh].
	62	Observer:	[laugh].
	63	Father:	You must be kidding! Why would I want to know the answer? You must be kidding! Why would I want to know the answer? One two # three four five six. These two. One two three four five +...
	% comment:	[omitted: inserted sequence of talk about dessert, five turns.]
	64	Father:	Okay, Ellen wise one. Which ones six do you take away?
	65	Mother:	You take away # four that form a cross on the interior +...
	66	Father:	Yeah?
	67	Mother:	And two at the corner.
	68	Father:	And you get two unequal size +/. Ok. Take away yeah? And now which other two?
	69	Mother:	Get out the square <xxxxxxxxxx +/.> [>]
	70	Father:	<Oh wise one oh> [<] [with realization]! # Yeah # team! Oh you knew the answer beforehand?!!
	71	Mother:	Not this one. It's a version of something I knew.
	72	Jordan:	<Wow!> [>]
	73	Father:	<Wow!> [<] stick with her, kids, and you'll go far Wow. Gee and I thought all your brains came from me. Oh well +...

In the first part of the exchange (turns 1–22), because it is obviously the father who is appointed to solve the problem, all explanations and clarifications are addressed to him, with the mother and (female) observer showing no indication of participating in the discourse of problem solving. This is evident in the mother's metacomment ("it's one of Torrence's [the teacher] creativity tests for children"). In the second part (turns 23–52), roles shift: The father indirectly admits having some difficulty ("I'll have to get a piece of paper and make some drawings") and then joins the boy in a joint (but futile) attempt to solve the problem. In this collaborative venture the mother participates minimally, making one highly significant contribution: "The squares don't have to be of equal size" (turn 31). The father acknowledges the mother's point (turns 33 and 35), but the child dismisses it ("I think they have to be all the same size," turn 41). For him it is the father only who is the knowledgeable adult found failing and who thereby represents the excessiveness of the demands made by the adult world on children:

Jordan: Daddy is having trouble with it, so is there any reason that *I* have to be able to figure it out right off the bat?

But the father won't admit failure:

Father: I'm not necessarily having trouble, Jordan. It's just that I'm having trouble picturing it in my mind without drawing a picture.

In the third part of the exchange (turns 53–73) the struggle over knowledge as power becomes clearly highlighted. The shift occurs with the mother's giggle (turn 50), which seems to signal either her knowledge (hinted at in turn 22) or her realization that she now has the answer. Her spouse, however, is reluctant to acknowledge defeat. She has to repeat "I can do that" or "I can do it easily" three times. Though it is seemingly accepted ("Oh," turn 54) when the explicit offer to help comes ("Want me to tell you what to do?") the initial "oh" is followed by further attempts by the father to solve the problem on his own (see turn 56). To highlight the gender struggle issue, I repeat (with some omissions) the exchange following her question that presupposes that she is the one in the know, omitting all but the metatalk:

(8a) Jewish Americans 4; Jordan (8m).

    59 Mother: Would you like to know the answer?
    60 Father: NO!
    61 Mother: [laugh].

62 Observer: [laugh].
63 Father: You must be kidding! Why would I want to know
                the answer? Okay, Ellen wise one.
64 Father: Yeah?
65 Mother: And two at the corner.
66 Father: And you get two unequal size +/. OK. Take away
                yeah? And now which other two?
67–70   [answer provided]
70 Father: Oh wise one oh [with realization]! # Yeah # team!
                You knew the answer beforehand?!!
71 Mother: Not this one. It's a version of something I knew.
72 Jordan: <Wow!> [>]
73 Father: <Wow!> [<] stick with her kids, and you'll go far.
                Wow. Gee and I thought all your brains came
                from me. Oh well +. . .

The father in this exchange manifests a gamut of characteristics attributed in the feminist literature to men only: fierce competitiveness, a reluctance to accept advice (grounded in the high value placed on autonomy and independence) and admit failure, and a claim for status through monopoly on prestigious bodies of knowledge (Maltz & Borker, 1982; Tannen, 1990). Granted that in the given case all these characteristics might be linked as much to personality as to gender, it is still instructive to analyze this example from the gender perspective. The exchange revolves around the novice–expert polarity. It shows the extent to which admitting failure to live up to the son's expectation (by not solving the problem) is perceived as a very serious threat to face. The fact that the exchange takes place in the family context is of crucial importance. This is not just competition between the sexes over who has the monopoly in the domain of science (defining the roles of expert versus novice between the sexes), but rather the striving for the status of "the knowledgeable parent" in this domain. The father's blunt refusal to hear the answer ("No!" said very emphatically) signals his difficulty in relinquishing the identity of the expert constructed for him by his son. The laughter of the two women shows understanding of the issue at stake. Next, very reluctantly and using sarcasm as a face-saving device, the father allows the answer to come forth (turn 63). The proliferation of admiring exclamations (notice the two "ohs" in turn 69), combined with an immediate attempt at minimization ("You knew the answer beforehand?") keep signaling the father's difficulty. Once the boy joins in celebrating his mother's solution ("woow" in turn 72) the father reverts to irony for face saving. Violating the Gricean maxim of quantity in his overuse of admiring exclamations (e.g., *wow, gee*), he frames part of his comment as a blatant violation of the maxim of quality ("And I thought all your brains came from me"). Though ostensibly addressing the children, the comment seems to be meant for the two other female participants.

Controlling Strategies: Instances
of Powerful Male Style

The language of the women in the Jewish American families does not seem to show any of the characteristics associated with a female "power-less" style (Lakoff, 1975, 1990; O'Barr, 1982) such as the overrepresentation of hedges and tag questions in women's speech. On the other hand, we found instances of a powerful style on the part of males, a style that might be interpreted as serving the need of men to present themselves as the source of authority and power in family and society. In the following extract, male assertiveness is manifested through the devices employed by the male speaker to maintain the topic of his choice on the floor by countering several attempts by others aimed at topical shift.

(9) Jewish Americans 1; Simon (13m); Jennifer (15f).
   The family is discussing Whoopi Goldberg films.

	1	Observer:	Did you see "The Color Purple"?
	2	Mother:	No.
	% comment:		[Simon comes into the kitchen where the family is eating].
	3	Observer:	Simon, how are you?
	4	Mother:	No, no, you have to sit there.
	5	Jennifer:	What?
	6	Mother:	You have to sit there.
	7	Father:	Okay.
	8	Observer:	Okay.
	9	Father:	Is that okay?
	10	Observer:	Okay.
>	11	Father:	Is that okay? Well, she did this thing the junkie. Did you see her do this thing on Anna Frank?
	12	Observer:	I don't think so.
	13	Mother:	We have one bread so eat it slowly not all at once.
>	14	Simon:	Wow!
	% comment:		[Said about the new VCR].
>	15	Jennifer:	Dad, I've started taping it.
	16	Father:	What? The news?
	17	Jennifer:	Mmhum.
	18	Father:	Okay.
>	19	Observer:	I hear you're a basketball star now.
	20	Simon:	A star is right.

21   Observer: xxx guys play you played once?
22   Simon: Yeah I got a basket.
23   Father: He scored two points. He scored a field goal for the season.
24   Observer: So now your record was uh +. . .
25   Simon: One thousand.
>   26   Father: For one shot he got it in. It's set very good.
                         Umm she did this thing on Anna Frank and +. . .

This segment is typical of the way in which several items on both the activity and the talk agenda demand attention simultanously: Simon's entrance interrupts the Whoopi Goldberg conversation, and the need to seat him focuses attention on the activity of shifting chairs, signaled verbally in turns 6 through 11. In turn 11 the father makes certain that the interruption is concluded and marks explicitly (by the discourse marker "well") the shift back to Whoopi Goldberg. But not for long. After a brief insert of dinner talk (turn 13), the new VCR draws Simon's attention ("wow") and occasions a side sequence (Jefferson, 1972) about taping the news (turns 15–18). It is again the father who closes the sequence ("Okay" in turn 18). Now the topic again changes, this time to basketball. But the father persists in returning to Whoopi Goldberg. Within the same turn (26), he combines a third-party-addressed compliment to Simon about basketball ("For one shot he got it in. It's set very good") with the topical back shift, signaled minimally by "Umm" ("Umm she did this thing on Anna Frank and . . .").

The brief exchange on basketball is also rich in messages about male behavior. Not only does the father celebrate Simon's achievement ("He scored two points. He scored a field point this season"), but when he does—following Simon's willing acceptance of being called a "star" (turn 20)—he also shows a favorable attitude to Simon's boasting about it.

The father's orchestration of the conversation is apparent in the way he handles the children's attempts at distraction. The children in this segment are directly or indirectly responsible for shifting the conversation from the main topic nonverbally, by causing the focus of attention to shift to seating Simon, and verbally, by Simon and Jennifer collaborating in initiating a side sequence about the VCR ("Wow" in turn 14 and "I have started taping it" in turn 15). It is the father who makes sure that the children's topics are clarified (turn 16) and acknowledged (turn 18). For a brief moment he collaborates in the introduction of a new topic by the observer (turn 19), allowing Simon to occupy center stage for its short duration (turns 19 and 26). Thus, the children's contributions are treated as legitimate but are not allowed to distract the conversation from the father's topic.

Despite these manifestations of a powerful style, it would be misleading to portray the men in these families as true to a domineering male stereotype. Interaction within a family context is not like interaction in cross-sex dyads; hence, perhaps it is not surprising that male–female differences true for conversation between couples do not hold in the family context. As a result, indices of control in the men's style tell only part of the story. Consider the issue of topical success. Fishman (1978) found that among young American couples women raised almost twice as many topics as men, but whereas topics raised by men were almost always accepted and elaborated, almost half the women's topics failed. Yet the women provided most of the interactional work that kept the conversation going. Neither part of these findings is repeated in the American Jewish families. Men raise more topics than women, but the rate of failure is similar in both: Among the 33 topics raised by women, 5 failed (13%), compared to 8 out of the 62 raised by men (11%). Failure of both sexes stems from the intergenerational participation structure of the talk: conversations in these families are dominantly child-focused (two thirds of the topics concern children), and both parents are equally active in (sometimes futile) attempts to involve children in the talk. Thus, topical failure in these families is mostly a feature of adult–child interaction.

Nor do Jewish American women do more interactional work than men. The analysis of narrative events in the family (see Chapter 4) shows that women and men in the Jewish American families support narrative by others conversationally—by brief utterances that show listenership—at similar rates, an average of one reaction per four narrative utterances.

Indexing Gender: Israeli Families

In the two Israeli groups, women do the bulk of all topical work, in terms of both the number of topics raised and topically relevant talk.[7] Yet the gender identities of women and men constructed through talk in the family scene fit neither the domineering, threatening, and suffocating image of the "Jewish mother" as depicted in Jewish and Israeli literature (by American Jewish authors and filmmakers like Philip Roth and Woody Allen and Israeli authors like David Grossman and Chanoch Levin) nor the overpowerful and assertive no-nonsense male macho image associated historically with Israeli Sabra men (Ben-Ari, 1989; Horowitz, 1993; Rubinstein, 1977). As in the Jewish American families, there is no qualitative difference between fathers and mothers in the thematic frames evoked during dinner. Both parents are active in controlling children and managing dinner within the instrumental frame, in eliciting from and sharing family news with their children and spouse, and in raising topics of no immediate concern. Nor do these parents

---

[7]In the native Israeli group, both mothers and fathers had only a single topical failure each. In the American Israeli families, mothers failed three times (of 61 cases) and fathers failed four times (of 41 cases).

differ in the degree of their topical involvement with the observer. Both parents engage (in a manner typical of the Israeli families) in topics designed to elicit personal information from the observer. When gender differences do appear, they tend to emerge as specific focuses in the framing of partici-pation structures, especially in a controlling strategy employed by mothers toward children.

Non-Gender Exclusiveness in Topical Choice

In the Israeli families, adults take up a higher proportion of talking space than children and engage in more adult–adult exchanges than Jewish Ameri-can families. One of the reasons for this trend may be the presence at some of the dinners of more than one adult outsider—the T.V. cameraman (families 5 and 10) or a male guest (families 2 and 9), for example. What is noteworthy in the choice of topics for the adult-focused exchanges is the degree to which both sexes show involvement in topics stereotypically associated with women, such as gossip and food, especially cooking. Although it was found (Liebes & Grissak, 1995) that when watching T.V. news, only the women show a high degree of interest in human interest stories like the nurses' strike, at the family dinner table the men are just as involved as the women in talking about nonpresent others. Consider the following extract:

(10) Israelis 5; Niva (13f); Yoav (11m); Tama (4f).
[Father is talking to the cameraman, Marcus, about the videotaping of the dinner]

1	Mother:	perfekcyonist. Amikam *ata* carix lehavin oto.	A perfectionist, Amikam [her husband] *you* should understand him.
2	Father:	kol ha-calamim kaele. calam im hu lo perfekcyonist hu lo calam.	All photographers are like that. A photographer who isn't a perfectionist isn't a photographer.
3	Mother:	ze yashar mazkir et <adam> [>].	That immediately reminds me of <Adam>[>].
4	Father:	<ma> [<]?	<What>[<]?
5	Mother:	haya, hikarnu, ata mekir et adam grinberg, hu calam [/] calam kolnoa.	There was, we knew, do you know Adam Greenberg? He's a photographer, a movie cameraman.
6	Observer:	hu zaxa [/] hu zaxa axshav be-eze pras.	He won, he's just won some prize.
7	Mother:	ken.	Yes.

8	Observer:	naxon?	Right?
9	Father:	lo, hu <cilem> [>] +...	No, he <filmed> [>] +...
10	Mother:	<az hikarnu oto>[<]. hu cilem sratim <shel xaverim shelanu [>].	<So we knew him> [<]. He made films <of some of our friends> [>].
11	Father:	<eze seret xx?> [<]	<What movie xx?> [<]
12	Observer:	ze hu she-cilem +...	He is the one that made +...
13	Father:	ken, ken et ha-mesima ha-zot. mashehu ha-sayens fikshn ha-ze.	Yes, yes, that mission movie. Something, science fiction like.
14	Mother:	be-kicur hu gam ken haya, ad she-ze lo haya <# tiptop perfekt +...> [>]	In short, he was also, <until it was absolutely perfect +...> [>]
15	Father:	<ex kor'im la-seret <she-raita, yoavi?> [<]	<What's the name of that movie you saw, Yoavi?> [<]
16	Mother:	+, lo, shum davar. ha-olam haya yaxol lehithapex.	+, No, nothing. The world could come to an end.
17	Father:	Yoavi, ex kor'im la-seret she-raita?	Yoavi, Whats the name of the movie you saw?
18	Yoav:	"shlixut katlanit."	"Terminator."
19	Father:	"shlixut katlanit" et ze hu cilem. menaxem golan lakax oto le-holivud. hu haya calam mispar exad ba-arec.	"Terminator." That's what he filmed. Menachem Golan took him to Hollywood. He was the number one cameraman in Israel.
20	Mother:	rega, ve-hu *gar* sham ve-ha-kol?	Wait a second, and he *lives* there and everything?
21	Father:	ken, hu +/.	Yes he +/.
22	Mother:	avar, azav et ha-arec?	Moved, left the country?
23	Father:	ken, yesh lo avoda bli sof sham.	Yes, he has tons of work there.
24	Observer:	ani agid lexa matay ani raiti oto? kshe-hu od lo haya kol kax yadua.	Should I tell you when I saw him? When he still wasn't so well known. In '64, no

		be-shnat 64, lo, 60, o 64 o 68 be- rexov ha-madregot 17. tish'alu oto im hu lo gar sham.	'60 or '64, or '68, at 17 Ha-madregot Street. Ask him if he didn't live there.
25	Father:	xxx blondini.	A blond xxx.
26	Observer:	rosh raxav?	Wide head?
27	Father:	ken, ha-sear xx.	Yes, his hair xx.
28	Mother:	haya blondini.	Was blond.
29	Observer:	ani zoxeret oto, ani kim'at +/.	I remember him. I almost +/.
30	Mother:	hu lo yisraeli.	He's not Israeli.
31	Father:	hu polani.	He's Polish.
32	Mother:	hu lo cabar.	He is not a Sabra [%com: not born in Israel]
33	Father:	yaxolt ledaber ito polanit. hu yelid polanya.	You could speak Polish to him. He was born in Poland.
% comment:		[5 turns omitted. Tama is trying vainly to catch her father's attention]	
38	Observer:	Ani garti sham pashut pa'amayim. garti be-'64.	It's just that I lived there twice. Once in 64.
39	Father:	efo ze rexov ha-madregot?	Where is Ha-madregot Street?
40	Observer:	be-naxlaot, naxalat axim.	In "Naxla'ot," "Naxlat-Axim."
41	Mother:	lo, hu lo gar sham, ani xoshevet.	No, he didn't live there, I think.
42	Observer:	lo aval hu +. . . tkufa kcara [/] tkufa kcara hu batuax gar sham, axeret ani lo hayiti zoxeret oto.	No but he +. . . For a short period, a short period he lived there for sure, otherwise I wouldn't have remembered him.
43	Father:	hu haya yerushalmi pa'am, lo?	He was a Jerusalimite once, wasn't he?
% comment:		[2 turns omitted. Niva is checking if the videotape is on.]	
46	Observer:	atem makirim oto tov?	You know him well?
47	Father:	hu avad im xaver shelanu she-be-zmano hayinu kaxa meoravim	He worked with a friend of ours who at the time we were kind of involved,

ve-azarnu lo	and we helped him with
ba-sratim she-hu	the movies he [filmed]
ba-hatxala.	in the beginning.
hikarnu oto, ken.	We knew him, yeah.

@End.

For the mother, the mention of Adam the cinematographer (turn 3) at first seems incidental to the point she is trying to make about perfectionism being a salient attribute of all photographers, professional (like Adam) and nonprofessional (like her husband). She pursues this point through several turns (3, 5, 10, 16), at first in perfect accord with her husband (turn 2) and later in competition, with the shift in focus introduced by the observer in turn 6. As of turn 6, the conversation is transformed into what newscasters would call a human interest story. The first task of the conversants is to establish Adam Greenberg as the common referent of the talk. This is done through naming the film he made, with the father turning to his 10-year-old son to aid him (turns 17 and 18). Next, the father elaborates Adam Greenberg's personal history and achievements (turn 19), surprising his wife with the information about his leaving the country (turn 20 and 22). She signals through stress ("He *lives* there? / He left the country?") not only surprise at receiving new personal information about Adam Greenberg but also the significance of this information from a cultural point of view. As for many Israelis, issues of immigration to and from Israel are rich in symbolic meanings; in colloquial Hebrew, one "ascends" ("oleh") rather than immigrates ("mehager") to Israel and "descends" ("yored") rather than emigrates when moving from Israel to anywhere else in the world. It is not clear if the mother is expressing a negative attitude with regard to Adam Greenberg's leaving the country, but she is clearly marking the event as highly sigificant, as important as Greenberg's jointly established identity as a non-native (turns 30, 31, 32). It is the lack of gendered talk here that is noteworthy; the man's achievements, past and present whereabouts, looks (turn 25, 26, 27, 28) and language, as well as the family's connections with him (turns 10 and 47), are established in a collaborative mode by both parents, with neither showing preference in highlighting one dimension of personality over the other.

Men in the Jewish American families also participate in talk about nonpresent others, but, whereas such talk in the Israeli families (with varying degrees of involvement by men) seems mainly to serve the interpersonal purpose of establishing social links with the observer (as in example 10, or as in other conversations about common acquaintances, see the section on observers), in the Jewish American families such talk is framed mainly as funny stories meant to entertain all present. Thus, both parents in Family 1 reminisce in a series of stories about their misfortunes at the hands of various weird house painters ("Do you remember the guy who used to paint my mother's apartment? What was his name, Sammy? . . . The guy was such a riot"). Talk about nonpresent others in the Israeli families is 'gossipy' by virtue of its referents being known to all adults present, whereas in the Jewish American families it fails to meet this condition and hence remains within the genre of storytelling for entertainment only.

Another topic stereotypically associated with women has to do with cooking. Because the talk takes place at dinner, it is natural that food is a frequent and universal topic of conversation. Food is more often topicalized in the Israeli families than the Jewish American ones and in the Israeli families is not female exclusive. It is interesting to note that, although in both groups the food is primarily prepared by the women, the men participate to some extent in cooking. "This is my creation," announces the father in Family 2 about the stuffed vegetables he contributed to dinner, and in one of the Jewish American families, the father is completely in charge of a barbecue dinner. However, only in the Israeli families did we find men actually engaged in talk about shopping and preparing food.

On the other hand, we found very slight indications for indexing any topic as exclusively male or female. Technical matters seem to be an accepted male domain, and hence when the television breaks down the father is expected to deal with it (in this specific case, by his own mother, who lives next door and is with the family at dinner) and when a child's toy airplane breaks (American Israeli Family 3), the mother frames the father as the fixer:

(11) American Israelis 3; Etan (9m); Noam (6m).

Mother: Dad, what do you think? You think we can improvise a stand for his plane?

Controlling Strategies by Mothers: Framing Children as Co-Present Others

In their ethnographic study of low-income families in South Baltimore, Miller and Byhouwer Moore (1989) found that the primary way in which stories of personal experience were available to young children in this community was through stories told *around* them, stories addressed to other persons. One subset of stories around the child encoded events about the child, with many of these "told pointedly in a way that included the child as 'ratified' participant" (p. 433). At the family dinner table children are included in storytelling events also in the two other participant structures mentioned by Miller and Byhouwer Moore, stories told specifically *to* them and stories told collaboratively *with* them as conarrators.

But whereas in all families both parents engage in collaborative conarration with children, the practice of telling stories (or making passing comments) *about* the child to another adult present seems the most prominent in the discourse of Israeli women.[8] Such stories may be addressed either to the father or to the observer. When addressed to the father, the practice follows the pattern observed by Perlman (1984), where at dinner mothers who do not work outside the home update the father about the child's doings during the day. In the Israeli families studied, all women are professionals who work outside the home, but either through special arrangements or because of their profession (e.g., teaching) they tend to be home earlier than their husbands. Stories about children may or may not involve the children as conarrators. For example, in telling a story (about how a rooster jumped on their daughter at nursery school), the mother in Family 5 shifts from the father to the child and back to the father ("D'you know that the rooster jumped on her today? They told the teacher that you cried and laughed." [the child laughs] "She said that Tali was crying through the tears ... rain and sun."). The story then unfolds with close collaboration among both parents (with the father asking the questions) and the child.

In contrast, the story of a bird that died (Israeli American Family 3) is a clear example of a mother excluding the child by talking above his head. The mother picks up a story already told by one of the boys (Noam, age 6) to the observer ("We have a bird that died. We buried her") to discuss the effects of the bird's death on the children with her husband: "Today we had a tragedy in the house, did you hear?" In response to the father's question ("Yeah, I heard. How did she die?"), she elaborates the circumstances of the bird's death and then emphasizes the emotional effect on the children: "There was a whole scene here. He was hysterical for an hour, Noam. Etan had his friend *lefaxot* [at least]. I hate to think what would happen if he didn't have his friend here." Turning to her older son (9 years old), she asks: "Did it help you Etan that Ze'ev was here?" The text is clearly framed as adult–adult interaction: Not only does the mother talk about the children in the third person, but she uses several distancing strategies (i.e., labeling the event "a tragedy" and the children's reaction as "hysterical") that invite the father to adopt a distanced adult perspective on the event.

When addressed to the observer, this practice may take the form of side remarks that talk "through" the children, transforming them into either side participants or even unratified overhearers. For example, in Israeli Family 10 the mother complains about her 4-year-old: "I am so stressed by him. He gets all excited and completely loses control." In another, more complex example, the mother actually talks to the children through the observer. The exchange (Israeli Family 1) opens with the mother addressing the observer directly: "You know, Rachel, today I came home especially because yesterday I barely saw the children because I had an awful day. I studied

---

[8]Note that the Jewish American mother's digression in Example 3 also exercises control by changing the recipient role of the child from addressee to side participant.

and then was busy and then worked, and then I come home and. . . ." She then elaborates her disappointment at finding signs of one of the boys having been at home but not meeting any of them. As the conversation unfolds, the children volunteer their whereabouts (i.e., one visited a friend, the other went to a youth movement activity) and on occasion engage in direct communication with the mother. However, the mother insists on formulating her message as third-party addressed: "This one visited a friend, the other went to the youth movement, and I was just so sad." The observer's response: "It seems as if they weren't sad at all" (said laughing) shifts the heavy tone of the interaction to a lighter one and is followed by a topic shift.

Parental control in the family is exercised both directly, through various forms of the language of control (see Chapter 5), and indirectly, through modes of discourse regulation. The practices described here show Israeli mothers especialy active in exercising one gender-linked mode of indirect control. By addressing topics related to their children's personal lives to other adults present they both monitor their children's participation roles (as addressee, side participant, or overhearer) and assert "authorship" (Goffman, 1981) for their children's autobiographies. Like the high-control mothers in Aronsson and Rundstrom's study (1988) of child discourse and parental control in pediatric consultations, mothers who engage in these practices reassert their authority over the children. When such strategies are used outside of the pediatric setting, where there is no need for the mother to accommodate herself to an expert professional, they add a specific mode of variation in participant structures to the repertoire of expressive forms of control in the family.[9]

Speech and Silence: What Does the Cultural Difference Mean?

We have seen that in the Jewish American families the fathers raise more topics and talk more than the mothers and that this gender balance is reversed in the two groups of Israeli families. We have also seen gendered forms of control in the discourse of American men, paralleled by (other) gendered forms of control in the discourse of Israeli women. However, the issues of gender, speech, and power are still puzzling. What do these findings tell us about the construction of gender identities through speech (or its relative avoidance)?

According to the credo of feminist literature, silence is to be deplored "because it is taken to be a result and a symbol of passivity and powerlessness:

---

[9]It should be stressed that the focus on Israeli mothers' controlling strategies follows from their prominence in the talk and does not necessarily imply a total absence of such strategies in the fathers' discourse.

Those who are denied speech cannot have their experience known and thus cannot influence the course of their lives or of history" (Smith-Rosenberg, 1985, as cited in Gal, 1989). In the context of family discourse, if silence symbolizes powerlessness, then American women, Israeli men, and children in both groups are relatively powerless at dinnertime. Many scholars, however, emphasize the paradoxical power of silence. As pointed out by Robin Lakoff (1990), in every context where one party is accountable to the other—in religious confessions, psychotherapy, gate-keeping interviews and police interrogations—it is the *silent* listener who has the right to judge and thereby exercises power over the one who speaks. A teacher or a parent can thus exert power over a child by simply listening to a child's account. This view of silence as power is congruent with Bateson's (1972) interpretation of American culture along the dimension of exhibitionism–spectatorship. Bateson claimed that, given hierarchical social relations, in America it is the powerless who are expected to display to the powerful (in Britain the reverse would be true). Within this framework, American women, Israeli men, and all children would be seen as exerting power by withholding talk. In fact, both of these interpretations err by assigning absolute values to the choice between silence and speech. As Gal (1989) stated, "silence, like any other linguistic form, gains different meanings and has different material effects within specific institutional and cultural contexts. Silence and inarticulateness are not, in themselves, necessarily signs of powerlessness" (p. 2).

The key to understanding the interrelations between culture and gender roles in these families seems to lie in different perceptions of the speech situation of family dinners in terms of the distinctions between public and private and formal and informal. As conceptualized by Habermas (1987a, 1987b) the "public sphere" in the modern world is the arena of political debate and participation, the arena where we function as citizens. The "private sphere," on the other hand, is the domain of the nuclear family, the arena involving the functions of socialization and cultural transmission. Together these two spheres constitute the socially integrated institutions of the "lifeword" engaged in functions of symbolic reproduction.[10]

---

[10]In Habermas' (1987a, 1987b) schemata of the institutional orders developed in the modern world, the private–public distinction holds for both domains posited by the theory: the system-integrated domain specializing in material reproduction (i.e., official economy and the beauracratic state) and the socially integrated domain of the "lifeword," engaged in functions of symbolic reproduction such as socialization, solidarity formation, and cultural transmission. The four elements (i.e., official economy, state, family, and political or public sphere) are all interrelated. One link connects the official capitalist economy and the modern restricted nuclear family (in the roles of workers and consumers) whereas another link connects the public state and the public opinion institutions through the roles of citizen and (welfare) clients. See Fraser (1990) for a critique of Habermas from a feminist perspective, claiming that he is gender blind and fails to thematize the gender subtext of the relations and arrangements he describes.

Although from a macro-perspective family dinners in all groups are essentially a private sphere occurrence, the Jewish American and Israeli families seem to differ in the boundaries they draw between the private and the public spheres and the gender roles assigned to each. One possible interpretation of the relative dominance of men in the talk in the Jewish American families is that it indicates a more public, or "on stage" (Goffman, 1981) framing of the family dinner than that drawn in the Israeli families. The question then is who represents the family in this semipublic event? In line with findings that show that American men tend to dominate talk in public meetings, such as academic sessions (Swacker, 1976) and faculty meetings (Eakins & Eakins, 1976), it is the men in these families who tend to take on themselves the responsibility for keeping the conversation going, including entertaining the guest, and thereby appear to dominate the talk.

Tannen's observation that men feel more comfortable doing public speaking whereas women feel more comfortable doing private speaking (Tannen, 1990) holds true for both Israelis and Jewish Americans. Apparently, it is precisely because Israeli families more clearly distinguish the public and private spheres (especially in terms of gender roles) that women gain prominence in dinner talk. Gender demarcation in the public sphere is symbolized for instance by soldiering: Israeli women serve in the army but do not do combat duty. The men fulfill the roles of fighters and protectors, with all the macho images that this role has cultivated in a country where in addition to regular army service, men become soldiers for up to a month each year doing reserve duty (Ben Ari, 1989).[11] There is little indication of the macho image in the talk of men at dinner. The Israeli fathers show as much interest in children, cooking, and gossip as the mothers, legitimizing these as male topics of the private sphere. Simultaneously, they also leave most of the discursive space to women, and as a result the women are the ones to exercise most verbal strategies of control toward children.

The second dimension that differentiates the groups is linked to degrees of formality. Of the four dimensions of formality posited by Irvine (1979), two seem relevant here: code structuring and (perhaps) the invoking of positional identities. The Jewish American dinners appear comparatively more structured, verbally and nonverbally, than the Israeli dinners. Verbal structuring is evident in specific rituals, like the "today" ritual of asking about "your day" (see Chapter 4), and in the metapragmatic awareness paid to perceived violations of turn-taking rules (see Chapter 6). Nonverbally, there is a higher degree of formality from this aspect in the Jewish American families, as seen from group differences in the physical array of the dinner table and in the degree of physical proximity.

---

[11]The general attitude to the Israeli woman–soldier as depicted by the texts of songs popular in the army is actually highly sexist, contradicting official proclamations of equality between the sexes in the army (Weiler, 1991).

As a second aspect of formality, Irvine suggested that "Formal occasions invoke positional and public, rather than personal, identities" (p. 778). Invoking positional, gender-linked identities in the family through talk may be viewed either as a replication in the family of patterns of gender identity found in the public sphere, or as a construction of positional gender identities specific to the familial context. The relatively higher formality of the Jewish American family dinners seems more susceptible to the import of wider societal positional gender roles, yet for both men and women, it also serves to enact parental gender identities specific to the family discourse. Thus, when in the domain of science Jewish American fathers dominate the discourse or compete for knowledgeability, they might be echoing male patterns observed in cross-sex dyads in the public sphere, whereas when they limit their discussion of sports to their sons, they might be enacting the fathering role expected in American culture.[12] At the less formal Israeli dinners, the scene is more clearly demarcated as private and familial. Hence, the gender roles constructed seem less susceptible to wider societal gendered patterns. When Israeli mothers dominate the discourse or assert their authority over children, and when Israeli fathers gossip or take an interest in the preparation of food, both are enacting familial rather than wider societal gender roles.

BEING AN OUTSIDER

The observers occupied a peculiar position at dinner. They were known to the family, either from previous visits or, occasionally, from former acquaintance, and in this respect fulfilled the role of a familiar guest. However, because they were also visiting on official business as representatives of the research project, their presence may have introduced an element of formality or self-awareness into the proceedings. Such perceptions may in turn have affected the parents' interaction with their children and the degree to which children participated in observer-raised topics. In all analyses of perceived and enacted role of the observer at the dinner table, the most consistent finding is that of *cultural diversity*: The Israeli families (including the American Israelis) differ dramatically from the Americans in attitudes toward the observer.

In both groups, the observers (with one exception) were invited to join the dinner table as a matter of course, but the nature of the interaction

---

[12]An illuminating illustration of the salience of sports as a key concept in the construction of American fatherhood is provided by one of the chapters in the series "Northern Exposure," which is entirely devoted (in an ironic tone) to the agony of the non-sports-loving husband who is afraid to admit this apparent failing as a father to his pregnant wife and his friends.

between them and the family differs in key and, consequently, in rules of interaction. In terms of Irvine's (1979) dimensions of formality, the generally prevailing key of family discourse (due to the intimacy of the participants) is that of informality. Yet there are differences of degree between the two groups, with Israelis seeming to celebrate the outermost informal end of the continuum. Consequently, the observer is drawn into the circle of conversation from the onset and interacts with all family members not only in the role of familiar guest but as an actual or potential friend. As one mother tells the observer, whom she had met only through the project, "Now that we became friends, you should come and visit us any time" (Israeli Family 11). This is in line with the ethos of solidarity in Israeli culture, which tends to minimize social distance symbolically (Blum-Kulka et al., 1985). Because topical activity and self-directed and other-directed narrative initiation are privileges granted to friends, the behavior of Israeli observers is similar to that of the parents for topical activity (see Figure 3.1) and for rates of narrative initiation (see Chapter 4). In the Jewish American families observers are far less active in both respects.

The mutual involvement of family and observer in the Israeli families is manifest at several levels of discourse. The observer is asked about and discloses personal information, acts as a mediator for interpreting children's utterances, and even takes sides in moments of conflict with the children. The Israeli need to domesticate the stranger is extended to the cameraman. He too is invited to eat with the family, is brought into the conversation, and is befriended through questions about his profession and personal life (e.g., "Do you also work for channel one?" "Isn't Marcus a South American name?" "When did you come to Israel?") In the following extract, the two women—Dalia the mother and Miriam the observer—discuss Miriam's health problems, a topic Miriam has apparently introduced on one of her previous meetings with the family.

(12) Israelis 6; Iris (6f); Lilax (6f); Miriam–Observer.

[The conversation takes place as the recording starts]

1	Mother:	at oxelet hayom hakol?	You're eating everything today?
2	Miriam:	ani oxelet ha-kol.	I'm eating everything.
3	Mother:	at nir'et tov.	You're looking good.
4	Miriam:	toda	Thanks.
5	Mother:	me-az razit.	You've lost weight since.
6	Miriam:	od raziti me-ha-shvuayim ha-axronim?	I've lost weight in the past two weeks?
7	Mother:	nir'a li.	I think so.
8	Miriam:	yaxol liyot. ani ered aval +...	Maybe. I might lose some but +...

hit'anyant ba-rofe	Did you ask about that
ha-hu?	doctor?

[At this point a child interferes, but the topic of Miriam's health is taken up again, leading to a discussion of alternative medicine.]

Miriam met the family through the project, but after a short period of acquaintance she apparently felt confident enough to disclose the reasons for her pickiness in food. At this second dinner, Miriam's health and the special diet are treated by the women as mutually shared knowledge; thus, the exchange that develops is marked by a degree of intimacy appropriate between friends (note the wording of the compliment in turn 3, "you're looking good" and Miriam's question in turn 6).

Probably due to our presence, the occurence of conflict at the dinner table is quite rare. Familial conflict at the dinner table places the observer in a difficult situation, momentarily framing his or her role as an unratified eavesdropper rather than a ratified participant.[13] Involvement by the observer at such moments runs the risk of being interpreted as illegitimate interference and being rejected as such. Hence it is not suprising that the standard path followed by both the Israeli and American observers at truly difficult moments, such as when the conflict involves husband and wife, is simply to keep silent. Still, in the Israeli families we found occasions when the observer chose to run the risk and manifestly affiliated with one of the participants. In the following extract, Ran, age 9, engages in a long negotiation with his parents and his sister to get their permission to play his recorder:

(13) Israelis 8; Rachel–Observer; Merav (11f); Ran (9m).
    Ran's request is preceded by a long stretch of adult–adult conversation.

1	Ran:	ima ani roce lenagen mashehu. ima ani roce lenagen mashehu.	Mom I want to play something. Mom, I want to play something.
2	Mother:	<Ran i efshar> [>].	<Ran, you can't> [>].
3	Merav:	<lo axshav [<].	<Not now> [<].
4	Mother:	gam lenagen ve-gam lishmoa <televizya ve-gam ledaber> [>].	Play and also listen to <the T.V. and talk>. [>].
5	Ran:	<az ani axabe et ze shniya> [<].	<So I'll turn it off for a second> [<].
6	Mother:	lo, lo, bevakasha lo.	No, no, please don't.

---

[13]I am indebted to Guy Aston (personal communication) for calling my attention to issues of alignment in the observers' discourse.

			ata roce ta'ale la-xeder shelxa ve-tenagen.	If you want, go up to your room and play.
>	7	Rachel:	hu roce she-ani eshma.	He wants me to hear him.
	8	Mother:	xuc mi-ze axshav shmone ve-esrim. ata carix lageshet ve-lehitkaleax.	Besides, it's eight twenty. You have to go and take a shower.
>	9	Rachel:	hu roce she-ani eshma.	He wants me to hear him.
	10	Mother:	bevaday she-hu roce she-at tishmei.	Of course he wants you to hear him.

[8 turns omitted, with the father joining in the same vein]

	19	Ran:	ima lama? rak et shoshana <ve-et ze +. . .> [>]	Mom why? Just "Shoshana" <and the +. . .> [>]
	20	Rachel:	<rak shir exad> [<] she-ani er'e ex hu menagen. hu roce lehashvic kcat.	>Just one song> [<] so that I see how he plays. He wants to show off a little.
	21	Ran:	rak kcat ani anagen.	I'll play just a bit.
>	22	Rachel:	nu az ma?	Well, so?
	23	Mother:	<xxxxxxxxxxxxxxxxxxxxx< [>].	<xxxxxxxxxxxxxxx> [>].
	24	Ran:	<az axshav et shoshana>[<].	<So now Shoshana> [>].
	% comment:		[Ran starts to play the song "Shoshana."]	

It is not clear from the transcript whether permission is ever explicitly granted (turn 23 is inaudible on the tape), but what is clear is that Ran does play, maybe because he feels permission has been negotiated for him by a third party. The observer uses her presence as a justification for the request (turns 9 and 20), negotiating terms ("Just one song") and even appointing herself spokeswoman for the requester (turn 22). Lines of affiliation are clearly drawn, with the observer aligning with one child against all the other members of the family. In another case, the observer steps in to reframe the key of the interaction. In contrast to the mother's emotional self-disclosure at feeling sad for finding her children not at home, the observer acts as spokeswoman for the children, voicing their feeling, but in a much lighter tone ("they don't look sad at all"). Another frequent practice found only among Israeli observers is to respond to queries from the children about food and other matters, in cases where the parents seem inattentive.

American observers are much more cautious, and their caution is nowhere more manifest than in moments involving a potential moral conflict. In the following extract the issue is normative behavior. Samuel, 10, is reporting his experience at camp. He finds it "weird" that "you are not allowed to throw things out of the window." Prompted by Susan, the observer, he then goes on to recount all the things he and his friends did in fact throw out of bus windows:

(14) Jewish Americans 3; Samuel (10m); Jeffrey (6m); Susan–Observer.

	1	Susan:	What did you throw out of the window?
	2	Samuel:	You don't want to know.
>	3	Susan:	Oh I do want to know. You mean like # not huge things.
	4	Samuel:	Make little paper planes # miniature planes.
>	5	Susan:	Right.
	6	Samuel:	Some of them are big but usually we'll make little ones. xxx right [/] right [/] right like right in people's parked, great parked cars.
>	7	Susan:	Ok.
	8	Samuel:	Jacob used to throw this crap from inside the bus seats. He used to take out these giant pieces like the size of the dinner plate +...
>	9	Susan:	Right.
	10	Samuel:	And throw them in parked cars [laughing].
	11	Mother:	Oh wonderful, the present camper could be your future vandal. I love it. I think the bus drivers must be the great unsung, unsung heroes.
	12	Susan:	Oh, it's horrible.

Acting as story recipient, Susan abstains from passing judgment on the kids' activities. Except for turn 3, she confines herself to showing listenership through brief back channels ("Right," "OK," "Right"). It is only when the mother clearly takes a critical stand (turn 11) that Susan also commits herself, supporting the mother's viewpoint (in turn 12) by providing a "matching assessment" (Aston, 1988). It is noteworthy that the mother frames her reaction not as a reprimand to the child but rather as a general comment to the other adults. Susan's comment follows in the same frame. She then goes on to provide a second justification through a story she tells about her difficulties at a summer job as van driver of a camp bus. This time, it is the mother who supports Susan ("It must have been gruesome") and Susan who agrees ("It was a nightmare").

Being a familiar guest at the Jewish American family's somewhat more formal dinner table does not bestow on the observer the privileges granted to friends; although partaking in the interaction, the observer does so cautiously, under the rules of interaction governing communication between non-intimates. Because lack of overt activity in topical contribution and narrative initiation is one of the ways in which such caution is exercised, it is not surprising that the observers in the American families have a mean rate of 7% for topical contribution (compared to 28% for the parents) and that they are engaged in less than 10% of story initiations.

One reason for these findings may be that for the Americans the very presence of the observer gives the occasion more formal overtones. Whereas it is mainly the mothers who serve the food, it is the fathers who take it upon themselves to *entertain the guest*—to introduce topics and to use narratives to keep the conversation going. In contrast, in the Israeli families the mothers seem to take charge of both activities. As suggested by Deborah Tannen (personal communication), it might also be the case that the American observers have different ideas about their obligations and about their rights. With the American scientific tradition of objectivity in the social sciences, they feel it incumbent upon them not to participate any more than necessary.

SUMMARY

The last two chapters show that dinners in Jewish middle-class families constitute a socioculturally unique speech event. The families all share basic organizational features of coherence but differ in the construction of discourse roles. Jewish American and Israeli families are alike in the ways they frame family dinners. It is a speech event that embodies built-in tensions between activity goals and talk goals, sociable talk and socializing talk. As a result, it allows for simultaneous coexistence of different planes of discourse, partially resolving the tensions by allowing for constant shifts between the instrumental, the family-focused, and the world-focused frames of discourse. These frames in turn evoke different genres: the highly contextualized, regulatory discourse of the instrumental task of having dinner, the spatiotemporally here-and-now-anchored discourse of family concerns (which assigns topical relevance by family membership and is highly sensitive to socializing goals), and finally, the discourse of non-immediate topics, which unfolds in the most sociable, ordinary-conversation-like manner, accepting with equal respect contributions from all participants, regardless of role in the family.

Despite this shared macrostructure, Israeli and Jewish American dinner table conversations differ in many ways. This discussion focused on modes of topical activity and their relation to the negotiation of power in the dynamics of dinner talk. The differences between the groups seem to reflect cultural diversity in the perception of the situation and the role expectancies built around it. Amount of talk and agenda setting (topical actions) are not equally distributed, favoring adults over children, Israeli women over men and American men over women, and cross-culturally, Israeli observers over their American counterparts. However, these unequal distributions do not index power in a simple way. The meanings associated with talk depend on a complex relation between perceptions of the situation, level of topical contribution, frame, and mode of participation. For gender and parent–observer differences, a cultural difference in the perception of the speech event places women predominantly in the less formal, private-like discourse world of the Israeli families, whereas men are in the foreground in the more formal, somewhat public-discourse-like world of the Jewish American families. The more formal and somewhat public Jewish American dinners further call for careful relations between the observers and the family; the acceptance and self-perception of the observers as potential friends is common within the more intimate Israeli dinner event. The Israeli observers' high level of involvement is expressed through levels of topical activity as well as conversational daring in stating opinions and taking a stand on moral issues. On all these accounts, Israeli observers are highly engaged; American observers are relatively passive.

Children's participation at dinner talk is universally professed by parents as a very important socializing goal. Indeed, parents engage in socializing practices to ease children's passage into adult discourse. Yet it is the parents who set the criteria for topical relevance and appropriate turn-taking. Hence, the parental conversational demands imposed on children index parental power. They set the terms for entry into the hegemonic, adult world of discourse.

For children, notions of power and talk are subject to variation by frame and mode of participation. When children act as topic initiators, for them power is directly associated with quantity of talk. When they respond to adult elicitation, the meaning of talk becomes ambivalent because self-disclosure and accountability in child–adult interactions are sensitive issues. Both modes tend to appear primarily within the frame of urgent family concerns, a frame in which ultimate control over discourse management remains the prerogative of adults. Children gain equal rights in the frame of non-immediate concerns, within which their contributions are accepted on par with those of adults. Although Jewish American children take a more active part in dinner talk than Israeli children, their activity tends to be confined to the frame of immediate family concerns, where adults are in control. Paradoxically it is the less active Israeli children, with equal participation in both immediate and non-immediate frames, who seem to gain easier access to adult discourse worlds.

4

TELLING, TALES, AND TELLERS IN FAMILY NARRATIVE EVENTS

My goal in this chapter is to apply a culturally sensitive analysis to the narratives told in the course of dinner in the Jewish American and Israeli families. Storytelling in ordinary talk between intimates is one of the most common enactments of narrative discourse. People tell stories to each other as a means of packaging experience in cognitively and affectively coherent ways (Labov & Fanshel, 1977; Sacks, 1974), or, in Bruner's (1986) terms, as a way to test the borderlines between the exceptional and the ordinary. Fisher (1987) considered the narrativization of experience a basic human need; the essential nature of human beings is captured by the metaphor of man as "homo narrans." Extending Burke's definition of man as a symbol-making and symbol-using animal, Fisher proposed an all-encompassing definition for the role of narratives:

> The idea of human beings as storytellers posits the generic form of all symbol composition. It holds that symbols are created and communicated ultimately as stories meant to give order to human experience and to induce others to dwell in them in order to establish ways of living in common, intellectual and spiritual communities in which there is confirmation for the story that constitutes one's life. (p. 63)

Although the narrative use of language is a universal function (Hymes, 1981), narrative use can vary culturally, as do other ways of speaking. Indeed, oral narrative styles vary by culture for both adults and children, as shown by work adopting a cross-cultural perspective (e.g., Scollon & Scollon, 1981; Tannen, 1980) as well as comparative studies in the context of language socialization (e.g., Heath, 1983; Schieffelin & Ochs, 1986). In this sample, the cultural styles emerge in regard to stories told in the course of ongoing conversation.

Conversational storytelling can be studied from a social interactionalist position, with a focus on how the narrative emerges in its context. It may also be studied as discourse, with a focus on the textual end product abstracted from the context. The first approach is represented by work on conversational storytelling from the perspectives of both ethnomethodology (e.g., Jefferson, 1978; Sacks, 1974) and discourse analysis (Polanyi, 1989; Schiffrin, 1984a; Tannen, 1984). Such work shows the manner in which the structure of oral narratives is conversationally accomplished. Particularly relevant here are studies focusing on narratives during family dinner table conversations (Erickson, 1982, 1988; Ochs et al., 1989; Ochs et al., 1992). A complementary, rich source of information on this dimension is provided by studies in folklore that highlight the poetic and social interactional aspects of performance (Bauman, 1986; Briggs, 1988; Hymes, 1981; Kirshenblatt-Gimblett, 1975; Shuman, 1986). By contrast, the discourse approach is best illustrated by Labov's influential work (Labov & Fanshel, 1977; Labov & Waletzky, 1967), which unveils the structural coherence of seemingly chaotic conversational renderings of personal experience.

The narrative events examined here, enacted by both adults and children, function as crucial socializing contexts for family interaction in general. A further perspective that needs to be added is cross-cultural variation in practices of narrative socialization, as suggested by cross-cultural and cross-ethnic studies of language socialization (Blum-Kulka & Snow, 1992; Heath, 1983; Miller, Potts, Fung, Hoogstra, & Mintz, 1990; Schieffelin & Ochs, 1986).

None of these approaches on its own suffices to capture the unique nature of family narratives. We need an approach that accounts simultaneously for family storytelling as an event, a social action unfolding in real time, and (at the discourse level) a text about other events. The links and transitions between these two realms are provided by performer–tellers. Dinner table narrative events are unique: They represent a three-way intersection of the act of narration, the textual content and form of the narrative, and the persons responsible. Taking all three dimensions together, narratives become *narrative events*.[1] Like all speech events, narrative events have specific norms governing the scene, participation rights, message content, message form, and rules of interpretation (Hymes, 1974). In narrative events, these features can be seen as subsumed under three dimensions of narrativity: *telling* (narration), *tales* (narratives), and *tellers* (narrators). In oral

---

[1]I borrow the term from Bauman (1986), who followed Roman Jacobson in distinguishing between the narrative context of the situation, namely the narrative event, and the story world evoked through the telling, namely the events narrated (Bauman, 1986).

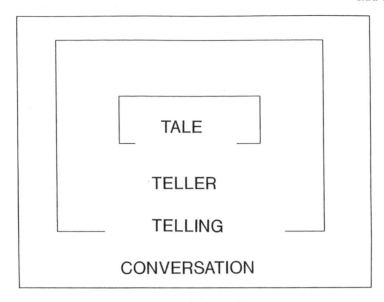

FIG. 4.1. Dimensions of narrativity. From " 'You gotta know how to tell a story':
Telling, tales and tellers in American and Israeli narrative events at dinner,"
by S. Blum-Kulka, 1993, *Language in Society, 22*, p. 363. Copyright 1993 by
Cambridge University Press. Reprinted with permission.

storytelling, the realm of telling is embedded (in an open-ended fashion) in
the realm of conversation, and the realm of tales is embedded within that
of telling, as depicted in Figure 4.1.[2]

Telling is the act of narrating in real time, the actual performance of a
story before an audience. The central issue of performance in family narratives is social interactional: who participates in whose stories and how. To
narrate "is to make a bid for power" (Toolan, 1988, p. 6); entering the telling
mode in the family context raises the issue of narrative participation rights.
Even when such rights are assumed by virtue of social role in the family,
as is the case for parents, they still need to be renegotiated conversationally
on each specific occasion (Jefferson, 1978; Polanyi, 1989; Polss, 1990). For
children, gaining participation rights and learning modes of story entry
remain goals to be achieved with some difficulty. The division of telling
space may vary by role in the family (i.e., children versus adults) as well as
by role and culture, as when children in one culture are granted storytelling
rights over and beyond their rights in another. Cultures also may differ in
the framing of transitions from the realm of conversation to the realm of
telling, as well as in how important the telling is relative to the tales.

---

[2]See Young (1987, especially Chapters 1 and 2) for a philosophically attuned discussion of
the phenomenological framework for the analysis of the different narrative realms (in her terms
storyworlds and *taleworlds*).

Tale is the stuff narratives are made of. It refers to the two dimensions of narrative captured in the poetics of narrative fiction by the distinction between "fabula" and "sjuzet" (in the Russian formalists' terms) or "story" versus "narrative" (Rimmon-Keenan, 1983). The fabula or the story of narratives "designates the narrated events, abstracted from their disposition in the text and reconstructed in their chronological order, together with the participants in these events" (Rimmon-Keenan, 1983, p. 3). In other words, in experience-based narratives, the fabula consists of the real-world building blocks used for the construction of the story. The sjuzet on the other hand relates to the way in which the story is shaped in the making, the "spoken or written discourse that undertakes the telling" (Rimmon-Keenan, 1983, p. 3). In the actual discourse, events do not necessarily appear in chronological order, and content is filtered through some perspective, sometimes called "focalizer" (Rimmon-Keenan, 1983, p. 74). It is the responsibility of the "author" (Goffman, 1981) to select the words in which the fabula is encoded in a way that is still retrievable for the audience. Cross-cultural variation in fabula choice may be expressed in spatiotemporal orientation of narrative plots (e.g., recent past vs. not recent past) or in the type of protagonists (e.g., self vs. other). However, cultural attitudes to the preferred style of sjuzet may be expressed through critical comments to children about the way they are telling a story. As one father told his son who failed to give a convincing performance of a joke learned from the father, "you gotta know how to tell a story."

Tellers take part in the act of telling as performers, but may or may not be the persons accountable for the story. In Goffman's (1981) terms, tellers first of all enact the role of the speaker as "animator," the one responsible for the sounds that make intelligible speech come into being. If they are also accountable for the tale, then they act as the "principal," the one committed to what the words say. In personal narratives, all three speaker roles proposed by Goffman (1981) (e.g., principal, author, and animator) can merge into one. In a personal narrative, it is the principal who has experienced the events recounted and claims authorship for the narrative, acting also as animator. In such narratives, response to the teller may signal a focus on the real person behind the story, the one whose personal meaning is expressed through the narrative. More generally, and especially when children are involved, the three speaker roles may well be realized by different speakers. A mother who repeats to the father a story of personal experience, recounted to her earlier by her child, may act only as animator (if she quotes verbatim), or may take authorship rights if she edits the child's version. In either case, the child remains the principal for the story. From a cross-cultural perspective, the relation of tellers to telling and tales raises issues of authorship versus performance: How is authorship culturally defined? Who, in each culture, is entitled to tell whose stories? A related issue is the attitude of audiences to telling tales and tellers: Can the granting and up-holding of telling rights be more important than getting the tale? In other words, do cultures vary in the relative support granted by recipients to tellers, telling, and tales?

METHOD

The database for the study consists of 264 narrative events that occurred during two dinner table conversations in the 8 Jewish American and 8 Israeli families defined as Stage two families.[3] **Narrative events** were defined broadly as conversations that recapitulate past events. Because the percep-tion of what constitutes a narrative may well differ from children to adults or across cultures, we deliberately avoided imposing any further structural criteria on tales (e.g., number of events mentioned).[4] The text segments extracted from full transcripts of the dinner conversations vary in length from brief exchanges of a few seconds to long elaborated discourses, lasting up to 10 minutes. Boundaries of the segments were decided textually, with agreement of three analysts, on the basis of transition markers signaling entrances and exits from the telling realm. Analysis of the texts proceeded by a set of quantifiable coding categories designed to capture variation on each dimension of narrativity.[5] The categories and the findings from the coding are integrated in the discussion that follows.

In the following I address the degree of cultural diversity of Jewish Ameri-cans and Israelis in their attitudes toward telling, tales, and tellers in family narrative events. I argue that, considered from this threefold framework, family narrative events of the two groups share certain features attributable

---

[3]Narrative events in the American Israeli families need to be analyzed separately due to the major role played by code switching in the telling. For an initial attempt in this direction see Olshtain and Blum-Kulka (1989).

[4]The common practice in studies of children's narrative development is to insist on a Labovian two consequent and causally or temporally related events (Labov & Waletzky, 1967) as a minimal requirement for a segment of text to be considered a narrative. On one occasion, we too have used this definition to allow for comparability across datasets collected under different conditions (Blum-Kulka & Snow, 1992), but we found the definition inadequate for capturing the richness of conversational narratives at dinner. For example, from a young child's perspective, recounting one past event (defying Labovian requirements for the existence of at least two events to make a story) during one short speaking turn (not an "extended turn," as in conversation analytical accounts of storytelling) may very well count as telling a story. Hence operational definitions of what constitutes a narrative need to accommodate the type of discourse the narrative is embedded in as well as variation in participants' emic perspectives.

[5]All narrative data were coded independently by two coders, Leslie Polss and Hadass Sheffer, who also participated in the analysis. Levels of agreement varied across the different dimensions from 75% to 85%.

to the speech event in which they are embedded. Yet the groups differ culturally in the structuring of each dimension of narrativity and in the relative importance granted to each: Jewish American narrative events highlight tellers and the act of telling, whereas Israeli narrative events focus on tales and tellers. I first discuss the degree of cultural diversity in terms of the division of narrative space between members of the family and styles of story initiation. Second, I address the spatiotemporal orientation of tales and the degree of conventionalization in the transformation of tales into telling. Finally, I address the relations between ownership of the tale and participation in the telling.

ISSUES OF TELLING

Gaining Access to Narrative Space: Children and Adults

Family dinner table narratives tend to be jointly constructed affairs (Erickson, 1988; Ochs et al., 1989). In our case, collaboration takes several forms: stories are co-narrated, constructed through question–answer sequences, or told with sporadic but meaningful contributions from an active audience. In all of these, telling is shared by several members of the family, sometimes including the observer. Collaborative process is at work in both Israeli and Jewish American narrative events. In almost half of the narratives (42%), more than four members participate; 31% are narrated in collaboration between three participants and 24% by two. Thus, only 3% of the narratives are performed by just one participant. What these numbers mask, though, are cultural styles of participation; Israeli and Jewish American families differ greatly in the way they draw lines of demarcation between *teller(s)* and *audience*.

Israeli and Jewish American families differ in their attitudes to the division of telling space as well as in members' modes of participation in narrative events. Consider attitudes to the division of telling space between adults and children. In both groups, dinnertime is perceived as a prime occasion for spotlighting children as narrators. To reveal attitudes toward children, we first divided narrative events by identity of the predominant *mainteller(s)* as either *child* (or children) or *adult(s)*. In a further analysis we identified the *initiator* of the narrative event by role in the family as *child*, *father*, *mother*, or *observer* (see Figure 4.2).

We found that across the two groups, children take up 42% of all narrative space. Their level of narrative participation further confirms that, as discussed in Chapter 3, children share at these dinners an official status as ratified participants.

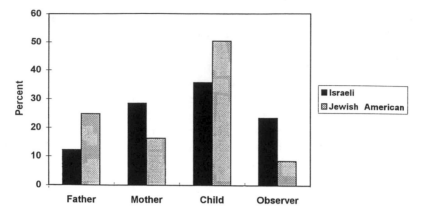

FIG. 4.2. Narrative initiation. From " 'You gotta know how to tell a story': Telling, tales and tellers in American and Israeli narrative events at dinner," by S. Blum-Kulka, 1993, *Language in Society, 22*, p. 368. Copyright 1993 by Cambridge University Press. Adapted with permission.

The pattern is most salient in the Jewish American families. Jewish American children act as maintellers in 66% of all narrative events, leaving the adults as maintellers of 34%. *The adults in the Israeli families take up a much higher proportion of narrative space*, playing the dominant role in 54% of narrative events. In line with the overall attitude to the division of narrative space between adults and children, Jewish American children are also more active (by 15%) story initators than Israeli children.

This difference points to a cultural distinction in modes of narrative socialization at dinner. Notions of tellability and cultural styles of telling are acquired by children by engaging in the telling as well as by being exposed to stories told by others. The Jewish American families tend to emphasize socialization by allowing the display of narrative practice, whereas in the Israeli families children are given a higher chance to act as active (or nonactive) story recipients.

This does not necessarily mean that Israeli children engage generally in less display of narrative than do Jewish American children; stories may be told by children at other points during the day, to siblings or one parent. It does mean, however, that dinner table conversations, where both adults and children jointly participate, are perceived by the Jewish American families as an occasion to focus on the children as narrators, whereas in the Israeli families narrative space is divided between adults and children. From the children's point of view, different gains are involved in each practice. Being encouraged to tell may be important in developing confidence in performing rights and the skills of narration (Blum-Kulka & Snow, 1992); however, acting as primary or even secondary audience to adult stories allows access to the experience of significant others, thereby expanding the bases for identification (Miller et al., 1990) and shaping cultural notions of tellability or *reportability* (cf. Hymes, 1981).[6]

Narrative Initiation:
Insiders and Outsiders, Women and Men

Adult roles also are differently distributed across the two groups, most notably in regard to the observer. In line with their general high level of participation in dinner talk (see Chapter 3), observers in the Israeli families initiate 15% more narrative events than do the observers in the Jewish American families (see Figure 4.2). In other words, the observers in the Israeli families seem much more confident in their storytelling rights than do their Jewish American counterparts. This result ties in with other observations on the relations between observers and families in the two groups: As discussed in Chapter 3, Israeli observers are drawn into the circle of conversation from the onset and interact with all family members, not only in the role of familiar guests but also as actual or potential friends. One privilege granted to friends is that of both self-directed and other-directed narrative initiation. Observers in the Israeli families accordingly share initiation almost equally with other members present.

Being a familiar guest at the Jewish American family's somewhat more formal dinner table does not bestow on the observer the privileges granted to friends; though partaking in the interaction, the observer does so cautiously, under the rules of interaction governing communication between nonintimates. Not being overtly active in narrative initiation is one the ways in which such caution is exercised. Hence, it is not surprising to find observers in the Jewish American families engaged in less than 10% of story initiations.

Another difference that emerges between Israelis and Jewish Americans is in the relative parts played by mothers versus fathers in narrative initiation. As in the case of topical actions, in the Israeli families mothers are much more active in story initiation than fathers. In the Jewish American families, fathers contribute more to the talk generally and also play a slightly more active role in narrative initiation. I suggested that one reason for these findings may be the Jewish American perception of the occasion as having formal overtones due to the presence of the observer. The serving of food is accomplished mostly by the mothers, and the fathers in the Jewish American families take it on themselves to entertain the guest, to introduce topics and to use narratives to keep the conversation going. By contrast, in the Israeli families, the mothers seem to take charge of the event both in instrumental terms (here, too, it is mostly the women who serve the food) and by keeping the conversation going.

---

[6]I use "reportability" here in the sense used by Hymes (1981): the knowledge competent members of a culture or community have as to what behavior is reportable in that community.

Styles of Narrative Initiation

The solidarity ethos of Israeli society, manifested in attitudes to the observer, finds a further expression in styles of narrative-event initiation. Consider story entry. In an independent study of the same corpora, Polss (1990) analyzed in detail the types of devices used by initiators and story recipients in the course of story-entry talk. Germane to the discussion of attitudes to telling is her analysis of the types of devices used in responsive utterances. Following Tannen's (1984, 1985, 1989) distinction between "high-involvement" and "high-considerateness" conversational styles, Polss distinguished between "high-involvement" and "low-involvement" narrative response strategies.

High involvement responsive strategies focus on the tale and the teller; in Tannen's terms, they show active "participatory listenership" (1984, p. 30). These include devices such as requests for information, confirmations of information, and listener contributions to the narrative. Low-involvement responsive utterances focus on the telling. They signal message reception, thereby confirming to the story initiator his or her success in aligning story recipients. These include different types of "uptakers" (Edmondson & House, 1981, pp. 62–63) such as neutral back-channeling responses (*mhmm, uhhuh, yeah, right, okay,* etc.) as well as emotionally colored ones (*really?, good, for heaven's sake*).

Polss found interactive, high-involvement style more characteristic of story entry in Israel than in America: The comparison of high to low involvement styles is 82% to 18% in the Israeli narratives, compared to 69% to 31% in the Jewish American stories. Thus, Israeli story openings exhibit a greater emphasis on coparticipation and more personal involvement. Israeli coparticipants frequently interpret story-initiator information, showing their concern with tale and teller:

(1) Israelis 7; Na'ama (16f); Tomer (12m); Gil (10m).
    The conversation takes place as the family is getting ready to sit down at the table.

1	Observer:	etmol hayinu, hayiti ecel pnina &ve +. . .	Yesterday we were, I was at Pnina's and +. . .
2	Mother:	ve-cvika?	And Cvika?
3	Observer:	ve-cvika ken.	and Cvika, yes.
4	Mother:	nu # ve-ex halax?	So how did it go?
5	Observer:	haya meod nexmad.	It was very nice.

[Story].

The fast rate of speech, lack of interturn pauses and dialogic unfolding of this story entry places it high on the involvement continuum. The story recipient's high engagement can further be seen by her use of what Tannen

(1984) called "cooperative promptings" at every turn (e.g., "So how did it go?"). Jewish Americans, by contrast, exhibit less relative focus on interpersonal involvement, devoting their efforts to floor-management tasks aimed at securing the telling:

(2) Jewish Americans 2; Marvin (8m); Daniel (6m); Tina (4f).
The conversation takes place at the middle of dinner.

1 Marvin: My best friend got about +. . .
You see me and my best friend were studying
rockets?
2 Observer: Uhhuh.
[story]

The shared features noted here are high degrees of collaboration and the inclusion of children in narrative events. Cultural diversity is revealed in attitudes to tellers (who participates) and styles of story entry. This trend for cultural diversity of a gradient nature, against a background of shared orientations, is also noticeable in attitudes to tales.

TRANSFORMING TALES TO TELLING

Cultural Variation in Tales' Spatiotemporal Orientation

Where do tellers find the tales for constructing narratives at dinnertime? Certainly not in fiction; the vast majority of narratives in both groups (90%) are derived from real-life experience. In predominantly adult narratives, fictional topics do not exceed 4%.

In child-involved narratives, fiction does play a role (14%). Israeli children mention fictional characters from storybooks (Aladdin is one) and tell the contents of movies and books. American children talk about fictional characters from television: Sesame Street, Bugs Bunny, and other shows.

We analyzed spatiotemporal framing by coding the two dimensions independently. First, because our definition of narratives included only stories of the past (see Ochs et al., 1989, for a different notion of temporal framing in family narratives), we distinguished narratives by temporal references included as **today stories** ("I finished my assignment today in um and . . ."), **recent past** ("I met an interesting man on the beach last week/last night Debbie . . .") or **distant past** ("that happened about five years ago"). Cases that were either timeless (such as jokes and fiction) or lacking in cues for us to reliably assign them to a recent or distant time frame were excluded from this analysis, leaving a corpus of 195 clearly time-frame-marked narrative events (out of 264). Second, we defined narrative spatial orientation as geared toward the **home**, the **world of school** or **work**, or any other location in the world. For example, a narrative about how the substitute teacher behaved that day would be considered a "today/school" narrative, a visit to the museum last week is a "recent past/world story" and a teenager's early childhood memory about a family pet is a "distant past/home" story.

In terms of their spatiotemporal framing, family dinner narratives defy the expectations of literary critics. Toolan (1988, pp. 1–2) defined narratives as "a recounting of things spatio-temporally distant." This might be true for fictional narratives, but most family narratives are definitely not temporally and only partially spatially remote from tellers and audience. Considered together for both groups, the majority of temporally marked narratives (63%) concerns events of the very recent past—today, yesterday, or last week—leaving 42% to focus on events from the distant past ($n = 195$); see Figure 4.3. In terms of location, half of the narratives fall into the third group, being located in the world; one third concern school or work, and the rest (12%) are located in the homes.

Within this general framework, we find cross-cultural preferences. The distribution by story time in Israeli and Jewish American narratives shows that story time is very different in the two groups. The most striking difference is revealed in regard to the "today" frame: In the Jewish American families, almost half of the time-marked narratives focus on today (46%). Telling about the happenings of the day thus stands out as the most important single time frame for Jewish American narratives. By contrast, in Israeli narratives, today stories take up only one quarter of narrative space (24%).

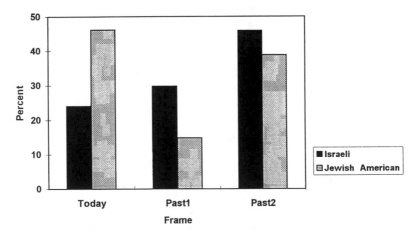

FIG. 4.3. Temporal tale frames. From " 'You gotta know how to tell a story': Telling, tales and tellers in American and Israeli narrative events at dinner," by S. Blum-Kulka, 1993, *Language in Society, 22*, p. 373. Copyright 1993 by Cambridge University Press. Adapted with permission.

For Israelis, the recent and nonrecent past are the preferred time frames, taking up over three fourths of narrative space (76%). The difference lies in general preference for time frames, not in choice of topics within the frames chosen. For example, for both Jewish Americans and Israelis, stories of the distant past cover a rich variety of topics. These include a series of humorous anecdotes about house painters the family employed over the years, the story of an exceptional shopping expedition, several camping and travel stories, as well as anecdotes from the children's earlier years.

Cultural preferences for the tales' spatial frame are less striking but still noticeable. They are revealed in the choices between home orientation and school or work orientation. For both groups, about half of the narratives are world oriented, concerning spatial frames such as museums, camping grounds, or shopping malls (48% Israeli, 53% Jewish American). The next choice is "work/school" stories: 41% in the Jewish American corpus, 33% for Israelis. However, Israeli narratives are markedly more home oriented than Jewish American narratives. In 20% of Israeli narratives the locus of the tale is at the home; by contrast, home stories are quite rare (6%) in the Jewish American corpus. The Israeli "home" stories include stories about birthday celebrations, family pets, grandparents visiting, or specific incidents linking the world and the home, such as the story of a mother's anxiety on coming home and not finding her two (early teen) sons there when she expected them.

An interesting corollary to the Israeli home orientation is provided by analysis of the types of protagonists in the foreground of family narratives. We divided protagonists as *self*, *other*, or *us*. For both Israelis and Jewish Americans, attention is divided almost equally between stories that involve the self as protagonist (47% and 52%, respectively) and stories concerning others (46% for Israelis, 47% for Jewish Americans). The prominence of the self as protagonist is not surprising, given that family dinners provide a unique opportunity for each member to use the narrative mode for raising issues of personal concern before a presumably supportive audience. Stories about others often involve the self, too, such as the self as critical observer, as when the story concerns a teenager recounting an incident between the teacher and another student. The third category, "us stories," are quite rare in both groups, but they are more likely to appear in the Israeli narratives (7.5%) than the Jewish American ones (1%). Furthermore, the 9 Israeli "us" narrative events are rather long and elaborated happenings, lasting up to 7 to 8 minutes each, whereas the two Jewish American "us narrative" events are much shorter (3 to 4 minutes) and less elaborated.

We have seen that the groups differ culturally on the dimensions of spatiotemporality. Furthermore, for the Jewish Americans the process of transformation from tales of today to the actual telling is enacted in a culturally specific, ritualistic way that is unparalleled in the Israeli narrative events.

Today Rituals: "To Who Will I Tell How My Day Goes?"

In a mock imitation of domesticity, a call girl in an American movie from the nineties ("Pretty Woman") greets her customer with "How was your day, dear?" Yet judging by the dinner table conversations, this conventional query functions socially in much richer ways than merely as a sign of wifely concern. Narratives about the day's happening figure in both Israeli and Jewish American dinner talk, but it is only in the Jewish American families that such narrative events take on the features of a proper "interaction ritual" (Goffman, 1967). Today narratives seem to combine three ritualistic features: the recurrent nature of the activity type and the role expectations that it entails; the formulaic, repetitive language of the opening phase; and the ritual constraints governing the type of conversational contribution expected.

As an activity type, today narratives resemble early childhood "formats of interaction" that are "standardized . . . interaction patterns between adult and infant that contain demarcated roles and eventually become reversible" (Bruner, 1983, p. 120). Within the family context, the roles of demarcation cut across insiders and outsiders: The observer at the family dinner table has in this case no participation rights, never asks (and is not asked) about others' or his or her day. This is not surprising, given that today rituals, like early childhood interaction formats, are based on a very high level of shared assumptions of both a cognitive and an affective nature. Members of the family have basic cognitive scripts about each other's activities during the day, and they act on the assumption that deviations from such scripts (the stuff narratives are made of) are a matter of mutual interest and concern.

Theoretically, within the family circle all members have reciprocal rights and duties to participate, but in practice, reciprocity is limited to spouses. Children either initiate participation or are invited by parents to do so, but, as a rule, they fail to show the same initiative toward their parents.

Childhood interaction formats act as a language acquisition support system (Bruner, 1983); in a parallel manner, today narrative events act as critical socializing contexts for the acquisition of narrative skills. As the analysis of the texts shows, the ritual can be performed with varying degrees of success. The processes involved in causes of success or failure provide contexts of socialization in regard to the choice of acceptable topics as well as appropriate ways of telling.

The opening phase of today rituals is marked by clear discourse boundaries at the point of initiation. The stylistic features of the opening gambit are of a formulaic and repetitive nature, allowing for only a limited degree of lexical and syntactic variation.

Consider modes of initiation. Transition from any other topic to the today narrative is enacted either by an other-initiated formulaic question (some variation on "How was your day?") or by a self-initiated today + action verb phrase ("I had lunch at the Park today").

(3) Jewish Americans 10; Andrew (10m); Jessica (8f); Jonathan (3m).
This today story is the first, followed by several others at the same meal.

> 1 Father: Jessie, how was your day?
  2 Jonathan: Ooooh aaah.
> 3 Mother: What was the best part of your day, Jessie?
  4 Jessica: After lunch.
  5 Jonathan: I get xxx.
  6 Jessica: xxx.
  7 Father: You were out playing in the rain.
  8 Jessica: Uu-huh. [affirmative]
 10 Mother: Do you have your templates, Jessie?
 11 Jessica: xxx.
 12 Father: [talking to Andrew] Really? What happened after lunch? You left for the beach yesterday?

The transition from the previous topic is often minimally marked by the use of a discourse marker (cf. Schiffrin, 1987), such as "so":

(4) Jewish Americans 2; Tina (4f).

> 1 Father: So, Tina, what did you do today?
  2 Mother: <xxxx help yourself> [>]?
  3 Father: <What'd you do today, Tina> [<]?

(5) Jewish Americans 9; Andrew (9.5m); Ellen (7f).

> 1 Mother: So what did you accomplish today?
  2 Father: xxx.
  3 Andrew: Uh, uh.
  4 Father: Yes.
  5 Mother: Yes. [laughing]
  6 Father: Well +. . .
     [Story]

The salience of the ritual becomes particularly evident through self-nomination. The right to tell your day is implicitly felt to be equally shared, as voiced by 4-year-old Sandra. With no preliminaries, Sandra at some point in the middle of the dinner turns to her mother and asks a question.

(6) Jewish Americans 4; Jordan (8m); Sandra (4f).
Sandra's initiation takes place half an hour into the dinner.

> 1 Sandra: Mommy to who will I tell how my day goes?
  2 Mother: Okay, let's hear your day.

> 3   Sandra: Well # I xxx played puzzles xxx I made xxx
>   [continued]

Sandra's question shows that she is already aware of her rights for displaying her day, and, moreover, that she offers her day as a gift to be received. It is the duty of her family to appoint a receiver for the gift, and indeed, her mother acknowledges the gift, accepting it on behalf of all present ("Okay, let's hear your day") and gives the signal for the ritual to begin. In other words, the ritual requirement in case of self-nomination is for recipients to display positive acceptance—not only yielding the floor for the teller, as is the case in all narratives, but also paying homage to the specific offering.

In other-initiated narratives, the opening gambit creates a slot that the recipient is expected to fill with a narrative of the *doings* and *accomplishments* of the day. In this way the ritual constraint that operates determines the type of contribution expected from both initiators and respondents. In example 4, the child is probed to conform to this "conversational demand" (cf. Dascal, 1983), whereas in example 5 the adult provides the expected narrative. What distinguishes the family today ritual from similar rhetorical routines in other types of interaction (e.g., "How was your weekend?" at the office) is apparently the notion of *accountability*. In the family, a question like "How was your day," especially when addressed to children, implicitly invites a narrative, no less than does an explicit query about the day's happenings. In other contexts, of course, a narrative may be neither invited nor much wanted. It is through the notion of accountability that we can understand how somebody's day can be topicalized, objectified, distanced, and contemplated with care.

(7) Jewish Americans 11; Gore (11m); Jacky (9f).
    The mother's move follows a request from Jacky to change the subject.

> > 1   Mother: I want to talk to Gore about his day, because
>   he said it was so horrible.
> > 2   Gore: It was not horrible, it was just boring.
>   3   Mother: Why was it boring, Gore?
>   4   Gore: It was really [//] actually that's not quite true.
>   This person who studies lungs came in for science
>   +/.
>   5   Mother: Lungs?
>   6   Gore: Yeah, and she said [//] she showed us some slides
>   and brought in a plastic dog's lung.
>   [continued]

As these examples show, both children and spouses are invited to participate in the ritual. However, nomination rights are not quite equally distributed. We encountered only one instance where a child tries to nominate a parent, rather than vice versa:

(8) Jewish Americans 9; Andrew (9.5m); Ellen (7f).

> 1   Andrew: What happened at work today Mother?
> 2   Mother: Well I bet you, one power trouble at work today.
> 3   Andrew: Oh really. [laughs]
> 4   Mother: [laughs] Oh God.
> 5   Ellen: You should drop your jobbie.
> 6   Mother: I know.
> 7   Ellen: Drop your jobbie.

This example shows one way in which the ritual may fail; neither party (certainly not the mother) seems to consider the question as a serious attempt to initiate a today ritual. When no narrative comes forth, another child offers a personal comment (turn 5) that serves to change the topic. In the case of successful today narratives, the same slot often is filled by prompts to continue, worded in no less formulaic ways than initiations:

(9) Jewish Americans 4; Sandra (4f).

> 1   Father: So what *else* did you today, Sandra?
> 2   Sandra: Um xx beads, puzzles and I played clock.
>   [continued]

(10) Jewish Americans 4.

> 1   Mother: What else did you do today, dear?
> 2   Father: That's all.

Such constraints on initiation and participation rights, as well as on modes of telling, turn today narrative events into clearly delimited speech events that impose specific rights and duties on all participants. For the gift of a today story to be well received, it must be a substantial gift. The first operating constraint is one of selection. Not all the day's happenings are worthy of telling. Adults explicitly call on nominated tellers to exercise criteria of interest in regard to the tale before launching into the telling. Thus, 8-year-old Jessica (turn 3 in Example 3) is asked to tell "the best part of [her] day." A long account of a soccer game by an 8-year-old boy is interrupted as follows:

(11) Jewish American 4; Jordan (8m).

1	Father:	Jordan, would you like to tell us something?
		Other than soccer, what happened today?

Child tellers are required to order the day's happenings by relevance ("Tell us the worst/best part of your day"; "What were the highlights of your day") prior to selecting one particular chain of events as a narrative topic. Children are also explicitly socialized in modes of telling. They are required, in Genette's (1980) terms, to turn "stories" into true "narratives." An extreme example of this process is illustrated by the narrative event I refer to as Everybody's Day:

(12) Everybody's Day; Jewish Americans 12; Dara (13f); Elizabeth [Beth] (10f) (also called Harriet); Daniel (4m).

	1	Father:	So how was your day, Harriet)?
			<You're supposed +/.> [>]
	2	Beth:	<Daddy>. [<] [offended]
	3	Father:	What?
	4	Beth:	Cut that out.
	% comment:		[Beth does not like to be called Harriet.]
	5	Father:	You're supposed to say "Oh it was wonderful xxx."
	6	Beth:	Daddy, [annoyed] no lousy <xxx lousy xxx [laughs]> [>].
	7	Father:	<laughs> [<]
	8	Mother:	Xx Why don't you tell us about your day now?
	9	Daniel:	My, your day.
	10	Beth:	Mine?
	11	Daniel:	xxx.
	12	Father:	Your first?
	13	Daniel:	And your tenth.
	14	Father:	[laughs].
>	15	Daniel:	Beth tell your day.
	16	Beth:	I woke up and I got dressed and xxx [speaks very softly].
	17	Daniel:	What?
	18	Father:	Speak up.
	19	Beth:	# Um # I woke up and got dressed and went to xx xx.
	20	Father:	You didn't bother to eat any of breakfast or lunch?
	21	Beth:	Nope.
	22	Father:	And I made you such nice French toast too.

23	Daniel:	No then <My day!>[>].
> 24	Father:	<Oh is it your turn now?> [<]
> 25	Daniel:	After Beth comes me [laughter]. # *My day* # washed and woke up, then go do nothing, then googo then doodo [laughs].
26	Father:	Daniel!
27	Daniel:	[laughs].
28	Father:	You can do any of that # whatever it was.
29	Dara:	Matthew now # can I go?
30	Daniel:	No. First I wake up # then go to bed # then wake up <then to to bed # then I wake up # then go to bed> [>] [laughing].
31	Father:	<Oh [laughs] you just lost your turn> [<].
32	Daniel:	First I wake up # then +/.
33	Beth:	Daniel!
34	Father:	No, stop.
35	Daniel:	xxx.
> 36	Beth:	Daniel you had a very <boring day>[>].
37	Daniel:	<Here go Mommy> [<].
38	Father:	First I wake up # then I go to nursery school.
% comment:		[imitates the way Daniel speaks].
39	Mother:	Listen to this family. First I woke up and then had breakfast.
40	Daniel:	Then you had NOTHING [laughs].
41	Mother:	Then I had my shower.
42	Daniel:	Then you had nothing [laughs].
43	Mother:	Then I did the wash. I made the lasagne +...
> 44	Dara:	Now it's *my* turn Daniel.
45	Father:	First I ate breakfast # then I got up.
46	Beth:	Daddy [annoyed tone].
47	Mother:	Oh [laughs].
> 48	Father:	Then I didn't take a shower. Then I brushed my teeth, then I went outside then I got dressed +/.
49	Beth:	Daddy! [shouting]
50	Mother:	Oh [laughs].
51	Father:	Then I took my shoes off and put my pajamas back on went to the basement # did some work # <made the pigeon for lunch> [>].
52	Daniel:	<Oh [laughs]> [<]
53	Father:	Then I drove you all to +... then I [/] then I went to Woolworths bought something that I had to return later in the day as usual because I always have to return *every*thing I buy.

54   Beth: You can't buy things.
55   Father: Um # then we went to the library.
56   Beth: And found nothing.
57   Father: And I went with a girl who found nothing. Then
                 we went out <of the library +/.> [>]
58   Beth: <Okay [shouting]!> [<]
                 [Turns into a discussion about whose books are on
                 whose library card]

Everybody's Day displays the typical features of the today ritual in its insistence on equality in rights of participation (on turn taking, see particularly turns 24, 25, 29, and 44), on the repetition of the formulaic questions (turns 1, 8, and 15), and on the type of sequential coherence built up from your-day questions responded to by action verb series. However, it is a ritual gone sour, negative rather than positive in affective outcomes.

Several indicators in the discourse combine to show us what is going wrong and thereby reveal underlying norms of the way it *should* have gone. First, there is a double message in the father's initiation: He uses the formulaic "How was your day?" but prefixes it with an unusual term of address (which his daughter does not like) and follows it up with a metacommunicative statement ("You are supposed to say . . ."). He thus sets a playful tone for the interaction, implying that this is not to be taken seriously. The mother shifts the key back to a serious tone (turn 8), and the children spend a considerable amount of metacommunicative energy—in line with the general tendency of Jewish American family dinner talk to topicalize turn taking (see Chapter 6)—arguing for their share in the family's today narrative space.

By shifting the argument constantly from the realm of telling, in which the issue at hand is a share in the today ritual, to the realm of conversation, in which the issue is floor management, that speakers indicate most clearly a dissatisfaction with the unfolding of the event. Consider turns 23 and 24. In 23, Daniel claims his share in the ritual of telling one's day; his utterance is an attempt to enter this specific telling realm. His father's response, "Oh, is it your turn now?" switches back to the realm of conversation, implicitly inviting talk for talk's sake rather than compliance with the demanding task (in terms of content) of telling one's day. In turn 24, the framing of the event shifts from the frame of "tell *my/your* day", in which it is meaningful to exchange and evaluate personally owned days, to the loosely defined "talk about *the* day" frame, in which the focus is on having a share in the talk rather than on telling your day. Subsequently, the realm of the tale is affected as well, yielding informatively poor today stories.

The first child to speak on topic, Elizabeth (turns 16–22), fails to provide an interesting narrative; she is interrupted by her younger brother, Daniel (turn 23) who is dismissed (turns 33–34) as having defied expectation for making a substantial contribution of any kind. Whereas Elizabeth conforms to the rules, though not very successfully, Daniel steps out of the rules completely. Deliberately or not, his account actually parodies the requirement for both informative substance (turns 25 & 31) and relevance. His father dismisses him by moving from the realm of telling to the realm of conversation, negating a conversational turn that fails the today requirements ("You just lost your turn"), but Elizabeth's evaluation of the tale ("Daniel, you had a very boring day") also implies a critique of the teller as principal (turn 36). The mother's metacomment in turn 39 ("Listen to this, family") suggests an awareness that things have gone wrong; yet her own attempt at a change of "footing" (Goffman, 1974, pp. 124–160) goes back to the earnest but not good enough report mode initiated earlier by her daugther (compare turn 16 to turns 40 and 44).

The event culminates with the father giving an echoed, free indirect speech mocking imitation of Daniel's account (turn 38) only to go on (turn 45) to offer a parodied version of a today report of his own. Framing the report as a parody of the real thing is indicated by an unlikely reversal of chronology ("First I had breakfast then got up") followed by reporting the negation of an event ("then I didn't take a shower"). Audience response (turns 46, 47, 49, 50, and 52) wavers between clear annoyance, which in the case of the daughter may mean taking offense (see turn 46), and laughter, which seems to indicate in this case that both mother and son align with the father's choice of telling frame.

The overall message of this failed narrative event relates to tales, telling, and tellers. In regard to the tale, it evokes the requirements of today tell-ability: To provide a significant contribution to the ritual, you have to select, order, and dramatize the events of the day. Failure to do so shifts the focus of the narrative event from the realm of telling back to the realm of conver-sation and changes its key: these transformations result in the disintegration of the today ritual. Tellers, encompassing in this event the role of animator and accountable principle (Goffman, 1981), are highly vulnerable to such transformations, finding themselves challenged on account of both their tales (e.g., "boring day") and their participation in the telling.

What is the overall function of the today rituals in the Jewish American families? In terms of discourse goals, they occupy a curious place in between transactional and interactional speech (Brown & Yule, 1983). The role of the ritualistic question, "How was your X?" can set off different types of speech events. When it is completed in a two-move exchange, as might be the case among coworkers in an office situation, it is an interaction ritual (in Goffman's sense) that tends to serve mainly phatic interactional goals, aimed predomi-nantly at the maintenance of social relations rather than the transmission of information. In the family, the same question sets off very different kinds of expectations. Here the transmission of (narratively filtered) information is not only tolerated but actually required, and the interactional goal achievable is not just social harmony but rather "affective convergence" (Aston, 1988, p. 255). The ritualistic mode seems to satisfy this variety of expectations; it provides conventionalized ways for the show of reciprocal interest and affect in the family, simultaneously serving as a socializing context for transmitting cultural notions of appropriate ways to transform tales into telling.

In contrast, the Israeli time-framed narratives exhibit only few features of the today ritual. We find the activity type enacted, especially by parents asking their children about the activities of the day. As in the Jewish American families, such questions expect a response in the form of a narrative, rather than phatic talk. Failure to provide a narrative is responded to by further probing:

(13) Israelis 10; Daffi (12f); Noga (8f); Yaron (4m).

	1	Mother:	Yaron, tesaper lanu <ma asita ha-yom ba-gan> [>].	Yaron, tell us <what you did at school today> [>].
	2	Daffi:	<ma [//] ex haya ba-gan> [<]?	<What [//] how was school> [<]?
	3	Yaron:	naim.	Pleasant.
>	4	Mother:	naim? ma haya naim? tesaper lanu ex haya naim.	Pleasant? What was pleasant? Tell us how it was pleasant.
	5	Yaron:	sixaknu.	We played.
>	6	Mother:	be-ma sixaktem?	What did you play with?
	7	Yaron:	be-misxakim.	With games.
>	8	Mother:	eze? ba-xuc? ba-xacer?	Which? Outside? In the yard?

[continued]

Initiation of such narrative events varies with child and family. Transition to a narrative concerned with the day's happenings is initiated either by a variant of a "What did you do in school (today)" question, as in Example 13, or more typically, by a topically specific question:

(14) Israelis 6; Lilax (6f); Iris (6f).

1	Father:	lean halaxtem hayom be-shiur teva?	Where did you go today during your nature lesson?
2	Lilax:	la-giva ha-zot she-pa'am she-avra halaxnu.	To this hill that we went to last time.

[continued]

The time-marker "today" tends to appear in stories told about children, rather than by children in response to today elicitations. An example is a story told mainly by a mother, with some participation from a child, about the adventure her 4-year-old daughter had at school when a rooster jumped on her; another is a story told by a mother about how 6-year-old Noam missed the bus to school. The need to mark narratives temporally tends to be reserved by Israelis for stories from the past. One device is the use of *pa'am*; literally *pa'am* means "once"; as in English, it figures in conventional story beginnings. Examples from the family narratives vary in topic (emphasis is mine):

(15) Israelis 2; Shlomit (12f); Riki (10f); Mira (5f).

    1 Father: hayiti *pa'am* be-shuk aravi   I visited *once* an Arab
                  ve-ani halaxti liknot   market and I went to
                  kishuim ve-hayu sham . . .   buy some zucchini and
                                          there were . . .

    [continued]

(16) Israelis 2; Mira (5f).

    1 Mira: ani roca lesaper bedixa.   I want to tell a joke.
               pa'am axat halax ish . . .   *Once* a man went . . .
               [continued]

(17) Israelis 1; Nadav (11m); Yoram (10m); Yoash is a guest, a friend of the family.

    1 Yoash: shamati *pa'am* et ex korim   I *once* heard, what's her
                  la, hagveret Milo . . .   name, Mrs. Milo . . .
                  [continued]

Other time marking devices used include concrete specifications of time (e.g., *last week, yesterday, last year, about a month ago*) as well as sequential ordering of events relative to self ("the first time I went to the university").

Talk about the day's activities lacks the ritual constraints on participation structure. We found no indication in the Israeli discourse of an expectation for all to participate, as in the Jewish American families. What seem to be missing are both the acccountability requirement in regard to the most recent time frame and the expectation for a display of reciprocal interest in each other's day.

The difference between the two groups in regard to today narratives seems to reflect a wider cultural difference in interactional style. Relative to Israeli society, American social interaction seems highly scripted, much more governed by fixed interaction rituals, such as phatic openings and closings, formulaic complimenting (Wolfson, 1983), and ostensible invitation sequences (Wolfson, D'Amico-Reisner, & Huber, 1983). By contrast, Israeli ways of speaking are considered by their own users as lacking in social convention (Blum-Kulka, 1992). From this perspective, the today ritual in the Jewish American families bears the hallmarks of an American ceremonial idiom. Apart from its specific familial functions for socialization and sociability, it is one more instance of an American accent on routinized performance.

CULTURAL STYLES OF COLLABORATION

Issues of Co-Ownership and Co-Performance

The degree of participation in the telling raises the issue of how access to the information contained in the tale, that is, "tale ownership" is related to the "entitlement" to tell the story (Shuman, 1986, pp. 137–141). In other words, whose stories in the family are told by whom and to whom? In discussing narratives that call for audience response, Sacks (1978) noted that it is the audience's "involvement in it [the story] that provides for the story's telling" (p. 261). Personal experience grants ownership, and shared experience grants joint ownership: "Parties who have experienced an event together are jointly in a position to describe it to someone else" (Goodwin, 1981, p. 159). As noted by Miller et al. (1990), "The conditions giving rise to joint ownership are more likely to occur in intimate relations than in non-intimate ones" (p. 298). Members of the family, being part of an intimate network, come to the dinner table with knowledge of both shared and unshared events. Although the conditions for claiming joint ownership may be met, the fact that several people are in the position to tell a story does not result necessarily in joint performance. Mothers regularly tell stories *about* children in the presence of the children (Miller et al., 1990), claiming sole performance rights on jointly owned stories. The reverse may be true as well; at least during the family dinner table conversations studied here, highly involved audience response to a personal experience (or knowledge) story may turn the telling into a joint performance, implying a process-motivated claim to joint ownership. Hence, ownership rights through access to the tale have no one-to-one correspondence to performance rights through access to the telling.

As the first step in exploring the interrelations between these two dimensions, I consider each independently and then explore the culturally preferred intersections observed in the family narratives.

One way to approach story ownership is by considering access to the knowledge of the events recounted: Is the narrated event(s) (the fabula) known to the teller only, or is it shared by any other participants? Abstracting the nature of the narrated events from the verbal narratives by considering textual indicators, we have followed Labov and Fanshel (1977) in distinguishing between individually known **A-events** (known to teller only), two-party shared **A-B events** (known to teller and one other participant), and generally known **O-type events**. Specific to the family scene is a fourth type of fabula, **F-events**, shared by all members of the family.[7] A breakdown of the data using these categories suggests that Jewish Americans and Israelis only partially share attitudes as to the degree of novelty expected from narratives around the dinner table.

In both groups, A-events dominate (66% and 69%). This is not surprising, given that dinner time provides a unique opportunity for all to share personal experiences with intimates. Family dinners with young children do not seem to occasion stories concerned with the state of the world; O-type event narratives are almost absent from this speech event (2.5% in the Israeli corpus, 0.7% in the Jewish American). For Jewish Americans, the next most frequent category following A-events is two-known A-B events (30% vs. 19% for Israelis). For the most part, these recount events experienced jointly by a child and one of the parents. For the Jewish Americans, these are the two dominant types of narrated events, with a marginal 3.5% F-event stories. On the other hand, for the Israelis, F-event narratives seem a viable category, representing 9% of all stories told. Furthermore, for Israelis, in child-involved narratives the percentage of family-event narratives rises to 15%, whereas in the equivalent set of Jewish American stories it drops to 2%.

Consider now modes of performance. We can distinguish three major modes of telling: *monologic*, *dialogic*, and *polyphonic*. Even though family narrative events are jointly constructed affairs, styles of collaborations vary on a continuum from low to high participation by people other than the primary narrator(s). At the dominantly single-voiced end of the continuum, we find monologic narratives in which one primary narrator remains in control of the floor throughout the event. The audience at such events responds indirectly, sustaining the telling but not involved in the tale. At the multivoiced, polyphonic end, we find narratives that defy the distinction of primary versus secondary narrator(s), as they are constructed in close collaboration between several participants. Between these two ends, we find dialogic narrations, constructed typically through a question–answer format.

A multiplicity of voices at the level of telling (in the polyphonic mode) can also transform relations between tellers. In Goffman's terms, at such events the audience is transformed into "fellow performers" who become "inhabitants of the same realm" (Goffman, 1974, p. 127). For Tannen (1989), it is an issue of involvement, "an internal, even emotional connection individuals feel which binds them together to other people as well as to places,

---

[7]Examples of textual indicators for event type would be "a funny thing happened to me today" (A-event); "remember the time I walked you to school?" (A-B event); "remember our last camping?" (F-event); "I was surprised by the results of the election" (O-event).

things, activities, ideas, memories and words. However, [it is] not a given but an achievement in conversational interaction" (p. 12). In Tannen's (1984) analysis of a dinner conversation between friends she found this achievement of high involvement through conversational style to characterize the three Eastern European Jewish speakers present.

Monologic narratives tend to be self-initiated, although they may follow a question from another participant. For example, in the robbery story analyzed by Polanyi (1989), the topic is put forward by a participant other than the storyteller, appealing to the appointed participant's expertise on the events to be narrated. Turning to the two women who got robbed, their friend asks, "I heard secondhand or whatever that you got robbed." "Yeah." "What happened?" (Polanyi, 1989, p. 66). Nor do tellers of monologic narratives necessarily have to claim experiential warrants for the tale, although around the dinner table, tales tend to be personal experience stories. The distinctive feature of monologic narratives is the recognizability of a single narrator's voice.

In the dialogic mode, narration proceeds through a question–answer format, regardless if the story is self- or other-initiated. This is the mode in which children get to tell stories from the very early stages of language acquisition (Ninio, 1988; Sachs, 1979). A well documented subset of such stories is the joint evocation of shared events, in which the caretaker and the child jointly recount the story (Heath, 1982; Snow, 1991). Whether or not the events to be recounted are known to both adult and child, elicited narratives with young children tend to remain collaborative, with story contributions distributed between adult and child (Snow & Goldfield, 1982).

Polyphonic narration is enacted in principle through both co-performance and co-ownership. Co-performance requires access to the tale, or at least shared access to its social context. This access takes into account both an individual teller's "information state" (cf. Goffman, 1974) as to "why events have happened as they have" (p. 133) as well as participants' familiarity with the underlying sociocultural scripts that make stories "ring true with the stories they know to be true in their lives" (Fisher, 1987, p. 63). Co-ownership may be culturally interpreted as entitling all co-owners to storytelling rights (but not necessarily so; see Miller et al., 1990, and Shuman, 1986[8]). The outcome is a jointly constructed narrative, where division lines between primary and secondary narrators are blurred. The issue of telling rights in such cases may vary culturally in regard to all participants or only in regard to children. If children are included in the circle of right holders, a child will feel licensed to contribute on topics felt relevant, whether the story is initiated by an adult or another child.

---

[8]As Shuman (1986) noted: "One must have information in order to talk about something. However, people with the information are not necessarily entitled to tell what they know" (p. 31).

TABLE 4.1
Styles of Participation

Event Type/Mode	Polyphonic	Monologic
Shared	Israeli Jewish American	Jewish American
Unshared	Israeli	Israeli Jewish American

Israelis and Jewish Americans seem to differ in preferences shown for these three modes of performance. Quantitative analysis of a subsample of the narratives included here (Blum-Kulka & Snow, 1992) shows Jewish Americans prefer the monologic, display mode in 60% of the cases, with a preference for the dialogic mode in 29%. Israelis, by contrast, make use of all three styles, preferring both the dialogic (49%) and the polyphonic (30%) to the monologic (24%).[9]

The cultural difference in regard to both ownership and performance rights is revealed mainly in the diverse ways the groups interpret the relation between these two dimensions. Excluding dialogic, typically adult–child narration from this analysis, we can detect four types of interaction between access to the tale and participation in the telling. The two groups differ in their preferences for these, as shown in Table 4.1.

Among the four possible configurations between event type and mode of telling, Israeli and Jewish American narratives seem to share two: telling shared experiences collaboratively in the polyphonic mode and allowing predominantly solo performances of personally known stories. However, the Jewish American families support monologic performances even when tales are known to more than one participant, and Israeli narration may unfold highly collaboratively even in cases of unshared tales.

The distribution between these four modes shows these preferences as representing a gradient phenomenon: Whereas in both groups shared experiences told collaboratively and single experiences told monologically constitute the bulk of narrative events (77% for Israelis, 83% for Jewish Americans), for Israelis the third choice is to *tell unshared events in a polyphonic mode* (18%), whereas for Jewish Americans it is to *tell shared events in the monologic mode* (12%). In the Israeli families, shared events are told in the monologic mode only in 5% of the time, whereas in the Jewish American families unshared events are told in the polyphonic mode in only 4% of cases. In the following section, I illustrate the way cultural styles are manifest within each of the two major modes of telling.

---

[9]Included in this analysis were narrative events from one meal of 10 American (5 middle-class and 5 working-class) and 5 Israeli middle-class families (*n* = 73).

The Monologic Mode: Telling Shared and Unshared Events

A culturally shared and highly prevalent mode of telling (43% for both groups) is the dominantly monologic performance granted occasionally to sole tellers recounting (mostly but not exclusively) personal experience. In one such case, an Israeli woman describes in great detail the nightmarish dream she had about getting lost on one of the campuses of the Hebrew University in Jerusalem. In another instance, a Jewish American teenage girl recounts a confrontation she had with a teacher in school. In the following example, the story offered by the observer terminates a series of stories concerning memories of food from childhood, all embedded in members' attitudes toward the religious practices of the parent and grandparent generations.

> (17) Israelis 1; Nadav (11m); Yoram (10m).
> The segment follows several exchanges concerning food and eating habits.

1	Observer:	aval ha-ax sheli Avner haya noda be-bareranuto be-oxel. hu mamash hayu shlosha dvarim she-hu axal ve-zehu.	But my brother Avner was well known for his pickiness in food. There were actually three things he ate and that's it.
3	Mother:	ma?	What?
4	Observer:	chips ve-stek ze haya ha-xx. ve-ani zoxeret she-od basar bishvil she-hu yoxal basar notnim lo. Sonya hayta notenet lo avatiax be-onat ha-avatixim xotexet lo she-yaani kaxa +/.	Chips and steak it was xx # and I remember that more meat so he'll eat meat they would give him. Sonya would serve him watermelon in season, would cut so +/.
	%comment:	[Sonya is the teller's stepmother]	
> 5	Mother:	++ lo yargish. bis mi-ze ve-bis me-ha-hu.	++ (that) he won't notice. A bite here and a bite there.
6	Observer:	ve-kshe-hu higia le-cava hu na'asa gorme kaze be-oxel ve-mitanyen be-misadot. hayom shuv ani lo yoda'at	And when he got to the army he became such a gourmet eater and interested in restaurants. Now again I don't know,

			ki hu dos. yesh lahem	'cause he became observant.
			mine isurim. aval ba-tkufa she-hu od haya xiloni, hu na'asa axlan bilti ragil ve-hu amar "axshav ani mictaer al kol ha-shanim she-haya oxel kol kax tov <ve-ani> [>] ve-ani lo neheneti me-*klum*".	They have all these rules, but during the while he was still non-observant, he turned into a great eater and said "Now I'm sorry for all those years when there was such good food <and I> [>] and I didn't enjoy it *at all*.
	7	Mother:	<ken?> [<]	<Yes?>
>	8	Nadav:	ani af pa'am lo ectaer.	I shall never regret.
	9	Observer:	lo, kol ze ba lomar lax she-ata lo yaxol lada'at ma yihye be-od +...	All this means that you can never know what will happen in another +...
>		@ END		

The story of Avner, the non-eating child transformed into a gourmet adult only to lose access (from the teller's point of view) to gourmet food through newly acquired religious practices, is exceptionally rich in cultural themes, negotiating transitions between life cycles in the Israeli context (child–soldier–adult) and Jewish life styles (nonobservant–observant) (see Polanyi, 1989, for analysis of cultural themes in American stories). For the purposes of the present analysis, the mode of telling is of main interest. The example illustrates that, even in the monologic mode, when someone is recounting unshared events, Israeli audience response goes beyond brief uptakers. In turn 4, the evaluative details added by the mother are her own logical inferences, never mentioned by the main teller. The child's comment in turn 8 indicates how carefully he had been listening to the story; in the Israeli families, children typically act as active audience to all stories told, regardless of tellers (adults or children) and topic. In the Jewish American families, child participation in the role of active audience seem more restricted to child-related topics (Blum-Kulka & Snow, 1992).

In the Jewish American families, *monologic telling is not restricted to unshared event*. Consider the following personal experience narratives told with the explicit purpose to entertain:

(18) The Bug. Jewish Americans 3; Samuel (10m); Jeffrey (6m).
    Talk about hikes precedes this segment.

    1 Mother: Daniel loves that.

		%comment:	[Daniel is her husband]
	2	Samuel:	Really?
	3	Mother:	I on the other hand [//] He *loves* to commune with nature. Me, I can take nature through a glass window.
	4	Samuel:	xxx.
>	5	Mother:	A glass window with the bugs out, and anything that's more than four feet removing themselves from my presence. I *can't* deal with them [laughs]! We had a bug once in the shower, and Samuel called me in on a Friday afternoon, wouldn't you know it, and he screams "MA!" and there is this thing, if it wasn't two inches big. # I thought it was the most *disgusting* and somehow as disgusting as they are small. # They get worse when they get larger. And there I was, it wasn't even afraid. It wasn't running, it was taking its time, it was sort of taking a little walk across the shower. I would at least appreciate it if they were afraid +/.
>	6	Observer:	But no.
	7	Mother:	+^But no, it sat there, very territorially, so I said "get rid of it." He said "I'm not getting rid of it, *you* get rid of it" and of course Daniel was nowhere around.
>	8	Observer:	Of course, right.
	9	Mother:	So we had to shpritz it to death.
>	10	Observer:	Of course.
	11	Mother:	Oh, it was horrible, and the darn thing was so resilient it wouldn't die, you know I find that absolutely appalling +/.
	12	Observer:	It wasn't xxx.
	13	Mother:	That's right, well by the time we finish with them, they would be +. . . Cockroaches are going to inherit this earth one of these days.
	14	Father:	Well, you weren't using insecticide though.
	15	Mother:	I was using mildew spray xxx and that bug had the nerve to walk around in it yet. But finally it gave up, the ghost, and then we had to dispose of it. So I said "go ahead, Samuel, dispose of it." He says "I'm *not* touching it, *you* touch it". So I took it out with thirty layers of tissue so that I wouldn't even [/] even feel its shape and I

			picked it up and I threw it into the bathroom toilet.

> 16 Observer: She hasn't gotten over it.

17 Mother: I'm still thinking about it. I can see that bug # and I have visions of it rising up yet like a phoenix to haunt me.

The Bug Story is initiated by the mother, who remains primary narrator for its duration. Though both father and older son (Samuel) are familiar with the events, audience response is limited to sustaining the act of telling through appropriate backchanneling and clarification comments (turns 6, 8, 10, 14, and 16). The teller's comment on her relations with nature ("I can take nature through a glass window," turn 3) serves as bridging talk to introduce her dramatic encounter with a spider in her bathroom on a Friday afternoon. She then manages to entertain her listeners by using several evaluative devices to highlight the turning points of her narratives (e.g., direct quotes, a shift to the use of the present tense; see turns 5 and 7). Her efforts are fully appreciated, as can be seen by audience reactions in turns 6, 8, and 16. Finally, she concludes by providing a Labovian coda (Labov & Waletsky, 1967); visions of the bug rising like a phoenix clearly linking the past to the present.

The Bug Story shows that co-ownership of the tale does not necessarily entail equal rights for the telling. Narrative events can distinguish tellers from experiencers. In the Bug Story, the teller is the chief but not sole experiencer in the narrated events, yet she is granted full telling rights, using her storytelling skills as individual performer.

The Polyphonic Mode: Telling Shared and Unshared Events

As listeners, we tend to expect collaboration in the telling when access to the tale is shared by several of the participants. Thus stories about a couple's trip abroad may be told to friends jointly, or in a monologic style, but with frequent interceptions from the other knowing participant. Shared ownership of the tale in the family may cut across generations, or create ownership affiliations between any group of members by true experience or claimed familiarity with the events. Events that happen to parents jointly, prior to the children's birth, are a source for generationally defined ownership. In one case the story of the parents' courtship is told in collaboration by both parents in response to a 10-year-old's question: "ex ata ve-aba higatem le-ahava me-aruxat-erev pshuta? [How did you and Dad get to love from a simple dinner?]."

The story of the parents' courtship is an example of the type of narrative that may be told again and again, due to its relevance to the history of the family. Memories from a shared past carry the potential of becoming part of the familial narrative repertoire, their telling triggered by the presence of a new audience. Our presence at the dinner table might have occasioned the retelling or construction of several such *family fables*. Consider the potential of the following recollection of a family reunion as a candidate of being or becoming a family fable:

(19) Jewish Americans 9; Andrew (9.5m); Ellen (7f).

	1	Father:	Yeah, anyway we had a big family reunion.
	2	Ellen:	What's a family reunion? [softly]
	3	Mother:	That was all the members of the family [//] all relations.
	4	Father:	Well, you can't be more specific.
	5	Mother:	Not all.
>	6	Ellen:	All the members of *his* side of the family.
	7	Father:	Yes, it was all of my father's [//] my father and both of his sisters and all their children, and all the grandchildren.
>	8	Andrew:	We were one of the grandchildren, right?
	9	Father:	Right.
	10	Mother:	Um hm.
	11	Father:	So all these people were at this big reunion. And there wasn't enough room to sleep inside the house. So a lot of people bought, had, or rented +/.
	12	Mother:	Rented. Nobody had, everybody rented.
	13	Father:	Yeah? Everybody rented RV's which are these motor homes which you sleep in. And are not real comfortable.
	14	Mother:	And they're not real private.
	15	Father:	xx didn't seem to mind.
>	16	Mother:	Well you just [//] you were so shy Ellen # you [/] you wouldn't talk to anybody. And you just stayed inside the RV and you never wanted to come out to see everybody. You just wanted to stay inside and read books and play with your toys.
	17	Andrew:	She could *read* then?
	18	Mother:	Well she had some books that she looked at the pictures, you know.
	19	Andrew:	Yeah.
	20	Ellen:	Picture book? Picture book?
	21	Andrew:	Pretended to read # pretended she was grown up.

	22	Mother:	Uh huh. And when anybody tried to talk to you [//] you'd run away and hide in the RV.
	23	Father:	Except for Pearson.
>	24	Ellen:	Yeah in the RV I would go.
	25	Father:	You visited xxx P. He picked you up. xxx feet and sat you on his back xxx started asking you about the pictures.
	26	Ellen:	Huh.
	27	Father:	You succumbed to his charms. xxx have [laughter].

The polyphonic mode of telling is particularly suitable for stories that have the family "us" as protagonist and that are relevant in terms of contribution to the building of familial and individual identities. The Family Reunion story is not about self or other but rather is reflexively about "us," the family, and the way we were then. Its relevance stems from stressing family continuity: It seems to be saying, "Here is something we did together, even if you children do not remember it all." Revealing several sides of her younger personality, the story is particularly relevant for the child protagonist. It provides her with a sense of the continuity with her own past, giving her the opportunity to reflect on her younger self as compared with her current self. The suggested key for reflection is a humorous one; the child is invited to join the others in laughing at her own shyness then and the attraction that broke it. The text contains indicators that the story has been told previously. Ellen's first contribution to the narrative (". . . all his side of the family," turn 6) suggests familiarity with the tale, or at least parts of it. A later remark ("Yeah in the RV I would go," turn 24) can be taken either as her recollection of the events or as her acceptance of her parents' version. The story is on its way to becoming a family fable.

Telling is carried by both parents, with a shift in appointed audiences. The father seems to be talking first to the observer, but the mother deliberately shifts perspective, appointing Ellen, the heroine of the story, as primary audience (". . . *you* were so shy Ellen," turn 16). Andrew, the older brother, takes the role of the challenger, doubting his mother's version (". . . she could read then?") and, once reassured, insisting on his sister's limitations ("[She] pretended to read," turn 21). The mother aligns with her son by picking up the third person reference to Ellen ("Well, she had some books . . . ," turn 20) and then treating the exchange with Andrew as a side sequence (Jefferson, 1972), she shifts back to addressing Ellen directly. Thus, although in different narrative roles, eventually all family members collaborate in constructing a narrative that may well become part of the family's fable repertoire.

In the Israeli narratives, by contrast, sharing the tale is no prerequisite for participation in the telling. Even when the specific events are strictly of the A-event, "only teller knows" type, in the family they are told against the background of shared sociocultural scripts that in turn provide occasions for nonexperiencer participation. Israeli dinner table participants seem to take full advantage of their familiarity with such scripts. In 18% of the nondialogic Israeli narrative events, singular tales get a polyphonic telling. In the Jewish American families, we detected only three such examples (4%). In the following Watermelon narrative the fact that the story concerns an A-event does not prevent other members from taking an active part in the construction of the story:

(20) Saving a Watermelon. Israelis 10; Daffi (12f); Noga (8f); Yaron (4m). The story of saving a watermelon follows an account, by the mother, of a car accident she was involved in the same day.

1	Father:	ani etmol [/] ani etmol hicalti avatiax.	I yesterday [/] yesterday I saved a watermelon.
2	Observer:	oh [laughs]	
3	Noga:	ex [/] ex?	How [/] How?
4	Daffi:	ex hu hicil?	How did he save?
5	Father:	atem lo ta'aminu. ani nasati li # hayiti ba-boker, ze haya etmol, ken, hayiti hare etmol ba-boker ba-bank <lifnei ha-caharayim>. [>]	You won't believe it. I was driving, in the morning, it happened yesterday, yes, I was at the bank yesterday <before noon>.[>]
6	Mother:	<avatiax al ha-sakin> [<].	<Watermelon by the knife> [<].
% comment:		[it's an expression used by watermelon vendors].	
7	Father:	lo ze lo al ha-sakin. mazal.	No it's not by the knife. Lucky.
8	Observer:	ani mekava she-lo <sikanta et acmexa>.[>]	I hope <you didn't endanger yourself> [>].
9	Father:	<ve-ani nosea li> [<] me-ha-super be-giva hacarfatit # ma at mekava?	<And I'm driving from> [<] the supermarket on French Hill # what do you hope?
10	Observer:	she-lo sikanta et xayexa.	That you didn't risk your life.
11	Father:	kim'at.	Almost.
12	Mother:	oy va-avoy li!	[exclamation]
13	Father:	ba-super lemata le-kivun ha-ramzor, ve-pitom ani	Near the supermarket in the direction of the

		roe holexet sham isha im ezo yalda ve-pitom ve-eze sakit matxila lehitgalgel ba-morad, ve-ha-yalda roca laruc <le-sham ve-*coraxat*>[>] ve-ha-ima maxzika ota.	traffic lights, and suddenly I see a women walking with a child (female) and suddenly a bag starts rolling down the slope, and the child wants to run <there and is *yelling*> [>] and her mother is holding her.
14	Observer:	<ha-yalda xx> [<].	<The child xxx> [<].
15	Father:	az ba-hatxala lo raiti ma ze aval ze hitgalgel be-merec.	So at the beginning I didn't see what it was but it rolled with vigor.
% comment:		[everybody is laughing].	
16	Daffi:	avatiax dafuk.	Shitty watermelon.
17	Father:	raiti [/] raiti she-lo keday la'acor et ze im ha-oto, maher acarti et ha-oto ve-racti ve-hiclaxti litfos et ha-avatiax she-hitgalgel be-tox sakit, ve-lo kara lo shum davar, bari ve-shalem hexzarti oto le-zro'ot ha-yalda.	I saw [/] I saw that it won't be good stopping it with the car, so I stopped the car quickly and ran, and managed to catch the watermelon that was rolling in the bag, and it came to no harm, I returned it safe and sound into the arms of the little girl.
18	Daffi:	+^ <ha-yalda ha-mityapaxat>. [>]	<The sobbing child>. [>]
19	Mother:	<acarta et ha-mexonit> [<] [/] acarta et ha +/.	<You stopped the car> [<] you stopped the +/.
20	Father:	avarti oto. acarti et ha-mexonit +/.	I passed it. I stopped the car +/.
21	Mother:	acarta ve-yaradeta me-ha-mexonit ve-hicalta et ha-avatiax?	You braked, got off the car and saved the watermelon?
22	Father:	natati la avatiax ve-hicalti et xaye ha-mishpaxa sham.	I gave her a watermelon and saved the life of the family there.
23	Mother:	ve-ma amru lexa ha-mishpaxa ha-zot?	And what did they say to you this family?
24	Observer:	[laughs]	
25	Father:	"toda raba be'emet toda ve-shuv toda."	"Thank you very much really and thanks again."

26	Mother:	be-amerika ish lo haya ose et ze.	In the States nobody would have done it.
27	Father:	be-amerika avatixim ze masoret lehacil.	In the States there is a tradition to save watermelons.
28	Mother:	ze rak be-erec <she-mishehu yored me-ha-mexonit> [>].	It's only here <that somebody would get out of the car> [>].
29	Father:	<ma at medaberet xx> [<>]? dvarim kaele +...	<What are you saying xx> [<>]. Such things +...
30	Daffi:	<be-amerika yesh xx xx xx> [<].	<You have in the States xx> [<].
31	Father:	hem meod adivim ba-dvarim ha-ele.	They are very polite in these things.
32	Observer:	aval avatiax: im ha-yalda hayta raca la-avatiax az haya yaxol lihyot nora mesukan.	But a watermelon! If the child would have chased the watermelon things might have become very dangerous.
33	Father:	lo. hayta sham beaya. Zot omeret ha-ba'aya shel ha-isha hayta o ha-avatiax o ha-yalda.	No, there was a problem. I mean the woman's problem was either the watermelon or the child.
34	Mother:	ve-hi hexlita ha-yalda <be-shlav dey mukdam> [>].	And she decided for the child <quite early on> [>].
35	Father:	<hi hexlita ha-yalda>[<] aval ha-yalda hexlita avatiax.	<She decided (in favor of) the child> [<] but the child decided (in favor of) the watermelon.

The story is offered as a humorous counterpoint to the preceding narrative by the mother, recounting her near escape from a car accident. The father embeds the upcoming story in the ongoing conversation by repeating the verb *save* (in the previous story, "saved from the incident") in the new and unexpected context of saving a watermelon. Unlike the Bug story, the Watermelon incident is based on events known to the teller only. Yet in the Israeli family, participants take an active part in the performance from the onset. The high level of involvement (cf. Tannen, 1984, 1989) can be glimpsed by just scanning the names of the participants making comments during the event (i.e., wife, observer, both older children) and by noticing the high proportion of overlapped talk.

The nature of audience participation changes with different phases of the narrative event. The event is composed of three phases (cf. Polanyi, 1989): opening (turns 1–13), which provides the abstract and the general setting (time and place), main body of narrative (turns 14–18), and discussion of its point (cf. Polanyi 1989), (turns 19–35). In the opening phase (turns 1–13), audience response takes the form of what Tannen (1984, p. 118) called "cooperative prompting": Both children display interest (turns 3 & 4), the wife debates jokingly the kind of watermelon in question (turn 6), and the observer expresses empathy for the teller experiencer (turn 8).

The teller presents the main events of the story—including setting, complication, and resolution in Labovian terms—in turns 13, 15, and 17. Audience response at this stage is diminished, recipients confining themselves mainly to backchanneling.

Once the happy ending becomes evident, the audience takes on a highly active part both in embellishing the story and in debating its point. In turn 18, Ruti uses a phrase borrowed from the language of written Hebrew fairytales ("the sobbing child"), which serves to dramatize the scene of the story's denouement. The child's sobbing is implied in an earlier statement by the teller ("she was screaming," turn 13) but is never mentioned again. This evaluation of the tale is offered because it coheres with the rest, not because the speaker has first-hand or vicarious proof for its being true.

The point of the narrative emerges in collaboration between several participants. In response to his wife's clarification question (turn 22) the teller reformulates the point of the story as concerning *the saving of a family* rather than *saving a watermelon* (turn 23). In the side sequence that follows, wife and husband disagree as to the plausibility of the event taking place anywhere but in Israel. The mother's attempts to explain the narrative's coda, in terms of cross-cultural variability as regards norms of politeness (turns 26 and 28) is rejected by both father and daughter (turns 29, 30, and 31). Note that the girl shows her alignment with her father's position by "cooperatively overlapping" talk (cf. Tannen, 1984) that actually completes the father's utterance (turn 30).

In turns 32–35 the three adults return to the issue of the point of the story. By rephrasing the "true" nature of the complication as a case of real danger (turn 32), the observer reinforces the transformation of the narrative's point from being an entertaining anecdote about saving a watermelon to being a serious story about saving lives. The discussion highlights the status of the narrative as a moral construct (cf. Fisher, 1987), giving it meaning through negotiating the nature of the moral dilemma at hand. Husband and wife collaborate in underscoring this new angle by shifting perspectives (turns 34 and 35) to the viewpoint of the woman with the child, for whom the problem was one of protecting her child rather than the watermelon.

This example shows that Israeli participants do not feel restrained by lack of access to actual experience when they claim authorship for the story. Although the fabula of the Watermelon is derived from the personal experience of the teller, the other participants in the event take a highly active part in the story's construction, especially in regard to negotiating its macrolevel point. The process culminates in a joint agreement as to the point of the story; this agreement, as well as the high degree of participation throughout, reveals a preference for a multivoiced modes of performance in this group. However, collaboration goes beyond performance: through the process of becoming *fellow performers* in the telling, participants claim joint ownership of the tale. In other words, in monologic unshared event narratives ownership rights are reconfirmed through the telling, but in the process of a joint performance of an (initially) unshared event, ownership rights may be generated performatively through the very act of participation in the telling.

These examples show that the two groups differ in attitudes to the relation between ownership and performance. Israeli families reveal a flexibility in regard to both dimensions; they strive toward joint ownership for all narratives. This trend is manifested by the high degree of participation in the telling of both personal narratives and shared family events. By partaking in the construction of the story, members of the Israeli family use "narrative authorship" (Shuman, 1986) to make claims for joint narrative ownership.

In the Jewish American families, by contrast, participation in the telling seems preconditioned by joint access to the tale. Thus the recollection of shared family memories (e.g., the Family Reunion story) is accomplished with the help of several family members. In contrast with the Israelis, story authorship is highly valued. There is a trend to allow for the display of individual storytelling skills even in cases where the tale is known to more than one participant (e.g., The Bug story). For these families, authorship through performance is used to assert and/or achieve individual ownership.

CONCLUSION

I have grounded my analysis of family narrative events in the threefold framework of telling, tales, and tellers. The distinction between the first two of these dimensions, under different guises, concerns students of narratology (e.g., Genette, 1980; Rimmon-Keenan, 1983) as well as folklore (e.g., Bauman, 1986; Briggs, 1988; Young, 1987). My inclusion of *tellers* within the same paradigm is meant to emphasize the social constitutive nature of oral storytelling and within it, the role of individual selves (e.g., in the presentation of self as performer and often also as protagonist) in relation to the other two realms.

This model permits us to isolate the shared and unshared properties of Jewish American and Israeli family narrative events. We found similar patterns in respect to multiple participation, the prevalence of personal experience stories, and a respect for children's storytelling rights. These patterns probably derive as much from a common Eastern European oral storytelling tradition as from modern narrative practices prevalent in middle-class families in the Western world. As documented by Kirshenblatt-Gimblett (1974/1989), oral storytelling has been a cultural focus in Jewish society from time immemorial; it was frequent and important in traditional Eastern European communities, it was egalitarian (i.e., everybody could tell), and it was not limited to specific speech events. By contrast, features like the dialogic nature of many oral narratives (Polanyi, 1989) or the deliberate involvement of children in storytelling (McCabe & Peterson, 1991) characterize White North American mainstream practices.

However, the two groups also differ in many respects, their differences bearing on practices of socialization and styles of sociability. The differences show up both in ways of construing each of the three narrativity dimensions independently and in the interplay between them. Access to telling, indeed to all dinner talk, is less available to Israeli than Jewish American children but is more available to Israeli than American observers. Socialization for storytelling in the Jewish American families relies heavily on adult–child engagement in narrative events focused on child tellers (and protagonists); by contrast, in the Israeli families adults take up a larger proportion of narrative space, and hence socialization for narrative skills (in the broadest sense, including notions of tellability), though including adult–child storytelling, relies more heavily on modeling and on allowing (limited) participation in adult-focused stories.

Differences in styles of sociability are apparent in the transitions between the realm of conversation and the realm of telling. Jewish American families search for clear demarcation lines, occasionally ritualized, as in the today stories. The high-involvement style of Israeli story entry tends to blur the boundaries between the two realms. Israeli narrative events often begin and end in a highly polyphonic mode; the opening phase establishes shared access to the tale, and the closing phase focuses on negotiating a shared interpretation of the story's meaning, seamlessly moving back to the realm of conversation.

The attitude of participants to the tellers, the tales, and telling is also perceived in culturally distinct ways. Jewish Americans support tellers by attending to individual telling rights, but Israelis tend to support tellers by attending to the tale. Access to story ownership in the Jewish American families is asserted through familiarity with the tale, whereas in the Israeli families it is also achievable through participation in the telling. As a result, monologic modes of telling in the Jewish American families extend to shared events, whereas telling of unshared events is celebrated by Israelis in the polyphonic mode. The proposition unique to the Jewish Americans seems to be "let me tell our story" and for Israelis "let us (all) tell your (singular) story."

Yet all these families share an Eastern European background. As such, all could be expected to manifest in narratives the high involvement conversational style found by Tannen (1984) as typifying Jewish New Yorkers from the same background. High involvement, in turn, seems linked to the ceremonial idiom of Eastern European Jewish traditions. Spolsky and Walters (1985) argued that a high involvement style typifies Eastern European learning styles of the yeshiva and styles of worship in Ashkenazi Eastern European synagogues. In the yeshiva, learning is accomplished dialogically, through high participatory listenership and rapid turn shifting; this high level of involvement is also apparent in style of worship in the Eastern European synagogue, which seems chaotic compared to the Oriental and Western European. In the latter case, this "chaos" is governed by underlying ideological principles that allow for higher involvement on the part of the individual worshipper.

Ideology is also a strong motivating factor in understanding Israeli conversational style. The Israeli style emerged against the background of a strong ideological opposition to all things associated with Eastern European diaspora traditions (Harshav, 1993), including ways of speaking (Katriel, 1986). On many dimensions of language use, the Israeli style has indeed been shown to break away from traditional modes (e.g., Blum-Kulka, 1992; Katriel, 1986). The study of narrative events suggests that the Israeli style is also strongly infused with the subtext of of the traditional style associated with the "old" Eastern European Jewish worlds of discourse. Compared to the Jewish Americans, the Israelis are more involved in all aspects of narrative disourse, sharing tellings and tales.

From this comparative perspective, the impact of Eastern European traditions is less noticeable in the narrative discourse of Jewish American families. In their case, American culture seems to have played the formative role. Hence the emphasis on individual rights and self-accomplishment, seen in attitudes to the telling, could be expected from sociological accounts of American society (e.g., Bellah et al., 1985). The Jewish American narrative style, like many other discourse practices, seems firmly embedded in American cultural practices, testifying to the Americanization of these families.

The differences in narrative practices suggest different interpretations to the dialectics of continuity and change in the respective communities. I return to this argument in the concluding chapter, where I am in a position to consider the accumulated evidence for cultural styles as it emerges from examining several dimensions of family discourse.

In the next section, I turn to practices of pragmatic socialization, as manifest in the language of control, metapragmatic discourse, and, for the American Israeli families, bilingual socialization. Practices of pragmatic socialization, while showing the impact of modernity on attitudes to children in all the families studied, also reveal many cultural differences.

"Its got this little tiny *xalon* (window) with all kinds of *kaftorim* (buttons)."
(American Israeli family 3, Father talking about his new computer).

"What do you want?" (American Israeli family 9, Ofer talking (in Hebrew) to
his baby brother).

"Shall I tell you when I saw him?" (Israeli family 5, Miriam, the observer, talking about a common acquaintance (translated from Hebrew; ex 10, chapter 3).

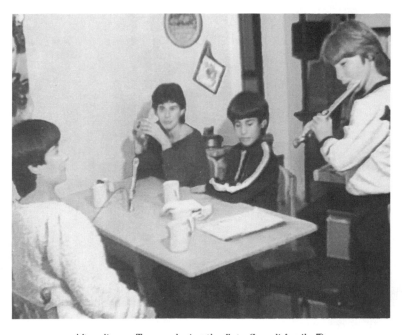

After dinner; Tomer playing the flute (Israeli family 7).

"Is he Jewish?" (Jewish American family 1, Simon asking about Woody Allen, example 6, Chapter 3).

After dinner: Yael doing homework (American Israeli family 12).

PRAGMATIC PATTERNS OF SOCIALIZATION

5

POLITENESS IN FAMILY DISCOURSE: THE TRAFFIC OF PARENTAL SOCIAL CONTROL ACTS

Dinnertime provides opportunities for both the negotiation of and the socialization for cultural styles of politeness. In the research tradition following the publication of Brown and Levinson's (1987) seminal book on politeness, politeness is taken to mean the culturally appropriate ways for what is said and how it is said relative to interactional goals, participants, and context. In other words, politeness is embedded in all aspects of human social interaction and as such is central to pragmatic socialization.

The following two chapters are concerned with two facets of pragmatic socialization for politeness: the language of social control acts and meta-pragmatic discourse. Family dinners invariably necessitate the use of **social control acts** (e.g., different types of directives). Even when no other conversation is taking place, there are occasions when participants have to express their dinner needs (like asking for the salt) and when adult participants need to verbally control the behavior of young children. Social control acts (Ervin-Tripp, 1982; Ervin-Tripp & Gordon, 1986) encompass a large class of verbal moves aimed at affecting the behavior of others (e.g., offers, requests, and orders), and these moves manifest complex relations between their modes of performance and contextual and cultural factors. All types of social control acts impinge on the recipient's freedom of action and constitute a threat to face; therefore, politeness becomes a major consideration in the choice of mode of performance. The enactment of social control acts in family discourse encodes both cultural and situational interpretations of politeness.

Comments made in response to perceived violations of conversational norms, **metapragmatic comments** exercise a different type of social control. For social control acts, cultural practices of pragmatic socialization focus on the conventional ways of performing single speech acts; metapragmatic discourse, in contrast, reveals the cultural norms for appropriate conversational behavior. As argued in Chapter 6, this is a central dimension of politeness, one hitherto much neglected in politeness research.

In the Goffmanian tradition, face concerns are the underlying social motivation for systems of politeness (Goffman, 1967). In this tradition, as elaborated by Brown and Levinson (1987), politeness is meant to satisfy self and other face needs in case of threat and is expressed by strategic choices affected by the social variables of social distance and power and the degree of perceived imposition. The two basic face wants—the need for freedom from imposition (i.e., negative face) and the need for the enhancement of a positive self-image—are satisfied through two different styles of politeness: *negative politeness*, which celebrates nonimposition and freedom of action, and *positive politeness*, which builds on indexes of solidarity such as in-group membership. Styles of politeness might differentiate cultures, so that societies that tend to minimize social distance and weight of imposition will tend toward positive politeness whereas other cultures will linguistically mark distance, power, and imposition by means including those of negative politeness.

But this sociologically oriented explanation of cross-cultural diversity in systems of politeness fails to take into account the possibility that cultures may already differ at the level of defining the constituents of face needs. In other words, underlying systems of politeness are cultural values associated with perceptions of *face* (for elaboration of this idea as related to Japanese culture, see Matsumoto, 1989, and Ide, 1989). Consider, for example, the notions of "sincerity" and "truthfulness" in two cultures as different from each other as the Chinese and the Israeli. For the Chinese, any outward show of politeness must be "made sincerely," yet a hostess will claim that there is nothing to eat even after she has laid a selection of different dishes before her guests (Gu, 1990). For the Chinese, sincerity seems a matter of symbolic persuasion, a necessary outward show, whereas actual truthfulness is waived in service of the principle of polite modesty (cf. Leech, 1983). The Israeli cultural notion of *dugriyut* (literally, "straightforwardness") as studied by Katriel (1986) involves no contradiction in marrying sincerity and truthfulness with politeness; redress to self and other's face might be expressed by stating sincerely the truth of a critical, threatening act. Cultural interpretations of face constituents should therefore be considered seriously in discussions of the universality of politeness systems. The study of politeness in the family further shows that face needs, and hence politeness meanings, are negotiated not only culturally but also domain specifically.

BALANCING POWER AND SOLIDARITY
IN THE FAMILY

The findings presented in this chapter show that parental language of control at the family dinner table is highly direct. To understand the motivation for and the meaning of this directness we need to consider how power and solidarity are balanced within the family as well as the specific needs of the dinner scene. From the microperspective of family discourse, I argue that *the* determining factor in shaping parental language of control is *the nature of the speech event.*

Consider the role relationships within the family. On the one hand, even in modern societies parents and children are bound in an asymmetrical power relation (see Queen, Habenstein, & Quadagno, 1985, for a sociological perspective). As one father put it, "I make no bones about the way I ask my son to do something; he is a child and should obey." Historically, in Steiner's (1975) elegant formulation, in most societies throughout history children (and women) were maintained in a condition of "privileged inferiority," suffering different modes of exploitation "while benefitting from a mythology of special regard" (p. 38). In his view, however, a principal gain of our recent past is "the entry of the child into complete adult notice, a heightened awareness of its uniquely vulnerable and creative condition," shown by the trouble taken in our society "to hear the actual language of the child, to receive and interpret its signals without distorting them" (Steiner, 1975, p. 38). But although children's voices are heard clearly in modern families, the structural asymmetry of power between them and their parents is bound to surface in the language of parental control. In Bernstein's (1990) formulation, the language of parental control thus becomes the intracontextual realization mode for power relations external to the context.

Indeed, previous research (Andersen Slosberg, 1990; Becker, 1988, 1990; Blum-Kulka et al., 1985; Clancy, 1986; Ervin-Tripp & Gordon, 1986) clearly shows that the discourse of social control acts of both adults and children in the family is highly sensitive to the asymmetric power relations among the participants. What may differ between families is the degree to which parental authority is *made manifest.* In Bernstein's (1971, 1990) terms, the difference is between "positional"-oriented styles of control, which make parental authority clearly visible, and "person"-oriented styles, which devote energy to making authority invisible. In the families studied, both orientations emerge; it seems that preference for one or the other is driven foremost by considerations of the goal of the control act and by cultural preferences.

Simultaneously, families are the prime symbolic enactment of intimacy. As one parent put it, it is the role of family dinners to enhance this solidarity, to "strengthen the sense of family" (lexazek mishpaxtiyut). Within this particular configuration of power and solidarity—the two dimensions essential to explaining sociolinguistic variation in all human interaction (e.g., Brown & Gilman, 1960)—each individual in the family is structurally bound in a double role, as an intimate but unequal member of the family group.

The expression of solidarity in the family is linked to two further dimensions: informality and affect. The key of the interaction between family members at the essentially backstage dinner event is necessarily informal. And as Garfinkel (1984) noted, this is the modality expected in family discourse: Deliberate switch from informal to formal style in the family is interpreted as impolite, disrespectful, and arrogant. Solidarity is further expressed through the indexing of affect. As in Shakespearean tragedies (Brown & Gilman, 1989), an increase in positive affect is associated with an increase in politeness, and decreased positive affect is associated with impoliteness.[1] Particularly in the discourse of Israeli parents, marking social control acts for affect mitigates their threatening edge hence serves as an important politeness resource.

For politeness to be expressed in the familial context, it needs to pay tribute to face wants *as emicly defined in the family domain*. When transferred to family relations, the basic face needs for nonimposition and positive support take on a sharp emotive edge. Parents need to balance a child's need for independence (the dictum of nonimposition) with his or her need for parental involvement. How to balance the two needs is a problem because, as noted by Tannen (1986), following Bateson (1972), anything said as a sign of involvement can in itself be a threat to the other's individuality, and anything said as a sign of distance threatens the need for involvement. As stated by one of the Israeli parents, conveying involvement without threatening individual space can be difficult; one needs "to find the right balance between involvement and interference" (using the same verb stem in Hebrew, "meuravut" and "hitarvut").

Jewish American and Israeli parents indeed seem to differ in this respect. The expressive mode of Jewish American parents reflects their concern with the child's independence and autonomy as prime values of socialization, whereas the rich affective display in Israeli parents' discourse with children highlights instead interdependence and involvement.

The next two sections examine the empirical evidence for the degree of politeness in the discourse of parental control in the three groups of families. The data are discussed from two perspectives. The first is the traditional "directness" perspective, which equates directness with impoliteness and indirectness with politeness. This perspective is rejected as invalid for

---

[1]Brown and Gilman (1989), contrary to Brown and Levinson's (1987) prediction, have found that degree of social distance per se has little or no effect on politeness in the tragedies. What matters instead is a positive change in affection, which in turn tends to be linked to interactive closeness.

family discourse. An alternative politeness scale is offered, and evidence is presented for the culturally varied ways in which it works in family discourse. This analysis leads to the conclusion that, contrary to the implications of the directness perspective, politeness considerations figure strongly in families' ways of speaking. In essence, my argument is that family discourse is polite but that it enacts its politeness in culturally and context- and role-sensitive ways.

The Direct Style of Parental Control Acts: Are Parents Impolite?

The analysis of control acts is derived from dinner table conversations of all 34 families who participated in the first stage of the study. Transcripts were coded for the speech act of social control (e.g., all directives) used by every participant during the first 20 minutes of every dinner, yielding a corpus of 4,120 control acts. A subset of the 903 control acts issued by parents to children served to examine parental styles of politeness in issuing directives. This analysis is complemented by insights concerning styles of socialization gained from the ethnographic interviews.

Control acts in the family data were first coded on a 9-point scale of indirectness and then collapsed into three major categories or modes, shown in previous research to represent cross-linguistically valid directness distinctions (Blum-Kulka et al., 1989).[2]

1. The **direct mode**: expressed by explicit naming of the act to be performed ("Close the window," "I want you to close the window," "You should close the window," "I am asking you to close the window").

2. The **conventionally indirect mode**: expressed via questions in regard to the preparatory conditions needed to perform the act, as conventionalized in any given language (for English, the habitual forms being "could you" or "would you do it?").

3. The **nonconventional indirect mode** expressed by hints (e.g., "It's cold in here," meant as a request to close the window, or "Dinner is on the table," meant as a request to come and sit down).

---

[2]Two coding schemes were used. One was the CIS (Cross-Cultural Interactional Styles Project) code for control acts, which is a revised version of Control Exchange Code prepared by Susan Ervin-Tripp and David Gordon at Berkeley and generously shared with us. The second was the Control Act Form code, developed for the Cross-Cultural Speech Act Realization project (Blum-Kulka et al., 1989). Esther Ziv and Abigail Neubach were the research assistants responsible for coding and analysis of control acts and patterns of compliance, Hadass Sheffer analyzed the nicknaming patterns in the families, and Simona Sarmoneta contributed several insights in a seminar paper she wrote on negotiations over requests with young children in the families.

Whereas the direct mode leaves the speaker fully accountable for his or her speech act, both types of indirectness allow for disclaiming communicative intents. Another way of saying this is that in the process of communication, direct control acts go on record as transparent to communicative intent, whereas the intent behind indirect acts can remain negotiable between speaker and hearer.

A second dimension coded for each control act was mitigation, that is, the types of linguistic devices used for softening the degree of coerciveness. As this dimension proved to be extremely important in family discourse, its various manifestations are exemplified here (all emphasis is added in examples 1–9).

Endearments and Nicknames Used for Targeting.

(1) Jewish Americans 4; Sandra (4f); Jordan (8m).

Mother to Sandra (4):   *Sweetie*, stop that please, OK?

(2) Israelis 8; Ran (9m); Merav (11f).

Father to Ran (9):   *Rani'le*, ta'azov et haofnayim.
[Rani'le, leave the bicycle alone.]

Point-of-View Manipulations in Naming the Actor(s). This involves adopting an inclusive perspective for an act to be performed by the hearer:

(3) Jewish Americans 3; Samuel (10m); Jeffrey (6m).

Mother to Samuel: *Let's* sit down.

This may also involve using the impersonal (e.g., "people," "one," "you") or passive:

(4) American Israelis 1; Neta (12f); David (5m).

Mother to Neta: *You* don't touch lettuce with your fingers.

(5) American Israelis 4: Yakir (16m); Ruth (12f); Batya (8f); Sara (6f).

Yakir to Ruth: *asur* lehagid et ze.
[*It's forbidden* to say that.]

External Modifications. These involve prefacing the control act by a prerequest:

(6) Israelis 2; Shlomit (12f); Riki (10f); Mira (5f).

Shlomit:	aba, ani yexola lish'ol otxa masehu?	Daddy, can I ask you something?
Father:	ken, ma?	Yes, what?
Shlomit:	yesh lexa kaseta reka?	Do you have an empty cassette?

or prefacing or following the request with reasons and justifications:

(7) Israelis 3; Dalit (11f); Orna (8f).

| Mother: | Daliti, tavi'i kapot. anaxnu crixim kapot le-mana axrona. | Daliti, get some spoons. We need spoons for the dessert. |

Internal Modifications.   These involve use of the politeness marker *please*:

(8) Jewish Americans 3; Samuel (10m).

Mother: Samuel, *please* finish your quiche.

or use of subjectivizers:

(9) Jewish Americans 3; Jeffrey (6m).

Mother to Jeffrey: *I believe* it's time for you to go to bed.

The two dimensions of directness and mitigation interact: Forms of mitigation can modify direct strategies as well as indirect ones. Also, mitigating devices appeal differentially to negative and positive face needs. By justifying the need for the act, for example, the speaker stresses the hearer's right to act as an independent agent (acting in a person-oriented mode). Appealing to negative face, on the other hand, by using an endearment term or a nickname as an opener for the control act to come, the speaker underlines his or her emotional bond with the hearer, emphasizing his or her positive face.

The distribution of control acts by levels of directness shows *a very high preference for the direct mode* in the speech of Jewish American, American Israeli, and Israeli parents to children around the dinner table. Simultaneously, parental discourse is very rich in forms of mitigation.

The overwhelming majority of control acts by parents in all three groups, 71.5%, *are phrased directly*. The speech event is a determining factor here. We know from studies of requests in American and Israeli societies that the directness levels of the parents' family discourse exceeds by far the general directness norms prevailing in adult speech in the respective cultures. In adult–adult talk (excluding families) in Israeli society, direct strategies are used only a third of the time (32%; Blum-Kulka et al., 1985; Blum-Kulka & House, 1989) and in American society even less often (28%; Rintell & Mitchell, 1989).

Yet culture interferes as well. Not surprisingly, Israeli parents are more direct than both Jewish Americans and American Israelis. Israeli parents opt for directness 85% of the time, whereas American Israelis use such strategies 67% of the time and Jewish Americans 60%. This finding is in line with the general Israeli ethos of dugriyut (Katriel, 1986), which calls for simplicity and sincerity in the encoding of illocutionary intent in expressive modes. Empirical studies of Israeli requests (Blum-Kulka et al., 1985) and complaints (Olshtain & Weinbach, 1987) show similar trends. Compared to Americans, Argentinians, Australians, (French) Canadians, Germans, and Danes (all student populations), Israelis come second only to Argentinians in their level of directness in requests (Blum-Kulka & House, 1989).

It is interesting to note that the style used by American Israeli parents conforms to neither of the two reference cultures but rather reveals a unique intercultural pattern of its own. The language spoken in the American Israeli families is mostly English, but regardless of language, *the pragmatic norms prevailing in these families vary with the dimension of discourse*. For the language of control, whether through directives or metapragmatic comments (see Chapter 6), the patterns are intercultural. On the other hand, in the domains of topical contribution and narratives (see Chapters 2, 3, and 4), the discourse of American Israeli families follows the pragmatics of the Israeli style but enacts this style mainly in English.[3]

However, directness per se does not tell the full story. A closer look at the direct strategies used by parents reveals an interesting phenomenon: In almost half the cases in all three groups—45%—*direct strategies are mitigated*, the coercive impact softened by the use of one or more of the devices listed previously.

Explaining the Family Politeness Paradox

How are we to interpret these results? If we judge family discourse by its choice of directness levels, then, at least as measured by the type of standards prevalent in the literature (Brown & Levinson, 1987; Fraser & Nolen, 1981; Leech, 1983), parents are quite positional and impolite. On the other hand, if we judge the parental language of control by its levels of mitigation,

---

[3]The mean percentage of English spoken in the American Israeli families ranges from 44% (in the four Hebrew-dominant families) to 74% (in the four English-dominant families).

we find politeness considerations at work, showing a person-oriented approach. The solution to this apparent paradox is in understanding that the politeness system of family discourse is highly domain specific and that within it *unmodified directness is neutral or unmarked in regard to politeness*[4]

Consider the interpersonal requirements of the family situation, specifically those marking the speech event studied, dinners. Given the basic properties of the social event, it is not surprising that the discourse of nonimposition is alien to American and Israeli family middle-class dinner discourse in the 1980s. Directness is preferred because for the parent it encodes indices of both power and solidarity. The parent's positional role as well as the need for efficiency give license to this mode, and the backstage, informal character of the event softens its potentially offensive edge. The medium also intervenes: In spoken language, tone of voice counts just as much if not more than lexicalization. During the ethnographic interviews, the standard response to the question "how polite would you consider a 10-year-old asking her mother for more ketchup by saying 'Mommy, bring me some ketchup' " was "Depends *how* she said it; it can be polite if said softly."

Certainly, one can soften degrees of coerciveness by mitigation as well as by varying the levels of directness. Yet the importance of this dimension has been relatively neglected in the politeness literature, and the contribution of mitigation devices have been seen as secondary to indirectness (Brown & Levinson, 1987; Edmondson, 1981; Faerch & Kasper, 1989; Fraser, 1980). Such accounts do not do full justice to the centrality of mitigation in indexing politeness. At least for family discourse, the politeness status of mitigation should be considered as equivalent to forms of indirectness.

---

[4]Contrary to prevailing theories, indirectness is not necessarily or universally a valid index of politeness. Current theories, such as those of Brown and Levinson and Leech, would want us to consider indirectness the correlate of politeness and directness the correlate of impoliteness. The logic of this argument is that by moving up on the scale of indirectness, the speaker leaves more and more options for mutual denial of a threatening communicative act. Hence a direct link is postulated between indirectness and politeness: Indirect acts are thought of as less imposing and less face-threatening than direct ones and hence are supposedly more polite. On the other hand, the choice of direct strategies is taken to indicate a lack of consideration for face concerns. Direct, bald on-record strategies are taken to be impolite. However, both equations have been seriously challenged. For both American and Israeli speakers, we have experimental evidence that shows that the most indirect strategies for performing requests *are not judged to be the most polite*. The highest ranking for politeness is granted to conventionally indirect ("could you" type) strategies and not to hints (Blum-Kulka, 1987). Work on Israeli straight talk and emic notions of politeness (Blum-Kulka, 1992; Katriel, 1986) furthermore shows that this direct cultural way of speaking functions for Israelis in certain speech events essentially as a positive mode of deference. Thus, for different reasons and by different methods, the equation of indirectness with politeness and that of directness with impoliteness breaks down completely for Israeli and partly for American speakers.

Redefining Politeness: A New Scale

How, then, is politeness expressed in this event? First, to be expressed it must serve the emicly perceived face needs of parental display of respect for the child's independence, balanced against the need to show the strength of the affective bond.

These two face wants find their linguistic counterparts in the two dimensions of variation in the request form, directness and mitigation. Although a move up on the scale of indirectness might serve the dictum of nonimposition, reliance on a rich use of mitigating devices, regardless of the level of directness chosen, can act to color the request affectively or express respect for the child's reasoning capacities.

Because the expressions of solidarity and involvement (i.e., redress to positive face) are of such prime importance in the context of family discourse, they must find a domain specific mode of expression. This mode can be found in the uses of *mitigated directness*, namely, mitigation used to modify direct forms.

Mitigated directness represents the case par excellence of *solidarity politeness* (Scollon & Scollon's, 1981, term for positive politeness). One essential feature of such devices lies in their being nonself-oriented: Whereas all forms of indirectness encode a self-face-saving element allowing for the denial of requestive intent, mitigated directness does not allow for such a denial and is clearly hearer oriented. By paying homage to the hearer's face, it enhances his or her positive face by appeals to in-group membership (adopting the we-perspective) by a stress on affective bonds (e.g., nicknames and endearments) and by giving reasons and justifications that assume cooperation and lead the hearer to the reasonableness of the act.

With mitigated directness representing an independent category, the options parents have in verbalizing their control acts to children can be placed on the following index of politeness: impoliteness, neutrality, solidarity politeness, hints, and conventional politeness.

Impolite. At dinner, complete disregard for face needs is expressed by aggravated directness. Forms of aggravation include prosody (e.g., raised voice) and lexical choices:

(10) Jewish Americans 2; Marvin (8m); Daniel (6m); Tina (4f).

Father to Daniel: Stop it, Daniel. You are making the most *horrible* noise.

Said in a raised tone of voice, this direct command is aggravated lexically by the use of the *horrible* "expletive" (cf. Edmondson & House, 1981).

Neutral. Given the domain specific requirements of the family code, directness per se in family discourse should not be taken to index either politeness or impoliteness. Although devoid of forms of either positional or person-oriented appeal, direct acts in neutral context do not manifest an "imperative" (Bernstein, 1971) mode of control.[5] Rather, unless marked as aggravated or mitigated, these direct acts represent the zero point of the politeness continuum. Requests such as (11) and (12) are thus considered unmarked for politeness:

(11) Jewish Americans 2; Marvin (8m).

　　Father:　Stop it, Marvin.

(12) Jewish Americans 9; Ellen (7f); Andrew (9.5m).

　　Mother:　Ellen, sit down.

Solidarity Politeness (Mitigated Directness). Solidarity politeness can take any of the forms listed in examples 1 to 9, including both internal modifications (such as endearments) and external modifications (such as appeals to reason). The following extract exemplifies the combination of such devices in actual practice:

(13) Israelis 6; Lilax (6f); Iris (6f).
　　The girls' books and toys are spread all over the dining table and the mother would like them removed so that the table can be set for dinner.

1	Mother:	Irisi, bevakasha tikxi et ha-devarim shelax, ve-Lilax tatxili gam lefanot, beseder? anaxnu holxim le'exol.	Irisi, please take your things, and Lilax start clearing up too, okay? We're going to eat.
2	Lilax:	rega, nu ani od crixa ligzor et ze.	Just a minute, I still have to cut this out.
3	Iris:	ima, rak rega tir'i.	Mom, look for a second.
4	Mother:	Irisi, ba-pa'am ha-axrona ani mevakeshet mimex lakaxat et ha-dvarim	Irisi, for the last time I'm asking you to take those things

---

[5]Bernstein (1971) distinguished between the imperative and the appeal modes of control and divided the latter further as either positional or personal. Positional appeals demand compliance by reference to traditional expectations from the child, according to his or her age, sex, and membership in the social group. Personal appeals focus on the child as an individual, basing control "in linguistically elaborated individualised meanings" (p. 184).

me-ha-shulxan ki ani	from the table because
crixa la'arox, beseder?	I have to set it, ok?
Lilax, gam at tigmeri.	Lilax, you finish up too.
anaxnu kvar holxim	We're going to eat in a
le'exol ki aba carix	minute because Daddy
lalexet la-universita.	has to go to the university.

The first appeal to the girls (turn 1) is mitigated through the addition of an affective suffix ("Irisi"), the use of the politeness marker ("please"), a tag question ("okay?"), and specification of the immediate justification for the request ("we're going to eat"). The second, more aggravated appeal ("For the last time, I'm asking you") repeats the nickname and tag and elaborates the justification, "We're going to eat in a minute, because Daddy has to go to the university" in a way that appeals to the girls' sense of family solidarity.

Hints. A parent's regard for children's face can further be expressed through the discourse of nonconventional indirectness, or hints:

(14) Jewish Americans 2; Daniel (6m).

    Father: Daniel, we don't usually sing at the table.

(15) Jewish Americans 2; Marvin (8m).

    Father: Marv, there is delicious food in front of you.

By no means do hints represent the most polite option. In children's speech, for example, underlying assumptions of cooperation transform formally indirect strategies into perfectly transparent "instrumental acts" (Ervin-Tripp & Gordon, 1986). A young child's statement of need, like "I am thirsty" is normally interpreted by nurturing parents as a request clear in illocutionary intent. The same utterance from an adult, however, is not necessarily intended or interpreted as a request. The same might be true of many of the highly contextualized hints used by parents to children. For example, in an Israeli family that lived down the street from Denmark Square, a recurrent comment to young children, voiced most often when they were particularly noisy in eating their soup, was "shom'im otxa ad kikar denya" ("You can be heard all the way to Denmark Square"). In such cases, the politeness status of the hints is seriously diminished. Furthermore, by trying to gain compliance by evoking a general norm, such indirectness goes against parents' expressed need for issuing control acts with a high degree of both "propositional transparency" (i.e., what the request is about) and "illocutionary transparency" (i.e., what is the communicative function of the utterance; cf. Weizman, 1989).

Parents interviewed in Israel stressed that especially between parents and children, intentions should be made perfectly clear. Yet the same parents found hints from children around the dinner table "quite polite" ("*dey menumas*").[6] Although hints might be perceived by both parties as potentially imposing by excessive cognitive burdening, in principle they are still perceived as encoding politeness. Hence, in line with previous results from rating experiment (Blum-Kulka, 1987), hints are viewed as representing one of several options for marking politeness.

Conventional Indirectness. This option represents the socially normative discourse of noninvolvement and is unequivocally polite on several acounts. In scaling experiments (Blum-Kulka, 1987), conventional indirect strategies were granted the highest marks for politeness by both Israeli and American informants. They are polite because they simultaneously encode both a relatively high degree of illocutionary transparency and the dictum of nonimposition (Blum-Kulka, 1989). In the words of the interviewees, asking a child "Would you mind going to the store?" is "a nice way to ask because it's not forcing him, and seems to allow him a way to refuse." Following are two examples of such polite indirectness from dinner conversations:

(16) Jewish Americans 2; Daniel (6m); Tina (4f).

Father: Daniel, can you wait until Tina finishes?

(17) Jewish Americans 12; Dara (13f); Beth (10f); Daniel (4m).

Mother to Beth: So, why don't you tell us about your day?

ENCODING POLITENESS IN FAMILY DISCOURSE

The language of parental control at dinner ranges from being contextually appropriate but unmarked for politeness to being polite—in other words, from the imperative to both the positional and person-oriented modes of control. We have found very few cases of offensive impoliteness in the speech of parents to children (see Figure 5.1). On the other hand, the second option, namely the use of unmitigated direct forms, *is quite frequent*, constituting a third of all cases, and this choice lacks a politeness marking. Licensed by the informality of the speech event and the real urgency of many requests, direct control acts lose their offensive edge in family dinners. Parents'

---

[6]During interviews, parents were asked to rate forms of requests from the dinner talk on a four-point scale: very polite, quite polite, neither polite nor impolite, or impolite.

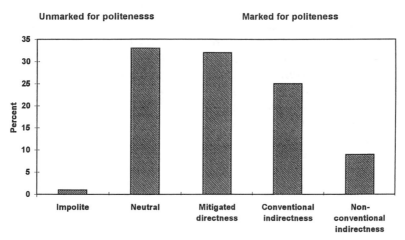

FIG. 5.1. Politeness strategies in the use of control acts. From " 'You don't touch lettuce with your fingers': Parental politeness in family discourse," by S. Blum-Kulka, 1990, p. 273. Copyright 1990 by Elsevier Science Publishers. Reprinted with permission.

interactional consideration for the addressee begin with mitigated directness. It is here that the effect of the speech event is most clearly felt: This option represents close to a third of all cases in parental discourse (32%), almost equal in proportion to the two forms of indirectness.

To be polite in speech to children, parents can choose essentially between two modes: the *solidarity politeness* mode, expressed by mitigated directness, and the *conventional politeness* mode, expressed by the two forms of indirectness. Mitigated directness redresses face by following the discourse of solidarity, stressing involvement. Its expression in family discourse is highly domain specific, drawing heavily on family in-group codes, such as nicknaming. On the other hand, by being unconventionally or conventionally indirect, parents are using the socially normative discourse of noninvolvement or redress to negative face.

The Effect of Context and Role

To what extent is a parent's style of control affected by contextual and individual factors? For example, are repeated tries phrased less politely then first tries? Do parents vary their styles according to the child's age or sex? Are parents less polite to their children than to each other?

We found politeness in family discourse around the dinner table to vary only by type of directive goal in all groups and by degree of power in the Israeli and American Israeli groups. We found *no* significant differences in politeness on the basis of either age or sex of the child addressee.[7] Nor did we find a decrease in politeness with repetition: Contrary to our common-sense expectation, we found that repeated tries for control were phrased in the same style as first tries. A parent's style of control does vary, however, with the type of directive goal. This result is not surprising; previous work on directives has shown modes of performance to be highly sensitive to goal. In a study of requesting styles in Israel, for example, the goal of the request was found to be the best predicting factor for level of directness (Blum-Kulka et al., 1985).

Control acts in family discourse are indexed under six types of goals:

1. Requests for action ("sit down"), 68%.
2. Requests to stop or prevent an ongoing activity ("stop that noise"), 15%.
3. Requests for goods ("pass the salt"), 7.5%.
4. Requests for verbal goods ("tell us what happened today"), 6%.
5. Requests for permission ("can I go upstairs"), 0.8%.
6. Requests granting permission ("you can go upstairs"), 1.3%.

The parents' need for behavioral control of children is reflected by the frequency of their requests for action or nonaction, which reaches 83%. The asymmetrical role relationship between parents and children explains why there are so few cases (only 6) of requests for permission addressed by parents to children. Immediate physical and conversational needs dictated by the speech event account for the remaining cases of requests for verbal and nonverbal goods (61%, 13.5%).

The type of request goal affects the mode of performance. Consider the difference between requests for action and requests for goods (Table 5.1). Requests for action tend to be uttered either in the neutral, direct mode (41%) or in the mode of solidarity politeness (34%). On the other hand, requests for goods are formulated half the time in the mode of conventional politeness, by the use of the neutral mode one third of the time (34%), and by solidarity politeness only 16% of the time. As shown in Examples 18 and 19, the canonical form for requesting goods is conventional indirectness.

(18) Jewish Americans 7; Max (14m).

Mother to Max: Could you pass the milk?

---

[7]Styles of politeness were similar regardless of the gender composition of the parent–child dyads or the child's age. It is noteworthy though, that in the corpus of children's control acts two thirds were addressed to the mother rather than the father. As discussed in Chapter 3, there are indications of gendered styles of control in discourse dimensions other than the speech act of requests.

TABLE 5.1
Politeness by Type of Goal

| | Goal Type | | | |
| | Action* | | Goods** | |
Style	N	%	N	%
Neutral	312	41.1	42	33.9
Solidarity politeness	261	34.2	20	16.1
Conventional politeness	188	24.7	61	50.0
Total	762	100.0	123	100.0

*Including requests to prevent action.
**Including requests for verbal goods.

(19) American Israelis 3; Noam (6m); Etan (8m).

Mother to Noam: Would you get the salt, please?

Role relationships were found to have a different effect for Israeli versus Jewish American discourse. For Israelis and American Israelis, parental status plays an important role: The speech of Israeli parents to children, as measured by the politeness scale, is less polite than their speech to each other.[8] No such difference was found for the Jewish American parents.

Do these results mean that Israeli families are more positional (in Bernstein's, 1971, sense of the term) than the Jewish American ones? The answer depends on the way we interpret Bernstein's notions of "positional" versus "person oriented." If the distinction is taken to imply a dichotomy between families with authoritative as opposed to egalitarian socialization ideologies and practices, then the answer is negative. Consider the case of reasons and justifications added to control acts. In positional families, conduct is expected to be regulated by appeal to ascribed roles, and in person-oriented families it is to be based on individuated negotiation. One would therefore expect Israeli parents to give fewer explanations and justifications than Jewish American parents, but the proportion of reasons and justifications is very similar for the groups (18% to 21%). Furthermore, despite appearances to the contrary, Israeli parents engage just as much in negotiations that reflect a person-oriented orientation to compliance as do Jewish American parents.

The distinction between positional and person oriented for Bernstein (1990) also means variation in degrees of ostensibility: namely, the degree

---

[8]Interactions between husband and wife in the Israeli families provide some instances of extreme indirectness. In Family 1, a very long and elaborate negotiation between the couple is initiated by the husband's information query ("What's on the menu?"). Closer analysis reveals in the ensuing dialogue several layers of misunderstanding, none of which surface in overt negotiation (Weizman & Blum-Kulka, 1992).

to which authority is made visible, or invisible, through the choice in modes of control. In this sense Israelis and Jewish Americans differ in positional orientations. By being more blunt with their children than with each other, Israeli parents invite a recognition of what counts as authority, as is typical of positional appeals. On the other hand, by issuing control acts to each other in the same modes as to their children, Jewish American parents make an effort toward making authority less visible, as required of person-oriented appeals.

Cultural Stances Toward Autonomy and Interdependence

Two central themes continually negotiated in Kaluli society, according to Schieffelin (1990), are the assertion of autonomy and the expression of interdependence. For the Kaluli, the tension is embedded in knowing "how and when to display one's autonomy and to express one's relationship to others" (p. 242). In a different manner, these two themes are also continually negotiated in family discourse. In the parental discourse of control, the dilemma is whether control is to be exercised through displaying one's respect for the child's autonomy or through an appeal to affective bonding. In juggling the needs for autonomy and interdependence, Jewish American parents seem to display verbally a respect for the child's autonomy at all ages, whereas Israeli parents manifest a greater display of emotional involvement, stressing interdependence.

Consider politeness markings. When American and Israeli parents choose to mark their directives for politeness, they do so in different ways. Given the choice between solidarity markers of politeness, which stress in-group membership, and conventional modes of politeness, which highlight the dictum of nonimposition, Israelis *tend to prefer solidarity politeness* markers, whereas American Israelis and *Jewish Americans tend to prefer conventional politeness* markers.

As can be seen in Figure 5.2, Israeli, American Israeli, and Jewish American parents differ in the ways in which they choose to mark their control acts for politeness. An Israeli parent's first choice for marking politeness is to use mitigation (39%); a Jewish American parent's first choice is to use indirectness (40%). American Israeli parents fall between the two groups: 32% of the parent's control acts are mitigated, 30% indirect.

The Jewish American stance toward autonomy follows a well-documented American cultural pattern. In exploring the notions of individualism and commitment in American life, the authors of *Habits of the Heart* cite Daniel Calhoun (1973, pp. 143–147) to stress this point: "Sometime after the middle of the eighteenth century, child-training practices began to change from an emphasis on peace and order in the family to the development of 'inde-

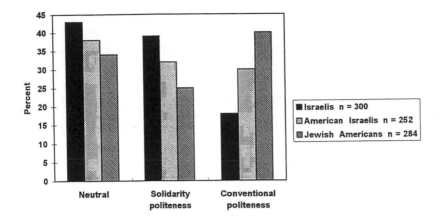

FIG. 5.2. Cultural styles of politeness. From " 'You don't touch lettuce with your fingers': Parental politeness in family discourse," by S. Blum-Kulka, 1990, p. 276. Copyright 1990 by Elsevier Science Publishers. Adapted with permission.

pendent self-sufficient individuals' " (Bellah et al., 1985, p. 57). Highly critical of this trend, Bellah et al. noted that "For highly individuated Americans, there is something anomolous about the relation between parents and children, for the biologically normal dependence of children on adults is perceived as morally abnormal," and they suggest that for most Americans the meaning of life "is to become one's own person, almost to give birth to oneself" (p. 82).

The Israeli stance towards interdependence within the family expresses the search for intragroup cohesion found in other contexts in the society, as well as the high value placed on familism. On one level, it might be understood as a by-product of a cultural focus on intragroup cohesiveness. In this interpretation, solidarity politeness, by stressing in-groupness, serves to solidify the family unit as a group, the communicative practice symbolically acting to enhance belonging rather than autonomy. In the Israeli educational system and in the Army, the general high value placed on creating collectivist frameworks is encapsaluted by the metaphor of crystallization ("*gibush*"), by which classes in schools as well as army units are expected to attain social cohesion. In the public sphere, it is the individual–society dialectic that is at stake; conscious efforts to crystallize the school class as a social unit are in the spirit of the rhetoric of communal orientation that prevailed in the early days of the State (Katriel, 1991; Handelman & Shamgar-Handelman, 1990; Shapira, 1989). In the private sphere of the family, because the social unit is demarcated by kinship, conscious efforts for crystallization seem less expected. Still, in several interviews, parents talked about the importance of doing things together as a family and mentioned activities geared towards this end, such as family meals and trips. Expressive modes that highlight familial interdependence—the familial code of politeness of the Israeli families, for example—are thus means for achieving intragroup cohesiveness. Simultaneously, the highly emotive coloring of these expressive modes is unique to family life; it is associated both with the interactional key of familial affect attributed to the traditional Jewish family (Zborowski & Herzog, 1952) and with the newly emerging value of familism in modern Israeli society (Bar-Yosef & Shamgar-Handelman, 1991; Katriel, 1991; Peres & Katz, 1981). Nowhere are these trends more clearly expressed than in the naming practices prevailing in the three groups.

Naming Practices

The role of modes of naming in control acts is closely tied to the general naming practices in the families. A detailed study of naming practices in the three groups (Blum-Kulka & Katriel, 1991) revealed clearly demarcated cultural patterns. In the Jewish American families and American Israeli families, children are addressed most of the time (85%–88% of all appellations) by their official names (e.g., David) or by abbreviated variations of their names that are also the institutionalized nicknames used in the wider society (e.g., Debra for Debora). On the other hand, in the Israeli families, in almost half the cases (45%), the appellation used is not the official name or institutionalized nickname but is rather a family nickname.

Israeli parents use a wide variety of innovative nicknames, yielding a rich repertoire of emotively colored terms of address per child at every meal. A child named Jonathan, who was 10 at the time of the recordings, was variously addressed by his parents as *yonatan, yoni, onton, yonti,* and *ontik.* Daniel was addressed as *dan, dani, danile, danilush,* and *dudu.* Many of the appellations used were made up on the spur of the moment, derived from the name by the addition or deletion of suffixes or infixes of various sorts, and the use of such nicknames is restricted to the family domain: During the interviews children expressed very strong objections to their parents addressing them by a nickname in front of others. As Noa put it, her affectively marked nickname "noale" is "a reserved name" ("shem shamur"). Interestingly, despite the conscious effort of native Israeli parents to choose for their children modern Hebrew names (Weitman, 1988), the innovative nicknames used in the family setting draw on Eastern European origins, echoing Yiddish and Slavic sound patterns: the /-le/ or /-ile/ suffix, as in *noa > noale* or *asaf > asafile*; the /-ik/ and /-ika/ suffix: *yaron > yaronik, gali > galika*; the /sh/ and /ch/ sounds embedded in the name, usually followed by one of the suffixes, as in *sivan > sivantchik* and *sivutsh; talya > tulish; mixal > mushkale.* Particularly with young children, this category yields some highly creative nonce nicknames (i.e., nicknames created on the spur of the moment, perhaps never to be repeated), such as *chapitchaika, tuchik,* and *tchapuka* for Talya. The effusive practice of nicknaming in the Israeli families is particularly salient in control acts. Nicknames, like names, are used to call a child to order (*"talush!"*), to reprimand (*"Uton, ma ata ose?* [Uton, what are you doing?]"), to draw the attention of the addressee, as prefaces to control acts (*"tulish, tavi'i mayim, tov?* [Tulish, get some water, ok?]") and to intensify, but foremost to mitigate, the impact of the control act. Intensification is expressed through repetition and variation, as in the following series of (unsuccessful) attempts by the father to get Dan to calm down: *"danile, day!, dan, tafsik! daːny!!* [Danile, enough! Dan, stop! Daːny!!]". The affectionate coloring embedded in the rich sound play on names is fully exploited to mitigate control acts. Thus a request to a girl called *xagit* to bring some spoons to the table is embedded within two free variations on her name: *xagitush, kapot, xavitush* [xagitush, spoons, xavitush].

In the usage of the Jewish American and American Israeli families, nicknames are few and standard and interchanged with conventional forms of endearment (Blum-Kulka & Katriel, 1991). Thus a girl named Jennifer, aged 8, is addressed either as Jennifer, Jenny, or darling, and a boy called Stephen is Steve. The demarcation line for the use of the abbreviated forms is along the formal–informal continuum: A teenager explains that she does not mind being called "Becky" around the house but prefers "Rebecca" for "dinner parties, weddings and the like." The interviews reveal that in the Jewish American families children were often given two names at birth, one American and one Jewish, but the Jewish names seldom surface at dinner, remaining a private and covert index of ethnic identity. In the Israeli American families, however, double (English/Hebrew) naming is common: Yael is "Jennifer" at home and "Yael" anywhere else, and like other children of American Israeli families she does not want her friends at school "to know that I have another name." Here the double naming marks the bicultural identity of the families as American born, non-native Israelis, signaling the family's own definition of its social identity.

The Yiddish and Slavic phonetic influence so visible in Israeli nicknaming practices come to the fore only in parental stories about their own childhood: "My grandfather used to call me things like *glansh* and *glantchik*—I can't even pronounce it anymore." Names and nicknames in these families have no special function in control acts beyond their vocative function.

For the Israeli families, innovative nicknaming serves as a means of indexing affect, comparable to the linguistic means used for this purpose in Samoan (Ochs, 1988). When it precedes control acts, it becomes the canonical form of mitigation. Asked to soften a bald-on record directive to a child in the course of the interviews, Israeli informants invariably responded by a shift in tone of voice and a questioning intonation, combined with a signal of endearment added to the name (from Tamar to *tamile* or *tamush*). Jewish American and American Israeli respondents, on the other hand, marked the command for politeness by a shift in strategy from the direct to the conventionally indirect, typically using "can you" or "could you." The cultural difference in naming practices reflects deeply rooted cultural attitudes to a child's personhood. Names, says Goffman (1963), are "identity pegs" that mark personal identity, "the unique combination of life-history items that comes to be attached to the individual" (p. 74) differentiating him or her from all others. Names, then, are means of differentation that distinguish the person thus marked from all other individuals. By shunning such means of differentiation through a free play on names, Israeli parents downplay the values of autonomy, emphasizing instead emotional involvement and interdependence. Jewish American and Israeli American parents, on the other hand, show deference to the child's individuality by avoiding such practices. Interviews with the families reveal differences in attitudes to naming along the same lines. In the Israeli families, interview questions regarding nicknames were met with general positive excitement, with all members of the family joining in to provide a full list interspersed with anecdotes. In the Jewish American and American Israeli families, nicknames were far from a positive family asset; on the contrary, they were frowned on as things that distort a person's claim to individuality. Even babies should know who they are: The Jewish American mothers pointed out that they insist on calling the newborn baby by the full name from his or her first day and discourage other members of the family from using nicknames. As one mother said about her 3-week-old infant: "Asher is Asher and I want him to know he is Asher."

PATTERNS OF PARENTAL COMPLIANCE

Just as control acts may vary in their modes of performance, encoding different levels of politeness, so do responses to control acts. From the speaker's point of view, control acts are face threatening because the speaker might encounter rejection, a speech act highly damaging to positive face. Indeed, sociolinguistic variation in ways of saying "no" abound, showing clear cultural preferences on a continuum of directness (e.g., Beebe & Takahashi, 1989; Kitagawa, 1980).

Children's requests to parents constitute 30% of the entire corpus of control acts. Beyond what they show about culturally varied attitudes to politeness, parental responses are also interesting as a rich site of information about socialization. Thus below the surface of an occasionally confrontational Israeli style in responding to children's requests we can detect a person-oriented middle-class preference for "invisible control" (cf. Bernstein, 1971, 1990; Hasan, 1992), shared by all families.

In Hasan's interpretation, an orientation to invisible control is manifest through efforts made to render authority invisible, especially in the efforts of parents in gaining their objectives through diplomacy and manoeuvering rather than through an open appeal to their own authority, much less by setting themselves up openly as the child's adversary. In the process they also transmit to the child a particular picture of how the world is organized and the place of the child's self in relation to that world. (p. 109)

The discourse of control within such an orientation is likely to be indirect and suggestive, inclined to contain reasons for commands and assertions that are supportive of the child's positive face. On the other hand, a visible orientation to control

cannot fail to engender a recognition of what counts as authority, so that authority cannot remain hidden from the child's consciousness, and so that irrationality must become part of the child's primary experience of life. (p. 109)

Hasan found that the two styles distinguish empirically between middle-class and working-class mothers, with the former, as expected, conforming to the norms of invisible control.

As we saw, in several respects the language of control at dinner in our middle-class families does not live up to the expectations of invisible control. It is inclined to be direct rather than indirect in a manner that makes authority clearly visible, and only a fifth of the time are control acts grounded in explanations and justifications. But though control is visible, it exhibits important features of the style associated with invisible control. First, parental control acts are sensitive to face needs. Second, in responding to children's control acts, the concern for face is translated into means that appeal both to positive face needs, through internal mitigation devices for refusals, and negative face needs, through the legitimacy granted to negotiations and through appeals to reason in grounding refusals. Due to the nature of the speech event, most control exchanges are brief, one-turn affairs, frequently with nonverbal compliance. When verbal responses do appear, they carry the messages associated with the invisible orientation that are supposed to be the trademark of person-oriented families, making *rationality* rather than irrationality an important part of the child's experience.

We classified the move immediately following the child's control act as choices between **compliance** ("Mommy, could you cut my chicken?" "Yes" [complies]; **negotiation** ("I wanna go outside." "Why?"); **ignoring** (no response), **refusal** ("I want to hear my voice [on the tape]" "Not now"). Figure 5.3 shows these patterns.

The three groups of families comply immediately with their children's requests to very similar rates but differ dramatically in their choices of negotiation and refusal formats. I refer to negotiation and refusals as formats rather than action categories because although verbal compliance closes the exchange, both negotiation and refusal moves are often followed by

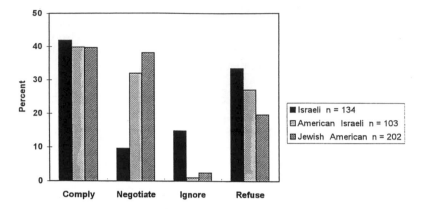

FIG. 5.3. Patterns of compliance.

further moves, with no predictable outcome in regard to compliance or rejection. *Hence the cultural differences should be interpreted as signaling preferences for interactional style, rather than as indicators for the degree of parental compliance.* Whereas in the Jewish American and American Israeli families 32% to 38% of requests are reacted to with a move that opens up a negotiation, in the Israeli families such moves appear only 10% of the time. On the other hand, both Israeli groups favor refusal formats (34% and 27%), a format relatively unfavored by the Jewish American families. The hybrid, intercultural pragmatic system of the American Israeli families is evident in the comparatively high preference for both negotiation and refusal formats. Unique to the Israeli families is the relatively high need for children to repeat their requests more than once (the first attempt having been ignored). This phenomenon is probably due to two factors: the lesser chance of Israeli children to occupy center stage at dinner (see Chapter 3) and the rapid tempo and high degree of overlap at the Israeli dinners, which make it physically more difficult for children's voices to be heard.

In the following section, three perspectives are interwoven in the discussion of parental patterns of compliance. The politeness perspective considers such patterns in terms of their degree of concern for face needs; the socialization perspective seeks to uncover the underlying norms of socialization implied by choices of parental style; and the cultural perspective traces the degree of cultural variation between the groups in their choices of response styles.

Granting Children's Requests

Immediate granting of children's requests at dinner is motivated by the parents' nurturant role on this specific occasion as well as by the general tendency to accommodate young children. The overall rate of compliance is similar to American norms for interaction with 2- to 8-year-olds in middle-class families (Ervin-Tripp, Guo, & Lampert, 1990) and it rises to 70% in our families with children younger than 6. The ready granting of the child's request is particularly evident when the request concerns food, provided the timing fits the parents' dinner agenda:

(20) Jewish Americans 2; Tina (4f).

> Tina: Can I have some ice cream?
> Father: Yes, you can have some dessert.

The format of compliance in Example 20 signals a preference for granting over rejecting, a feature Wootton (1981) claimed is typical of (in his case, Scottish) parents' interaction with young children. It is this preference that explains why even in cases where there is only very partial compliance, the phrasing has an affirmative format:

(21) Jewish Americans 4; Sandra (4f).

> Sandra: Mommy, can I have some more cookies?
> Mother: One more. You may have one more.

However, in the families studied such concern with face is not a universal norm. Especially in the Israeli families, even compliance may be phrased in negative rather than affirmative syntax:

(22) Israelis 5; Niva (13f); Yoav (11m); Tama (4f).

> Niva: I want to sit by the microphone today, Daddy. Okay?
> Father: I have no objection.

Cultural Styles of Negotiation

The coding for negotiations masks two related but distinct phenomena: cases of ostensible negotiation, where the sequence developed in response to the initial request serves only to delay a rejection of the request, and cases of true negotiation, where one party either changes his or her initial position or becomes convinced of the need for compliance or rejection of the original request. In both types of negotiation, the style prevailing in the Israeli families shows a clear preference for initial refusal formats, whereas in the Jewish American families blunt initial refusals are dispreferred.

In the following extract, in effect no real negotiation takes place. Looked at retrospectively, the final rejection seems forthcoming from the first move, but its bald on-record realization is tactfully delayed through four parental moves:

(23) Jewish American 3; Jeffrey (6m).

1	Jeffrey:	Excuse, can I be excused?
2	Mother:	You haven't finished your sandwich.
3	Jeffrey:	I don't want it.
4	Mother:	We're having dessert. You're going to like it.
5	Jeffrey:	I don't want it.
6	Mother:	Where are you gonna go?
7	Jeffrey:	Outside.
8	Mother:	No, you're not going outside. I'm sorry. This is the dinner hour.

The next extract exemplifies a more overt type of ostensible negotiation. Although both parent and child ask for explanations, only the child answers a "why" question seriously.

(24) Israelis 5; Niva (13f); Yoav (11m).

1	Yoav:	ima mutar la'alot lemala?	Mom, can I go upstairs?
2	Mother:	bishvil ma?	What for?
3	Yoav:	kedey lehavi batariya.	To get a battery.
4	Mother:	lama?	Why?
5	Niva:	ani lo marsha me-ha-tep sheli.	Not from my tape.
6	Yoav:	lama?	Why?
7	Niva:	ki ani lo marsha. bishvil ma ata carix?	Because I won't allow it. What do you need it for?
8	Yoav:	bishvil lehaf'il et xx.	To turn on the xx.
9	Mother:	tishkax mi-ze.	Forget it.
10	Yoav:	lama?	Why?
11	Mother:	ya'ani kodem ten lanu harca'a po al ha-mifrakim.	Well, first give us a lecture on joints [of the body].

Yoav's polite request for permission to go upstairs is responded to by questions for clarification (challenging because of the implied suggestion that going upstairs needs a strong justification), but before Yoav can fully reply, his sister intervenes with a control act that anticipates his intentions only to reject them ("not from my tape," turn 5). When he tries to ask why, she responds with a clear positional statement of authority: "Because I won't allow it." Although the mother fully aligns herself with her daughter ("forget it," turn 9), she closes the exchange politely: Her redressive action (turn 11) is a counterproposal, an attempt to save face through a change of topic.

In contrast to cases where negotiations (ostensible or not) lead to final rejection, we also find cases where negotiations lead to compliance. This pattern typifies Israeli families, where often *initial refusal followed by nego-tiation eventually leads to compliance*.[9] In the following extract, Nir is trying to enlist his mother to help at a Purim school fair:

(25) Israelis 11; Meni (11m); Nir (9.5m); Natan (8m); Gila (7f).

1	Nir:	ima, at yexola beyom shishi lavo la'azor be-bitan "ha-ma'arav-ha-parua"?	Mom, can you come on Friday and help at the "Wild West" booth?
2	Mother:	be-shum panim va-ofen lo.	No way.
3	Nir:	lama? be-yom shishi.	Why? On Friday.
4	Mother:	be-yom shishi aval ani crixa leargen po kol mine devarim, ben.	But on Friday I have a lot of things to arrange here, son.
5	Nir:	rak me-tesha ve-xeci ad eser ve-xeci.	Just from nine-thirty till ten-thirty.
6	Mother:	ve-matay nikne le-nili matana la-yom huledet? la-bat micva?	And when will we buy Nili a birthday present? For the Bat Mitzva?
7	Nir:	be-shmone.	At eight.
8	Mother:	aba yavo.	Dad will come.
9	Nir:	ken. aba ata yaxol?	Yes. Dad, can you?
10	Father:	eze yom?	What day?
11	Nir:	shishi. mi-tesha va-xeci ad eser va-xeci.	Friday. From nine-thirty till ten-thirty.
12	Father:	yaxol lihiyot she-ken.	Possibly yes.
13	Noam:	yaxol lihiyot?	Possibly? [not happy]
14	Mother:	beseder, ten lo lehit'argen. lo manxitim ve-miyad bicua.	Okay, let him get organized. You can't expect immediate results.

The mother's first reaction is a very emphatic "No." In response to Nir's question, she explains her reasons for the refusal, rejects (implicitly) Nir's attempt to find a solution that will free her to come to his school (turns 6 and 7), and suggests that her husband go instead. This suggestion (turn 8) opens a new round of negotiation, which ends in a promise for compliance

---

[9]It proved exceptionally difficult to trace negotiated control acts to their final outcome because even on videotapes it was often unclear whether the negotiation ended in nonverbal compliance or was simply dropped. From the 97 cases we identified on video, the rate of a positive outcome in the two groups of Israeli families is 40%, compared to only 25% in the Jewish American dataset. This result is not surprising, given the general tendency in Israeli society to treat all refusals as negotiable (Blum-Kulka, 1992).

that Nir thinks is not binding enough (turn 13). On the whole, however, what seemed from the child's point of view absolutely unattainable becomes an almost certain possibility.

Despite the cultural difference in preferences for initial refusal and granting formats, all the families share a set of underlying norms with regard to socialization. Thus, in Example 23, although it seems that the mother's mind is made up from the start (she is not going to permit her son to leave the dinner table), before evoking authority she makes two attempts to convince the child to stay at the table of his own free will. Furthermore, her attempts form part of an argument–counterargument sequence that legitimizes his right to plead his case and her parental willingness to take his reasons seriously, thereby blurring status differences.

In Example 24, Nir's "why?" signals that he is entitled to an explanation for the initial rejection of his request. Furthermore, in providing the explanation the mother shifts from using "I" ("I have a lot of things to arrange") to "we" ("When will we buy a Nili a birthday present?"), transforming compliance with Nir's request into a family problem that all can share in solving. Nir's suggestion for a solution (turn 7), although implicitly rejected, thus becomes part of a serious negotiation of the family's search for a way to comply with his request.

What needs to be emphasized is that, as in all child–adult negotiations, whether ostensible or not, the right granted to children to argue their case and the respect shown to them by providing counterarguments to their own, is itself a mark of parental politeness. As a socializing practice, negotiations over parental compliance teach children that the culturally legitimate way to challenge parental authority is through an appeal to reason. Whether succeful or not in changing parental attitudes, for children just being listened to seriously while evoking rational arguments is meaningful in this regard. The effort invested in rationally convincing a child why his or her wishes cannot be fulfilled carries the same message. As the next example shows, appeals to interpersonal phenomena, to use Hasan's (1992) terms, figure along with appeals to logic:

(26) Jewish Americans 2; Father; Tina (4f).

1	Tina:	I want Daddy to carry me.
2	Father:	Tina, maybe Daddy doesn't want to carry you.
3	Tina:	Maybe you?
4	Mother:	Maybe I don't want to carry you?
5	Tina:	But you haven't carried me since *all* day.
6	Mother:	I haven't carried you all day?
7	Tina:	Yeah.
8	Mother:	I think I have been carrying you around all day.

9   Tina: I wanna. [whining]
10 Mother: Once or twice I had to carry you today, like I
                remember when you thought the pavement was too
                hot and I had to carry you down the stairs.
[Father carries Tina out of the room].

The negotiation in Example 26 follows the format suggested by Wootton (1981) for delayed compliance: initial reservation, expressed via refusal formats in the first response, followed by final (in this case nonverbal) granting. Differing from the previous examples, here the reasons for initial reservation are interpersonal; they refer to the parent's inner preference for carrying or not carrying the child, suggesting that the addressee needs to consider other people's feelings as warrants for action. By turning to the other parent Tina accepts this empathy principle (turn 3) and calls on parental obligation to conform to her wishes (for being carried at least once a day, turn 5). From this point, the mother's counterarguments make no impression on Tina, who reverts to childish means (i.e., whining) to achieve her goal.

The longest sequence of negotiation we have (spread over 270 lines of transcript) concerns the attempts by Jeffrey's (age 5.5) to get his mother's permission to invite his friend Adam over the same night "to see an experiment." During most of the dinner, the father and older son discuss experiments they have done and are planning to do from instructions in the book that accompanies the T.V. show "Mr Wizard." Jeffrey, who is too young to follow all the details of this conversation, is still part of it by virtue of having done such experiments with his father in the past. When he mentions his wish to have his friend over to see an experiment, it is not clear from the wording whether he means the one planned by his father and brother or whether he is indirectly trying to convince his father (through a third-party targeted request) to do one with him the same night. The negotiation that ensues is based on the second interpretation; the mother takes it on herself to respond for the father on the issue of doing an experiment and on her behalf on the issue of having a friend over for the occasion.

(27)   Jewish American 3; Jeffrey (6m).

1   Jeffrey: Mom.
2   Mother: Jeffy, what?
3   Jeffrey: Could I tell Adam if he wants to see an experiment?
4   Mother: Jeff, listen to me.
5   Jeffrey: Mom, xxx Mom, MOM!
6   Mother: What?
7   Jeffrey: Could I tell Adam if he wants to see an experiment?

8	Mother:	xxx.
9	Jeffrey:	Dad, remember when we did an experiment for Mr. Wizard? We pressed a string into ice cubes and sawed and it stuck together after a few days.

[132 turns omitted]

10	Jeffrey:	Can I ask Adam if he wants to see an experiment?
11	Mother:	Can I see, did you ask me a question? Then listen to my answer. After supper you can either do an experiment or Sara is coming over to watch "Karate Kid." You have the choice of two things. Sara would like to watch "Karate Kid" with you.
12	Jeffrey:	Or watch it with xxx.
13	Mother:	The one that we have and some time this week +/.
14	Jeffrey:	I've seen that one five hundred times.
15	Mother:	You're the one who always wants to see it again. Sometime this week, Jeffy, I'm gonna take you and Samuel to see "Karate Kid 2."
16	Jeffrey:	Oh okay, okay, *okay* Mom. Which day? Which number?
17	Mother:	I'm gonna have to figure it out. We're gonna have to find out what day you're available.

[12 turns omitted]

18	Jeffrey:	Mom, could I tell Adam if he wants to see an experiment? *Please*, could I tell him?
19	Mother:	Jeffy by the time you're in to do an experiment, we'll be going to the movies. Daddy said he was going to do an experiment with you tomorrow xxx. Then you can invite Adam upstairs, okay?
20	Jeffrey:	But can I tell Adam if he wants to see an experiment?
21	Mother:	But you're gonna do your experiment tomorrow, I thought. Don't you want to see "Karate Kid" with Sara?
22	Jeffrey:	Yeah, ok.
23	Mother:	Okay, so tomorrow.
24	Jeffrey:	xxx.
25	Mother:	You know what I think, Jeffy? There are so many things you want to do, you can't decide.

The sequence contains no fewer than six repeated attempts by Jeffrey (distributed over 20 minutes of dinner talk), with no change in wording, aimed at having both his parents help him realize his plans for the evening—the father, by doing the experiment, the mother, by allowing Jeffrey's friend to come over. The child repeats the request three times before his mother ever gets a chance to respond. Her response is framed in a way that fore-shadows rejection: Although it opens with a mitigating nickname (turn 4), it follows with a metapragmatic comment, demanding attention, that would be superfluous if a positive answer were coming. Next, she presents the boy with a choice of two alternatives, hinting at her preference (turn 11). When Jeffrey is not convinced to watch a movie instead of doing the experiment ("I've seen that one five hundred times") she offers a bribe ("Sometime this week Jeffy, I'm gonna take you and Samuel to see Karate Kid 2"). The fourth attempt, including several intensifications (repetition, "please," and a whin-ing tone) is responded to by a move that includes a number of attempts at mitigation: the use of affective nickname ("Jeffy"), an affirmative rather than negative syntax, a promise for delayed compliance ("tomorrow"), and an appeal for agreement, signaled by a tag question ("okay?"). When Jeffrey still persists, she shifts to a businesslike tone, stating the facts ("But you're gonna do your experiment tomorrow") and even getting Jeffrey to accept what was first offered as a second alternative (watching a movie on T.V.) and has by the end of the sequence become the only one.

This sequence is ambivalent in its control messages. At one level it can be taken to illustrate a concern for both negative and positive face: The child is reasoned with and cajoled until he agrees, making the change in his original plans seem like one reached by free will. Despite Jeffrey's nagging persistence, all his repeated requests are responded to by attempts at persuasion rather than by evoking authority. On the other hand, being led to agree with the adult's rejection of one's wishes might be perceived by children (and adults alike) as more coercive and intrusive than simply having one's request rejected outright. In this sense, the exchange manifests the "ambiguity in the sense of social identity" that Bernstein (1971) attributed to control through personal appeal (p. 181).

Refusals

In describing the ways in which children learn to say no, Garvey (1984) stated that "For adults, at least, the rule is: in refusing, disagreeing or contradicting, don't just say 'no'; provide an account" (p. 141). She then described how children learn to progress from simple negatives to reasons, counterpro-posals, postponements, evasions, and hedges. As in all dimensions of lan-guage socialization, family discourse is an important source for acquiring such skills. At dinner children learn such skills despite parental response to control acts that fail to meet the ideal of rational argumentation. In all groups, parents provide accounts, delay compliance, and hedge, but at least part of the time, and especially in the Israeli families, they also just say no.

Verbal responses were classified as **agreements**, **conditional agree-ments**, **noncommittals**, or **disagreements**, and are presented in Table 5.2.

TABLE 5.2
Verbal Response Patterns to Children's Requests

	Israelis		American Israelis		Jewish Americans	
	N	%	N	%	N	%
Agreement	13	12	27	26.7	44	31.2
Conditional agreement	7	6.5	9	8.9	7	5.0
Noncommittal	32	29.6	35	34.7	34	24.1
Signals of disagreement	18	16.7	12	11.9	32	22.7
Disagreement	38	35.2	18	17.8	24	17.0
Total	108	100.0	101	100.0	141	100.0

- Agreements: cases of an unambiguous cooperative reply ("Can we go to that?" "We'll go there again, absolutely").
- Conditional agreements: cases where the response specifies a condition or a delay ("Can I play with that now?" "As long as you don't make a mess"; "Dad, let's do that telepathy game." "Not now. We're eating. After dinner").
- Noncommittals: cases where the utterance contains a clarification question, a metacomment, or a joke, all of which may under certain circumstances act as preparation for disagreement ("May I go upstairs?" "What for?").
- Disagreements (plus or minus an account): cases with an unambiguous negative reply ("No, you can't") or where the need for the request is nullified ("There is a knife missing." "No, Esther does not need a knife").

In line with the distribution of patterns for compliance, verbal response styles reveal clear cultural preferences. Jewish American families show a preference for agreement, using such formats 31% of the time, more than any other category. Israelis, on the other hand, prefer disagreement, opting for this as the most frequent category (35%). American Israelis again have a pattern of their own, opting for noncommittal responses as their first choice (35%).

The Israeli overindulgence in "no" is apparent even in simple, nonmitigated refusals. When Jewish Americans bluntly refuse their children's request, they just say no; when Israelis opt for blunt refusals, they do so emphatically, repeating "no" more than once:

(28) Jewish Americans 1; Jennifer (15f); Simon (13m).
    Simon: Can you get out the peaches?
    Mother: No.

(29) Israelis 6; Lilax (6f).

1	Lilax:	ani kofecet.	I'm jumping.
2	Father:	*lo*, ani amarti *lo* Lilax.	*No.* I said *no* Lilax.
3	Lilax:	Iris, ani roca lir'ot rega mashehu.	Iris, I want to see something a minute.
% comment:		[she wants to leave the table.]	
4	Mother:	*lo*, ani *lo* maskima.	*No.* I will *not* allow it.

This structure of a twice-repeated negative typifies Israeli discourse. In those cases where the response embeds a promise for compliance at a latter point in time, the Jewish American parent will say "not now," whereas the Israeli parent says "no, not now." Even when the blunt refusal is followed by an explanation, in Israeli discourse the explanation is embedded in a series of emphatic nos:

(30) Israelis 5; Niva (13f); Yoav (11m).
Yoav is looking for a battery, and he wants to take one from the flashlight in the camera.

1	Father:	Yoav, ata lo lokeax me-ha flesh sheli	Yoav, you're not taking (it) from my camera.
2	Yoav:	xxx.	xxx.
3	Father:	lo ata lo lokeax me-ha-flesh. axar kax yihiye li xxx +/.	No, you're not taking it from the camera. Because then I'll have xxx +/.
4	Yoav:	exad, exad xx xx +/.	One, one xx xx +/.
5	Father:	lo. az tikax &me-ha me-ha-ze shelxa.	No. Take it from from that thing of yours, then.
6	Yoav:	xxx xx +/.	xxx xx +/.
7	Father:	lo ani lo marshe, Yoav.	No, I won't allow it, Yoav.
8	Yoav:	tip tipa.	Just a little bit.
9	Father:	*lo roce* nu. ani carix et ze. axar kax lo yihye li.	*I don't want* you to. OK? I need it. Because then I won't have any.

This brief exchange contains no fewer than eight nos, six of which are in refusal formats. The most typical structure is that of "No, I won't allow it, Yoav [*lo, ani lo marshe, Yoav*]" where the refusal is signaled by an initial no and then rephrased, the utterance ending with a vocative. Because such double negatives are semantically redundant, their only function is to enhance the illocutionary force of the utterance as a refusal. Although the tendency to intensify through repetition (as in "*ani mamash mamash sone ota* [I really really hate her]") typifies Israeli ways of speaking, its use in refusals is more than just a stylistic feature. The structure of the double negative is common in Israeli discourse in general (as in "No, I don't think so" instead of just "I don't think so") and it ties in with a preference for disagreement that prevails in this culture. In sharp contrast to cultures where disagreements are dispreferred (like American; cf. Sacks, 1973, and Pomerantz, 1984; or even more, Japanese; cf. Kitagawa, 1980), the prevalence of disagreement in Israeli culture extends even to cases where no real difference of opinion exists. In the family data examples are utterances like "No, what I want to say is" or "No, I agree, you're right" where closer examination fails to reveal a prior utterance (or conversational inference) being negated.

It seems, then, that in their style of refusal to children Israeli adults are not so much displaying a culture-specific orientation to socialization as they are enacting a cultural way of speaking. Such patterns of use have been previously described as typical for Jewish communities of Eastern European origin (Kirshenblatt-Gimblett, 1974/1989; Schiffrin, 1984b; Tannen, 1981a, 1984). As Schiffrin elegantly showed, in the Jewish community she studied (a lower middle-class urban neighborhood in Philadelphia), the overt confrontational style of the participants is inherently sociable, the sustained adversative formats masking underlying solidarity. Within the discourse of control in the family, arguments over compliance may well be truly conflictual, yet in the Israeli families the degree of confrontational marking in the style of negotiations over compliance does not necessarily reflect the level of underlying conflict.

Not all refusals are stated as bluntly as in Examples 29 and 30. In all families, parents engage in a variety of means for mitigating the face threat involved in refusals. From among the variety of means available, family discourse manifests two major types:

> **Internal mitigation**, expressed through tone of voice, affective nicknaming, and solidarity markers such as choice of pronoun. Thus, parents soften refusals by using a term of endearment ("Darling, not now" in response to a child's request to hear her voice on tape), an affective nickname ("Tamush [for Tama], you can't leave the table now" in response to a request to leave the table), or a switch to an inclusive "we," as in Example 25. As in issuing control acts, this approach appeals to positive face and is hence oriented toward solidarity politeness.
>
> **External mitigation**, expressed through appeals to reason. As in control acts, explaining the grounds for a refusal signals respect for the other's individuality and hence manifests deference politeness (Scollon & Scollon's, 1981, term for negative politeness). Differing from modes of realization in control acts, where the two types of politeness distinguish

between the groups, the choice for types of mitigation in refusal formats shows no cultural division.

Beyond their politeness function, grounded refusals, like grounded control acts, transmit messages about the range of reasons culturally acceptable in turning down a request. In many brief request refusal sequences at dinner, the dominant function is politeness: The request is turned down, but the child is shown respect when told why and is socialized through modeling to the need to provide accounts for refusals. For example, in Israeli family 6, the twins (age 6) are helping to set the table, competing with each other as to who does what. When one of the girls begins to lift the tray with soft drinks the mother says, "No, I'll take it because it's very heavy." Her sister then announces, "I'm handing out the plates. I'm doing it," but she is stopped by her father's "No, Mommy is filling them first."

In the next example, strictly speaking there is no verbal realization of the child's request: Stephen comes into the kitchen, where the family is about to sit down to dinner, and helps himself to potato chips from a plate on the counter:

(31) Jewish Americans 1; Simon (13m).

1	Mother:	Put it away [the plate with the potato chips].
2	Simon:	Why can't I have +...
3	Mother:	Because it fills you up.
4	Simon:	No, it doesn't [puts the plate down].

The reason given describes an outcome (in a logical cause and effect relation) that is undesirable in terms of an underlying norm of behavior with regard to eating habits (if dinner is being served, junk food should be ignored and dinner food preferred). Stephen's retort ("No, it doesn't") is interesting in that it accepts the norm but argues with its relevance to his particular case.

Talk about reasons for a refusal may, depending on the topic, directly instruct children in factual information, as well as train them in logical reasoning:

(32) Israelis 1; Nadav (11m); Yoram (10m).

1	Nadav:	aba, ani yaxol lakaxat et ha-maclema sheli lecalem ba-gremlin?	Dad, can I take my camera along to take pictures at "Gremlins"?
2	Father:	lo.	No.
3	Nadav:	lama?	Why?
4	Father:	ki ze lo holex be-bet kolnoa.	Because you can't [do it] in a cinema.
5	Nadav:	Aba lama?	Daddy why?

6	Father:	biglal she-en sham maspik or xxx.	Because there isn't enough light there xxx.
7	Nadav:	ani sam flesh.	I'll use a flash.
8	Father:	aval ha-flesh hu tov mimxa ve-od xamesh meter kadima.	But the flash is only good for about 5 meters.

This example illustrates several features of the Israeli refusal style. The response opens with a blunt brief "no," followed by an attempt to provide an explanation only in response to the child's query in turn 3. After two sequences of "why" answered with "because" (and a reason; turns 3, 4, 5, and 6), the exchange ends with two adversative turns, with the child's "but" (turn 7) countered with that of the father's (turn 8). Despite the markers of the confrontational style, in fact the exchange is highly cooperative. First, Nadav's question in turn 1 is an indirect speech act, ambiguous in its illocutionary force; it can be read as a request for permission to take the camera or a question of feasibility, as asking whether it is possible to photograph in a movie house. In response to the second interpretation (which is the one taken, as seen from subsequent turns), the father's "no" is informative and not face threatening, as it would be if a permission request were intended. Within this interpretive frame, Nadav's question in turn 5, "Dad, why?" signals that he has found the father's first response lacking on the maxim of quantity in terms of informativeness. He counters the logical explanation ("there isn't enough light") with a logical argument of his own ("I'll use a flash"), which is then dismissed as not valid for the circumstances. By the end of the exchange, Nadav has not only learned some new facts about photography but has also gained some experience in reasoned argumentation. As also shown for Italian families, learning to argue is thus one of the socializing functions achievable through intergenerational talk during family dinners (Pontecervo & Fasulo, in press).

CONCLUSION: IMPLICATIONS FOR THEORIES OF POLITENESS

We have examined politeness in family discourse by isolating the speech act of control as issued from parents to children. Our findings indicate that cultural perceptions of the given speech event determine the social motivation for politeness, its forms of linguistic encoding, and the social meanings attached to these forms in family discourse across different cultures.

From the microperspective of family discourse, *the* determining factor in shaping the politeness system is *the nature of the speech event*. The asymmetrical role relationships within the family, combined with a feeling of high intimacy and informality, license the prevailing direct style, lending it a solidarity politeness interpretation.

Three key notions combine in setting the tone of family politeness: power, informality, and affect. Asymmetrical power between parents and children explains the level of directness; the level of informality expected in the family helps us understand the social meaning attached to its interpretation. The importance of affect is revealed by the salience of linguistic devices indexing positive affect.

As Garfinkel (1984) showed, families expect informality. A deliberate switch from informal to formal style in the home is interpreted as impolite, disrespectful, and arrogant. Garfinkel suggested that whether one speech style is interpreted as more polite than another in a given situation depends largely on the listener's expectations at the moment the speaker makes his or her stylistic choice. Our results lend systematicity to such situational expectations: It is the particular configuration of asymmetrical power, interactive closeness, and "relationship affect" (cf. Brown & Gilman, 1989) embedded in family life that provide the interpretive framework for its politeness system.

The importance of affect in family discourse is revealed through the use of mitigation. In this discourse, this parameter explains the salience of linguistic devices drawing on in-group membership and stressing bonding. In our presence, parents shift in their speech to children from neutral, direct forms of control, licensed by the informality of the event, to more polite, mitigated forms that extend affect, reverting much less frequently to conventional indirect modes of politeness. Their withdrawal of affection is marked by aggravating devices added to direct forms. Maybe due to our presence, this end of the politeness continuum did not much find its way into our data.

Despite the domain specificity of the system, *culture plays an equally important role in shaping politeness*. Culturally varied perceptions of children's face needs are reflected in differential styles of politeness, with Israeli parents drawing heavily on the emotively colored language of mitigation and nicknaming and Jewish American parents paying homage to the child's independence by adherence to first names and the use of conventional indirect forms. The Israeli style of politeness acts to *minimize social distance* between members of the family; the Jewish American style is directed toward allowing each member his or her *individuated personal space*. For Israeli parents, distance minimization combines with an acknowledgment of the power disparity between adults and children; Israeli parents are more polite to each other than to their children. The Jewish American parents' language of control seems to be governed by a principle of symmetrical solidarity; Jewish American parents are equally polite to each other and to their children.

Choices among patterns of compliance are motivated by the discursive structure of the event as well as by cultural preferences. As elaborated in Chapter 2, talk at dinner moves from being occupied with the imposing needs of the activity at hand, through concern with the immediate family concerns (i.e., the family's latest news), to an open-ended range of non-immediate topics. Compliance with requests is a matter of complex interaction between frame of talk, age, and culture. The dinner-related topical frame may intervene with all other frames, but as long as talk concerns requests for food, chances for compliance are very high in all groups. The age of the requestor is another factor: Younger children's requests stand a higher chance of compliance than those of older children. Culture comes to the fore in two ways, in preferences shown between four modes of immediate verbal and nonverbal response to control acts (i.e., compliance, nonresponse, negotiation, and refusal) and in styles of responsiveness. Whereas Israelis make choices that cluster around the two extreme categories of compliance and rejection, Jewish Americans react frequently by opening up a sequence of negotiation. The preference is one of style, not behavioral norm: Levels of immediate compliance versus overall rejection are similar across the groups.

A parallel phenomenon is noted in styles of responsiveness. Jewish Americans tend to mark positive responses explicitly, whereas Israelis tend to mark negative responses explicitly. One way of interpreting the Jewish American preference for negotiation over immediate refusal is to attribute it to the American ideology of prizing individuality over community, expressed here by providing opportunities for discussion that, regardless of outcome (which often is negative), index a respect for the other person's need to have the issue explicitly laid out. The preference for signaling agreement over disagreement shown by this group is in line with findings that indicate the American tendency to enhance the other's positive face. The Israeli style, on the other hand, can be seen as a fusion of the *dugri* (straight) way of speaking claimed to characterize this society (Katriel, 1986; Blum-Kulka, 1992), with the argumentative yet sociable style described by Schiffrin (1984b) as characteristic of Jewish communities of Eastern European background in the United States (see Chapter 8).

A final word is in order in regard to the implications of the study of politeness in family discourse for a general theory of politeness. There is a need to incorporate the hitherto neglected dimension of speech events as a determining factor for evaluating politeness values. Furthermore, the relative importance granted to different strategic dimensions in indexing politeness should be reassessed. For directives, the status of mitigation needs to be considered as equivalent in value with choices on a directness continuum. Finally, it is suggested that the scope of pragmatic phenomena studied for politeness move beyond specific speech acts to incorporate wider discourse phenomena such as discourse management.

Though the speech act of control has been repeatedly shown to be highly sensitive to politeness considerations, it is certainly not the sole carrier of politeness in discourse. Other important areas include turn-taking, turn allocation styles, and participants' reactions to perceived violations of conversational norms. The culturally differential emphasis in these domains is captured by the analysis of metapragmatic comments presented in the next chapter.

CHAPTER

6

METAPRAGMATIC DISCOURSE

As discussed in Chapter 5, variability in directive use is an important resource for understanding cultural diversity in styles of pragmatic socialization. Cultural notions of interactional style and pragmatic socialization can
be further educed by what people say they do with words, namely, by their
metapragmatic discourse. *Metapragmatic comments* made in regard to linguistic and conversational behavior reveal the pragmatic norms underlying
such behavior. In Silverstein's (1976) terms, metapragmatic comments are
nonreferential indexes. Just as language use can index nonreferentially social
dimensions such as degrees of deference, so comments made in regard to
the perceived violation of a conversational norm may index for the members
of the particular speech community the network of interactional norms
governing its particular language use. Such comments relate to the smooth
flow of discourse and include calling attention to breaches of turn-taking
rules and to perceived violations of conversational maxims, as laid out by
Grice (1975). Thus, metapragmatic comments are one of the explicit ways
in which members discuss criteria for verbal appropriateness.

Parental metapragmatic comments around the dinner table relate to all
aspects of verbal and nonverbal behavior considered worthy of attention.
Such comments are part and parcel of the discourse of control, their affective coloring often critical. They point to the lack of adherence to a norm
in the immediate past or direct the child as to how to behave or speak in
the near future. Children's comments may bear witness to the internalization
of a given culture's pragmatic norm or express age-related concerns. The
types of comments made by both adults and children in different cultures

indicate cultural preferences: Cultures may differ in the relative importance that adults give to metapragmatic comments as a tool of socialization and, in the discourse of all members, to the relative salience of one type of comment over another.

Research in the development of communicative competence in childhood reveals that the process is highly dependent on culturally varied adult input. Caretakers across cultures differ in their preferences for the amount and type of talk expected from children and in the degree to which they deem it essential to explicitly teach language to children (Heath, 1983; Ochs, 1988; Schieffelin, 1990; Schieffelin & Ochs, 1986). In Western societies it is the manner of speaking—politeness in the narrower sense—that tends to be explicitly attended to. American middle-class mothers systematically prompt the use of politeness formulae and condemn any perceived lack of polite behavior (Becker, 1988, 1990; Gleason et al., 1984; Gleason & Weintraub, 1976; Grief & Gleason, 1980). However, as argued in the previous chapter, politeness is a culturally relative notion that is best understood as a cover term for social criteria applied to the distinction between socially appropriate and inappropriate verbal and nonverbal behavior. In this wider sense, metapragmatic comments play a crucial role in socialization for politeness.

TYPES OF COMMENTS USED

In the data we identified three types of comments related to verbal behavior:[1]

1. **Discourse management**: These are comments made to regulate the smooth flow of turn-taking. They include **bidding for turn** ("Can I say something?"), **allocation of turns** ("OK, let's hear about your day"), **negating a turn** ("Wait till David finishes"), **upholding a turn** ("I'm talking now"), and checking that the listener is attending ("Are you listening?").

2. **Maxim violations** (conversational norms): These are comments signaling the perceived violation of one of the four Gricean (1975) maxims (see also Pellegrini, Brody, & Stoneman, 1987). Comments in regard to the maxim of **Relevance** prompt the child to respond to a conversational demand ("Beth, there is a question on the floor") or delegitimize what was said ("One should not say that"). Comments in regard to **Quality** cast doubt on the truth value of a child's proposition (for example, in response to a child reporting having seen a "giant turtle," the mother inquires, "How giant is giant? Have you really seen it?"). Comments in regard to **Quantity** set limits on the degree of informativeness of stated propositions ("We heard that")

---

[1]The analysis of metapragmatic comments is based on two meals (normalized to 1,000 transcript lines for each) from the 24 families included in Stage two of the project.

and also elicit information or a response when it is lacking ("Aren't you participating with us today?"). Comments in regard to **Manner** prompt the use of politeness formulae ("say please"), correct ungrammatical language, condemn the use of slang and vulgar language, and note improper forms of address and reference (Child: "that stupid teacher . . ." Mother: "Who?" Child: "Varda, the math teacher").

3. **Metalinguistic comments**: This category includes all talk about language—queries and responses about word meanings as well as comments topicalizing language, including cross-linguistic comparisons ("Did you know the Eskimos have a hundred words for snow?").

Jewish Americans show the highest degree of metapragmatic awareness. During two dinners they made 571 comments (54% of all the metapragmatic discourse), as compared to only 259 comments made by American Israelis and 222 by Israelis (see Fig. 6.1). This pattern is similar for both adults and children. In proportion to the total number of utterances, metapragmatic discourse constitutes 6.5% in the Jewish American families, 3.4% in the Israeli American families, and only 1.5% in the Israeli families. Each Jewish American adult made an average of 10 comments per dinner, and each child made 7, whereas Israeli adults averaged 4 and children averaged only 3.

Talk about talk in the Jewish American families *shows the salience of metacommunication as a cultural category in American speech*. This phenomenon is not restricted to metapragmatic comments; as discussed in Chapter 4, Jewish American families pay much more explicit verbal attention to aspects of story performance (i.e., the telling) than do Israeli families. In Liebes and Katz's (1990) terms, the Jewish Americans tend to reveal a critical

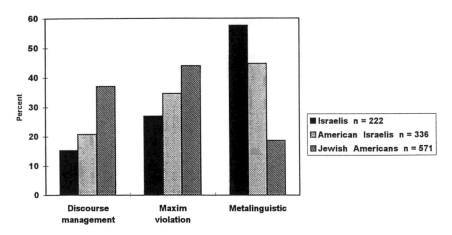

FIG. 6.1.   Types of metapragmatic comments used.

rather than a referential attitude to discourse. The difference is exemplified in the types of framings manifested in the retelling of a T.V. program: Critical framings treat the aesthetic aspects of the program cognitively, whereas referential framings treat the story as depicting real events, requiring a viewer to suspend disbelief and become emotionally involved in the characters' fates. In Liebes and Katz's study, the two types of framings distinguish between ethnic groups: Modern groups (e.g., Americans, Russian Israelis, and native Israeli Kibbutz members) tend toward critical framings, and traditional groups (e.g., Arabs and Moroccan Israelis) tend towards referential framings. Tannen (1980) found a similar trend in comparing Americans to Greeks, with the Americans more inclined to talk in metacommunicative, aesthetic terms about a silent film they had viewed than the Greek viewers, who related more directly and emotionally to the story itself. In family discourse, these different orientations are manifest with regard to the ongoing talk, with the Jewish Americans more inclined than the Israelis and American Israelis *to engage in critical talk about talk.*

The three groups also show culturally differing attitudes to pragmatic norms, placing different emphases on discourse management, Gricean conversational rules, or language per se. In the Jewish American families, the importance of conversational behavior overrides the importance of language as topic; in the Israeli families this trend is reversed. In the Jewish American discourse, the two conversational behavior categories (maxim violation and discourse management) take up 81% of all metapragmatic discourse space; in the Israeli discourse, they constitute less than half of all comments made (42%). The American Israelis occupy an interim position between the other two groups: 65.5% of the comments relate to turn regulation and conversational rules, whereas 45% are metalinguistic in nature.[2] In the discussion that follows, the themes of overall cultural preferences—and specifically, parental cultural norms for pragmatic socialization—are discussed in relation to the three domains of metapragmatic discourse.

---

[2]Hadass Sheffer was the reseach assistant responsible for the analysis of metapragmatic comments. Statistical analyses, based on discourse management and metalinguistic scores computed per speaker, reveal significant group differences in preferences for types of comments made for both adults and children. On the measure of discourse management, Israeli adults differ from Jewish American adults ($p < .001$) and from American Israeli adults ($p < .001$). The American Israeli adults also differ from the Jewish Americans ($p < .05$). Scores for metalinguistic comments differentiate Israelis from Jewish Americans ($p < .001$) and American Israelis from Jewish Americans ($p < .001$), but not American Israelis from Israelis. For children, the differences between Israelis and Jewish Americans are significant for both discourse management ($p < .001$) and metalinguistic comments ($p < .005$). The same pattern is repeated for the differences between American Israelis and Jewish Americans (for both, $p < .001$). The scores for children in the American Israeli families do not differ significantly from those of Israelis (see Blum-Kulka & Sheffer, 1993, for more detail on these tests).

Discourse Management

Discourse management is an important domain of socialization for Jewish Americans. During interviews, Jewish American parents express a firm belief in the need to teach children turn-taking rules explicitly ("It is important that they learn to speak in turn"). The discourse management model echoed in such comments is the mainstream, middle-class American one: Fair turn allocation and the censure of untimely interruptions seem to represent the discourse corollary of American ideals of individual rights and equal opportunity for all. Individualism, with all that it entails for mutual respect for individual space, has long been noted by observers of American society such as De Tocqueville and has more recently been studied extensively from both sociological (Bellah et al., 1985) and social psychological (Brown, 1991) points of view. Cross-cultural research has amply shown that the discourse manifestation of such ideals—namely, the systematics of turn-taking (Sacks, Schegloff, & Jefferson, 1974)—are by no means universal (e.g., Reisman, 1974). Even in American conversations, regular turn-taking is not necessarily adhered to in all domains (Edelsky, 1981). However, as the Jewish American adults' metapragmatic discourse shows, the rules appear to have an unquestionable normative status in American society. In this respect, Jewish Americans approximate mainstream American ways of speaking.

In the Jewish American families, turn-taking rules are seriously and explicitly negotiated, floor space being granted to each individual child in response to metabids for turn. As we saw in Chapter 4, floor space may be semiritualized, with time set aside for each child's today story:

(1) Jewish Americans 4; Jordan (8m); Sandra (4f).

Sandra: Mommy, to who will I tell how my day goes?
Mother: Okay, let's hear your day.

As illustrated by the next segment, Jewish American parents share with their children a very high degree of metapragmatic awareness in regard to discourse management, especially to turn-taking.

(2) Jewish Americans 2; Marvin (8m); Daniel (6m); Tina (4f).

> 1 Marvin: Can I say something? Is it my turn?
> 2 Mother: I don't know
> 3 Daniel: *No!* You have to wait until I finish!
> 4 Marvin: [whining] You had a long turn, so there.
> 5 Daniel: You had a longer one!
> 6 Marvin: No, I didn't.
> 7 Daniel: Yes, you did.
> 8 Father: Daniel, are you finished saying what you were saying?

9 Daniel: I am in the Poliwogs, but you know how high Adam is?

10 Father: How high?

11 Daniel: He is *right* into the highest thing.

12 Father: He is in beginners too?

13 Daniel: Yeah, he is right under advanced beginners.

14 Father: That's very good.

15 Daniel: Do you want me to tell you what go on # one time, well, the beginners, *Daddy # Marvin!* The beginners isn't exactly the beginners, you know. Why?

16 Father: Why?

17 Marvin: Well, why do they call it the beginners?

18 Father: Let Daniel answer that.

19 Marvin: You call it the [xxx] (laughter).

20 Daniel: Quit it Marvin because +/.

21–28   [for the next 8 turns Daniel manages to engage Marvin in discussing the swimming pool]

> 29 Marvin: Now can I start talking?
          [no response; parents engaged with Tina]

> 30 Marvin: Can I start talking?

31 Daniel: You guys! I am in the Polliwogs but Adam is really big, he is in beginners too!

> 32 Father: Okay, we heard that.

33 Daniel: [goes on for 50 seconds]

34 Marvin: So Adam swims at a different time from you?

35 Daniel: Yeah.

> 36 Marvin: My turn!
    %comment: [children screaming]

> 37 Mother: I think it's Tina's turn. Yes, Tina?

38 Tina: Uh . . . Uh . . .

39 Father: Do you want me to give you some? Do you want it yourself?

40 Mother: With those hands, Jack?

41 Father: What? # She doesn't have any others # Tina xxxx. Yes, Marvin?

> 42 Marvin: Okay, starting now I get a *long* turn.

> 43 Mother: No it won't be. It will be a reasonable turn.

44 Marvin: Okay, well you know we swim in Chapel Hill.

This unusually dense example of talk about talk reveals several aspects of the Jewish American parents' concept of discourse management politeness. The exchange opens with a permission request for a turn, combined with a comment indicating awareness of turn-taking rules ("Daddy, can I say something? Is it my turn?"). Securing a turn through metatalk typifies the discourse of Jewish American children; bids for turn constitute half of the Jewish American children's discourse management comments ($n = 115$).[3] Once a turn is granted, the speaker has exclusive rights: It is up to him or her to decide when enough has been said (turn 8: "Daniel, are you finished saying what you were saying?"), and others are discouraged from contributing to the talk (the father's comment in turn 18: "Let Daniel answer that"). Turn-regulation rules are *worthy of explicit mention*: out of 44 turns in this example, 15 explicitly concern turn-taking. The children bid for turns (turns 1, 30, and 42) and argue about speakers' rights and floor space (turns 2–7). Parents are clearly in charge, and they allocate turns and divide floor space (turns 2, 8, and 43), taking care that all children get a chance (turn 37), yet adhere to the maxim of informativeness (turn 32).

The Jewish American level of metapragmatic awareness with regard to turn-taking sharply contrasts with that of Israeli families. The generally low level of meta-awareness paid to discourse management is well illustrated by the Israeli children's pattern for securing the floor. The typical format is to use a direct attention-getting device ("Listen") with or without vocatives ("Mommy, listen") or a vocative followed by a question ("Daddy, you know what happened today?"), and a pause. In the following example, a vocative is repeated in a second attempt to secure attention:

(3) Israelis 2; Shlomit (12f); Riki (10f); Mira (5f).

1	Mira:	tishmeu mashehu	Listen to something.
[15 turns omitted, while Mira gets no response]			
2	Mira:	ima, ima.	Mommy, mommy.
3	Mother:	ma?	What?
4	Mira:	tishmeu bdixa.	Listen to a joke.
5	Mother:	nishma.	Let's hear it ...

Mira first targets her bid to all present, using the second person plural of the verb *listen*. When she gets no response, she appeals to her mother to secure the attention of at least one adult. As witnessed by turn 4 ("Listen [2nd person plural] to a joke"), the mother is acting here as the gatekeeper to the family's floor space, allocating the turn in the name of all present ("Let's hear it," using the first person plural of the verb).

Another typical bidding pattern is to combine the attention-getting device with the upcoming narrative or comment in the same turn. The Israeli parent grants the child permission to talk implicitly by showing interest in the topic raised:

---

[3]The other half of American Israeli children's discourse management comments are focused on arguing a turn and negating somebody else's turn.

(4) Israelis 6; Iris (6f); Lilax (6f).

> 1   Iris: aba, ata yodea,   Daddy, you know, we
                 halaxnu la-giv'a   went to that hill today.
                 ha-zot hayom.
  2   Father: eze? al yad malon   Which one? The one near
                 holiland?   Holyland Hotel?
  3   Iris: ken, ve-hem mac'u   Yes, and they found
                 kalanit.   an anemone.
  4   Lilax: ani macati, ani macati   I found it, I found it
                 ve-karati la-mora.   and called the teacher.
  5   Father: ani od lo raiti   I haven't seen an anemone
                 hashana kalanit.   yet this year.
        [continued]

Not all bids for turn are so successful, and fairness in floor space division between siblings is as much a concern of Israeli children as of Jewish American ones. Although occasionally Israeli children may try to negate a sibling's bid for a turn by an explicit "now it's my turn," their metapragmatic energy seems more focused on upholding their turn and getting their message across to all present. For instance, a 16-year-old girl, Na'ama (Israeli family 7), in response to her mother's inquiry, tells how she felt about her math exam the same day ("No, really, Mom, you don't know what happened, do you hear? Today you remember I came out of the exam in math with such a good feeling"). Her account is interrupted by a phone call for the mother. While the mother is on the phone, the conversation focuses on Tomer's (12, m) upcoming T.V. appearance and then, when the mother returns, on the T.V. program the mother produces. But Na'ama insists on resuming her topic:

(5) Israelis 7; Na'ama (16f); Tomer (12m); Gil (10m).

  1   Na'ama: hayiti be-emca   I was in the middle
                 ha-sipur.   of the story.
  2   Mother: slixa.   Sorry.
  3   Na'ama: rega, al ma siparti?   Wait a minute. What was I
                 ani crixa lehizaxer,   telling about? I need to re-
                 ani crixa lehizaxer ma   member. I need to remember
                 hitxalti lehagid lax.   what I started to tell you.
                                             [you = 2nd person singular]
  4   Gil: im ha-mivxan   About the math test +/.
                 be-xeshbon +/.
  5   Na'ama: ah!   Oh!
  6   Gil: she-hu shafax et libo.   That he poured his heart out.

| 7 | Na'ama: | ken. | Right. |

[story]

Three points are worth noting about this example. First, the renewed bid is typically justified in terms of the tale ("I was in the middle of the story") rather than the telling (as would be a comment like "It's my turn"). Second, as shown by the mother's apology in turn 2, the norm upheld is that a speaker has the right to bring his or her narrative to completion. Finally, when Na'ama has difficulty recalling her own story, she is aided by her younger brother, Gil, whose comment indicates how carefully he has listened to her earlier account.

Examples 3, 4, and 5 show a further cultural difference in modes of recipient design. Although both Jewish American and Israeli children often turn to their parents for turn allocation, in the Israeli discourse we also find indications that the discourse to follow is actually targeted for the general audience, as in the use of "Listen" in the second person plural in Example 3 or as in Na'ama's comment (added to another story she tells at the same dinner), "I wanted to tell you xx not only you, everybody [*raciti lesaper lax* [2nd person singular feminine] *xxx lo rak lax, le-KUlam*]." Such meta-insistence on group cohesiveness in listenership is absent from the Jewish American discourse. Linguistic motivation may be lacking, as the format of the English bids for turn ("Can I say something? Is it my turn?") focus on the speaker rather than the listener and leave no room for marking the audience. It may also be that targeting for all is taken for granted and not considered worthy of mention. In this context, 3-year-old Sandra's active search for an audience ("to who will I tell how my day goes?") is an exception.

American Israeli parents share with Jewish American parents a firm belief in the need to socialize their children to turn-taking rules:

(6) American Israelis 6 [interview] Father; Mother.
[Asked about their attitude to interruptions].

1	Father:	It's very important that they don't interrupt others. It's a principle here. In fact, sometimes we say to the other "wait, your brother is still talking," or "Jessica is still talking."
2	Mother:	And sometimes it ends up where they have to raise their hands even. [laughter]
3	Father:	Oh, yeah.

By paying attention to this particular aspect of discourse, the American Israeli adults reveal a sensitivity going back to their own socialization: *they are trying to preserve a positively evaluated feature of American interaction in their children's talk*. It is important to note that, by its very nature, this feature is not bound to any specific language; potentially, it is equally applicable to conversations in both Hebrew and English. But though the American Israeli parents highlight this domain both during interviews and at dinner (one fifth of their metapragmatic energy is concerned with discourse management), their children's discourse lacks the metacommunicative marking typical of the Jewish American families. Thus, when the children bid for a turn, they do so in a style that differs from both the explicit metatalk we saw in Example 3 and the attention-getting strategies of Examples 4 and 5.

(7) American Israelis 6; David (15m); Irit (13f); Noa (5f).

1	Noa:	{*ima*} (Mom), now can I tell you what they do?
% comment:		[talk around continues]
2	Noa:	Should I tell you what they do, what the {*gananot*} (nursery-school teachers) do? Should I tell you what they do?

Similar to the Israeli child's attempts in Example 4, Noa's attempt to get the floor acts as a pre-exchange move (Edmondson, 1981), inviting confirmation. However, the wording of her question is reminiscent of the American format of bids for the floor: "tell" is used as a "linguistic action-verbial" (Verschueren, 1985) that names the move to be performed. Hence what is exhibited is an interim, interlanguage-type pattern that shows the influence of both contact cultures.

Conversational Norms

Maxim violation comments can relate to the perceived violation of any one of the four Gricean submaxims of conversation: relevance, quality, quantity, and manner. The distribution of maxim violation comments by type shows that Jewish American and Israeli families differ in preferences for the type of conversational rule most likely to be noticed explicitly (see Fig. 6.2). This mode of pragmatic socialization is altogether much less prominent in the two Israeli groups. The two dinner conversations (of equal length) examined yielded only 63 comments made by the Israelis and 93 made by the American Israelis, as compared to 252 made by the Jewish Americans.

Jewish Americans emphasize foremost adherence to the maxim of quality, the factuality of the proposition asserted (63%). Israelis distribute their attention more equally between all four aspects of discourse. For Israelis, manner (mainly politeness) is highly attended to (42%), followed by quality (28%) and relevance (25%). Degree of informativeness and volubility (quantity) are rarely spoken about (6%). The American Israeli families fall between

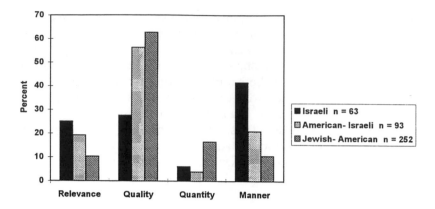

FIG. 6.2. Types of maxim-violation comments used.

the two other groups in their order of preference. Quality is very important (56%), followed by attention to violations of manner (21%) and relevance (19%). Overt attention to the maxim of informativeness (quantity) is negligible (4%).

Metapragmatic comments represent an overt, explicit mode of pragmatic socialization to conversational norms. Pragmatic socialization to discourse norms may take many other covert modes of expression such as the choice of the types of questions asked in response to a story told. Hence, in discussing how the families foster such norms as factuality, informativeness, and relevance, I also incorporate examples where underlying discourse values are detectable through types of responses made rather than through metapragmatic comments.

Quality: A Stress on Factuality and Evidence

The salience of comments in regard to factuality in the Jewish American and American Israeli families deserves special attention. Prompting adherence to the factuality of stated propositions is by no means a universal norm of pragmatic socialization. Israeli families, as the two other groups, though less prominently, echo the literate traditions described by Heath (1983). Heath found an emphasis on factuality to typify both White working-class people of Roadville and middle-class townspeople, but not the Black community of Trackton. In Roadville, children are expected to "stick to the truth" in retelling nonfictional stories of shared events that the adults are aware of. The middle-class townspeople parents insist on the factuality of personal experience stories not only in the retelling of shared events but also in encouraging children to engage in the telling of A-events (Labov & Fanshel, 1977) only they know. Heath interpreted such an insistence on factuality as associated with literate traditions. As Olson (1977) noted, literacy is associated historically with verifiability: Written texts carry a potential for verifiability absent from oral accounts. The demand for verifiability for an oral account enhances its status as historical (i.e., "true") rather than mythical (i.e., "fiction").

On the other hand, in the Black working-class community of Trackton, oral traditions dominate, and adherence to factuality is suspended in favor of *storyness*. The purpose of narratives above all is to entertain and "to establish the story-teller's intimate knowledge of truths about life larger than the factual details of real events" (Heath, 1983, p. 188). Similarly, Miller et al. (1990) found that caregivers from Chinese and from low-income Black families "were relatively tolerant of fictional embellishments of experience, whereas those from the White working-class community demanded a fairly strict adherence to the literal truth" (p. 301).

True to their middle-class modern literate background, all families we studied required children to learn to distinguish fact from fiction.[4] Factuality is highlighted through various types of questions interpretable as challenging the accuracy of an account as well as by metapragmatic comments explicitly denying its truth value. Furthermore, common practice in all families is to directly challenge a child's account if it seems illogical or counterfactual. In the following example, a child's report of her actions after school is challenged by both parents and her older brother:

(8) American Israelis 6; David (15m); Irit (13f); Noa (5f).
    Irit addresses the question to Noa.

1	Irit:	Did you have a good time at Leora's?
2	Noa:	I wasn't at Leora's.
3	Father:	Yes you were, this afternoon.
4	Mother:	You weren't? Where did you go from {gan} (nursery school)?
5	Noa:	To a home.
6	Mother:	Not to *this* home. [laughs]
7	Noa:	Yes to this home.
8	Mother:	I wasn't here.
9	Noa:	Hm?
10	David:	You went to Nevo's Naomi? I mean to Leora's and then from there to Nevo's?

[Noa does not answer and the family goes back to the previous topic, which was David's flight to the States.]

---

[4]Preliminary findings from an ongoing investigation of lower-class family discourse in Israel suggest that social class interacts with culture in this domain. The lower-class families seem to demand strict adherence to factuality on all occasions of personal storytelling, whereas in the Israeli middle-class families adherence to factuality is sometimes suspended in preference for other values such as familial bonding.

Among siblings, challenges at the factual level are often organized in sequences of "reciprocal counters" (cf. Goodwin, 1990) in which the first challenge is answered by a counter to it, which in turn provides the ground for a further counter.

(9) American Israelis 1; Neta (12f); David (5m).

	1	David:	She plays {*xamesh avanim*} (marbles).
	2	Neta:	We don't play. We play *after* you go to sleep.
	3	David:	No, you play *before* I go to \<sleep> [>].
>	4	Neta:	\<Thats> [<] *not* true.
			Last time we didn't.

Challenge may take the form of verifying questions, which, depending on tone of voice, express varying degrees of disbelief. For example, in their coconstructed account of their visit to the Science Museum in Boston, Marvin (8), Daniel (6), and Tina (4f) marvel about what they saw:

(10) Jewish American 2; Marvin (8m); Daniel (6m); Tina (4f).

1	Marvin:	A real um # um a real rat.
2	Tina:	And # it was +/.
3	Daniel:	\<I know, that played basketball> [>].
4	Tina:	\<xxxxxxxxxxxxxxxxxxxxxxx football> [<].
5	Father:	That rat plays basketball?
6	Tina:	Yeah.

[continued]

The phrasing of the father's question is an interesting example of how a reaction to a story may act as an attempt at reconstruction (Ochs et al., 1992). The question accepts the first part of the proposition, acknowledging the rat ("that rat") but challenges its second part, casting doubt on the rat's abilty to play basketball.

The next extract takes the notion of factuality several steps further, showing, as argued by Ochs (1992), how families, through conarration, draw upon and stimulate cognitive and linguistic skills that underlie scientific discourse in the modern world.

(11) Jewish Americans 3; Samuel (10m); Jeffrey (6m).

1	Samuel:	Um Jacob # xxx and then they tipped over and there was this, ya know, a GIANT turtle, it was coming *right* at them.
2	Mother:	Where? On the lake?

3	Samuel:	On the lake.
4	Mother:	They have giant turtles on the lake? I want to understand.
5	Samuel:	Yeah. Four.
6	Father:	In the lake like that a giant turtle? Thats only six inches across.
7	Mother:	Have you seen it?
8	Samuel:	Oh, *yeah.*
9	Mother:	How giant is giant?
10	Samuel:	How giant is giant? About three feet.
11	Mother:	Show me with your hands how big it is.
12	Samuel:	I can't fit it. My arms aren't that big.
13	Mother:	You really saw a giant turtle? In the lake?
14	Jeffrey:	About this big? This big?
15	Mother:	Were they like friendly?
16	Samuel:	Its claws were like that long.
17	Father:	xxx.
18	Jeffrey:	xxx and its claws xxx I'm sure its fins are that big.
19	Father:	xxx.
20	Mother:	Did you see it, or did Jacob see it?
21	Samuel:	Jacob saw it and I saw it too.
22	Mother:	You saw a three-foot turtle?
23	Samuel:	I didn't say it was exactly three foot, but approximately three feet.
24	Mother:	Was it like this?
25	Samuel:	No. Is that three feet?
26	Father:	Was it bigger than the plate you're eating?
27	Samuel:	Much.
28	Jeffrey:	Bigger than a house? Bigger than a house?
29	Mother:	I hope not. I wouldn't want to meet that turtle.
30	Jeffrey:	Me either. Yuk. xxx! [making funny noises].
31	Father:	I don't think xxx turtles grow that big.
32	Mother:	xxx if Jacob says he saw it, it doesn't surprise me.
% comment:		[There is a long pause]
33	Samuel:	He didn't say it was three feet.
34	Mother:	You said it was three feet.
35	Samuel:	By the look of its head and tail it looked like three feet.
36	Father:	By the look of its head, or did you see the body?
37	Samuel:	I saw part of his body.
38	Father:	But you didn't see its whole body.

39 Samuel: No.
40 Father: Now we have more of an understanding.
41 Mother: That's called an unconfirmed assumption. You know
                    what that's worth?
42 Samuel: What?
43 Mother: Nothing.
44 Father: xxx.
45 Mother: Do you remember the story of the four blind men
                    and the elephant? I was about to tell you a story
                    as I tell you now xxx. The part that's relevant to
                    you is that four blind men were asked to describe
                    an +/.
46 Jeffrey: Mom!
47 Mother: +, Elephant. Wait, sweetheart. An elephant is *very*
                    large. Each blind man was stationed at a different
                    part of the elephant. And they each described him
                    by what they were touching. So one blind man was
                    near his trunk and he said "Uh, it feels like a
                    long tube with sharp points." That was the tusks.
                    Another blind man was near his legs. "Oh
                    my goodness, its *so* tall, it must have # pillars."
                    Another blind man was near his tail # and said,
                    "Oh my goodness, it xxx very strange, very small
                    tail. It feels very *hairy*. It must have lots of fur
                    all over its body." The fourth blind man—What's
                    left of this poor elephant? I guess was near his
                    ear, and he thought, because the ear was very flat,
                    that the elephant was covered with flat scale
                    skin. And they all came to a different conclusion
                    based on what area they were touching, because
                    they didn't have the entire picture before them.
                    Had they seen, which of of course the couldn't do,
                    that if you see the entire picture that's one
                    thing, and if you see parts of it, you can't assume
                    from that a whole picture if you only have certain
                    parts of it. So, if you see a head of a turtle and
                    a little bit of its body, you can't assume that
                    it's three feet # # if you didn't see the whole
                    turtle.
@ End.

Evidently giant turtles on the lake are not considered by the adults in
this family a part of natural phenomena. Faced with the child's claim of

having experienced an unnatural phenomenon, the parents put the burden of proof on the child. Like a scientist claiming a new discovery, he is required to provide reliable evidence for his claim. As the exchange enfolds, the reliabilty of the evidence is challenged on several grounds, the challenge culminating not only in total dismissal of the claim but also in an explicit didactic statement defining the nature of scientific evidence in general.

As the exchange opens, Samuel's use of "giant" as a description of the turtle he saw on his trip to the lake immediately triggers doubt ("Where? On the lake? They have giant turtles on the lake?"), which gradually and systematically builds up to the explicit expression of disbelief. For a while, Samuel holds his ground, claiming experiential warranties for his story ("Have you seen it?" "Oh, yeah"). With repeated questioning his account begins to lose credibility, and from the point he begins to admit doubt (hedging his claim for the turtle's size with "approximately," turn 23) his mother's challenge gathers momentum, systematically undermining each of Samuel's claims until the final collapse of his story in turns 37–39 ("I saw part of its body." "But you didn't see the whole body." "No."). Next, from turn 47 on, the mother takes it upon herself to dismiss the account in unequivocal terms, to formulate the scientific principle behind the dismissal ("That's called an unconfirmed assumption") and to illustrate the result of the lack of critical thinking through the story of the four blind men and the elephant, which she modifies from memory as she goes along.[5]

---

[5]The story of the elephant, as told by the mother, is a wonderful example of the transformation of an old religious fable to suit modern needs. The story is Indian in origin and can be found in several versions in anthologies of Indian folktales. The following is one of those versions:

Six blind men once described an elephant that stood before them all. One felt the back. The second noticed perdent ears. The third could only feel the tail. The tusks absorbed the admiration of the fourth. While one of the other two grasped the trunk, the last sought for small things and found four thick and clumsy feet. From what each learned, he drew the beast. Six monsters stood revealed. Just so the six religions learned of God, and tell their wondrous tales. Our God is One.
[Written in the higher dialect of Pattanatta, in poetic form. Robinson, E. J., *Tales and Poems of South India*, T. Wolmer, London, 1885]

I am grateful to Udo Fries for bringing to my attention a rhymed version of the story, called "The Six Men of Indostan," written in a humorous tone and lacking all trace of the religious moral, as can be seen from the last stanza:

And so these men of Indostan
Disputed loud and long
Each in his own opinion
Exceeding stiff and strong,
Though each was partly in the right,
And all were in the wrong!

Informativeness and Relevance

In Grice's account, the maxim of quantity relates to the requirement to provide as much information as needed relative to the general direction of the exchange but not to provide more information than necessary. Because the requirements are subject to considerations of relevance in terms of the general goal of the exchange, the two submaxims are interrelated. This interrelationship is particularly evident in family discourse, where negotiations over degree of informativeness are guided by considerations of situational and topical relevance.

The information requirement is only rarely implemented in family discourse through metapragmatic comments. The common practice is not to say "tell us more about that" but rather to pose information-seeking questions that shape both the amount and the nature of information required in connection with the topic at hand. With young children, the issue is to get the child to verbalize his or her experience in a manner that can be judged informative enough from the adult's point of view.

(12) Israelis 10; Daffi (12f); Noga (8f); Yaron (4m).

	1	Mother:	Yaron, tesaper lanu ma <asita ha-yom ba-gan.> [>]	Yaron, tell us what <you did in nursery school today.> [>]
	2	Daffi:	<ma [//] ex haya ba-gan>?	<What [//] how was school>? [<]
	3	Yaron:	naim.	Nice.
>	4	Mother:	+^ naim? *ma* haya naim? tesapper lanu ex haya naim.	Nice? *What* was nice? Tell us how was it nice.
	5	Yaron:	sixaknu.	We played.
>	6	Mother:	be-ma sixaktem?	What did you play?
	7	Yaron:	be-misxakim.	Games.
>	8	Mother:	eze? ba-xuc? ba-xacer?	What kind? Outside? In the yard?

[continued]

The parental effort to elicit a story in this case highlights the relevance of his experience at school as a topic of conversation at dinner and simul-

---

The mother's version of the story builds on and expands the modern interpretation of the parable, as used, for example, in an advertisement for *Time* magazine, where the caption above the picture of an elephant behind bars in a zoo reads, "What you see of the world depends entirely on how you look at it" (meaning in the context of the ad that you need of course to read *Time* for the global perspective).

tanously sets up criteria for the degree of informativeness that needs to be contained in the verbal recounting of such experiences. In other words, through this highly contextualized, dialogic mode of story coconstruction the child is invited to learn the requirements for eventually constructing decontextualized, autonomous accounts (Blum-Kulka & Snow, 1992). In this case, the events recounted are known to the teller only, but similar probing is apparent in cases where attempts at coconstruction relate to the retelling of shared events. For example, during the same dinner, the mother turns to Yaron and asks him "Tell Rachel [the observer] where we were during the vacations, where did we go," thereby marking the retold events as memorable and relevant for the child's autobiography (Snow, 1991).

With older children, as among adults, negotiations over informativeness are more overtly linked to questions of relevance, namely to the types of information considered most relevant to the topic at hand. In the following extract (continuing the exchange in example 4) relevance is defined in terms of a specific type of scientific knowledge. The details required by the father highlight basic principles of the observational method in natural science— careful observation, attention to detail, and logical classification. Accordingly, the child is asked which flowers were seen, whether she learned to differentiate the various botanical parts of the flower, and whether she learned the names of these parts.

(13) Israelis 6; Lilax (6f); Iris (6f).

1	Father:	ve-hayu eze xayot meyuxadot? macatem xargol lemashal?	And were there any special animals? Did you find a grasshopper for example?
2	Lilax:	ken, ani raiti xargol.	Yes, I saw a grasshopper.
3	Iris:	hem mac'u kalanit.	They found an anemone.
4	Father:	kalanit?	An anemone?
5	Lilax:	*ani* macati ve-karati la, la +...	*I* found one and called the, the +...
6	Iris:	la-mora nili.	The teacher, Nili.
7	Lilax:	la-mora ve-hi amra le-kulam: "tir'u, tir'u macanu kalanit."	The teacher and she said to everybody: "Look, look, we found an anemone."
8	Father:	ani od lo raiti ha-shana kalanit.	I haven't seen an anemone yet this year.
9	Lilax:	ani raiti. ani macati et ha-kalanit.	I have. I found the anemone.
10	Father:	kvar ptuxa?	Already open?

11	Lilax:	ma?	What?
12	Father:	ha-alim, ale ha-koteret.	The leaves, petals.
13	Lilax:	ken. ve-rainu afilu et ha-lavan shela.	Yes. And we even saw its white.
14	Father:	ma ze? eze lavan yesh la?	What? What white does it have?
15	Lilax:	et ha-lavan be-tox ha-ale koteret. yesh la lavan # im ha-adom.	The white inside its petals. It has white # with the red.
16	Iris:	LO, YESH GAM xx SHAXOR. [shouting]	NO, IT ALSO HAS BLACK xx. [shouting]
17	Lilax:	ken ha-avkanim hem shxorim.	Right the stamens are black.
18	Iris:	xashavti shaxor.	I thought black.
19	Lilax:	ha-lavan hu yaxad im ha-adom betox ha # le-yad ha +...	The white is together with the red in the # near the +...
20	Father:	az ulay ze &civ # hi amra she-ze kalanit?	So maybe it's a &tul # Did she say it was an anemone?
21	Mother:	yesh kvar kalaniyot ba-ir. lama lo?	There are already anemones in town. Why not?
% comment:		[Iris is busy cutting cucumbers.]	
22	Father:	ve-ma ha-madrixim hisbiru laxem?	And what did the guides tell you?
23	Lilax:	yesh li rak madrixa axat.	I have only one guide.
24	Father:	ma hi hisbira?	What did she say?
25	Lilax:	she-ze KALAnit!	That it's an anemone!
26	Father:	lo, ma hi hisbira bixlal?	No, what did she explain in general?
27	Lilax:	hi hisbira she-kalanit yod'im she-ze kalanit biglal ha-lavan shela. ve-pereg hu adom aval rak bli ha-lavan.	She explained that an anemone, you know it's an anemone by it's white and a poppy is also red but without the white.
30	Father:	xxx.	xxx.
31	Mother:	lo, aval +/.	No, but +/.
32	Iris:	ima, ma efshar od? laxtox?	Mom, what else is there to cut?
33	Lilax:	Kshe-nir'e parag az hi [/] hi tagid.	When we see a poppy she [/] she'll tell us.

34	Father:	hi tasbir.	She'll explain.
35	Lilax:	hi tasbir.	She'll explain.
36	Father:	et ha-hevdel?	The difference?
37	Lilax:	ken.	Yes.
38	Father:	hi codeket.	She's right.

@End

The particular rendition of an experience encouraged through parental questioning shows children which events are reportable, what components are worthy of elaboration, and what is important about them. Importance may be defined in terms of reportability, as in Example 1, specific observational detail, as in Example 13, or in terms of a causal explanation that seeks to provide motivations for the event(s) reported. In the joint account by two children of their visit to the Science Museum (Example 10), as the story enfolds the smallest child (Tina, 3) reports that the rat is placed in a small cage to play basketball, that "he's very good at throwing the ball," and that when the rat gets the ball in the basket he receives food pellets. At this point the mother intervenes to ask, "Do you think that's why he was so eager to get it in the basket? So he could get something to eat?" encouraging the children to engage in logical, inferential thinking, to attribute to the rat the type of intentional goal-directed motivation that can explain human actions.

Such "why" questions may also relate to the overall significance of a story, demanding verbalization of its focal relevance. In coconstructing with Yoram (Israeli family 1) his experiences during a school trip to "a school for teachers or something like it," the adults present pose not only clarifying questions ("Who organized it?" "Did you go with your teacher?") that signal to the child the shortcomings of his account in terms of the maxim of quantity, but also questions that direct him to think about the overall significance of the event ("Did they explain to you what the goal was? Why did they take you there and what they are trying to find in this?").

Censoring forthcoming information, in line with the second part of the informativeness requirement (not to say more than necessary) may be implemented on the grounds of redundancy ("we already heard that") or be subject to considerations of relevance. The following exchange exemplifies the requirement for novelty. The father's "Oh, yes, you told me, I forgot completely" (turn 6) serves as indirect apology for having asked the same question twice.

(14) Israeli 6; Lilax (6f); Iris (6f).

1	Father:	ma at asit be-shiur xonxut ha-axaron shelax?	What did you do in your last tutoring lesson?
2	Lilax:	ehm ani asiti ani osa ehm +. . .	Ehm, I did, I'm making ehm +. . .

	3	Lilax:	od lo gamarti et ze.	I haven't finished it yet.
	4	Father:	ma ze?	What?
>	5	Lilax:	aval ani osa # simaniya.	But I'm making a book mark.
	6	Father:	ah naxon, amart li. shaxaxti legamre.	Oh right. You told me. I forgot all about it.

@End

Censorship may be also self-directed, implying conversationally that the topic raised is not relevant to the occasion, possibly due to the presence of the children:

(15) Jewish Americans 1; Jennifer (15f); Simon (13m).

> 1 Father: I won't say in detail what Nancy Black told me. Just let me say there's verification.
> 2 Simon: For what?
> 3 Father: Never mind.
> @End.

Both adults and siblings engage in curtailing forthcoming information on the grounds of irrelevance in terms of the interests of one or some of the participants present at dinner:

(16) Jewish Americans 2; Marvin (8m); Daniel (6m).
Marvin and Daniel are telling the story of "The Flight of the Navigator."

> 1 Daniel: And the alien says: "I told you that turnpike would be hectic. Then they stopped xxx. They didn't find on the way, you know, # and, well, first they ask +/.
> 2 Marvin: Hey leave that! xxx He escapes in that +/.
> 3 Mother: You know what, Susan might want to see this movie. Don't tell us every detail. [continued]

(17) Jewish Americans 1; Jennifer (15f); Simon (13m).
Simon is telling what's going to happen on the coming chapters of some soap opera.

> 1 Simon: What happens is that she and Patrick, you know, they got drunk and they, and then +/.
> 2 Jennifer: Shut up, Simon!
> 3 Simon: +, She walks out.

4 Jennifer: Simon, shut up! Forget it!
@ End

Comments on Manner

The maxim of manner relates to how things are said. In Grice's (1975) formulation it requires speakers to be clear, avoid ambiguity and prolixity, and be orderly. A further important aspect of how things are said, included here, relates to politeness: the use of politeness formulae and protest against certain words.

The demand for clarity is especially prominent in the case of storytelling. For children, family discourse provides opportunities to develop the ability to construct autonomous, self-contained texts, texts that allow the audience to identify participants and events in the story world. This is a focal dimension of language socialization, the dimension referred to by Snow (1984, 1989) as "contextualized" versus "decontextualized" language. Contextualized language relies heavily on shared knowledge. Decontextualized language is more self-contained and is associated with literate traditions (Scollon & Scollon, 1981), because a written text by definition needs to be more autonomous than an oral rendition. In turn, the use of language in literate societies is characterized by decontextualized modes of expression, regardless of the medium used. It is these modes that are required in schools, and the success of children in school may well depend on their skills in the uses of decontextualized language skills (Snow & Dickinson, 1997).

One of the ways in which children may acquire the ability to construct texts in the decontextualized mode is through audience reactions to perceived violations of the submaxim of clarity. Such reactions may transmit criteria for the degree of explicitness needed in identifying characters in a story and in making clear the chronological order of the events related. The demand for clarity is particularly relevant in the case of personal experience stories, which require a higher degree of text construction effort on the part of the child than stories shared with one or more of the adults, as shown by Example 18.

(18) Jewish Americans 3; Samuel (10m); Jeffrey (6m).

1 Jeffrey: One day we stayed that much, all the way from xxx it's so smell.
2 Father: What smells?
3 Jeffrey: It's xxx.
4 Father: What smells?
5 Samuel: We don't know what you're talking about. Who, what smells?
6 Jeffrey: The ice cream.
7 Father: The ice cream?

8 Jeffrey: Yeah, it does.
9 Samuel: Whose ice cream smells?
10 Father: I never smelled bad ice cream, Jeffrey.
11 Jeffrey: I *smelled* it.
12 Father: You did? Where?
13 Jeffrey: At school.
14 Samuel: Oh, at school.
15 Father: That's most unfortunate.
16 Jeffrey: Yeah, it stinks. That's the baddest in +. . .
17 Samuel: The best or the baddest?
18 Jeffrey: The baddest.
19 Father: Not the baddest, the worst.
20 Jeffrey: The worst.
@End.

The issue of clarity is best epitomized by 10-year-old Samuel: "We don't know what you're talking about. Who, what smells?" As of turn 9, attention to clarity becomes confounded with concern about quality (i.e., truth-value) because the questions about the whereabouts of the bad ice cream seek information while signaling disbelief.[6] Finally, the issue becomes one of language, with Samuel trying to clarify meaning (repeating Jeffrey's wrong usage) and the father correcting Jeffrey's use of "baddest."

In Example 18, clarifying the focal point of reference for the story is an essential condition for communication because the listeners truly do not know what Jeffrey is talking about. In Example 19, the focus is on eliciting a coherent account for events known to the mother.

(19) Jewish Americans 4; Jordan (8m); Sandra (4f).

1 Mother: Wait Sandra. Were you going to tell Elisabeth something about the pop-up mouse?
2 Sandra: Okay. and xxx <whenever I go to sleep> [>], she pops up # I open my eyes!
3 Jordan: <Where in the refrigerator Mom?> [<]
4 Sandra: Pops down # I close them. Xxx she lives # I'll show you all where's. <Just xxx where I am. Walk> [>] and I'll show where's, ok?
5 Jordan: <xxxxxxxxxxxxxxxxxxxxxxxxx> [<].
> 6 Mother: Could you begin to tell us in words?

---

[6]See Burton (1980) for an illuminating analysis of how repetitions and clarification questions (in her case in literary texts) can act as challenging moves by virtue of holding up the topic introduced in the previous turn. See Blum-Kulka (1983) for an application of this idea to the discourse of political interviews.

```
7  Jordan:   xxx.
8  Sandra:   xxx he lives in +...
9  Mother:   He lives in a couch, the pop-up mouse.
             It's her explanation for waking up in the middle
             of the night.
   @End.
```

Obviously, Sandra's attempts to cooperate with her mother in telling Elisabeth about her fantasy pet fail to meet the adult requirements for coherence and clarity. This dissatisfaction is expressed by the exasperated question, "Could you begin to tell us in words?" which implies a global rejection of all that Sandra has said so far.

It has been widely noted that parents use direct teaching to induce children to use conventional politeness forms (Becker, 1988, 1990; Gleason et al., 1984; Gleason & Weintraub 1976; Grief & Gleason, 1980; Snow et al., 1990). Examples of this practice in family discourse follow the patterns noted, by which parents elicit the required "please" or "thank you" through conventional question forms that signal the need for reformulation:

(20) Jewish Americans 4; Jordan (8m); Sandra (4f).

```
1  Father:   Jordan, would you like some more meat?
2  Sandra:   Meat!
3  Mother:   How do you ask, dear?
4  Jordan:   xxx.
5  Sandra:   Please.
6  Mother:   Okay.
```

(21) Jewish Americans 10; Andrew (10m); Jessica (8f); Jonathan (3m).

```
1  Jonathan:  Can I have some more orange juice?
2  Mother:    What's the magic word?
3  Jonathan:  Please?
```

It is especially noteworthy that in the bilingual American Israeli families metapragmatic comments are indices of the families' perception of correct discourse *regardless of the language they are uttered in or commented on*. This can be seen by the tacit agreement of participants to ignore completely the language spoken if the issue at hand concerns pragmatically proper behavior, as in the following case:

(22) American Israelis 4; Yakir (16m); Ruth (12f); Batya (8f); Sara (6f).

```
1  Sara:     Mommy, {tavi'i li od} [bring me more] fish.
2  Mother:   Excuse me?
```

> 3 Sara: {bevakasha, tni li od}[please give me more] fish.

The child's mixture of Hebrew and English here is typical of the bilingual family (see Chapter 7). However, the mixing is irrelevant to the main issue discussed. After first using a colloquial slang expression in Hebrew (literally "bring me" instead of "get me" or "give me") the child interprets her mother's reaction as a reprimand for her lack of politeness, although it might as easily have been interpreted as a negative reaction to mixing the two languages. Next, Sara adds the required magic word ("*bevakasha*") and shifts register ("*tni li*" instead of "*tavi'i li*"). But the fish remains "fish," and the exchange is double-coded, the mother never saying a word in Hebrew. *Pragmatic socialization is hence taking place independent of the language used for its implementation.*

Another way in which the "how" of speaking is attended to is through the censuring of bad words. On one occasion, Tina (4, Jewish American family 2) deliberately uses the word "shit" to test reactions, turning to each participant in turn to ask "Did you hear what I said?" She is met by supportive giggles and chuckles from her brother and father, but her mother emphatically and repeatedly forbids her to use the word ("Don't say it/No, don't say it/Sandra don't say it"). Eventually Jordan (8) evokes the taping situation to stop his sister:[7]

(23) Jewish Americans 4; Jordan (8m); Sandra (4f); Ellisabeth–observer.

1	Jordan:	What will Catherine Snow think when she finds out that the average family says bad words at the, at the dinner table?
2	Father:	[laughs].
3	Jordan:	[giggles].
4	Sandra:	[giggles]. Did you hear what I said?
5	Jordan:	<*Yes!*> [>]
6	Father:	<Yeah yeah> [<] [laughing]!
7	Sandra:	Ellisabeth, did you hear what I said?

Comments about "bad" words also appear among siblings, such as an Israeli 6-year-old telling her sister not to say "*mag'il*" [disgusting] about food and an Israeli 10-year-old reacting to her 12-year-old sister:

---

[7]Metacomments about the taping situation appear sporadically in several dinners. In this particular case, the quoted reference to Catherine Snow (who supervised data collection in Boston) is preceded by Jordan responding to his father—who jokingly referred to the tape as "the evil eye"—with "Daddy, what will Catherine Snow think when she hears the whispers of the evil eye?"

(24) Israelis 6; Iris (6f); Lilax (6f).

1	Lilax:	ze mag'il. ze fixsa.	It's disgusting. It's yukky.
2	Father:	ma mag'il?	What's disgusting?
3	Observer:	[laughs] xxx.	xxx.
4	Iris:	ha-beca ha-zot ze lo mag'il.	This egg is not disgusting.
5	Lilax:	xx az at xx.	xx so you xx.
6	Iris:	bixlal lo omrim al oxel mag'il.	Anyway, you don't say disgusting about food.
7	Father:	mi amar lax?	Who said so?
8	Iris:	ani yoda'at.	I know.
9	Lilax:	mi yoda'at?	Who knows?
10	Father:	ze gam naxon.	It's true, too.

Metalinguistic Comments

Awareness of matters of language is salient in both the American Israeli and Israeli families but negligible in the Jewish American families. In the American Israeli families, English is the main language spoken at home, although it is often mixed with Hebrew. Adults and children alike are fully bilingual in both languages, English being the dominant language for the adults and Hebrew for the children. Both adults and children practice their bilingualism not only in speaking (using mainly English at home and Hebrew at school and work) but also in reading (see Chapter 7). Given their active bilingualism and the adults' recent history of second language learning, it seemed reasonable to expect from these speakers a relatively high level of explicit attention to matters of language. Indeed, the bilingual families exceed the Jewish Americans by far in their degree of language awareness, but, surprisingly, they still fall below the Israeli norm. For American Israeli adults and their children, metalinguistic comments constitute almost half of all metapragmatic talk, whereas for Jewish Americans such comments do not exceed a fifth of metapragmatic discourse. For Israelis, matters of language figure as the most prominent aspect of discourse commented on for both adults (62%) and children (51%).

Jewish Americans. The comments that do appear in the Jewish American families have to do with three aspects of language use: correcting children's grammar, noting children's use of slang, and commenting generally on language. In Example 25, Andrew (9.5) is having problems with pronunciation and verb formation of the word "competition." He tries "competitioning" (the logical but wrong derivation) and is immediately corrected by both parents. In Example 26, the parents challenge the extensive use of "like"

("you can like save a half like of the tuition that you pay") through joking
question repetitions, without ever explicitly expressing their objection.

(25) Jewish Americans 9; Andrew (9.5m); Ellen (7f).

1	Andrew:	By the way # who's winning in this competition? Drugs, um for getting this drug thing?
2	Mother:	Well, I think the BU has dropped out of the competition.
3	Andrew:	Well, are you competion [//] competitioning with anyone else then?
4	Father:	Competing.
	%comment:	[correcting Andrew.]
5	Mother:	Competing.

(26) Jewish Americans 1; Jennifer (15f); Simon (13m).

1	Jennifer:	He said that if you take a certain amount of courses you can like save a half like of the tuition that you pay.
2	Observer:	Well, there happen to be a lot of courses.
3	Father:	Like again, like really?
4	Mother:	Like really?
5	Father:	Like really?
6	Mother:	Like.
7	Father:	Like.
8	Jennifer:	Okay. [everybody laughs]
9	Jennifer:	Like yes!!
10	Simon:	Shh.
11	Jennifer:	Okay.
12	Father:	Like are we having dessert? Like +/.
13	Simon:	Like no.

The third type of metalinguistic comments relate to language use in
general. On occasions when the Jewish American families topicalize lan-
guage-related issues, they make general comments in regard to the language
of others, not their own ("Did you know the Eskimos have a hundred words
for snow?").

Israeli Families. In contrast, the high level of attention to matters of
language in the Israeli families challenges the issue of linguistic awareness
as a hallmark of bilingualism. This seems due to the peculiar history of the

revival of Hebrew, which provides the sociolinguistic context for the Israeli preoccupation with all matters of language (Harshav, 1990, 1993; Rabin, 1976).

Issues of language that are discussed by the Israelis include all the linguistic dimensions: phonology, morphology, syntax, lexicon, semantics, and pragmatics. Speakers comment on pronunciation (e.g., how /x/ and /r/ are pronounced in different registers); children query the meaning of loan translations used with Hebrew phonology and morphology ([*dilemmot*]>di-lemmas; [*fotogeni*]>photogenic; [*privilegya*]>privilege) or rare words, and all speakers discuss word origins ("does x comes from"), the acceptability of slang, and foreigners' or newcomers' ways of speaking.

With regard to both grammar and lexicon, the families echo the wider societal debates between prescriptive and permissive attitudes to language use. The prescriptive attitude, represented by several popular books on correct usage, as well as by programs such as "A Moment of Hebrew" on the radio, often object to grammatical forms and expressions of Modern Hebrew, labeling them as wrong on the grounds that they are not true to the historical tradition of the Hebrew language. Permissive linguists, on the other hand, evoke the notion of *acceptability* as a legitimate criterion in judging new developments in Hebrew. We find both attitudes in the families. On the one hand, speakers comment on "correct" usage, accepting the prescriptive attitude:

(27) Israelis 8; Merav (11f); Ran (9m).

1	Father:	at yoda'at she-carix lehagid *klavot* ve-lo kalbot?	You know that you're supposed to say *klavot* (bitches) and not *kalbot klavot*?
2	Mother:	klavot?	
3	Father:	ken, kmo *melaxot*.	Yes, like *melaxot* (queens).
4	Mother:	ken?	Yeah?
5	Father:	ken, ze nora muzar.	Yeah, it's very odd.

@End.

On the other hand, the acceptance of new usages in spoken Hebrew can become a matter of debate:

(28) Israelis 5; Niva (13f); Yoav (11m); Tama (4f).

1	Observer:	be-tosefet shel ha-ivrit she-kalateti, nidme afilu she-kalateti et ze kan, ba-poal *tavi li* bimkom *titen li*.	An addition to Hebrew I've noticed, I think I even heard it here, is the use of the verb *tavi* (bring) instead of *titen* (give).
	% comment:	["tavi" means "bring" and "titen" means "give"]	

2	Mother:	tavi li ze kvar +/.	Give it to me is already+/.
3	Observer:	tavi li bimkom ten li.	*tavi li* instead of *ten li.*
4	Father:	ze yerushalmi. tavi li ze yerushalmi, chaxchaxit yerushalmit.	It's Jerusalemese. *tavi li* is Jerusalemese street talk.
5	Mother:	tavi li ze +/.	*tavi li* is +/.
6	Father:	ze xxx.	It's xxx.
7	Observer:	lo, ze aval lo rak kan. ani kvar shamati et ze kama peamim, ve-ba-sof, shamati et ze kvar gam ba-radyo mi-yardena arazi. samti lev bimyuxad.	No, but it's not just here. I've heard it several times, and recently, I heard it on the radio too, Yardena Arazi (singer) said it. I noticed it specially.
8	Niva:	ma?	What?
9	Mother:	ma?	What?
10	Observer:	hi amra "hu hevi li" bimkom "hu natan li," ve-ze hikpic et ha-ozen.	She said "he brought me" instead of "he gave me" and that made me jump.
> 11	Niva:	aval ma ra be-hevi li?	But what's wrong with "brought me"?
12	Observer:	en shum ra, ani lo omeret she-yesh.	Nothing. I'm not saying it's wrong.
13	Niva:	hevi, hu hevi.	Brought, he brought.
14	Observer:	lo, ani lo omeret she-yesh ra, ani omeret she-ze shimush xadash shel ha-poal *hevi*, ki be-ivrit ha-shimush ha-normali haya: "hu natan li" ve-lo "hu hevi li."	No, I'm not saying it's wrong, I'm saying that it's a new usage of the verb *hevi*, because in Hebrew the normal usage was: "he gave me" and not "he brought me."
15	Mother:	lo, ze lo naxon lehagid et ze.	No, it's not correct to say that.
16	Yoav:	ma, ma ze "hevi"?	What, what's "hevi"?
17	Observer:	"hu hevi li" ze +/.	"hu hevi li" is +/.
18	Father:	ze sleng, ze lo, ze lo ivrit nexona.	It's slang. It's not correct Hebrew.
19	Yoav:	az ma ze, aval "hevi"? ma ze?	But what is "*hevi*"? What is it?
20	Observer:	ma ze "lehavi"?	What is "*lehavi*"?

21	Yoav:	ken.	Yes.
22	Observer:	aba nasa le-amerika ve-*hevi* lexa mi-sham # matana, *natan* lexa et ha-matana kshe-hu ba hena. yesh hevdel?	Daddy went to America and *brought* you # a present from there, he *gave* you the present when he came here. Isn't there a difference?
23	Yoav:	ken.	Yeah.
24	Observer:	naxon? kshe-lokxim mi-makom exad la-sheni ze lehavi, ve-latet +/.	Right? When you take from one place to another that's to bring, and to give +/.
25	Niva:	natan li matana.	Gave me a present.
26	Observer:	hevi li matana, az afilu lo, axshav she-omrim "hevi li matana" ze ma she +...	Brought me a present, is not even, now when you say "brought me a present" it's +...
27	Niva:	ani yoda'at she-omrim "natan li," aval +/.	I know you say "gave me" but +/.
28	Observer:	ze lo nir'a lax, ze lo nishma lax muzar? at hayit metakenet et ze le-mi she-ba mi-xuc la'arec ve-at hayit omeret lo "anaxnu lo omrim hu hevi li."	It doesn't seem, sound strange to you? You would correct someone who came from abroad, and say to him "we don't say he brought me."
29	Niva:	lo, lo hayiti metakenet.	No, I wouldn't correct him.
30	Observer:	lo, aval hayta lax hargasha keilu hu medaber kmo she-lo medabrim po.	No, but you'd feel like he was talking in a way that isn't used here.
31	Mother:	ivrit yafa miday.	A too beautiful kind of Hebrew.
32	Father:	ze kmo im ha, ze kmo im ha-misparim, zaxar ve-nekeva she-hofxim otam be-xavana.	It's like with, it's like with numbers, masculine and feminine that are reversed on purpose.
33	Observer:	mi hofex otam be-xavana?	Who reverses them on purpose?
34	Niva:	lo hofxim otam be-xavana.	They are not reversed on purpose.

35	Father:	be-sleng be-sax ha-kol hofxim be-xavana.	In slang on the whole it's done on purpose.
36	Observer:	ma pit'om? amiram, lo maxlifim be-xavana, ze nora kashe lilmod ve-anashim +/.	No way, Amiram, people don't mix them up on purpose. It's really hard to learn and people +/.
37	Father:	ha-inyan hu ha-inyan shel nekeva ba-zman ha-axaron,# ba'ayat ha-sfaradim ze ba'ayat ha-likud ve-ha-lo likud. ze mamash kmo mexa'a lehagid shgia.	The thing, the thing with feminine lately # the problem of the Sephardim is the problem of the Likud and non-Likud. It's like a (political) protest to make mistakes.
% comment:		[Likud is a right-wing political party that is supposed to have a strong Sephardic (oriental Jews) support].	
38	Observer:	ma ata omer!	You don't say!
39	Father:	lehagid be-min zaxar.	To speak in the masculine.
40	Observer:	ani lo xoshevet she-ze be-xavana, pashut nekeva harbe yoter kacar me-ha-zaxar be-misparim, la'asot dvarim yoter kacar.	I don't think it's on purpose, just that the feminine is much shorter than the masculine in numbers, to make things shorter.
41	Father:	ze lo haya kaxa.	That's not the way it was.
42	Niva:	shte ve-shne ze oto davar, oto orex.	*shte* (feminine two) and *shne* (masculine two) are the same, the same length.
43	Father:	ze lo haya xarif kol kax.	It wasn't that bad.
44	Observer:	ze haya me-az u-mi-tamid she-lo yad'u ex la'asot, az kevan she-yod'im she-carix la'asot mashehu az +...	It has always been that they didn't know how to say it, So since they know they have to say something, so +...
		yesh hare et ha-ma'arxon ha-ze she-omer "shlosha	There's this sketch that says "*shlosha* (3m)

kvucot" az ha-hu masbir lo "shalosh kvucot," az ha-hu masbir lo "ani sidarti otam. *ani* yodea ex sidarti otam!"	groups" so someone tells him, "*shalosh* (3f) groups." So he explains "I arranged them. *I* know how I arranged them!"
% comment:	[The word "group" is feminine in Hebrew, so the correct form is "shalosh kevucot"].
@End.	

In this exceptionally long metalinguistic discussion, led by the observer, several linguistic matters come to the fore: the legitimacy of replacing "give" [*latet*] by "bring" [*lehavi*] in requests for goods ("bring me" instead of "give me") and its extended use ("he brought me" in the sense of "gave me"), the semantics of "give" and "bring" in general, and the participants' attitudes to the common practice in spoken Hebrew of ignoring the grammatical rule that calls for gender differentiation in the use of numbers.[8] On the issue of "bring," each of the participants takes a different stand. The observer first objects to it (when she heard it on the radio, it "jumped her ears") but later accepts it ("not that it is wrong, but"); the father dismisses it as local slang; the mother rejects it ("it's not correct"); and the daughter (13) seems to find nothing wrong with it ("What's wrong with 'bring me'?") This vacillation between normative and permissive attitudes is typical of educated native speakers of Hebrew, who are aware that the grammatical rules learned in school do not apply to much of common spoken Hebrew. The result is that, like the linguists, speakers differ in drawing the lines between what is considered acceptable (even if only as slang) and what is dismissed as "wrong." With regard to the use of numbers, for instance, the adults seem united in their critical attitude to the common practice not to differentiate between feminine and masculine forms and spend their energy in theorizing about the reasons for the phenomenon (turns 37–40).[9] It is noteworthy that topicalizing language in terms of normative use simultaneously occasions discussions about the semantics of the expressions discussed, thus serving goals in language socialization. The discussion about the meaning of the verb *bring* in Hebrew is a case in point: Initiated by Yoav (10), it develops as a lesson in the semantic components of *bring* as opposed to *give*.

---

[8]During interviews with the Israeli parents, children's lack of gender differentiation in the use of numbers was universally mentioned as an example for the type of incorrect usage the parents felt needed to be corrected.

[9]The comment in turn 37 draws on a cultural presupposition (that the Likud is known to attract the Sephardic vote) to offer a sociolinguistic explanation to a case of incorrect grammatical usage, in essence claiming that choosing (or not choosing) to speak correctly is a strategic move meant to mark political and ethnic identity.

Metalinguistic discourse further occasions language socialization in cases where the issue concerns the use of foreign words. At one level, this type of discourse is again related to the fact that Modern Hebrew is a revived language that borrows heavily from other languages (currently mainly from English) yet also constantly coins new words in Hebrew. Many loaned lexical items in use have a Hebrew equivalent (coined most frequently by the Academy of Language), and a current metalinguistic practice in family situations and elsewhere is to appear knowledgeable by reminding others of the Hebrew term. For instance, talk about the best way to prepare chocolate mousse includes a comment on the Hebrew term for mousse ("You want to know in Hebrew? Mousse is *kcifa*"). This type of talk represents the purist attitude, which objects to borrowing and prefers the Hebrew term.

Talk about commonly used borrowed terms that have an equivalent term in Hebrew may also turn into an elaborate discussion of the concepts involved:

(29) Israelis 2; Shlomit (12f); Yoash (a guest).

1	Yoash:	ma she-nir'a li she-ken, be-eze muvan ze paxot prominenti.	What I do think is that in some way it's less prominent.
2	Shlomit:	ma ze prominenti?	What's "*prominenti*"?
3	Yoash:	paxot bolet, klomar ze davar lo murgash.	Less striking, that is it's something not noticeable.

When a "what's x?" question about a foreign word is posed by a child, it might be interpreted metalinguistically, as requiring a translation equivalent, or conceptually, as requiring an explanation. Example 29 is typical of the way in which adults tend to respond to both aspects: Yoash, a guest at the dinner table, provides the Hebrew equivalent for the phrase with the foreign word ("less striking") and goes on to supply a clarification of the concept involved ("that is it's something not noticeable"). In the next example, the search for the exact Hebrew equivalent of "dilemma" leads to an extended discussion on the semantics of a whole set of related terms, including "problem" [*beaya*], "vacillation" [*hitlabtut*], "possibility" [*efsharut*], and "question" [*she'ela*].

(33) Israelis 7; Na'ama (16f); Tomer (12m); Gil (10m).

1	Na'ama:	ani be-dilema.	I have a dilemma.
2	Tomer:	ma ze dilema?	What's "a dilemma"?
3	Mother:	dilema ze ba'aya. ba'aya ve-hitlabtut ben kama efsharuyot.	A dilemma is a problem. A problem and vacillation about several possibilities.

4	Na'ama:	ze ma she-haya hayom be-talmud, tomer.	That's what there was today in Talmud, Tomer.
%	comment:	[Referring to a lesson in Talmud on the educational channel of the Israeli Television].	
5	Mother:	be-derex klal ben shte efsharuyot, aval yaxol gam yoter, naxon? dilema.	Usually it's between two possibilities, but you can have more, right? A dilemma.
6	Na'ama:	dilema zo ba'aya. dilema, ha-tirgum shel ze ba'aya.	A dilemma is a problem. *dilemma*, the translation would be "problem."
7	Mother:	ken? ze ba'aya? lo hitlabtut?	Really? It's a "problem"? Not "vacillation"?
8	Na'ama:	gam hitlabtut aval yoter. lo ki ba'aya, ki ba'aya +...	"Vacillation" too, but more. No because "problem" +...
9	Observer:	dilema zo lo ba'aya.	A "dilemma" is not a "problem."
10	Mother:	problema ze ba'aya.	*problema* is a problem.
11	Na'ama:	aval ima, ba'aya ha-hesber shel ze ze efsharut shel bxira ben shte draxim o yoter. az im dilema ze gam kaxa, az dilema ze ba'aya.	But, mom, problem the explanation is having the option to choose between two ways or more. So if that's a dilemma, then *dilemma* is "problem."
12	Mother:	ba'aya ze lav davka efsharut shel bxira ben shte draxim.	A problem is not necessarily the option of choosing between two things.
13	Na'ama:	ben shte draxim o yoter, ken.	Between two things or more, yes.
14	Mother:	ulay be-txum mesuyam, be-maxshevim o mashehu kaze. ba'aya ze lav davka, ba'aya ze yaxol lihiyot be-kol mine +...	Maybe in a particular field, computers or something like that. A problem is not necessarily, a problem can be in all kinds +...
15	Na'ama:	ben shte efsharuyot, shte efsharuyot klaliyot.	Between two options, two general options.
16	Observer:	ulay yesh rak efsharut	Maybe there is only one

		axat ve-at lo yoda'at. ha-pitaron hu ulay rak exad.	option and you don't know. There may be only one solution.
17	Na'ama:	lo pitaron she-yesh lo, ulay pitaron exad. ze she'ela yoter kshe-yesh xxx. ze haya hayom be-talmud, hisbiru et ze.	Not the solution, maybe there's one solution, it's more a question when you have xxx. It was mentioned today in Talmud, they explained it.
18	Mother:	be-talmud? ba-televizya?	In Talmud? On T.V.?
19	Na'ama:	she'ela ze kshe-yesh pitaron exad.	A question is when there is one answer.
20	Mother:	bifne ze ani nixna'at.	To that I surrender.
21	Na'ama:	ima tishmei, she'ela ze pitaron exad she-lo yod'im oto, ve-ba'aya ze kama pitronot she-carix livxor benehem.	Mom, listen. A question is when you have one answer which you don't know, and a problem is when you have several solutions that you have to choose from.

@End.

Discussions of word meanings do not necessarily concern foreign words only. For example, in trying to reassure her teenage daughter that she is not too slim, the mother in Family 7 states "you are not thin," using a distorted version of an expression (*shxif* instead of *shaxif*) unknown to the daughter. The word used originally meant "a thin board," but it is used figuratively to denote an exceptionally thin person. The adults, unaware of the origin of the word, attempt to explain it first by providing a definition ("somebody with the skin hanging with no fat") and an incorrect etymology ("it comes from tuberculosis") then by differentiating it from expressions with a similar sound pattern ("like *shaduf*") and finally by suggesting familiar collocations ("thin bones"). Though from a linguistic point of view the exchange fails to provide a satisfactory account of the origins and exact meaning of the word, it is noteworthy as an illustration of the amount of interest matters of language can raise in Israeli families.[10]

---

[10]The historical origin of the word *shaxif* is not clear. It certainly is not connected to either of the words, evoked probably because of their sound patterns, *shaxefet* [tuberculosis] or *shaduf* [withered]. The original idiomatic expression, derived from *shaxif*, is *sxif ec* [thin board] used to denote a thin person. In the conversation it gets confused with the Aramaic expression *shxiv mera* [dying person]. The two other variation mentioned, *shaxuf* and *sxuf*, are nonce words, made up on the spur of the moment.

(31) Israelis 7; Na'ama (16f); Gil (10m).

1	Mother:	at lo shxif, aval at beseder. at behexlet nir'et beseder.	You're not a *shxif*, but you're okay. You definitely look okay.
2	Gil:	ma ze shxif?	What's a *shxif*?
3	Mother:	shxif ze mishehu "Shxif" she-ha-or taluy al ha-acamot bli basar.	is someone whose skin hangs on his bones with no flesh.
4	Observer:	ze ba mi-shaxefet.	It comes from *shaxefet* (tuberculosis).
5	Mother:	ani lo xoshevet she-ze ba mi-shaxefet. shaxuf, naxon?	I don't think it comes from *shaxefet*. *shaxuf*, right?
6	Gil:	ma ze shaxuf?	What's *shaxuf*?
7	Mother:	shaxuf ze +. . . lo? *en* mila kazo?	*shaxuf* is +. . . No? There is *no* such word?
8	Na'ama:	yesh shaduf.	There's *shaduf* (withered).
9	Mother:	[laughs] lo, aval yesh kmo shaduf, shaxuf.	No, but there is like *shaduf, shaxuf*.
10	Na'ama:	yesh shaduf.	*shaduf* exists.
11	Mother:	shxif, lo, ze shxiv me-ra. shxif acamot, nu.	*shxif* no, it's *shxif mera* (dying). *shxif acamot* (a bag of bones).
12	Observer:	ken?	Really?
13	Mother:	shxif acamot, shxif, shxif acmo, ze lo meshane she-ze ulay kashur.	Bag of bones, *shxif* itself, doesn't matter that it may be connected.
14	Observer:	ulay et ha-shaxefet kar'u al ze?	Maybe they called tuberculosis (*shaxefet*) because of it?
15	Mother:	ulay et ha-shaxefet. bediyuk. ulay be-le-hefex me-ha-shxif.	Maybe the tuberculosis. Exactly. Maybe the other way around, from [the word] *shxif*.
16	Na'ama:	nu, az ma?	Well, so what?
	[continued]		

Talk about language may also relate to sociopragmatics—for example, the way "others" (non-natives or other cultures) use language. As the next example shows, Israelis are sensitive to ways of speaking that deviate from native norms:

(32) Israelis 5; Yoav (10m).

1	Father:	kol davar ele	Everything all those
		ha-amerikaim bixlal,	Americans,
		superlativim kaele.	superlatives like that.
		hakol "fantastik"	Everything is "fantastic"
		ve-"gorjes." anaxnu	and "gorgeous." We
		korim lahem "gorjesim."	call them "gorgeouses."
2	Yoav:	be-mivta ivri.	In an Israeli accent.

The American Israeli Bilingual Speakers. A close look at the metalinguistic comments made in the bilingual families reveals several unique features. First, although clarifying word meanings to children is a favorite pasttime, in these families it is carried out in a multilingual fashion. Both Hebrew and English words may be explained in the language in which the query was made ("What's garlic? It's a spice") or explained and translated, with the degree of translational equivalence between items in a given semantic field becoming the topic of lengthy discussions. For example, a 13-year-old's test question (Heath, 1983) to her 5-year-old sister, "What is *oger* [hamster], Naomi, do you know?" sets in motion a discussion of the biological differences between a hamster and a guinea pig, combined with the linguistic quest for the Hebrew names of these animals (Olshtain & Blum-Kulka, 1989).

Word meaning queries in these families serve different functions for adults and children. Children's queries concern the meaning of English words or ask for equivalents between the two languages.

(36) American Israelis 4; Ruth (12f).

1	Ruth:	What are physicists {*fisikaim*?}?
2	Mother:	Yes.

The mother confirms that "fisikaim," a phonological loan translation, is indeed the equivalent of "physicists."

(37) American Israelis 4; Ruth (12f).

1	Ruth:	How do you say {*soter*}, aba?
2	Father:	Contradictory.

The adults, on the other hand, rely on their children's Hebrew expertise to clarify the meaning of Hebrew words:

(38) American Israelis 6; David (15m).

   1   Father: What's {*kraza*}?
   2   David: Poster.

Code switching is the topic of another language game. One the one hand, on many occasions code switching goes unnoticed, as in the exchange concerning a request for fish (Example 22), where a child, speaking Hebrew, is prompted (successfully) in English to use a politeness marker. On the other hand, differing from Gumperz' (1982) findings that show bilingual speakers to be unaware of the language they are speaking, we found indications that our bilingual speakers are aware of actually *using a hybrid language variety*, one that draws on both languages. This variety is alternatively referred to as "Hibbish" or "Hebrish" as exemplified in the following exchanges:

(39) American Israelis 2; Eran (8m); Mira (6f).

   1   Eran: (to sister) You're talking gibberish.
   2   Father: Hibbish
   3   Eran: Oh, ya.

A few minutes later, Eran comments on his mother code switching from English to Hebrew:

(40) American Israelis 2; Eran (8m).

   1   Eran: Those two words, {*ima*}[Mom], were in Hebrish.
   2   Mother: You're right. I changed in the middle.

The language game at work is one of naming: By trying to find an appropriate label for their own mixed dialect, these families are indicating their high degree of linguistic self-awareness.

Metalinguistic awareness allows for self-directed humor:

(41) American Israelis 3; Etan (9m); Noam (6m).

   1   Father: Noam, show Marit (the observer) how you speak Hebrew with an American accent.
   2   Noam: {*lo*} (no).
   3   Observer: Yes, please.
   4   Noam: What?
   5   Father: Say something like when you imitate Mommy and me like {*ani raiti*} (=I saw).

6 Noam: {aba amar pa'am "hatarnejol"} (Daddy once said
"*hatarnejol*"—replacing /j/ for /g/ in
pronouncing the Hebrew word for rooster).

The children's high proficiency in Hebrew can also lead to a power game. After being reassured by his parents that he speaks both English and Hebrew well, a child criticizes his mother's Hebrew. Sister and father alike find the comment face-threatening, to the extent that the father feels it necessary to come to the mother's defense:

(42) American Israelis 2; Eran (8m); Mira (6f).

1	Eran:	ani samti lev, ima, et hatauyot shelax ksheat koret li mixtavim ve-hakol, at koret li im tauyot, bli mivta ivrit.	I've noticed your mistakes, Mom, when you read me letters and stuff, you read to me with mistakes, without a Hebrew accent.
2	Mira:	It's not nice to say that.	
3	Mother:	I really am pretty bad.	
4	Father:	But actually that's not true, Eran. There are some words that you know, but I think there are still some things that {ima} (Mother) can express more clearly, even in Hebrew.	
5	Eran:	I know {aba} (Daddy), except I am better in reading and talking in Hebrew.	

Finally, the awareness of code switching is combined with ambivalent feelings toward the benefits of such practices.

(43) American Israelis 12; Yael (8f); Yoash (12m).

1	Interviewer:	ma atem medabrim babayit bederex klal? anglit?	What do you usually speak at home? English?
2	Father:	We try to speak English xxx.	
3	Yael:	We talk part English and part Hebrew xxx. ani kmo medaberet nagid be-emca ha-mishpat ani osa, overet me-anglit le-ivrit ve-me-ivrit le-anglit.	 I like talk say in the middle of the sentence I make, I switch from English to Hebrew and from Hebrew to English.
4	Father:	As a matter of fact, I have been puzzling	

<table>
<tr><td></td><td></td><td>over it for the last year. I used to think it was cute when they mixed the sentences together.</td></tr>
<tr><td>5</td><td>Mother:</td><td>I still think it's cute. I do it.</td></tr>
<tr><td>6</td><td>Father:</td><td>I don't. I think it's bad for their Hebrew and their English, so I fuss at them for the last year now, "Speak either English or Hebrew but not the two of them together."</td></tr>
</table>

CONCLUSION

Metapragmatic discourse is a powerful resource of pragmatic socialization in all families. The "discourse world" (cf. Scollon & Scollon, 1995) of the family is particularly rich in talk about talk. Through metapragmatic discourse families index and construct their attitudes to discourse management, conversational norms, and language. All the families share a set of conversational norms that is expressed in reaction to perceived violations of these norms. Insistence on factuality, informativeness, relevance, clarity, and politeness in discourse tie all the families to the wider secular rationality of the discourse world(s) of Western modernity. I return to this argument in the concluding chapter (Chapter 8) to show the manifold manifestations of the impact of modernity on all the families studied.

However, the metapragmatic discourse of the groups also differs in several respects. The norms of discourse management figure high in the conversational values emphasized in the Jewish American families. We find here a heightened awareness of the systematics of turn-taking, an awareness probably linked to American respect for fair play and individualism as well as to the prominence of ritualistic aspects of performance in American discourse. The corollary in the Israeli families is found in metalinguistic talk; for historical reasons, language figures in these families as the most salient feature of metapragmatic discourse. The American Israeli families occupy an interim position in this and in many other dimensions of discourse; their unique intercultural interactional style, realized through bilingual usage, is the subject of the next chapter.

7

BILINGUAL SOCIALIZATION: THE INTERCULTURAL STYLE OF AMERICAN ISRAELI FAMILIES

In this chapter I discuss the discourse of the American Israeli families from two points of view: bilingualism and interlanguage. As has been seen, particularly in the metapragmatic discourse discussed in Chapter 6, for American Israeli families bilingualism is an active social practice. All members of the family are competent English–Hebrew bilinguals, and all alternate freely between the two languages during dinner. There are several questions that need to be answered in regard to bilingualism. What goes on in this kind of interaction generally? Do parents and children differ in their preferences for Hebrew or English and in their switching behavior? Is there uniformity among the families in their language choice? Is there evidence in the interactions that parents are promoting the maintenance of English? If so, do children collaborate with their parents in this maintenance?[1] Interestingly, the issue of interlanguage arises in this context with regard to a native language spoken by an immigrant community, namely English. Our findings show that at least in its pragmatic aspects, the English spoken in the homes of the American Israeli families differs from (but is influenced by) both native American English and native Israeli Hebrew. In other words, I argue that the

[1]Permission to use data from Brenda Kurland (1992) in this chapter is gratefully acknowledged. Kurland's study on language choice and language mixing in the project's American Israeli families was carried out at Harvard University as an Honors Thesis for the Department of Psychology for the Degree of Bachelor of Arts under joint supervison of Catherine Snow and myself during my sabbatical at Harvard during 1990–1991. A paper based on this project, entitled "Language Maintenance and Accommodation: Two Processes in Code Switching Behavior," by Kurland, Blum-Kulka, and Snow, was presented by Catherine Snow at the 1993 AILA conference in Amsterdam.

discourse style that emerges realizes features of a first-language-based interlanguage.

Issues of code switching and language maintenance have been widely described and discussed but are rarely linked. Issues of language maintenance tend to be discussed from a historical perspective, with reference to the processes of language shift and language attrition of whole communities in situations of language contact (e.g., Fishman, 1985; Gal, 1979; Weinreich, 1953). In the case of immigrant communities, the prevalent pattern is a total shift to the dominant language in the course of two to four generations (Hamers & Blanc, 1989; Sharwood-Smith, 1983; Weltens, 1987) with a few exceptions (Heredia-Deprez, 1990). Only in specific cases of self-imposed symbolic or geographic boundaries do communities continue to maintain the native tongue, as in the case of the Poles and Greeks in Australia (Clyne, 1982) and of Hasidic Jewish communities in Israel, where Yiddish is the dominant spoken language of the community and parents may send their children to Yiddish-speaking schools (El Or, 1990). For children of immigrant parents, bilingualism is the exception rather than the rule. For example, Saville-Troike and her colleagues (Saville-Troike, 1994; Saville-Troike & Kleigfen, 1986) found that in the United States, children who emigrated from other countries at the age of 3 acquired productive dominance in English within two years and at the age of 6 could hardly speak their native tongue, even in homes where the parents continued to speak the native language.

In Israel, speaking good Hebrew is regarded as a sign of successful acculturation (labeled in Hebrew "klita," meaning "absorption") and the general language policy of the State has been to encourage the universal use of Hebrew by immigrants, even if this means abandoning the minority language (Gold, 1989). Ben Rafael's (1994) recent field studies among several Ashkenazi groups in Israel reveal, for example, that despite strong aspiration in the immigrant generation to retain their languages of origin, in all cases enduring speech communities have failed to emerge. The second generation speaks principally Hebrew, and the third is totally Hebraised. Strongly motivated by Zionist ideology, which sees in the revival of Hebrew a cornerstone to national identity (Harshav, 1990, 1993), Israel has no heritage language programs (like Canada) or bilingual education programs (like Wales), and all institutional support is channeled into the teaching of Hebrew to new immigrants. Against this background, the successful maintenance of English by the American Israeli families is an exception to the norm. There are several external facilitating factors for this situation, such as the prestige of English as an international language and the instrumental, educational, and social gains associated with high English proficiency in a society where "the mastery of English constitutes a genuine marker of privileged class positions" (Ben Rafael, 1994, p. 128). To understand the success of this process we need to consider how the actual bilingual discourse of the families promotes bilingualism as a goal of language socialization.

As elaborated in this chapter, both the choice of language and conversational code switching in American Israeli families are geared towards bilingualism. Conversational code switching has been studied in a wide variety of languages in contact situations, mostly in naturally occurring, unstructured interactions between participants of symmetrical power relations. The linguistic tradition in code switching studies (e.g., Berk-Seligson, 1986; Pfaff, 1979; Poplack, 1988) typically focuses on the syntactic position of switches and the linguistic constraints on the coexistence of two varieties within a sentence. Such analyses are carried out from the point of view of one focused speaker, the target subject, and ignore the dynamics of the interaction as a whole. Our analysis follows in the tradition of anthropological and sociolinguistic perspectives on code switching (e.g., Auer, 1988; Gumperz, 1982; Halmari & Smith, 1994; Mashler, 1994; Scotton, 1988, 1990) that consider the wider social context, including the value placed on the two languages involved and the social and discourse functions achievable through switching.

However, the situation described here differs from that of previous studies in several respects. The speech event under consideration is a relatively structured, commonly occurring interaction between participants of unequal power. Moreover, the parents, who obviously have more power within the family than the children, revealed during interviews that they view English as the home language and expressed clear desires regarding maintenance of their children's English. Hence, patterns of language choice and code switching are examined against a background in which bilingualism is a socially valued goal for the parents, who are highly motivated to promote the use of English by the children. Still, English is not universally used: All the participants—typically children and guests—occasionally show a preference for Hebrew. The parents' desire to promote English might, at certain points in an interaction, clash with their wish to maintain sociability and friendly, nurturant family interactions.

To account for the mechanisms needed to achieve such opposing goals, I consider code switches not only from the perspective of the single speaker (i.e., who switches to which language and to whom?) but also in terms of the dynamics of the entire interaction. This approach takes into account two perspectives on code switching, that of the **speaker** (e.g., whether he or she shifted languages within a turn or from his or her previous turn) and that of the **floor** (i.e., if a change in the language of the conversation has occurred). Incorporating the floor perspective broadens the definition of code switching beyond that traditionally applied.

The second point of view brought to bear on these bilingual conversations is that of interlanguage pragmatics. Traditionally, interlanguage pragmatics is concerned with the difficulties of second language learners in acquiring the pragmatic system of the target language (e.g., Kasper & Blum-Kulka, 1993). The comparison of the discourse patterns of the American

Israeli families with those of the two other groups reveals that *interlanguage pragmatics can also be realized in the first language*. In effect, for bilinguals in conditions of twofold cultural contact, pragmatics is the first area affected by exposure to the sociocultural influence of the second language.

The bilingual families we studied are in contact with two incongruent pragmatic systems, each realized by a culturally specific style of language use. The possibility of a two-way interference under such conditions was recognized by Weinreich (1953): "Those instances of deviation from the norms of either language which occur in the speech of bilinguals as a result of their familiarity with more than one language, i.e., as a result of language contact, will be referred to as interference phenomena" (p. 1). I demonstrate that, as implied by Weinrich, language contact creates bidirectional effects, from the first language to the second and vice versa, not only for specific language and discourse phenomena (e.g., Clyne, 1982) but as the organizing principle for the pragmatic system of the language variety used.

FAMILY BACKGROUND AND PATTERNS OF ACCULTURATION

The parents in the families studied were all born in the United States and lived in Israel for more than 9 years at the time of the study. Most of the children (16 of 29) were born in Israel and had not spent more than a month or two in an English-speaking environment. Six of the children had spent 2 years abroad, and two had spent 5. Of the four children born in the United States, two moved to Israel at the age of one; another moved at the age of 4½.

All members of the families are competent English–Hebrew bilinguals. Although Hebrew has unquestionably become the dominant language for the children, English plays an important role. To varying degrees English is spoken in all the homes, though it is often mixed with Hebrew. Adults and children alike practice their bilingualism not only in speaking (speaking English at home and Hebrew at work and at school) but also in reading. All the adults report reading in English for pleasure, and 13 of the 14 school-age children report reading in both languages.

During the ethnographic interviews with the families, all parents expressed a strong desire to foster their children's bilingualism by maintaining English in the home. The maintenance of English is considered important for both practical and symbolic reasons: Parents are aware that a high level of proficiency in English is an asset for academic achievement (providing an advantage in school, where English is taught as a foreign language and is extremely important for success in higher education), and they recognize the high status of English in Israel, as elsewhere (Ben Rafael, 1994; Fishman,

Cooper, & Conrad, 1977; Gold, 1989). As in the case of mother-tongue maintenance in all immigrant communities, socializing children in the parents'
mother tongue also means preserving across the generations family ties with
parts of the family who did not immigrate, as well as providing the children
with first-hand access to the culture their parents were brought up in.

The families' active bilingualism goes hand in hand with their maintenance of a bicultural social reality. The families maintain in practice and in
attitude close contact with two languages and two cultures and therefore
are exposed to two systems of pragmatic and discourse rules. Of course,
there is individual variation among the families, with some showing a higher
degree of "convergence" (Giles, 1979) with the Israeli culture than others.
However, as illustrated by the two following extreme cases on the convergence continuum in our sample, even the least American family in the group
maintains an intimate link with the language and cultural heritage of its
country of origin. Consider the cases of the Bells (Family 6) and the Darnos
(Family 12).

The Bells represent the Anglophone extreme of our bilingual continuum.
They have chosen to live in a Jerusalem neighborhood known for its density
of Americans and Canadians. They claim that at least on the street they live,
English is the dominant language even for the children. Indeed, during the
interview I was surprised to detect a trace of an American accent in the
Hebrew speech of their Israeli-born, 8-year-old daughter. At work, the husband uses only Hebrew (at a very advanced level, given his occupation); at
home, only English. As an instructor of English, the wife speaks English in
most of her professional and private lives. The family spends most summers
in the United States, and all the children are balanced Hebrew–English
bilinguals. In line with the general language policy of English maintenance
in the family, conversation at mealtime was dominantly (96%) English.

Whereas the Bells invest familial effort in preserving English, the Darnos
vacillate between a desire to raise their children as bilingual speakers and
the equally strong desire to acculturate to the Hebrew-dominant Israeli
culture. They mainly, but not entirely, speak English at home and Hebrew
at school and work. For the children, Hebrew is the preferred and unquestionably the better-known language; their English is more advanced than
that of their peers, but it still remains definitely a second language. For the
parents, mastering Hebrew to the degree that would allow them to read
literature in Hebrew presented a challenge within the family context. Thus,
the father worked through all his son's literature assignments from high
school, a process he considered extremely beneficial for his own acculturation. Yet despite the strong emphasis on acculturation to Hebrew, the conversation at mealtime still preserved English 70% of the time.

Both of these families, like all the families studied, show ties to the
community of American Israeli immigrants. The parents reported that many

of their friends are fellow Americans, and, in fact, phone calls received during mealtimes tended to be from other English speakers.

THE SOCIAL PRACTICE OF BILINGUALISM

In Israel, as in the United States—countries where minority languages are not valorized—the most common pattern is for the second generation of immigrants to make the language of the majority the dominant one, with varying degrees of first-language proficiency, and for the third generation to show a complete shift to the language of the majority (Ben-Rafael, 1994; Bratt-Paulston, 1986). Interviews with the parents of the families in the United States and Israel show this pattern for Yiddish: In the United States, Yiddish was spoken in the home of the first-generation immigrants, our subjects' grandparents, was known but less used by their parents, and was rarely known and never used at home by our subjects. The Israeli families, as second generation to immigrant parents, remember their parents speaking Yiddish and other languages (e.g., Russian, Polish) at home, but even if they know these languages, they never use them with their own children (see Appendix B for a summary of languages spoken over two family generations).

There are, of course, exceptions to this pattern, as when a minority group exercises self-imposed boundary maintenance (e.g., the Yiddish spoken by Hassidic groups in Israel; El Or, 1990) or maintains a native tongue due to social or geographic isolation (i.e., Gaelic in the Hebrides). In diglossic situations, bilingualism prevails but the two languages are distinguished functionally (e.g., Guarani and Spanish in Paraquay; Bratt-Paulston, 1986).

Against this background, the active bilingualism of the American Israeli families deserves special attention. These families succeed in socializing their children for additive, balanced bilingualism in a social environment that, as in the United States, ideologically has strongly favored shift and attrition. It has been shown that in such settings young immigrant children are much more likely to lose or fail to develop native language skills fully even when parents continue to speak the native language at home (Ben-Rafael, 1994; Saville-Troike, 1994). Most children in the families studied were born in Israel; however, despite the pressures of the Hebrew environment, the families succeed in providing support for dual-language development.

Choice of Language

Kurland (1992) examined the patterns of language choice and code switching in a 20-minute segment of one dinnertime conversation in eight of the families in the project. The findings showed variation between the families in the use of English. The rate of English used varies by family from 30% to 96%, with five of the families using it more than half the time (see Fig. 7.1).

The division of English use according to the speaker's role and the addressee (see Table 7.1) also shows the importance of English. English is the dominant language used by the parents to all the other speakers (76%) and is used by the children more than half the time (56%). The guests (observers and friends) use much less English than the family members (36%).

The parents are the main promoters of English: They speak it almost exclusively to each other (97%), and it is their dominant language in speaking to their children (86%, with a range of 78% to 100%). The fact that this is a matter of choice, not necessity—that it is not due to lack of Hebrew skills—can be seen in the lower proportions of English used to address all other participants present (73%) and in speaking to the outsiders (49%). The parents clearly prefer English but use Hebrew as well. There is no gender difference, with mothers and fathers using an equal percentage of English.

The parents' success in socializing their children to bilingualism can be seen in the way children vary their language choices according to addressee. In addressing all participants and guests, Hebrew is preferred (only 23% to 35% English). In the speech among children, English is used half the time (51%), and, most important, it *is the dominant language in speech to parents* (81%, with a range of 10% to 96% by individual child). This finding is opposed to the more common type of pattern described by Harding-Riley (1986), who found that as the children of immigrant parents grew older, they refused more and more to speak their parents' native language.

The outsiders present at dinner included friends of the children (at two meals). Both were teenagers, one an American Israeli and the other a native Israeli. The observers present (at all meals) in four families were native (bilingual) Israelis, with a preference for Hebrew; in four others were (bilin-

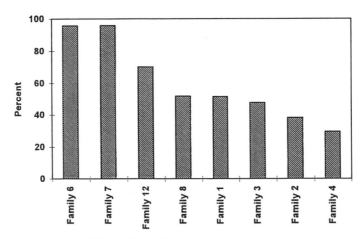

FIG. 7.1. Percent English used in 8 families.

TABLE 7.1
Language Choice: Mean Percentage of English
Spoken by Speaker and Addressee Roles

	Addressee									
	Parent		Child		Guest		All		Total	
Speaker	%	(s.d.)	%	(s.d.)	%	(s.d.)	%	(s.d.)	%	(s.d.)
Parent n = 2,086	96.8	(7.8)	86.1	(13.7)	49.3	(40.7)	73	(28.8)	75.9	(21.8)
Child n = 1,714	80.5	(14.9)	56	(30.5)	23.5	(36.4)	34.9	(32.4)	55.4	(23.7)
Guest n = 1,025	44	(45.6)	32	(45.4)	0.6	(1.3)	40.8	(46.3)	36	(42.5)

Note. Based on 30 minutes of one meal in eight American Israeli families.

gual) American Israelis with a preference for English.[2] The video technicians, present at four meals, were all Israelis but participated negligibly in the talk. The outsiders spoke less English than the family members; 41% to 45% of the time when they addressed the parents or all present, and 33% of the time when they addressed the children.

Because the families live in a Hebrew-speaking environment, having Israeli Hebrew-speaking dinner guests is common and might be expected to affect the choice of language. Indeed, variation among the families in mean rate of English use is affected by the perceived and actual language preferences of the guests, particularly of the observers. In the four families where the observers preferred to speak Hebrew, English was spoken only 44% of the time, whereas in families where the observers preferred English, English was spoken 74% of the time. However, these language preferences do not fully account for the variations found. For example, Sarah, one of the observers, an American Israeli who admits to mixing languages in her own home, observed Families 12 and 8. She used a similar rate of English in both (55% of the time in 8, 56% in 12), yet in Family 12 the overall rate of English was considerably higher (70%) than in 8 (52%). Similarly, in the families (2, 3, and 4) observed by Marit, who preferred Hebrew, the rate of English varied from 30% to 48%.

In the four families with lower than 52% rates of English (Families 1, 2, 3, and 4), the rates derive from interactions between the outsiders and members of

---

[2]During initial interviews with the families, several told us they use both English and Hebrew at home and asked which language we would prefer them to speak during the recorded meal. The answer was "speak as you do normally." When we realized that the language preference of the observer might be a factor, we chose bilingual observers with varying degrees of English or Hebrew dominance.

the family, *not* from interactions between the parents and the children. Parents address English-speaking guests in English 87% of the time, but the rate of English drops to 12% when they address guests who seem to prefer Hebrew. Children follow similar patterns of accommodation to the language of the guest, but *the language preference of the guests does not affect the language choices in parent–child interactions*. Even in the presence of Hebrew-speaking guests (in Families 1 to 4), parents still prefer to speak English to their children (77%) and children prefer to speak English to their parents (80%). Thus, the patterns of language choice among parents and children remain constant, regardless of the language preference of the guests.

The interviews help to place these findings in a wider perspective. There is no exception to the expressed desire to maintain English in the home and raise the children as bilinguals. To this end, all the parents read English story books to their children when young and try to speak English to the children (although some are aware of mixing the two languages). Simultaneously, for the parents mastering Hebrew is seen as an important symbol of accultura-tion. Several went to Jewish schools abroad and learned some Hebrew before coming to Israel; many participated in the intensive 5-month Hebrew courses (*Ulpan*) provided for new immigrants. Parents and children alike emphasized in our interviews that the choice of language at any particular social event in the family is affected by the language preferences of the guests.

Happy Hebrish: Familial Codes of Mixing and Switching

As evidenced by the metalinguistic comments of the families studied (Chapter 6), the bilingual proficiency of all family members allows them to draw freely on the two languages at any point in a conversation. Furthermore, our bilingual speakers are aware that they speak a hybrid language variety, referred to as "Hibbish" or "Hebrish" (see Examples 40 and 41 in Chapter 6).

The interviews with the families show that awareness of code switching and mixing is combined with ambivalent feelings toward the benefits of such practices:

(1) American Israelis 12; Yoash (12m); Yael (8f).

1	Interviewer:	ma atem medabrim ba-bayit bederex klal? anglit?	What do you usually speak at home? English?
2	Father:	We try to speak English xxx.	
3	Yael:	We talk part English and part Hebrew xxx. ani kmo medaberet nagid be-emca ha-mishpat ani osa, overet me-anglit	I like talk say in the middle of the sentence I make, I switch from English

		le-ivrit ve-me-ivrit le-anglit.	to Hebrew and from Hebrew to English.
4	Father:	As a matter of fact, I have been puzzling over it for the last year. I used to think it was cute when they mixed the sentences together.	
5	Mother:	I still think it's cute. I do it.	
6	Father:	I don't. I think it's bad for their Hebrew and their English, so I fuss at them for the last year now, speak either English or Hebrew but not the two of them together.	

This exchange shows two of the norms that govern bilingual usage during mealtimes. A question asked in one language may be answered in another, as in the case of the father's English response to the question asked in Hebrew, and a speaker may switch languages within a turn, as formulated (and practiced) by Yael in turn 3. The prerequisite for mutual comprehensibility in such bilingual conversations is the high proficiency of all family members in both languages. Its social implication is in creating familial codes unique to American Israeli bilingual families.

In a previous paper, we defined language contact in practice as taking two basic forms (Olshtain & Blum-Kulka, 1989): **mixing**, the insertion of a linguistic element from language B within the clause boundaries of language A, and **switching**, a shift from language A to B (or vice versa) minimally involving a clause.

Mixing

Inserting Hebrew words into English sentences is more common than inserting English into Hebrew. In the parents' speech in English, 11% of the utterances contain a Hebrew element; in the children's English speech, the rate of mixes rises to 16%. Mixes of English into Hebrew sentences are much less frequent for parents (6%) and negligible for children (1.5%).

Most of the mixes involve noun phrases (77% to 91%); the next categories, for all speakers, are adverbs (2% to 11%) and discourse markers (2% to 7%). Only the children also mix verbs (2%). The following conversation between parents illustrates how mixing can be interwoven in the discourse to a point that makes mutual comprehensibility wholly dependent on a knowledge of the two languages.

(2) American Israelis 3; Etan (9m); Noam (6m).

	1	Mother:	We're making a {kaytana} [summer camp] in {bituach leumi} [(the institute of) Social Security] in July # # for fifty to a hundred kids.

2 Father: Why not with the <{*ovdey medina*}> [state
             employees]?
3 Mother: <We're also having that> [<]. We're also having it
             for {*ovdey medina*}, but there are so many workers
             that we're interested in some kind of {*sidur*}
             [arrangement] for July.
4 Father: {*ovdey medina*} is when? From July?
5 Mother: The 30th of July to 19th of August.
6 Father: Why {*davka*} [especially] the second month?
7 Mother: They always do it the second month because usually
             the first month there are all kinds of {*kaytanot*}
             [summer camps] from xxx.
8 Father: xxx?
9 Mother: Yeah and this year they have {*kaytanot*} in the
             {*matnas*} [Community Center] but not in the schools.
10 Father: xxx {*kaytanot*}[3] xxx?
11 Mother: Pardon me?
12 Father: They'll be able to set up a {*kaytana*} for our
             workers also soon.
13 Mother: Yeah.
14 Father: *tuxlu la'asot xayim* [You'll be able to have fun].
15 Mother: It'll inspire you to hire yourself new workers.

The inserted Hebrew elements are like cultural pegs; they seem to point
to islands of acculturation, to domains in the immigrant's life in Israel, which
by virtue of being unique to the Israeli experience cannot be labeled in
anything but Hebrew. Several such unique institutions are mentioned in
Example 2—the speakers refer to summer camps, community centers, and
State employees only by their Hebrew names. Such patterns for language
mix in the bilingual families repeat the pattern for mixing that has been
noted in other immigrant communities, as, for example, the case of Mexican
Americans (Huerta-Macias, 1981) who speak Spanish in the home but tend
to use English words with English-speaking contexts. Other typical contexts
associated with the Israeli experience are schooling (e.g., nursery schools,
teachers, the Ministry of Education, reading comprehension, and various

---

[3]*Kaytanot* is the plural form (with the addition of the suffix -*ot*) of the word *kaytana*. In this
instance the speaker respects the free morpheme constraint proposed by Poplack (1980),
namely that a mix cannot take place between the stem of a word and its affix (bound morpheme)
unless the stem has been phonologically integrated. The conversations contain many other
cases where this constraint is not respected; thus, the same speaker forms the plural of the
word *ganenet* [nursery school teacher] once in accordance with Hebrew morphology as *gananot*
and once with the English -*s* (*ganenets*). Similarly, speakers form the plural of *kartiv* [popsicle]
both as *kartivim* [popsicles] and as *kartivs*.

high-school exams are all referred to in Hebrew by everyone, even one
father who teaches English at the university level) and army experience
(including all issues of personal security). In these two domains the cultural
gap is perhaps more noticeable than in others. The following extract combines both worlds:

(3) American Israelis 8; Nira (13f); Aya (6f); Natan (5m).

 1   Mother: Daddy is in {*miluim*} [reserve duty]. He's managed
                 to have {*miluim*} so far on Natan's days so that I
                 had to do {*shmira*} [guard duty] in his {*gan*}
                 [nursery school] and now on your {*shmira*}.

School life is associated with Hebrew, even if the subject studied happens
to be English:

(4) American Israelis 1; Neta (12f); David (5m).

 1   Neta: They're going to do me a {*mivxan*} [test] in English
                 and in the {*mivxan*} they'll see I'll get {*mea*}
                 [a hundred].[4]

Example 2 contains three other features typical of mixing and switching
in these families. First, note the use of the word *sidur* by the mother. As an
action verb it literally means "arrangement,"[5] but it is typically used in
colloquial Hebrew to refer broadly to child care arrangements, as in "ein li
sidur la-yladim ba-xofesh" [I don't have an arrangement for the kids during
summer vacation]. The mix here seems motivated linguistically rather than
culturally, drawing on the resources of colloquial Hebrew for an expression
felt to be untranslatable. The use of the discourse marker *davka* (turn 6) is
an even clearer case, for *davka* represents a true lexical void in English.
Depending on the context, it can mean "especially," "exactly," or "(just)
because!" but none of these expressions captures its exact meaning.

The insertion of Hebrew discourse markers in English conversation represents the second general feature of these bilingual conversations; by
preferring Hebrew to English discourse markers the speakers seem to be
indicating that the pragmatic resources of English are insufficient and that
they must turn to Hebrew for pragmatic shades of meaning. This point is
connected with my claim (developed in the second part of this chapter) that

---

[4]There is a clear transfer effect from Hebrew in the use of the phrase "to do me [a test]"
instead of "have a test." Similarly, in Example 10, the child is translating from Hebrew when
she says "you didn't give me my present *till the birthday*."

[5]The word also has a religious use: *sidur hatfila* is the collection or arrangement of Jewish
prayers.

the language variety spoken in these families represents a case of interlanguage pragmatics realized in the first language.

The third typical feature, further elaborated in the next section, is the easy transition from language mix to language switch. In turn 14 of Example 2, the father chooses to respond in Hebrew but is answered in English. Such inter-turn "ping-ponging" is a recurring pattern among all members of the family.

A further domain that serves to anchor the families in the surrounding Hebrew-speaking environment and form a cultural link with Israeli society at large is the choice of address and reference terms for parents. Children frequently use Hebrew terms (e.g., *ima* [Mommy] and *aba* [Daddy]) for both address and reference (e.g., "ima, I finished my corn; aba said I can go.").[6] What is more remarkable is that in some instances—especially if the message is intended for a child as well as for the spouse, as in Example 5—parents borrow this usage when speaking to each other:[7]

(5) American Israelis 3;

    1   Mother: {*Aba*} what do you think? You think you can improvise a stand for his plane?[8]

Borrowings

The Hebrew terms cited so far represent diachronically a midpoint in the process of borrowing[9] in language contact situations. At one end of the

---

[6]The distribution of the kin terms used by the children as vocatives in the American Israeli families is as follows: *aba* was used 47 times, compared to *Dad* or *Daddy*, which were used only 26 times. The English and Hebrew vocatives for "mother" are more equally distributed: There are 84 occurrences of *ima* and 80 of *Mom* or *Mommy*. See Wilson and Zeitlyn (1995) for an analysis of all person-referring expressions in the project's Jewish American families.

[7]The mother's choice of *aba* here is a highly marked (and unusual) instance of mixing, which functions to target the overhearing child as the recipient of a message ostensibly addressed only to the father.

[8]The conversation about Etan's broken toy plane also includes a comment that shows grammatical interlanguage effects in bilingual usage. Talking about the plane, Etan remarks: "The one that you show me *leharkiv*" [to put together]. Etan uses a Hebrew verb form, a type of mix that appears only in children's language. Even if the Hebrew infinitive is replaced by an English one, the sentence remains ungrammatical due to the verb tense ("you show me") and the omission of "how to." Ungrammaticality is not a result of direct transfer from Hebrew because if literally translated the sentence would also be ungrammatical in Hebrew.

[9]There is considerable disagreement among researchers about the use of the terms *borrowing, mixing,* and *switching.* I am using "borrowing" here in the classical diachronic linguistic sense: the adoption of a linguistic item from one language to another, a phenomenon that by definition begins with individual usage and might eventually be codified in dictionaries. For further discussions of these issues in the context of bilingualism, see Clyne (1985), Pfaff (1979), Romaine (1989), or Scotton (1988).

borrowing continuum are borrowed terms integrated into the host language, such as, in the case of the American families, Middle Eastern food (*xumus, pita, falafel*) and references to Jewish holidays and customs (*bar mitzva, kidush, shabat*). Such borrowings are not limited to the American Israelis; they are also used by the Jewish American families in this study in the United States and might appear in the discourse of any English speaker. References to schooling and army experiences in Hebrew, on the other hand, are specific to this speech community. The systematicity of such borrowings shows them to be an integrated component of the language variety spoken by the bilingual families. At the other end of this continuum are borrowings that might typify a given family or nonce borrowings used only on one occasion.

As an example of family-specific borrowings, consider the language used by members of an American Israeli family when enacting a regular family ritual of compliments and complaints:

(6) American Israelis 1; Neta (12f); David (5m).

    Father: David, David is the {*yoshev rosh*} [chairman] so you start.

(7) Father: I have a compliment for Neta for handling her turtles.

(8) Father: I have a {*maxma'a*} [compliment] for David for handling the bonfire.

(9) Mother: And I have a {*maxma'a*} for him for going to the {*makolet*} [grocery store] so many times.

The key words of the ritual, "compliment" and "chair," have Hebrew labels, but though the Hebrew terms are used most of the time (see Examples 6, 8, and 9), they are interchangeable with the English words (see Example 7). In a similar fashion, "bonfire" is used both in English (in 8) and later in Hebrew ("David is tired because he stayed late by the {*medura*} [bonfire] last night"). It seems that for this family the speech acts of complimenting and complaining tend to be associated with the borrowed Hebrew names of these speech acts, but neither these nor other borrowings are fixed.

The last point to be noted with regard to mixing is its function in the maintenance of English. Beyond being part of the general tendency to encourage English in the home, both mixing and switching are used as strategies for promoting bilingualism. One way in which this is accomplished is through collaborative metalinguistic talk concerned with the search for translation equivalents (see Examples 36 to 40 in Chapter 6). In several instances, the establishment of the Hebrew–English parallels leads to a double learning process in which Hebrew terms are clarified for the Eng-

lish-dominant speakers (mostly the parents) and English terms are clarified
for the Hebrew-dominant speakers (mostly the children).

(10) American Israelis 6; David (15m); Irit (13f); Noa (5f).

1	Noa:	David.
2	David:	What?
3	Noa:	Now I understand why you didn't give my present to me till the birthday when [/] when the other one xxx. Now I understand because it was a guinea pig.
4	David:	Remember I told you that? Were you surprised?
5	Noa:	Yeah.
6	David:	What did you think it was going to be when you saw the big box?
7	Noa:	{oger} [a hamster].
8	Irit:	What is an {oger} Noa? # # You know?
	%comment:	There is a long pause (2.8).
9	Noa:	Radiator [/] radiator.
	%comment:	[The verb le'egor means to 'collect' and an oger xom is a heater (heat collector).
10	David:	A hamster Noa.
11	Father:	{oger}? No [/] no, it's a {shorek}.
12	Irit:	No.
13	Noa:	No.
14	Irit:	A {shorek} is a guinea pig.
15	Father:	Oh.
16	David:	Or a {xazir yam} [guinea pig], whatever.
17	Mother:	Or a &yam. What's it called?
18	Noa:	{xazir yam}.

In this example, the children use English as their means of communication
in a child–child interaction, and it is the older sister who in turn 8 builds on
Noa's insertion of a Hebrew word to initiate an English-language teaching
sequence. When Noa confuses the two meanings of "oger" (turn 7), her
brother (ignoring the source of the confusion) provides the contextually
appropriate translation equivalent in English. His translation is contested by
the father (turn 10), who in turn is contested by Irit and Noa (turns 12 to 14).
Note that the father accepts the children's bilingual expertise (turn 15) before
the introduction of a third Hebrew term (turn 16) confuses matters further.
The following example illustrates the more common expert–novice situation,
where the adults serve as teachers of English to the children:

(11) American Israelis 2; Eran (8m); Mira (6f).

1	Father:	How do you say {*geves*} in English?
2	Eran:	I don't know.
3	Father:	Cast.
4	Eran:	Cast?
5	Father:	Uh-huh.
6	Eran:	Cast, cast, cast.

The overall assumption prevailing for the American Israeli parents is that for their children language acquisition means learning two languages simultaneously. Although explicit language-teaching sequences like that in Example 11 are rare, this assumption of bilinguality is upheld through metalinguistic discourse (as in Example 10) as well as by drawing on two codes simultaneously in interaction with young language acquirers. In the next example, a 5-year-old boy engages his baby brother in a repetition game, choosing the objects of repetition through free association (Grandma> thank you) and sound patterns (*toda*> bottle) rather than language. In listening to the tape, we found it noteworthy that although the child keeps the languages phonologically distinct, he does not seem to feel a need to mark the transition from one language to the other.[10]

(12) American Israelis 10; Yair (5m); Yossi (1.5m).

1	Yair:	Say Grandma!
2	Yossi:	Gramma.
3	Yair:	Say {*toda*} [thank you].
4	Yossi:	{*toda*}.
5	Yair:	{*toda*}. Say bottle.
6	Yossi:	Bah.

As the final example of language mixing, consider the way mixing may combine with code switching in socializing children for bilingualism.[11]

---

[10]For code switching and language socialization, see Harding-Riley (1986), Goodz Singerman (1989), Lanza (1990), and Saunders (1988). Lanza showed how very young children (under two years of age) are socialized to mix languages.

[11]One of the basic issues in the analysis of code switches is the difficulty in defining the language that serves as the *base language* of the conversation. In the following discussion, the base language is identified relative to topically definable exchanges, namely, the segment bounded by two topical actions (see Chapter 3). By tracking code switches sequentially following the initiation of the topic, we can determine which of the languages serves as the base language for the exchange and map the nature of the switches in terms of socialization and sociability functions.

(13) American Israelis 12; Yael (8f).

    1 Father: Is that {*lordim*} [magic markers] you're using,
                 Yael? What is that stuff?
    2 Yael: {*lo, cvaim*} [no, colors].
    3 Father: Ah what kind of colors do you call those? Just
                 crayons? Colors?
    4 Observer: Colors.
    5 Yael: {*ken*} [yes] crayons.
    6 Father: Is that from school or just here?
    7 Yael: {*lo, shel ima*} [No, mother's].
    8 Father: Ah, it's {*ima's*}.

When this exchange opens, the father expresses his interest in the type of
colors Yael is using; to this end, he borrows the colloquial Hebrew term for
markers (based on the brand name), perhaps to make certain that he is
understood. When Yael responds in Hebrew, the father uses his next turn (3)
for language teaching in an indirect way—first by expanding *in English* the
previous Hebrew utterance and second by shifting attention to the metalinguistic aspect of talk about colors and asking for the English terms. With the
help of the observer, Yael (turn 5) mixes her first English word ("crayons") in
her response. In the next three turns, when his question in English (turn 6) is
again responded to in Hebrew, the father acknowledges, through repetition
in English (turn 8), the previous Hebrew utterance. Techniques such as
expansion and echoing are well-known mechanisms in adult–child interaction
in the early stages of language acquisition (e.g., Snow, 1984). What is surprising
is to find the same strategies used with older children in a bilingual situation.

Code Switching

In contrast with code mixes, which occur within clause boundaries and
usually involve single words only, a code switch has been defined as a
change from one language to another involving clauses and larger-than-
clause units. To account for the effect of code switching on the dynamics
of the interaction, code switches are considered here in two ways (Kurland,
1992). First, **speaker switches** consider the switch from the point of view of
the speaker: Does the speaker change languages from one utterance to the
next? Regardless of whether the switch occurs within one turn or across
turns (in response to another speaker or following several turns by other
speakers), a **speaker switch** is defined as a change from the language used
by the same speaker in his or her previous utterance. Second, code switches
are considered in terms of their locus in the sequential organization of the
discourse. From this point of view, the question is what language follows

what language on the floor? **Floor switches** consider the switch in terms of sequential organization; a **floor switch** is defined as a change in language that occurs from one turn to the next.

When both of these perspectives are taken into account, three combinations emerge. The first possibility is that of a speaker switch that does not involve a floor switch. This can occur when a speaker joins a conversation that has been going on in language A and makes a contribution in language A despite that he or she had used language B in a previous utterance. In such a case, the speaker switches languages, but this switch does not affect the language of the floor.

The second possibility occurs in the reverse situation: a conversation is going on in language A, and a speaker joins in using language B, which is the language the same speaker used in his or her previous utterance. In this case, a floor switch occurs (or is at least attempted) with no speaker switch.

The third possibility is a combination of both speaker and floor switches. A speaker using language B joins in a conversation that has been going on in language A, whereas in his or her previous utterance the same speaker also used language A.

It is important to keep this distinction in mind when considering the role of code switching in balancing the opposing goals of socialization and sociability in the American Israeli families. In our bilingual context, a major goal of socialization concerns the maintenance and promotion of English. Sociability, on the other hand, is associated with the use of Hebrew. On one level, the use of Hebrew and the switches to Hebrew on the part of the adults in the families may contribute to sociability by signaling consideration for the perceived or anticipated language preferences of children and guests. On another level, such switches index sociability for all members of the family in a wider sense, as a symbol of the family's enculturation in Israeli society at large.

With these considerations in mind, code switches to English are considered **maintenance** switches, and code switches to Hebrew are considered **acculturation** switches. In the turn following a maintenance or an acculturation switch, an **accommodation** switch may occur. In accommodation switches, speakers change languages to accommodate previous speakers, be it from Hebrew to English or vice versa. Code switches have been summarized accordingly into four main categories.

1. *Hebrew to English maintenance switches* (socialization). Code switching geared towards the maintenance of English involves attempts to change the language on the floor from Hebrew to English. Included here are both speaker and floor switches and floor switches only, as long as the switch involves a change of the language on the floor to English. Across turns in a multiparty

conversation the schematic sequence of maintenance switches will be (where the switch considered is performed in turn 3):

Speaker x, turn 1	English or Hebrew
Other speaker(s), turn 2 (or more):	Hebrew
Speaker y, turn 3	English.

2. *Hebrew to English accommodation switches*. The success of maintenance code switches finds its expression in the turn following a maintenance switch. This is the case when, following a floor switch to English by a previous speaker, the current speaker accommodates and performs a speaker switch to English. Across turns, the sequence of Hebrew to English accommodation switches will be (where the switch considered is performed in turn 4):

Speaker x, turn 1	Hebrew
Other speaker(s), turn 2 (or more)	Hebrew
Speaker y, turn 3	English
Speaker x, turn 4	English

3. *English to Hebrew acculturation switches* (linked to sociability). English to Hebrew acculturation switches have the same structure as English maintenance switches, with a change in the direction of languages:

Speaker x, turn 1	English or Hebrew
Other speaker(s), turn 2 (or more)	English
Speaker x, turn 3	Hebrew

4. *English to Hebrew accommodation switches*. English to Hebrew accommodation switches have the same structure as Hebrew to English ones, category b, with a change in the direction of languages:

Speaker x, turn 1	English
Other speakers, turn 2 (or more)	English
Speaker y, turn 3	Hebrew
Speaker x, turn 4	Hebrew

Hebrew to English Maintenance and Accommodation Switches. The numbers for maintenance and accommodation shifts (see Fig. 7.2) point to the success of bilingual socialization. Thus, the effort invested in maintaining English pays off and is signaled by accommodation shifts: *The more parents invest in maintenance shifts, the more children accommodate to them*. Figure 7.2 also shows that, although the parents are the dominant maintainers, children take part in this practice as well.

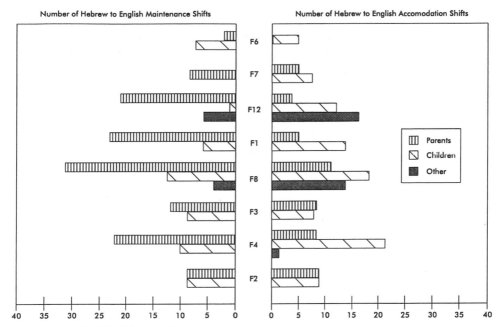

FIG. 7.2. Hebrew to English maintenance and accommodation code switches.

In the following discussion, code switches are analyzed sequentially, in relation to the topical unit in which they appear and their socialization and sociability functions. The classical pattern of a maintenance shift occurs at the onset of a topically definable segment of conversation, when one speaker initiates a new topic in Hebrew, to be responded to immediately in English:

(13) American Israelis 4; Yakir (16m); Ruth (12f); Batya (8f); Sara (6f).

   1   Ruth: {*ha-yom be-kalkala # asinu orez im gezer*} [today in Home Ec. # we made rice with carrots].

   2   Mother: Oh that's a good one, that's a good recipe.

However, maintenance switches can also occur at any other point during the development of the topic on the floor, in response to a switch to Hebrew.

In Example 14 the topic is initiated and developed for several turns in English. English serves as the base language of the exchange until Noa switches to Hebrew in turn 5. From the point of view of language maintenance, the relevant switch occurs in turn 6, where the mother ignores the switch to Hebrew and responds in English. Her choice of English at this point in the sequence constitutes a floor switch with no speaker switch.

(14) American Israelis 6; Noa (5f).

1	Noa:	Should I tell you what they do? What the {gananot} [kindergarten teachers] do? Should I tell you what they do?
2	Mother:	What?
3	Noa:	{ima} [Mom].
4	Mother:	Tell me.
5	Noa:	Well if you eat and you're still there +... Then, then you {lemalot et ha-kosot be-mayim # o be-petel o be-te} [fill the glasses with water or with juice or with tea].
6	Mother:	But I think I'll be there after you finish {aruxat eser} [the ten o'clock snack]. I'm coming at eleven, eleven-thirty. I'm coming for the last hour and a half of {gan} [kindergarten].

In Example 15 the base language of the exchange is Hebrew, but when the mother joins the conversation (in turn 7) she chooses to phrase her contribution in English. Though no accommodation switch follows and the language on the floor remains Hebrew, she persists in her attempts to steer the conversation to English (turn 15). As is the case in all instances of mixing and switching, here too the coherence of the discourse is coconstructed through the use of both languages, in a way that makes bilingualism (or at least passive bilingualism) a precondition for full participation.

(15) American Israelis 8; Nira (13f); Aya (6f); Natan (5m); Yael (13f), a friend of Nira. The children are trying to clarify a misunderstanding with regard to the observer's name.

1	Aya:	korim lax yael?	Is your name Yael?
2	Nira:	yael?	Yael?
3	Observer:	lo yael, laxavera \<shel nira> [>] korim yael.	No, \<its Nira's> [>] friend who's called Yael.
4	Aya:	\<ani yoda'at> [<].	\<I know> [<].
5	Observer:	sara korim li.	Sara is my name.
6	Aya:	az lama amart yael?	So why did you say "Yael"?
> 7	Mother:	because she you know +/.	
8	Yael:	he hitkavna elay.	She meant me.
9	Observer:	hi hitkavna eleha [//] hitkavanti eleha.	She meant her, I meant her.
10	Observer:	ah lo, az ani [/] az ani	Ah no, it's me, it's me.

		lo shamati. slixa.	I didn't hear anything. Sorry.
11	Aya:	ah xashavt she-ani medaberet *eleha*.	Ah you thought I was talking to *her*.
12	Observer:	lo. lo shamati shum davar.	No. I didn't hear anything.
13	Nira:	lo xashuv, lo xashuv.	Never mind, never mind.
14	Observer:	[laughs]	

> 15 Mother: By the end of the evening we'll all be confused.

The full success of maintenance switches is signaled by accommodation. In a sense, one could argue that even if a parental switch to English is countered by a child's response in Hebrew, such bilingual exchanges testify to the child's understanding of English and carry the message of the importance of English in the home. As the numbers show, however, in the American Israeli families *children generally cooperate with parental efforts to maintain English*. This cooperation takes the form of accommodation switches, as in Example 16.

(16) American Israelis 4; Yakir (16m); Ruth (12f); Batya (8f); Sara (6f). The topic is Yakir's reading habits.

1	Mother:	You see # you're not illiterate.	
2	Yakir:	No, I just don't read.	
%	comment:	[two turns about food omitted.]	
3	Yakir:	kama ze ole lihyot manuy le-sifria? ze eze 20 elef shekel.	How much does a library subscription cost? It's about 20 thousand shekels.
4	Mother:	ma pit'om?	No way.
5	Yakir:	ken.	Yeah.
6	Mother:	eze sifriya?	At which library?
7	Yakir:	rene kasen.	Rene Casin.
8	Mother:	Oh no. Sara, sit in your seat or go away.	
9	Sara:	aval yakir +/.	But Yakir +/.
10	Mother:	Oh no.	Oh no.
11	Yakir:	aseret alafim lihyot manuy ve-axat esre bishvil pikadon bishvilam.	Ten thousand for subscription, and eleven as a guarantee.
%	comment:	[The prices mentioned reflect the high rate of inflation in Israel at the time.]	
12	Observer:	rega aval le-shana?	Wait a minute. For a year?
13	Yakir:	le-shana.	For a year.

	14	Observer:	ze lo nora.	That's not bad.
>	15	Mother:	You're sure it's that much money?	
	16	Yakir:	Oh yeah.	
	17	Mother:	I don't know +/.	
>	18	Yakir:	I don't know, maybe upstairs it's different but nah, upstairs they don't keep books, that's what she told me.	

In all these examples, maintenance switches are the mother's domain. This is not surprising, given the parental emphasis on the importance of maintaining English in the home. Yet parents are not the sole employers of this practice. In both Examples 17a and 17b it is the children who perform the switches to English.

(17a) American Israelis 4; Ruth (12f); Batya (8f); Sara (6f).
The family is co-narrating to the observer the story of a recent weekend they spent together on an organized tour on the shores of the Dead Sea, which included walking tours in the area. Up to the segment quoted, the conversation on this topic has been carried on in Hebrew.

1	Batya:	rak tesha anashim yardu le-naxal arugot. ze haya haxi mesha'amem.	Just nine people went to Nahal Arugot. It was so boring.
2	Ruth:	kol ha-shar hayu paxdanim.	Everyone else was afraid.
3	Observer:	be'emet?	Really?
4	Sara:	*ima!*	*Mommy!*
5	Batya:	kol hashar gam hayu zkenim <ve-yeladim ktanim ktanim> [>].	And everyone else was old people and <and very small children> [>].
6	Sara:	<Could I go [//] can I go> [<] get some &cina cinnamon?	
7	Mother:	Yes you can. [continues in Hebrew]	

Later in the same conversation the topic shifts to the explanations of the guide during the hike, specifically those concerning the persimmon perfume, made from the fruit by the same name, in first-century ancient settlements near the Dead Sea.

(17b)	1	Mother:	ze carix lihyot mashehu meod +...	It's supposed to be something very +...

2	Observer:	++ meod meyuxad.	++ Very special.
3	Mother:	meyuxad mefursam ve-yadua, ve-ani af pa'am lo shamati al ze kamuvan.	Special famous and well known, and I've never heard of it of course.
4	Observer:	ah, lo lo lo.	Ah, no no no.
5	Mother:	lo?	No?
6	Observer:	lo, ze lo kol kax. mi she-lo mitasek ba-inyanim ha-ele ze lo +... yesh kama agadot &ba ba-talmud aval ze lo +...	No, it's not that much. People who don't deal with this stuff, it's not +... There are a few Talmudic tales but it's not +...
7	Mother:	lo, ki hi omeret she-ze [//] mi-ze hitparnesu mi-ze. hayu rak yehudim be-eyn-gedi kol ha-shanim &ve she-asku rak be-ze.	No, because she said that it [//] from it they made a living from it. There were only Jews in Ein Gedi all the years and that they lived only from that.
8	Yakir:	ken beseder, aval ze pa'am.	Yes okay, but it was in the past.
9	Mother:	ze carix lihyot me-xx ha-historia shelanu keilu, ve-ani af pa'am lo +...	It must be from our own xx history like, and I've never +...
> 10	Yakir:	It was before Chanel Number 5.	
11	Mother:	Before Chanel Number 5 that's right. Way before.	
12	Sara:	Who before who? # {aba}?	
13	Father:	That's a famous perfume.	

Whereas in Example 17a because it is not on the topic, Sara's switch to English can be considered a borderline case, Yakir's code switch to English in Example 17b (turn 10) is clearly marked as a maintenance switch. Technically Sara performs a floor switch (which is accommodated by the mother, who responds in English), but the two turns (6 and 7) constitute a digression from the thematic frame of the exchange and hence can easily be ignored. Indeed, the conversation continues in Hebrew until Yakir's comment in turn 10 of Example 17b. Here the maintenance switch to English triggers a complete change in the language on the floor, with all speakers, including the youngest, continuing the conversation in English.

English to Hebrew Acculturation and Accommodation Switches. The pattern for switches to Hebrew is different from that of switches to English. In switches to Hebrew, the observers play an active part (note the relatively high rate of observers' English to Hebrew switches in families 8 and 12; see Fig. 7.3), with children being the next most active participants. Accommodation is practiced by both parents and children. For example, in Family 3, the parents' 5 acculturation switches and the children's 14, are matched by 13 accommodation switches by the parents and 15 by the children. Thus, sensitivity to the language games of others plays an important role for both parents and children.

As in the case of language choice, switches to Hebrew during the conversations were affected by the attributed and expressed language preferences of the observers and the video technicians. Thus, the mother in Family 4 offers wine to her husband in English ("Would you like some wine?") but switches to Hebrew in making the same offer to the video technician. For the children, observers seem to have been perceived as representatives of the Hebrew-speaking Israeli society; sociability finds its expression in the children's switch to Hebrew even in cases when an observer talks mostly English with the parents (see Example 14). The adults are more discriminating, switching to Hebrew mainly with those observers who clearly prefer Hebrew.

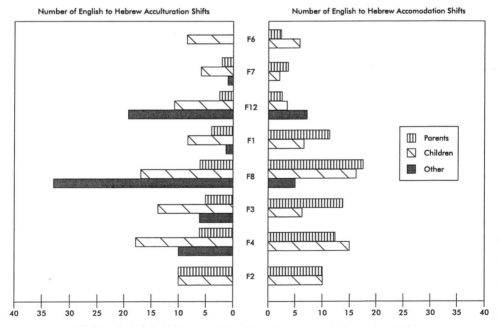

FIG. 7.3. English to Hebrew acculturation and accommodation code switches.

The two final extracts in this section (18a and 18b) manifest a dense practice of language shifts, illustrating the tension between socialization and sociability goals in bilingual conversations. The outsiders in this case are Yael (13f), Nira's friend, and the observer Sarah.

(18a) American Israelis 8; Nira (13f); Aya (6f); Natan (5m); Yael (13f, a friend of Nira's).

1	Nira:	Ask me about the movie.
2	Mother:	{*nu*} [well] how was the movie?
3	Nira:	Great.
4	Yael:	Great.
5	Mother:	What was the movie about?
6	Nira:	Like John Travolta was em he was a journaler em # # &j &journal {*uf!*} [oof!].
% comment:		[Nira is having difficulty pronouncing the word "journalist"].
7	Aya:	Which movie?
8	Observer:	A reporter.
9	Nira:	No yeah a &jou +/.
10	Mother:	A journalist?
11	Nira:	Yeah a reporter journalist whatever. So he was [//] so he wanted um to +. . . ## You know he made a story about somebody that was like making um never mind.
12	Yael:	To make them a &s+. . . His article and xxx +/.

> 13 Nira: {*tedabri be-ivrit.*} [speak in Hebrew].

14 Observer: {*lama?*} [why?]

15	Yael:	anashim <racu &she-ha> [>] [/] she-katava shelo tihiye ha-pa'am ha-merkaz shel ha-iton.	they <wanted the> [>] [/] his article to be the main piece in the newspaper.
16	Mother:	<ken> [<].	[Yes] [<].
17	Yael:	az hm em az hu halax le-moadon briut kor'im le-ze, ze mashehu xadash keilu she +/.	So ehm so he went to a health club they call it, it's a new thing like +. . .

> 18 Nira: A health em +. . .

> 19 Aya: ++ club.

> 20 Nira: Yeah.

> 21 Mother: Yeah, so?

> 22	Yael:	So kulam sham mit'amlim ve <rokdim erobika> [>].	Everybody there works out and does <aerobic dancing> [>].

> 23 Nira: <No he wanted to tell about> [<] and he wanted to tell that you know couples that meet there get married you know and all and fall in love. So he was you know going around you know asking and this and everybody showed him. And then he saw +/.

24 Mother: Showed him what?

25 Nira: You know what they do and this and all kinds of things.

26 Mother: Ah.

27 Nira: So uh <he saw> [>] he went to a room and he saw this woman em giving a [//] an aerobic class.

28 Yael: <He went to> [<] +/.

29 Nira: And her you know he fell in love with her and this and they came together and he wanted to interview her but she didn't want to 'cause she said she got hurt before from that you know. Cause she had a long time ago you know she was having an affair with a coach and this and then it got published +. . .

> 30 Observer: ma hem lo yod'im? | What don't they know?
  ze ma she-ani roca | That's what I want to
  lada'at. | know.

> 31 Nira: Yeah so +/.

> 32 Yael: ve-ha-bigdey balet shela | And her ballet clothes
  hayu *mesha*gim. kol | were fabulous. Every
  xazara hi lavsha | rehearsal she wore a
  mashehu axer ve +. . . | different outfit and +. . .

33 Nira: Yeah.

> 34 Observer: <She's really xxx> [>].

> 35 Mother: <aval ze haya seret> [<] | <But was it an
  mat'im le-yeladim | appropriate> [<] movie
  ba-gil shelaxem? | for children your age?

36 Yael: at rait at ha-seret, | Did you see the movie,
  Sara? | Sarah?

> 37 Observer: <lo, aval ani raiti> | <No, but I saw> [>]
  [>] +. . . | +. . .

> 38 Mother: <No Yael> [<] Nira ah Yael said it wasn't a film <for you guys> [>].

> 39 Nira: <ze lo haya la-gil | <It wasn't for kids
  shelanu] [<]. | our age> [<].

40 Aya: naxon, ze haya la-gil | Right, it was for my
  sheli. | age.

	% comment:	[All laugh.]	
	41 Nira:	shel Natan.	Natan's.
	% comment:	[All laugh.]	
	42 Father:	ze lo bishvil ha-gil shelo.	It's not for his age.
	43 Mother:	ha-gil shelanu?	Ours?
	44 Aya:	lo.	No.
	45 Nira:	lo.	No.
>	46 Observer:	aval hi be'emet rokedet yafe.	But she really dances beautifully.
		<She's Tony Curtis' daughter this actress> [>].	
>	47 Mother:	<xxxx be-gil esrim [<]. mashehu.	<xxx twenty years old>. [<] Smashing.
>	48 Nira:	She's so thin <and she> dances so good.	
	49 Aya:	<Who who>?	
	50 Observer:	Jamie Lee Curtis.	
	51 Mother:	Jamie Lee Curtis?	
	52 Observer:	She is Tony Curtis' daughter.	
	53 Mother:	No kidding.	
	54 Observer:	Do you know who Tony Curtis is?	
	55 Mother:	Yeah sure. I remember +/.	
	56 Observer:	She looks just like the mother, as a matter of fact.	
	57 Aya:	Yeah.	
	58 Observer:	Like Janet Leigh.	
>	59 Yael:	hi *meshaga:'at*.	She's *fanta:stic*.
>	60 Observer:	Terrific.	

[continued: The father joins in and the discussion develops the theme of dancing in movies. The topic shifts with turn 1 of 18b, as Yael mentions another film.]

(18b) American Israelis 8.

	1 Yael:	Nira at roca lalexet lirot "shoter im kavod"?	Nira you want see "An honorable policeman"?
	2 Natan:	ani roce lir'ot.	I want to see.
	3 Nira:	<ani lo>. [>]	<I don't.> [<]
	4 Aya:	<al ma ze> [<]?	<What's it about?> [>]
	5 Natan:	<ani roce> [>].	<I want to.> [>].
	6 Mother:	<lirot ma?>[<]	<To see what?> [<]
	7 Yael:	"shoter im kavod."	"An honorable policeman."
	8 Nira:	ze becarfatit.	It's in French.

			(Hebrew/transcription)	(English translation)

      9 Aya: al ma ze?   What's it about?

    10 Mother: ma ze?   What is it?

    11 Yael: ze al shoter im kavod.   It's about an honorable policeman.

>   12 Father: Nira do you think I'll <like the movie> [>]?

    13 Mother: <matay ze> [<]?   <When is it> [<] (playing)?

    14 Yael: ze al shoter she-ishto ve-bito nircaxot +...   It's about a policeman whose wife and daughter are murdered.

    15 Mother: [laughs].

    16 Yael: nircexu ve-hu roce legalot mi asa et ze, az eze baxura axat ozeret lo +...   They're murdered and he wants to find out who did it, and some girl helps him +...

>   17 Mother: Daddy would like it as long as it wasn't scary.

>   18 Father: ze lo bishvili. ani sone et ze ani sone <dvarim kaele> [>].   It's not for me. I hate it, I hate things like <like that> [>].

>   19 Nira: <beseder nu> [<] maspik.   <all right> [<] enough.

    20 Natan: haya seret exad +/.   There was a movie +/.

>   21 Mother: Daddy likes it if it was scary then he could yell.

>   22 Father: No, I get scared of those things like the Goonies and <xxxxx> [>].

    23 Aya: <Daddy xxx> [<] Indiana Jones and when Nira went to see it with him there was xx "Ooohh" and everybody looks and turns around and it's a grown-up screaming.

    24 Nira: xxxxx.

    25 Father: But that's the end.

    26 Mother: It's embarrassing to go to the movies with xxx. You never know when he'll yell from fright.

>   27 Natan: ze kmo im eze sipur +...   That's like with some story +...

    32 Natan: kmo ba-sipur im &s im ha-sus she-hu dahar alav ve-hu tava.   Like the story with &h with the horse he rode on and he drowned.

    33 Nira: ha-sipur she-lo nigmar.   "The Never Ending Story."

@End.

The first general feature to note in 18a and 18b is that, with the exception of Natan, all speakers use both English and Hebrew. In 18a, Nira speaks

English mainly (for example, turns 1, 3, 6, 11, 23, 29, and 48), but she uses Hebrew as well (turns 13, 39, 41, and 45). In 18b she uses Hebrew only (turns 3, 8, and 19). Her friend Yael, who obviously prefers Hebrew and speaks it most of the time, also switches to English part of the time (see turns 12 and 28 in 18a). The mother alternates between the two languages in both 18a and 18b (turns 10 and 35 in 18a; turns 6 and 17 in 18b). The father speaks less than the others in this exchange, but when he does his choice of language also varies (compare turns 12 and 18 in 18b). The younger children in the family do not deviate from this pattern: Aya uses both Hebrew and English (compare turns 4 and 23 in 18b) and though Natan speaks only Hebrew in this particular exchange, he does use English in others. The observer's choice of languages repeats the same bilingual pattern (compare, for example, turns 46 and 52 in 18a).

A closer look at the code switches in 18a and 18b reveals the tensions between socialization (as expressed by the maintenance of English and accommodations to such moves) and sociability (as expressed through acculturation to Hebrew and accommodation to such moves). To highlight these tensions, I analyze the flow of the two exchanges, noting only the code switches particularly relevant in this context.

The topic of movies is introduced by Nira in turn 1 of 18a and continues in English for 12 turns. In turn 13, Nira switches to Hebrew, using a metapragmatic comment, to urge Yael to speak Hebrew (probably in accommodation to Yael's language preferences). Her move succeeds and is accommodated to by the observer (turn 14), Yael (turn 15), and the mother (turn 16). The mother's backchannel in turn 16 is especially noteworthy as an accommodation switch: Her previous utterances (turns 5 and 10) were in English, and her response in Hebrew to Yael is clearly in the spirit of sociability.

Interestingly, it is Nira who reintroduces English in turn 18. Her attempt at English maintenance is endorsed by Aya, who completes for her the term she is looking for ("a health club," turns 18 and 19) and is further supported by the mother, who again switches languages (turns 21 and 24) to accommodate her daughter. For a while (turns 31 and 33), Nira persists in maintaining English even when both the observer (turn 30) and Yael (turn 32) try to steer the conversation to Hebrew. It is only when the mother switches to Hebrew in addressing both girls (turn 35, another English to Hebrew accommodation switch, the overlap signaling that she is ignoring turn 34) that Nira accommodates her and switches to Hebrew in her next utterance (turn 39).

Between turn 35 and Nira's reponse to it (turn 39) the mother makes another attempt at English maintenance by switching to English (turn 38). At turn 39 Hebrew is accepted as the language on the floor by four different speakers and is maintained as such for seven turns.

Turn 46 triggers another shift in the languages on the floor. This time it is caused by the observer, who switches the floor back to English. Before this move succeeds, however, she is accommodated to by the mother, who follows the first, Hebrew part of turn 46 (overlapping with the English part) with a Hebrew utterance of her own. As of the next turn (48), all speakers except for Yael continue the conversation in English.

The shift in topics introduced by Yael in turn 1 (18b) triggers a new Hebrew accommodating sequence. The first switch occurs in turn 12, with the father addressing Nira in English. Because the question is overheard by all, it is an attempt to change languages on the floor in the interest of socialization. The question remains unanswered, and Yael continues to dominate the floor in Hebrew for two further turns. The indirect response to turn 12 is given by the mother in turn 17: Though she speaks about her husband in the third person, her utterance echoes turn 12 (note the repetition of "like" in turns 12, "do you think I'll like the movie" and 17, "would like it as long as . . ."). By speaking English, she is again accommodating, this time to her husband.[12] Perhaps to fend off the implied criticism, in his next turn the father fails to accommodate and instead performs a speaker switch to Hebrew (turn 18). Nira's response in Hebrew (19) is technically an accommodation shift, but on another level it signals alignment with her father against her mother because it is an attempt to delegitimize the subject of her father becoming frightened at the movies. But the mother persists (turn 21) and is successful on two accounts. First, the floor changes back to English and the other speakers (except Natan who has an agenda of his own) collaborate with the switch (turns 22, 23, and 25). Second, the switch functions to map alignments: Despite Nira's objection, the mother's topic is pursued by both her and Aya, the younger daughter aligning with the mother against the father. With turn 27, the conversation shifts once again to Hebrew, Natan pursuing the topic he raised in turn 20. Hebrew remains the only language on the floor till the children leave the dinner table three minutes later.

Socialization and Sociability in Bilingual Conversations

In the context examined, bilingual socialization means bilingual practices in the process of socialization as well as socialization toward balanced bilingualism. On the first account, the bilingual practices typifying these families help create a bilingual interactional style (i.e., "Hebrish") felt by members to index familial cohesiveness. As elaborated in the next section, this style is marked not only linguistically, by bilingual practices, but also pragmatically, by the norms of interlanguage pragmatics governing its patterns of use. On the second account, the high levels of English used by both children

---

[12]The mother's accommodation code switching to all others in this example is reminiscent of the high accommodation of mothers to young children in middle-class White American families, a communicative strategy through which, Ochs (1992) argued, mothers actually help construct a low image of themselves.

and adults, the parents' consistent attempts at English maintenance, and the children's accommodation to this practice testify to the success of bilingual socialization. This success is facilitated by the high prestige of English and by the cultural and instrumental benefits associated with high English proficiency. However, the process of bilingual socialization can be at odds with family internal sociability and nurturing needs as well as wider societal pressures valorizing Hebrew. For the parents, accommodating children and guests may ask for the use of Hebrew. For the children, the tension is even greater, with all secondary language experience (i.e., school, peers, media) being counter to the primary language experience at home. Furthermore, on a wider societal level, the prevalence of English in the family domain may be interpreted by the society at large as indexing a degree of group disindentification (Goffman, 1963) from Israeli culture. As discussed in the next section, bilingual practices are one component in the building of the intercultural (or bicultural) identity through language enacted in the American Israeli families.

INTERLANGUAGE PRAGMATICS
IN THE FIRST LANGUAGE

The bilingual families maintain their first language under conditions of intensive sociocultural contact with a second language. As a result, the pragmatics of the first language is the primary domain to be affected by this contact. Ironically, although pragmatic competence is the most difficult aspect of language to master in learning a second language (e.g., Kasper & Blum-Kulka, 1993), it seems also, under certain conditions of bilingualism, to be the easiest to lose in the first language. Furthermore, the specific case of bilinguals studied suggests that *interlanguage is not necessarily a second-language phenomenon*. The discourse style realized by the bilingual families, mostly in their first language, shows that pragmatic systems can be bidirectionally transferable, from both the first to the second language and from the second to the first. The resulting hybrid style of the bilinguals constitutes a prime example of interlanguage pragmatics. To evaluate this proposal, reconsider the major findings for the discourse patterns of the Israeli American families as presented in Chapters 2, 3, 5, and 6.

The patterns for interlanguage pragmatics phenomena differ according to the discourse dimension. On some of the dimensions, the discourse of the American Israeli families we observed manifests a bicultural or *intercultural* style that is systematically different from both the Israeli and American patterns. On other dimensions, it manifests an acculturated style, approximating Israeli norms. On a few others, the norms prevailing are those of the Jewish American discourse.

In the area of discourse dynamics (Chapter 3), the American Israeli families interact like native Israelis in construing the role of the observer and in respect to gender of parents, but they show a culturally mixed pattern with regard to the role of children. The case of the observers is especially dramatic: In both Israeli groups observers are treated as potential friends, participating in the talk to a degree similar to that of the parents (20% to 28% of topical action turns in both Israeli groups, see Fig. 3.1). This is in sharp contrast to the situation in Jewish American families, where observers play a much more subdued role than the parents (8% topical action turns only). The observers' mode of reception in the Israeli American families seems to signal the adoption of native Israeli norms of social interaction, at least as far as it is part of the trend to minimize the social distance between the family and the visitors, in the spirit of the ethos of solidarity politeness prevailing in this society.

The pattern for genders also follows native Israeli norms. Mothers talk more and are more active in the traffic of topical actions (60%) than are fathers (40%), in contrast to the reverse trend in the Jewish American families. This result seems to indicate a shift in the perception of the dinner situation with a guest that occurred after years of living in Israel. As in native Israeli families, dinner is perceived as an informal, private occasion in which women dominate, in contrast to the more formal and public enactment of the Jewish American dinners, where men tend to dominate.

The role of children in the talk is connected with the attitude to the observers. In both Israeli groups, adults take up a larger proportion of talking space (and topical control) than children. This differs from the Jewish American families, where the rate of children's contribution is closer to that of adults. Although the topical agenda of dinner talk is clearly controlled by adults in both Israeli and American Israeli families, the children in the American Israeli families still participate more in the talk than do Israeli children. The mean number of utterances for an Israeli child is only 27, whereas for an American Israeli child it is 33.5 and for a Jewish American child it is 37.8. Thus the attitude toward children's participation in American Israeli families retains in part the Jewish American trend for construing dinner talk as highly child-centered, allowing children central stage for relatively long stretches of time.

In most other discourse dimensions, the discourse patterns followed by the Israeli American families clearly manifest an interim pattern, which conforms to neither Israeli nor Jewish American norms. The language of control in these families is enacted in a true intercultural manner (see Chapter 5). Parents in the bilingual families realize requests less directly than native Israelis but more directly than Jewish Americans. In the politeness style of the American Israelis, solidarity politeness, so typical of Israeli parent–child interaction, is as frequent (32%) as conventional politeness

(31%), whereas in Jewish American families, politeness tends to find its expression mainly through conventional politeness (see Fig. 5.2). Furthermore, this intercultural style is realized regardless of the language spoken; the distribution of strategy types follows the same request patterns for English as for Hebrew. Pragmatic interlanguage effects are also detectable in patterns of compliance, as analyzed for parents' immediate responses to requests. Chapter 5 showed that Israeli responses tend to be categorical, either complying with or refusing the children's requests, whereas Jewish American parental responses tend to favor negotiation. The Israeli American parents in this case are closer to the Jewish American pattern, favoring negotiation over categorical yes or no. Yet the children in these families follow an interim pattern of their own: They negotiate more than the children from native Israeli families (27% vs. 17%) but less than children in the Jewish American families (39%).[13]

Metapragmatic discourse follows similar intercultural patterns. The parents in the bilingual families try to socialize their children according to a normative system of pragmatic rules shaped on the American example, yet in practice they deviate from the Jewish American norms (see Chapter 6). A case in point are metapragmatic comments with regard to discourse management. Although both Jewish American and American Israeli families place a high value on discourse management, turn-taking is not attended to as frequently in the discourse of American Israeli families as in the Jewish American discourse, but it is still more important than in the native Israeli families. Furthermore, in phrasing their metapragmatic comments, speakers in the American Israeli families often create a style of their own, as witnessed, for example, in the case of children's bids for turn (see Example 7, Chapter 6). Yet it should be kept in mind that certain features of metapragmatic discourse seem more linked to the social practice of bilingualism rather than to cultural influences. Thus American Israeli families, like native Israelis but for different reasons, valorize matters of language and frequently engage in metalinguistic talk, a practice almost completely absent from the Jewish American discourse.

A third pattern that emerges points to the preservation of some of the hallmarks of the Jewish American style. American Israeli parents, like Jewish Americans, avoid nicknaming almost absolutely (we found 20 cases of nicknaming in the two American groups, compared to 163 in the Israeli families), reflecting a preference for showing respect for children's independence over the expression of affective proximity. Furthermore, in narrative events focused on child main tellers, De Ber (1995) found a strong emphasis on today

---

[13]"Negotiation" represents one of the four choices for immediate response to requests: no response, compliance, rejection, and negotiation (see Chapter 5). The rate of adult negotiations is 10% for Israelis, 32% for American Israelis, and 38% for Jewish Americans.

stories (37% from all time frames chosen, versus only 16% in the Israeli narrative events) although in actual performance the today narratives are not as highly stylized as their Jewish American counterparts. In a similar pattern, American Israeli narrative initiators are less concerned with aligning future listener-participants than the Israelis are, and the topics of their stories tend to move further away from the home than do Israeli stories (De Ber, 1995).

This hybrid, intercultural nature of the American Israeli ways of speaking is thus revealed in two ways. On the microlevel, mixed patterns are related to a given discourse dimension (as in the case of the language of control). On the macrolevel, the peculiar tapestry of style is woven from acculturated patterns on some discourse dimensions and from preservation and the mixing of cultural patterns on others.

Metapragmatic Awareness and the Negotiation of Social and Cultural Identity

To what extent are the members of the American Israeli families aware of any incongruence between the two pragmatic systems represented by the languages they speak? How far are they aware of their own interlanguage pragmatics? What is the cultural model for their practices of language socialization? To answer these questions, I draw on the bilingual speakers' explicit metacommunicative responses to questions on language use during our interviews with the families in the project. We asked the parents both to rate the degree of importance attached to socializing children in various aspects of appropriate language use and to comment on perceived differences between their own ways of speaking and those of native Israelis. It is from responses to the first type of question that we learned about the bilingual parents' conscious efforts to socialize their children to systematic turn-taking norms. The second type of question followed from discussions of the families' discourse practices and attitudes in a certain domain. For example, we asked the families to tell us about their naming practices and attitudes to nicknaming (Blum-Kulka & Katriel, 1991) and encouraged their attempts to compare their own practices and attitudes with those of both Americans and Israelis. The following extract is a good example of such a comparative, reflexive effort:

(19) American Israelis 12; Mother (Lydia); Father (Bob); Interviewer.

1	Mother:	I grew up in the South where they say "Yes, Ma'am" for a woman.
2	Interviewer:	Any woman?
3	Mother:	Any woman other than me, anybody other than me—my mother's friends, to my mother "Yes, Ma'am" and "Yes, Sir" to a man.

4	Father:	We had those things too.
5	Mother:	And to this day. Now I don't expect anybody to say "Yes, Ma'am" to me. I don't even want people to call me Mrs. Joss. I like to be called Lydia—by everybody. Even Jason's friends, Jennifer's friends, everybody calls me Lydia. In the States, if I were to call my mother's friend by her first name, why there isn't anything like that! So here I <like being called> +. . .
6	Interviewer:	<Still today?>
7	Mother:	You know that's funny. When I go back, I still call my mother's friends Mrs. such and such. I think.
8	Father:	Here it is different.
9	Mother:	Anyway, here I don't mind being called by my first name by my children's friends because it's that way here.

Lydia draws a clear distinction between past and present, here and there. While shunning the habits of her childhood, she accepts the difference in terms of address between Israel and the States as a given, surprising herself (i.e., raising tacit knowledge to the level of consciousness) by the realization that she has adapted to this difference in norms ("you know that's funny"). This metapragmatic awareness of cross-cultural, and in this case also regional, variability in ways of speaking is presented in an emotionally favorable light: She "likes" or at least "does not mind" being addressed by her first name even by status inferiors (children) because "it's that way here." In Schumann's (1978) terms, Lydia is describing her own process of acculturation, as motivated by social and affective factors.

The issue of names and forms of address indexes the formation of social identities in a multiplicity of ways (Goffman, 1963). In the American Israeli families, the stances and practices in this domain are as polysemic in their social meanings as most other dimensions of discourse. Even the repertoire of children's first names in the American Israeli families signals a certain ambivalence toward fully embracing Israeli identities: Alongside uniquely Hebrew names, such as Noam and Ofer, we find Biblical names such as Rachel, Ya'akov, and Sarah, a category not represented in the repertoire of the children's names in the Israeli families.[14] Another common practice is double naming, as Jason & Yuval, Jennifer & Yael. These two children are

---

[14]See Weitman (1988) for a historical study of personal names as cultural indicators in Israeli society between 1882 and 1980.

known by their Hebrew names to their friends and addressed by their English names at home. Indeed, Yael insisted that she does not want her friends at school to know she has an English name. In the segment quoted from the interview, Lydia welcomes the informal Israeli practice of first-name address by children to adults, taking an Israeli stance toward naming, but she also refers to her own children by their English names, distancing herself and her family from the Israeli custom.

Attitudes expressed with regard to pragmatic socialization, as compared to actual practice, testify further to the ongoing negotiation of the desired and adoptable cultural model of interactional style. In actual use, we found no difference between Israeli and immigrant adults in the relative salience of comments eliciting politeness formulae from children. In the interviews, however, adults in the immigrant families claimed that they insist on such formulae, with such insistence occasionally cast in half-apologetic terms (note the use of "still" in Example 21), as a conscious cultural transfer strategy:

(20) American Israelis 3; Father.

    1   Father: A request is a request, and it should have a "please" joined to it.

(21) American Israelis 4; Mother.

    1   Mother: It's also still important to me, the "pleases" and "thank yous."

Are the adults in these families aware that their process of acculturation has affected the pragmatic system of their native English? That they are instantiating an interlanguage pragmatic system both in the way they realize speech acts and in their metapragmatic discourse in the course of natural conversation? The answer is negative. As illustrated by Examples 20 and 21, the norms claimed are not necessarily the norms enacted. On the contrary—metatalk about pragmatic socialization seems motivated by the underlying assumption that *by maintaining English in the home one also maintains American ways of speaking.* During the interview, adults often took a critical stance toward Israeli ways of speaking (". . . like 'thank you' and 'excuse me,' which people don't know in this country"), unaware that the system of politeness they enact in their families actually approximates native Israeli practices. In no part of the interviews did we find any indication of a self-awareness related to the pragmatic aspects of the style used. Self-awareness seems to stop short at the borderline between linguistics and pragmatics. Although both dinner table conversations and interviews are particularly rich with metareferences to linguistic issues of language choice and code switching, they are remarkably devoid of reference to the pragmatic issues of how either of the languages differs in style from native American or native Israeli usage.

IN CONCLUSION: SOCIALIZATION
AND SOCIABILITY IN BILINGUAL FAMILIES

In the context examined here, bilingual socialization means two things: bilingual practices in the process of socialization and socialization toward balanced bilingualism. The bilingual practices typifying these families help to create a bilingual language variety ("Hebrish"), felt by their members to index familial cohesiveness. This intercultural style is marked not only linguistically by bilingual practices but also pragmatically, by the norms of interlanguage pragmatics governing patterns of use. The families' bilingual practices realize the parents' socialization goals, which not only include the promotion of English in the family but also tend to value the American cultural ways of speaking that the families associated with English. Yet in actual practice the interactional style prevailing in the families (regardless of language) is strongly influenced by Israeli practices. Theoretically, this intercultural style could have been enacted in either English or Hebrew; in practice, it is enacted in both. In the context of interlanguage studies, this finding has important implications for the way we think about language learning and language attrition. It opens new possibilities in thinking about interlanguage, showing that it is not necessarily a second-language phenomenon. In the context of language socialization studies, it raises questions regarding the role of pragmatics in a situation of bilingual socialization.[15]

The high levels of English used by both children and adults, the parents' consistent attempt at English maintenance, and the children's accommodation to this practice all testify to the success of socialization toward bilingualism. We have seen that this success is facilitated by the prestige of English and by the cultural and instrumental benefits associated with a high level of English proficiency. We have also seen that the process of bilingual socialization can be at odds both with internal family sociability and nurturing needs and with wider societal pressures valorizing Hebrew. For the parents, accommodating children and guests may invite the use of Hebrew. For the children, the tension is even greater because all secondary language

---

[15]A full pragmatic perspective on bilingual language socialization, only hinted at here, would need to include the ways pragmatic systems develop under conditions of bicultural and bilingual input.

experience in school, with peers, and in the media run counter to the primary language experience at home. Furthermore, on a wider societal level, the prevalence of English in the family domain may be interpreted by the society at large as indexing a degree of voluntary group "disidentification" (Goffman, 1963) from Israeli culture.

How do language practices affect the social identity of the families? On the family level, the choice of language is constitutive of the family itself. Families constitute themselves through eating together, through conversing at dinner, and through using a bilingual style peculiar to themselves, a style that becomes one of the resources for claiming membership in the family. Such bilingual practices also have important implications for how the different members of the family negotiate their social identities within the family unit. Of the two languages known, parents have an obvious advantage in English, and in most cases children have just as obvious an advantage in Hebrew. The parents' knowledge of English serves to reinforce their social identities as knowledgeable parent–teachers, underscoring asymmetries of knowledge (cf. Keppler & Luckman, 1991) in the specific domain of English and occasioning teaching sequences geared toward bilingual socialization. On the other hand, the children's advantage in Hebrew allows them to challenge this role, as when a child corrects a parent's grammatical mistake, comments on his or her accent, or takes on the role of language teacher.

On another level, bilingual practices are also relevant for the formation of social identity within the larger society. The parents' policy of speaking English in the home and socializing their children as bilinguals is their solution to the dilemma faced by all immigrant families—whether to try to maintain their native language in the home, raising their children as bilinguals, or to accommodate to the pressure of the new society and move, if they can, to the new language. Both choices will eventually affect identity formations—in Ochs's (1993) terms, the resources available to family members for constructing their social identities.

For Richard Rodriguez (1980), as a child immigrant in the United States, Spanish was the language of the home, standing for the "pleasing, soothing, consoling reminder that one was at home," in contrast to the language of "los otros" (the others), namely English (p. 27). Yet loyalty to this private family language carried the risk of "pain of public alienation" and the eventual replacement of Spanish by English is retroactively commended by Rodriguez as a necessary step in his Americanization.[16] For the children in

---

[16]See Doleve-Gondelman (1989) for the discussion of a case where a switch to the majority language implied alienation within the family. Doleve-Gondelman did an ethnographic study of an Ethiopian family in Israel, in which the mother chose to accommodate to the child, speaking to her in Hebrew and making no effort to maintain Amharic in the home. Because the mother spoke only broken Hebrew, the end result of the process was a dramatic impoverishment in patterns of mother–child interaction as well as a diminished social status of the mother whose identity as a parent had to be constructed through impoverished linguistic means.

the American Israeli families, no clear-cut boundaries can be drawn between the private language of the home and the public language of "the others," namely Hebrew-speakers. English is very much a language of the public sphere as well as the private one, and knowing English is valued on several accounts. Yet bilingualism even in this context is not devoid of the fears or pains of alienation. The child who did not want her friends at school to know her English name was expressing such fears; for her, bilingual naming (or for that matter, any bilingual practice) represents an undesired bicultural identity. Such tensions are interactionally relevant, with language choice and language alternations signifying language games associated with both socialization and sociability goals.

8

FAMILY, TALK,
AND CULTURE

This book is about patterns of language use at dinner in native and non-native Israeli and Jewish American families. The examination of dinner table conversations has provided insights into the specific nature of interactional practices at this speech event. Because cultural and social meanings are continually constructed through talk, the findings also point to the relation between language and culture in the wider sociocultural context.

The stories of the families in these groups are deeply embedded in collective Jewish history and the specific histories of their respective communities. I turn to this historical perspective, endorsing Harshav's (1993) theories on the Modern Jewish Revolution to develop my argument that the commonalities between the groups can be traced to the impacts of modernity, and I draw on Vygotskian theories of development to locate the translation of modernity in this context into patterns of pragmatic socialization. Next, I discuss the diversity in cultural practices between two of the groups studied. In this discussion, the two contrasting reference groups are the native Israeli and the Jewish American families, setting aside, for the sake of a sharper contrast, the complex bilingual and intercultural patterns of the immigrant families.

The fine-grained discourse analytical methods enabled me to detect similarities and differences in the discursive practices of all three groups of families. From the detailed analyses of family interactions, in conjunction with individual statements about language use and socialization and in view of the relevant wider sociocultural contexts, three general points emerge.

First, dinner talk for all is both sociable and socializing. The tension between sociability and socialization provides the key to understanding the shared features of the speech event within the middle-class families studied. Because the event is construed simultaneously as a familial social gathering and as a verbal (and nonverbal) mediated socializing interaction, the talk can and does move freely between different thematic frames and a rich repertoire of genres such as control talk, narratives, and metapragmatic talk. I interpret this finding as related to the *impact of modernity* on all these families and argue that the commonalities observed in cultural discursive practices are diachronically and synchronically related to their modern consciousness as Western, urban, middle-class, secular, and Jewish.

Second, despite the commonalities, Israeli and Jewish American families manifest *culturally bound interpretations of the notions of sociability and socialization.* The Israeli families are sociable and socialize their children in an interactional style bearing the hallmarks of the ideologies that forged modern Israeli society, including those directly associated with the revival of Hebrew. Yet this ostensibly "new" Israeli–Hebrew style is strongly infused with the *subtext* of the traditional style associated with Yiddish and the old world. On the other hand, from the book's comparative perspective, the discourse world of the Jewish American families seems firmly embedded in American cultural practices. I see these findings as representing two distinct interpretations of the dialectics of continuity and change in the history of these communities.

Third, the distinctiveness in the cultural styles of native Israeli and Jewish American families is accentuated by the liminal position of the American Israeli families. The language choices and interactional style of these families offer an unusual pattern in the history of immigration to Israel. The American Israeli families successfully implement a policy of English-language maintenance at home, yet their linguistically and pragmatically *hybrid interactional style* is in essence an *interlanguage* that bears the marks of a unique intercultural identity.

MODERNITY: THE COMMON DENOMINATOR

Throughout the book I have argued that the discourse world of the families (in all three groups) is in many ways similar and in many others different. To understand the commonalities in discourse practices we need to take into account the quintessential modernity of these families. Differing from former generations and from other communities in the same countries, these urban, secular, middle-class families are modern in the ways this concept was historically interpreted in the framework of Jewish history in the last century.

From Harshav's (1993) perspective on the cultural history of the Jews in the last century, "the internal response to culture and consciousness" (p.

viii), the shared discourse features may be attributed to the modern Jewish revolution, a revolution that entailed a total transformation of the modes of extrinsic and intrinsic existence of the Jews and their descendants in the post-Christian modern world: "It was the most radical change in the historical situation of the Jews in the last two thousand years, entirely transforming their geography, modes of living, languages, professions, consciousness, culture, politics, and place in general history" (p. viii). Harshav traced the extrinsic axis of this revolution to the end of the 19th century, with the great waves of immigration from Russia to America and the Zionist immigration to Palestine/Eretz-Israel. This is the shared historical past of our families, the period when their forefathers moved out of the *shtetl*, the East European small town, both physically and symbolically. For Harshav, this move symbolizes the great leap from traditional Jewish existence to the creation of a new Jewish civilization and the participation in the general culture of modernity. It is this intrinsic stratum of modern Jewish consciousness that, despite the differences in recent history, language, modes of living, ideologies, and self-perceived identities, unites the families and provides the theoretical framework for understanding the similarities in their discourse worlds.

Harshav described the intrinsic aspect of the revolution in semiotic terms as the negation of the three deictic axes of traditional Jewish existence: *I*, *here*, and *now*. Although the rhetoric of negation is most clearly associated with Zionist ideology, Harshav convincingly demonstrated that historically this rhetoric was much more widespread. Its manifestations appear in Yiddish and Hebrew literature of the late 19th and early 20th centuries, autobiographies of the period, and ideological writings, and, significantly, it was associated with a wealth of ideological and political solutions, including the Zionist option. The personal deixis is perhaps the hardest one to experience; it was translated into "not as we were" or "not the public image of 'us,'" implying a sharp dissociation from all that was perceived as wrong with the Jews themselves. The call for a change of character and way of life found its sharpest expession in the Zionist ideal of creating a New Jew, healthy in mind and body, but the negative attitude to things past and to communities that represented traditional ways of living (like that of the German Jews toward Eastern European Jews) was shared by various trends. Harshav quotes from the article of Walter Lippman, written in 1922, as an example of the highly critical view of the first generation of Jewish immigrants to the United States and then summarizes: "For both assimilationists and Zionists, Yiddish language and 'behaviour' symbolized the contemptible world of the shtetl" (p. 18). "Not here" was, of course, one of the central tenets of the Zionists, but it was also the instinctive response of millions who turned to immigration. "Not like now" was expressed on the public level in the struggle for political change and on the personal level "in the future oriented aspiration for learning and personal education and professional change of every individual for himself and his children" (p. 17).[1]

For many of the Jewish American families we studied, the revolution in ways of life, occupations, and learning is a matter of the past. The generational shift in religiosity, professions, language, and level of education and the modern consciousness entailed throughout three generations in the family history of just one of our subjects (the father in Family 1) is typical: The father is a professor of Economics who speaks some French and Hebrew but no Yiddish. His father immigrated to the United States at the age of 3 and became a teacher; his mother was born in America and was a bookkeeper and housewife. The family spoke English in the home and was traditional but not observant. His grandparents on his father's side emigrated from Poland in 1903; the grandmother was a housewife, the grandfather a tailor, and the family was observant and spoke Yiddish in the home. On his mother's side, his grandparents emigrated from Russia in 1905; his grandmother was a garment worker and his grandfather an actor on the Yiddish stage. The family was not observant and spoke both English and Yiddish in the home. In the current generation, both parents are occupied professionally outside the home, and no one speaks Yiddish. One of the children goes to a Hebrew day school, the other goes to a regular American high school.

The family histories of the Israeli families present a more diversified picture (see Appendixes A to C). As noted, most are first generation to immigrant parents; the break from the old world is very much a matter of recent history. The families also know less about their grandparents, several of whom perished in the Holocaust. The professions of our subjects' parents' generation are more varied than in the equivalent generation of the Jewish American families and include several academics (e.g., a physician, a professor of History, an agronomist) as well as merchants, housewives, and, most notably, three pioneer farmers. For example, in Family 2 the father is a statistician; his father went to Palestine as a Halutz (pioneer) from Latvia at the age of 28 and is known in the family as having spent many years actually drying swamps before he became a clerk. The mother was a housewife who emigrated from Russia; the family spoke Russian, Yiddish, and Hebrew at home and was nonobservant. None of the grandparents immigrated. On both sides, the women were housewives; on the father's side,

---

[1]Not all sociologists and cultural historians would agree with Harshav's emphasis on the common roots of the modern Jewish revolution. Sociological studies of American Jewry stress instead that the ideologies of European Jews, which are the base of modern Zionism and Israeli culture, were not carried over into the arena of public Jewish life in the United States and that the real history of the American Jewish community "begins after the most critical problem that faced other Jewries in modern times—the problem of the emancipation of the Jews" (Halpern, 1983, p. 26). According to Biale (1986), American Jews developed ideologies that "serve to create a Jewish identity that is equally American" (p. 195), including a cultural ideology "that sees Jews as one ethnic group in a pluralistic society" (pp. 195–198).

the grandfather was a wood merchant and on the mother's side, a teacher. In the current generation, both parents are college graduates, speak only Hebrew at home (their second language is English), and like all the families in the project, are nonobservant and work professionally outside the home.

These family histories, like the discourse practices themselves, manifest both similarities and differences. Common to all is an actual and ideological distancing from the shared traditional East European Jewish world. Among its many manifestations, this distancing finds its symbolic expression in current beliefs and practices of socialization for pragmatic competencies. In this domain the shared modernity of the families finds its clearest expression in family discourse.

Socialization: The Primacy of Talk

The tensions observed at dinnertime between sociability and socialization could not exist without the underlying modern cultural practices that highlight the primacy of talk as an agent of socialization. Viewed from a developmental perspective, this talk at dinner serves as the major means for "guided participation" (Rogoff, 1990). In the essentially Vygotskian approach to development from which this concept stems, child development is seen as occurring "through [a child's] active participation in culturally structured activity with the guidance, support and challenge of companions who vary in skill and status" (Rogoff, Mistry, Goncu, & Mosier, 1993, p. 5). I find this theoretical perspective particularly useful in interpreting the role of dinner talk for socialization. In all of these middle-class families, dinners are an intergenerational, language-rich activity type, in which both the direct and indirect participation of children in family discourse serves as a primary mode of mediation in the developmental passage to the adult discourse world. The shared, modern principles of this process are apparent both with respect to the primary role of talk in socialization for pragmatic competencies and in the availability of parental facilitation for cognitive development along the lines of modern, analytic, and scientific ways of thinking.

Children's modes of participation in cultural systems of practice vary with the degree of their embeddedness in the everyday life of adults. In medieval Europe (Aries, 1962), the black working community in Trackton (Heath, 1983), or the Mayan Indian town in Guatemala (Rogoff et al, 1993), children were not (or are not) segregated from the work and social life of adults, and hence guided participation can unfold through an emphasis on nonverbal fostering of observation and engagement. In the middle-class modern families we studied, daily routines separate adults from children for most of the day: Dinnertime is one of the few regular time frames for intergenerational gathering. As in other modern middle-class communities (Heath, 1983; Keppler & Luckman, 1991; Rogoff et al., 1993), the emphasis shifts to interpersonal communication. Guided participation evolves through an emphasis on verbal rather than nonverbal forms of mediation.

Asked during the interviews where they differ in parenting styles from their own parents, the adults in our study repeatedly mentioned discipline, children's status in the family, involvement, and talk. As the following extracts show, the topics are interwoven by their shared emphasis on socialization through interpersonal communication (all emphasis added).

> We are more *liberal* with our children ... My parents just laid down the law and "pulled rank." *No arguing or discussing*. We are more *attentive* and *sharing* with our children (American Israeli Family 8, Mother).

> I don't think we're the disciplinarians our parents were. I mean it was very black and white discipline with my father. We try to be *more rational*. And I'm much more *involved* than my parents. We try to do things together (American Israeli Family 3, Father),

> I think [the children] are more *coequal* members of the family than I certainly was. I *listen* more. We will tend to *explain things longer* than my parents would to me as a kid (Jewish American Family 4, Mother).

> The gap between me and my children is much smaller than between me and my parents. In all areas, there is *much more openness* (Israeli Family 5, Mother).

All the topics mentioned have their correlates in discourse practices, although the underlying messages do not always correspond in a simple manner to declared parenting ideologies. The comments seem to fall into two clusters of interwoven themes: an overall ethos of child-centeredness, expressed in terms like *involvement, attentiveness, sharing,* and *listening*; and an egalitarian attitude to socialization that stresses diminishing intergenerational gaps and the importance of language for socialization (i.e., children are *coequals*; there is more *openness*; children get things *explained* to them and are encouraged to *argue* and *discuss*; parents are more *rational*).

The families manifest the hallmarks of child-centeredness that characterize White, middle-class mainstream American families, differing from societies like the Kaluli or Samoan (e.g., Ochs & Schieffelin, 1984). A basic tenet of child-centeredness is the need for adult accommodation: The child is perceived as an incompetent member of society who has to have the situation adapted to his or her needs. Whereas the practices of adaptation described in the literature tell the story of how language acquisition is facilitated through dyadic interaction between the young child and his or her caretaker, the family dinner conversations we studied demonstrate how, through guided participation in multiparty, intergenerational talk, adults ease the passage of preschool and school-age children into adult discourse worlds, helping them to acquire the pragmatic skills needed to become communicatively fully competent.

At dinner, the most obvious expression of adaptation to children's needs is seen in the attention paid to the food needs of children of all ages: "Daniel, you want apple juice?" "Is this too much spaghetti, Jessie?" "Are you hungry, Marvin?" Such queries show that children's wishes and preferences are taken into account (with intentionality attributed to their utterances), their personhood as autonomous beings respected by parents. Furthermore, parents adapt by guessing children's wishes not only for food ("Mommy!" "I'll get it for you") but also with regard to conversational needs, picking up bid for turn cues ("Mommy, do you know what?" "Yes, dear") and engaging in conversational scaffolding, especially in collaborative storytelling. Such scaffolding rests on the assumption that at the family dinners even the youngest children are ratified conversational partners.

We find the discourse correlate of parents' allusion to being *more involved* with and *listening more* to their children than to their own parents in their tendency to grant center stage to children's topics at dinner and in the modes of facilitation through which adults help children participate and gain the skills needed for full and equal participation. Seen from this perspective, the many adult–child coconstructed discourse sequences exemplified throughout the book are further manifestations of facilitation strategies. Parental questions and responses, especially in the thematic frame of immediate family concerns, set the criteria for norms of conversational coherence while exercising an indirect form of control and help children acquire those norms and advance their skills as conversationalists. Family dinners also provide opportunities for children to celebrate acceptance into adult discourse worlds, as happens, especially in the thematic frame of non-immediate concerns, when children's contributions are woven seamlessly into the web of dinner talk.

The status of children as *more coequal* translates on one level into participatory roles in dinner conversations. At dinner children of all ages are granted participatory rights as ratified conversational partners. They engage others in topics of their own interest and are included in discussions of topics of general interest. Although undoubtedly discourse space in these families is more equally distributed than in traditional families within the same communities (see, for example, Stahl, 1993, for descriptions of father-dominated Friday meals in traditional Sephardic families in Israel), adults still retain control in subtle ways by the occasional delegitimization of children's topics and by the overall prevalence of adult topical control as well as by adult questions to children and the occasional framing of children as side participants. Responding to the conversational demand of adult questions requires children to adhere to conversational norms as set by adults. As demonstrated by Goffman (1967), the articulation of norms often surfaces when violations occur. Indeed, we found that all families attend metacommunicatively to perceived violations of conversational norms, commenting on the apparent lack of topical relevance ("Dalit, we don't want to talk about that now"), on verbosity, on nonsatisfactory levels of informativeness or factivity, and on manner ("You don't say 'disgusting' about food").

In cases where the topic of conversation directly concerns children's lives, parent–child dialogues further index adult dominance by showing that in these societies children are *accountable* to parents for their deeds and decisions. Thus we saw high levels of parental conversational involvement with regard to many facets of children's lives, ranging from school work and school attendance to moral issues in peer relations such as whether to tell on a school friend who had stolen a prized possession from the child.

Nowhere are power ambiguities more apparent than in the language of control. As Bernstein (1990) noted, modern, "new middle-class" pedagogies replace authoritarian, clear-cut positional styles of control by person-oriented, powerwise more implicit, yet verbally complex forms of control through interpersonal communication. I find Bernstein's comments on such forms of "invisible pedagogy" pertinent to all child-involved discourse dimensions at dinner. The visibility of talk renders adult power less noticeable but carries with it for the children a whole new set of ambiguities. Modes of children's participation in child- and adult-initiated topics are one example; the patterns observed in the explicit language of control are another. Notwithstanding cultural differences (which I return to), the characteristic pattern for control acts in the families manifests a preference for high levels of directness. *However, this directness does not necessarily reflect a positional, authoritarian stance toward compliance.* I have argued that the frequency of imperatives seems licensed by the intimacy between the participants, the informality of the activity type, and power asymmetries negotiated between adults and children. It represents a speech-event-specific interpretation of appropriate forms of facework.

Two features nevertheless signal that the language of control is person-oriented rather than positional: the types of explanations provided and the negotiation sequences that often follow initial direct forms. As parents claim they tend to explain more; thus, the simplest directive for realizing action may be accompanied by an explanation that provides the rational basis for the need for compliance ("It'll be a bad thing to eat b'cause it will get in your braces," "Don't lift that; it's too heavy for you" "Come sit down; we have to start dinner because Daddy has to get back to work"). Such justifications counterbalance the authoritarian implication of the direct forms (e.g., Do it because I [your parent] said so) by potentially making room for negotiation even when no reason is provided. In this way children learn to implement in their requests the discourse of rational reasoning ("Well, can I go over to her house 'cause Amy is going to be there too?"), which typifies the rhetoric of modern scientific discourse. Negotiation sequences for gaining compliance contain a similar message: Children are indeed encouraged (or at least allowed) to argue and discuss as they seek and provide reasons for compliance and noncompliance. However, the rhetoric of mutual rationality can serve to mask power imbalances. Although parents may provide reasons and invite children to do the same, not all cases represent true negotiations with initially unclear outcomes. In some ostensible negotiations, the final outcomes in response to children's requests are predetermined by parents, and talk serves only to render power less visible.

As a guiding principle, *rationality* penetrates several genres of family discourse in all the families. The concept of rationality should be seen in the wider context of parental facilitation of cognitive development along the lines of modern analytic, scientific ways of thinking. The striking feature of this process, as demonstrated throughout the book, is that it occurs as a by-product of several genres of talk, not necessarily of talk identifiable as explanatory or scientific. The emphasis on rational explanations goes beyond the reasons and justifications that are part of the genre of the language of control; we also find it in the language of explanation and definitions provided in response to children's questions, where it is expected, and, most prominently, in the types of parental questions that guide parent–child coconstruction of narratives. In the way in which they respond to children's narratives, parents highlight the importance of finding rational goals and explanations for the action of human agents (as when a father questions his son about the overall educational goal of the school trip he is recounting); emphasize the importance of the scientific principles of careful observation, attention to detail, and rational, taxonomic classification (as in response to an account of the flowers observed during a hike); stress the need for factuality in personal narratives, and, when appropriate, demand verifiability (as in the story of the giant turtle, where the mother goes to great lengths to demonstrate the need for verifiability, calling on the rhetoric of science to formulate her reaction: "that's called an unconfirmed assumption"). The point here is that, as argued elsewhere (Blum-Kulka & Snow, 1992), what underlies discourse socialization along these lines, in spite of important cultural differences, is the construct of the types of decontextualized discourse worlds associated with Western literate traditions, including the discourse of modern science.

The concept of modernity provides a key element for understanding some of the commonalities in the discourse practices observed in all the families. To account for the differences in cultural styles of sociability and socialization between the discourse of the native Israeli and the Jewish American families, we need to consider the interactional styles of the families in these two groups as semiotic systems operating within the *cultural polysystems* of the respective societies. The concept of "polysystem," as defined by Even-Zohar (1990a), is a coherent system of systems, a whole cultural network, composed of interrelated textual genres and social institutions in a society, each of which is a dynamic system in its own right.[2]

---

[2]Originally suggested by Russian formalists to describe literature, this concept is developed by Even-Zohar and adopted by Harshav as a cultural historical perspective on the emergence of new cultural trends in modern Jewish semiotic systems, including but not restricted to trends in canonical and noncanonical literature.

Synchronically, the interactional styles observed at dinner in educated, middle-class, secular Israeli and Jewish American families represent one dynamic semiotic system within the complex network of interwoven systems that constitute Israeli and American cultures. Diachronically the emergence of these two systems as culturally distinct cannot be understood apart from the historical backgrounds of the communities in question; they represent two orientations to the dialectics of continuity and change in the history of modern Jewish communities.

THE DIALECTICS OF CONTINUITY AND CHANGE

Emending Horowitz and Lissak's description of Israel as the result of "an ideological trend that created a society that became a State" (Horowitz & Lissak, 1989, p. 9, quoted in Harshav, 1993, p. viii), Harshav (1993) saw Israel as the result of "*an ideology that created a language* [i.e., Modern Hebrew] *that forged a society that became a State*" (Harshav, 1993, p. viii). It was in the spirit of this ideological trend that the first University in Palestine was named "The *Hebrew* University," replacing the then-current identification "Jew" or "Jewish" with "Hebrew." The name, like the language, symbolizes the transformation strived for in collective identity, in ways of life, and, most important in the context of this book, in ways of speaking. As vehemently argued by Dina, one of the mothers, Diaspora mentality as well as Diaspora-associated ways of speaking were consciously rejected in preference for the creation of the new *dugri* ["straight"] style (Katriel, 1986). This style, like other semiotic systems within the new Hebrew culture, had to be created anew because the first pioneers had no culture to assimilate to (Even-Zohar, 1990b).

But how truly new is the Israeli interactional style? The question is not often asked. As noted by Even-Zohar (1990a), "the struggle of Hebrew or new recognition and revival, so intimately linked with the social and political struggle for national revival, did not encourage treatment of an undesirable past which one wanted to shed" (p. 151). His own polysystem studies represent one of the very few exceptions to date.[3] In these studies, Even-Zohar

---

[3]An interesting parallel in the domain of political culture is Shlomo Avineri's claim that the roots of Israeli democracy are to be sought in the political traditions emanating from the countries of origin of Israel's founders. Paradoxically, "not in the political traditions and mores of the general, that is Gentile, society out of which those Jewish immigrants came, but in the traditional mores and actual behaviour of the Jewish communities in the Diaspora" (Avineri, 1985, p. 4). Thus, even the pioneers in the Kibbutz, the most novel and revolutionary expression of the new society, "were revolutionaries and socialists, rebelling against the ossified rabbinical and *kehilla* [community] structure of the European *shtetl*; but the modes of their behavior were deeply grounded in the societal behavior patterns of the shtetl, the force of dialectics" (p. 7).

traced the role of Russian models in the shaping of several native Hebrew cultural forms (such as theater, poetry, and reported speech in literature) and the role of Russian and Yiddish in the making of Modern Hebrew, arguing that "side by side with the penetration of new constituents, there remained a substantial mass of 'old culture' " (Even-Zohar, 1990b, p. 182). Katriel (1991) demonstrated such continuity within an ideology of change in the creation of youth movement ceremonies that drew selectively on traditional Jewish as well as European cultural forms. Our study demonstrates such continuity in a domain hitherto undocumented: the interactional style of family discourse.

On the Israeli public scene, it is very much a matter of debate whether the Zionist interpretation of the Jewish revolution (in Harshav's sense) is indeed over, challenged as it is by recent claims that Israel is now living in a Post-Zionist era.[4] On the personal level, for at least a part of the generation studied, it is a compelling and poignant issue, addressed in emotionally charged language. Consider how one mother expresses her Zionist credo in unequivocal terms, voicing clearly the rhetoric of negation. I repeat here, with some omissions, her response to my question, "How would you say you differ, as parents from your own parents?"

> In EVErything. Being Israeli for me . . . well, it's a major subject. *I couldn't live anywhere else* [my emphasis]. My mother—she never really assimilated, she had difficulties with Hebrew, she spoke Polish with me (we were a single parent family, I did not know my father) and I couldn't always understand her. And often she did not understand what I wanted to say. It was like the Tower of Babel . . . [The contrast] is really between the Diaspora and the Israeli generation. For instance, I think about her attitude to the grandchildren—"If you do so and so for me I'll give you . . ." It's her attitude, it's so *very* much the Diaspora (*galuti*) mentality . . . I believe we don't have that any more. I grew up here, mine is an *Israeli* home, because I grew up here and for me this

---

[4]The public debate between Zionists and Post-Zionists cuts across Israeli society, involving scholars from the social sciences and the humanities, creating fierce personal divisions and a heated debate that finds its way into the daily press. The debate raises questions about the definition of Israeli identity: past, present, and future. It concerns the very premises of Zionist ideology, the way its history has been written, and the future direction of Israeli society. For example, the political scientist Ze'ev Shternhal, in responding to attacks on Post-Zionist attitudes, claimed that the argument is not about the legitimacy of the Israeli existence but rather is about the "Zionism of tomorrow" in a society that has passed the period of having to fight for its very existence and can now leave behind the values of "a closed tribal society" (*Ha'aretz*, Israeli daily 15.9.95). The epitome of Post-Zionist attitudes was recently captured on Channel One Televison by a satirical program called *haxamishiya hakamerit*, which in the second week of February (1996) depicted a scene of 'Yuppi' Tel-Aviv youth at a party, dancing in ecstasy and smoking hash to the tunes of "Hatikva," the national anthem. Curiously, this scene did not meet with a general public outcry, unlike many other challenges to canonical ideologies in theater, film, and historical writing.

State—I don't want to go into politics but for me it's the only place we can live in, I have *no doubt* at all. I don't know about them. The young generation. I think Dalit [her daughter] won't have a problem [living elsewhere]. For me it will be a catastrophe [if she leaves], because it will separate between us (. . . .) With all the problems we have, and I am aware of them, I am not blind. Maybe this is my mother's contribution, or the Diaspora, or the Holocaust. Call it whatever you like, this unequivocality of our existence here for me. Maybe more than for others—I can see that among my students, and among young people, you don't find that *xad mashmaiyut* (singlemindedness) of my generation, or at least a *big* part of my generation.

The rhetoric of dissociation from the immigrant mother is infused here with revulsion for anything that stands for the Diaspora (*galuti*) mentality. The cultural opposition invoked is that between the old Jewish ways and the new Israeli ones, and it voices all three of the deictic axes mentioned by Harshav: *here* and not *there* ("this State . . . it's the only place"), *us*, an Israeli home that is radically different in its attitude to children from the bargaining style of the older generation, and finally the future-oriented interpretation of *now*, expressed less confidently with regard to the younger generation ("among young people you don't find that singlemindedness of my generation"). Yet paradoxically, the discursive practices in Dina's family, as in the other Israeli families studied, are not as clearly divorced from the past as is ideologically claimed.

Before we reconsider the evidence in the Israeli style for elements of continuity with the past, we need to locate the relation of the Jewish American families studied with their own past. In the concluding chapter to his historical account of the life of first-generation Jewish immigrants from Eastern Europe to the United States, Howe (1976) asked from a sociological perspective the very question we have been trying to answer in specific sociolinguistic terms: "To what extent . . . did the culture of the East European Jewish immigrants leave a significant imprint on the lives of their children and grandchildren?" (p. 618). Howe's conclusion in essence is that with the move from immigrant neighborhoods to Americanized suburbs, "American society, by its very nature, simply made it all but impossible for Yiddish culture to survive" (p. 641). Nevertheless, Howe argued for the presence of deep continuities with the immigrant past, detectable for him in the choice of vocations, hopes for children, moral views, emphasis on education, and strong conservative feelings for the family.

The sociological literature on American Jewry suggests that for post-emancipation Jewry, the issue of the relation with the past was historically framed not so much in terms of an ideological negation of the Old World as in terms of the need to relinquish its habits to avoid clannishness, to integrate better into the American open society (Biale, 1986; Halpern, 1983). For the present-day community, the issue tends to be framed in terms of identity formation—identity as an ethnic group in a pluralistic society, with the inherent tensions between the forces of assimilation and those of sustained group continuity (Biale, 1986; Cohen, 1989). Against this background it is no wonder that when asked about the difference between their own parental practices and those of their parents, Jewish Americans evoked two themes: that of modern parenting (i.e., their involvement in children's activities, treatment of children as coequals, and the expression of feelings) and that of Jewish parenting (i.e., sending children to Hebrew schools and visiting Israel with the family). For them, the crucial historical transformations are a thing of the past. The difference between them and their parents is mainly a generational gap in a continuing process of assimilation to modern American culture, with a certain degree of variation between the families in the importance they attach to practices aimed at the preservation of an ethnic Jewish identity.

The discourse at dinner suggests that the "Jewishness" of these families is taken for granted and serves as a constant cultural presupposition in relating to people and events (recall the conversations about Whoopi Goldberg and Woody Allen, emphasizing the non-Jewishness of the former and the Jewishness of the latter). For the families we studied, it is a Jewishness defined in ethnic rather than religious terms. For some, Jewish self-identification has no correlate in private or public Jewish activities; for others, it is translated as an educational goal and is manifest by sending the children to all-day Hebrew schools. Yet there is no question of the impact of American culture on all; the English spoken and the discursive practices of these families tell the story of a great transformation in interactional style, parallel to the transformations in religiosity and profession that occurred through this century.

Our findings support Even-Zohar's (1990c) suggestion about the infusion of Jewish elements in the Israeli interactional style, but we see them in a different light from the one he suggested. Even-Zohar located the phenomenon diachronically for Israeli Hebrew and from a synchronic point of view argued for similarities between a Jewish American variety of English and Israeli Hebrew, in the semiotic structure "which in concrete terms manifests itself on the level of argumentation (conversational negation) patterns of persuasion and influence, stock attitudes toward events, joys and troubles and the like" (1990c, p. 120). I agree with Even-Zohar that the most important manifestation of the phenomena is indeed in the semiotic structure of the text rather than in linguistic detail, in our case detected in family discourse, but the lines of similarity he drew (between Israelis and Jewish Americans) do not hold for the variety of English spoken by the Jewish American families we investigated. In the context of our comparative study, the phenomenon needs to be located diachronically; by now, the high-involvement Jewish style seems largely a matter of the past for at least the assimilated, middle-class Jewish Americans like the ones in the study.[5] On the other hand, the impact of the Eastern European past on the Israeli style has been firmly consolidated and integrated (although continuing to be a constant source of influence).[6] However, it should be remembered that the Jewish elements teased out for analytic purposes merge with a wealth of other cultural inputs—cultural practices brought with waves of immigration from oriental and occidental cultures; the discourse world of the religious sectors in the society penetrating the public scene; recent American influences and many other cultural contacts, which all take part in the dynamic construction of the discourse worlds of Israeli culture at large.

It is true that in comparison to Gentile middle-class families in the United States, the Jewish families in our study would stand out as Jewish by features of discourse showing continuity with their Eastern European origins. However, in the context of this study, in comparison with the Israeli families and from my perspective as an Israeli observer and interpreter, the elements that stand out are those that bear the hallmarks of assimilation to mainstream American culture. It is from this perspective that the Jewish American interactional style emerges as highly Americanized.

Two Orientations to Levels of Conversational Involvement

One of the most memorable scenes in Woody Allen's film, "Annie Hall," contrasts on a split screen two dinner conversations as seen from the perspective of the Jewish author–protagonist. One is of an American Jewish family, and the other is of an American Gentile family. The two families seem worlds apart in the ways they construct the speech event; the seemingly chaotic, high-involvement style of the first family, where everybody seems to be talking (and arguing) at the same time, contrasts sharply with the orderly, formal, and smooth conversational ambience of the second. With

---

[5]No doubt, there are different degrees and shades of Americanization among various social strata in the Jewish American community. The speakers in Schiffrin's (1984b) study, who manifested a highly argumentative style probably linked to Eastern European traditions, all came from lower middle-class and were occupied in blue-collar or low white-collar jobs. Although Schiffrin suggested (personal communication) that they were assimilated to mainstream American culture, they seem less so than the professional, academic, middle-class Berkeley and Bostonian families in our project.

[6]A recent example is provided by the campaign for safe sex, figuring an ad on the back of public buses in Israel. It reads, "*shelo neda miaids*," a Yiddish sounding phrase confirmed by a teacher of Yiddish (Leah Skirah, personal communication) to be a direct calque from Yiddish: *me zol nisht visn fun AIDS* [that we shouldn't know from AIDS]. The effect in Hebrew is quite humorous. Another example is the abundance of diminutive suffixes added to all parts of speech found in the gossip columns of the daily press, some borrowings from Russian with Yiddish mediation (as *ik* in yael*ik* and *behexletik* [definitely+ik]) and others directly from Yiddish (like *ke* in *dietke* [diet+ke]) (Mochnik, 1995).

all its oversimplification, this scene provides a key metaphor for understanding the cultural styles of sociability (and in part, socialization) in the families studied here, not because of simple resemblances to any one of our groups, but because the scene represents different levels of conversational involvement, one of which is presumably linked to Jewish Eastern European origins. Conversational involvement represents a gradient phenomenon with many manifestations. I argue that, of the two specific Jewish groups we studied, the Israeli families are higher on the scale of conversational involvement. Not that the Israeli families resemble the stereotypical Jewish family in "Annie Hall"; rather, Israeli speakers have developed a unique interactional style, a style that reconciles the opposing elements of continuity and change in the manifold ways in which it displays conversational involvement.

The subtext of links to the past in the Israeli style cannot be appreciated without first considering the novelty of this interactional style as manifest in family discourse. Its vehicle of expression, namely Modern Hebrew (and Hebrew only), is by now completely taken for granted, testifying to the success of the revival of Hebrew as a spoken language. From a linguistic point of view—a dimension not systematically analyzed in this study—one is struck by the richness and pliability of the language. Even a cursory glimpse at the segments presented in the book shows that the speakers draw freely on several registers of spoken discourse, take care to point out imprecisions in children's use of language, and have no difficulty in reverting to a literate style when appropriate. Yet curiously, this native Hebrew is not fully accepted by its own speakers. From its very beginnings, native spoken Hebrew has met with opposition from purists who fought (and are still fighting, although to a lesser degree) against new linguistic developments thought to abuse the historical heritage of the language. The penetration of native spoken registers into literature, for example, has been a very slow process, with characters in plays and prose in original and translated texts made to speak (until approximately two decades ago) in a highly stylized, unnatural language (Ben-Shachar, 1994; Toury, 1977). This lack of confidence toward native spoken Hebrew is reflected in the abundance of metalinguistic comments in family discourse. The Israeli families topicalize a wide variety of language issues and are highly concerned with correct usage. The high degree of language awareness relates to both socialization and sociability: In interviews and actual speech, the grammaticality of children's speech is a highly valued goal. Also, semantic differentiation between the shades of meanings of apparent synonyms and the acceptability of the accent of announcers in the mass media are important topics of conversation for all participants.

Language is of no topical importance in the Jewish American families. The use of English as the sole medium of communication is absolutely taken for granted, testifying to full Americanization on the purely linguistic level. Instead we find a high degree of concern with the performance aspects of talk; by highlighting turn-taking rules metacommunicatively, the speakers distance themselves from the flow of discourse, underscoring the importance of conversational demeanor (Goffman, 1967). This distancing, associated with several other dimensions of Jewish American discourse, marks this style as less involved than the Israeli style.

In analyzing levels of conversational involvement I am using Tannen's (1985) term to refer specifically to two loci of conversational involvement (Chafe, 1985): involvement with the other interlocutor and degrees of involvement in the discourse per se. On both accounts, the families manifest different patterns of involvement in five of the discourse dimensions examined (see Table 8.1). The Israeli style encompasses several oppositions. In the case of language, the opposition is between usage and attitude, the richness in the actual use of Modern Hebrew as opposed to the note of doubt that accompanies this use on the metalevel of awareness. In the realm of discourse practices, the opposition derives from the ideologies underlying the different worlds of discourse infused in the interactional style.

Consider the opposition between chosen names and actual naming practices. In naming the children, the parents in the native Israeli families chose the modern Hebrew names (e.g., *dalit, merav, niva, tomer, noga, nir*) that were fashionable in the 1970s and 1980s, when the children were born (Weitman, 1988). Yet in addressing the children, the personal given name is rarely used; it is replaced either by derivates or by a rich repertoire of nonce appellations, some made up on the spur of the moment. It is in this dynamic system of expressive nicknaming and endearments that the imprint of Slavic languages and Yiddish is felt most strongly: *nir* is transformed to nir**chik**, merav to merav**ush**, and noga to noga**le**, with each of the children given four to five different appellations during a single dinner. Not only are the sound patterns appropriated from Yiddish and Slavic languages; perhaps even more important, it is the *emotive display* of expressive nicknaming that

TABLE 8.1
Levels of Conversational Involvement at Dinner

Israeli	Jewish American
Display of affective proximity with children	Show of respect for children's independence
Preference for solidarity politeness	Preference for deference politeness
Involvement in narrative events is tale-centered and encourages collective construction and appropriation of the tale.	Involvement in narrative events emphasizes telling rights and allows for the celebration of individual performance
Non-family members accorded full participatory rights	Non-family members accorded limited participatory rights
Responsibility for sociability rests with the women	Responsibility for sociability rests with the men

bears the influence of another cultural phase. Familial affect figures prominently in the folklore surrounding the celebrated warmth—or, depending on
point of view, the suffocation—of the traditional Jewish family (Howe, 1976).
Although exact documentation of its linguistic expression is difficult to come
by (Stahl, 1993), we know that a rich system of expessive derivations and
terms of endearments is widely used in Slavic cultures and has been interpreted as reflecting the high cultural value placed on the display of warmth
and affection, notably in Polish culture (Weirzbicka, 1991).

Free nicknaming signifies a high level of involvement with the interlocutor.
This emphasis on interdependence sharply contrasts with the respect for
independence that is displayed by naming practices in the Jewish American
families. In these families, Jewish identity finds partial expression in the choice
of names: Some of the names are typically Jewish (e.g., Max, Samuel), and
some of the children have been given an additional Hebrew name. In actual
naming practices, however, the American ethos of individualism comes to the
fore. Usually the names chosen are the names used; nicknames and endearments are purposely rare. Like the mother who insisted on addressing her son
from birth by one name and one name only, these families seem to pay homage
to the value of names as identity pegs, as symbolic lines of self-demarcation.

The display of familial affect in the discourse of the Israeli families is
often associated with the language of control. In issuing directives and
negotiating compliance, parents turn to nicknaming and endearments as
one of many forms of mitigation. Forms of mitigation, in turn, are combined
with an extensive use of imperatives. As I have suggested, there are several
explanations, such as asymmetrical relations, informality, affect, and intimacy, for the license given to the use of imperatives in family discourse, a
usage particularly prominent in the Israeli families. From the perspective of
the dialectics of continuity and change, the distinctive feature of the Israeli
language of control is its preference for mitigated directness, a solidarity
politeness style that indexes another opposition between old (and presumably soft) and new (and presumably tough) elements. In the language of
control we find a typical combination of the new, Israeli-created cultural
practices in Hebrew associated with the negation of old ways of being and
speaking, and traces of the old, presumably Eastern European elements of
expressive language, especially those for marking affective attitudes.

The specifics of the language of refusals illustrate this point. The ethos
of directness calls for sincerity and simplicity in the encoding of illocutionary intent. Indeed, in response to children's requests, in cases of noncompliance Israeli parents show a preference for initial blunt rejection ("no")
over the opening of negotiation ("why"). If this ethos alone was adhered to,
negotiation over noncompliance would end either with the first "no" or, in
the spirit of modern, person-oriented attitudes to socialization, would develop further with reasons and justifications grounding the initial move. A

closer look at the Israeli family negotiation sequences shows otherwise: Request sequences rarely end with the first refusal. Despite their bluntness, initial refusals in these families are negotiable and have unpredictable outcomes, with many ending in a reversal of the initial position. Moreover, there is an overindulgence in adversative formats: Signals of disagreement abound and, as noted by Even-Zohar (1990a) for Israeli parlance in general, are sometimes used as discourse connectors void of semantic and pragmatic meaning. All in all, these negotiations recall Jewish sociable arguments (Schiffrin, 1984b) where the overtly confrontational style does not map on to underlying levels of conflict.[7]

In contrast to the dictum of solidarity politeness, which calls for the show of involvement, the dictum of deference politeness[8] favored by the Jewish American families calls for a show of respect for the independence of others. As noted in Chapter 5, the language of control in the Jewish American families when not direct—the overall high level of directness in all the families being motivated by the nature of the speech event—opts for the conventional markers of considerateness, expressed by forms of conventional indirectness such as "can you" and "would you" questions. The Jewish American preference for negotiation in immediate responses to requests provides a further example. In discussing the impact of modernity on all the families, I have argued that by inviting children to argue and discuss the grounds of compliance for their own and their parents' requests, parents are projecting a modern, person-oriented attitude to socialization. The Jewish American families go a step further in this direction, displaying their adherence to the notion of a democratic family by overt marking. Both parents and children abundantly insert "why" in the second slot of request sequences, including sequences opening ostensible negotiations. Hence, in all the families the actual negotiability of requests marks their modern attitude to socialization, whereas the differences in styles of negotiation signify culturally different interpretations of face needs. The net result is two quite different face systems. In the quest for a balance between the two paradoxical aspects of face (i.e., the need for a show of involvement and the need to show respect for others' independence), the balance in the Jewish American families is tipped toward the independence end, whereas in the Israeli families it is tipped toward the involvement end. Both choices seem linked to historically

---

[7]Katriel (1986) suggested that the *dugri* mode itself encapsulates a parallel discrepancy between overt confrontational style and underlying sociability: "despite the discordant note associated with it, the *dugri* ritual manifests the functional nature of conflict as an integrative force in the life of individuals and groups" (p. 59).

[8]My labeling of the Jewish American politeness system as deference politeness shows the cultural relativity of such constructs. For Scollon and Scollon (1995), in a comparative framework that considers Anglophone and Oriental cultures, North American politeness is predominantly solidarity politeness oriented, in contrast to the deference politeness of some Oriental cultures.

shaped attitudes to family interaction. In this respect, the Jewish American interpretation of face needs in the family evokes the egalitarian aspirations and respect for individualism noted by observers of American society since Tocqueville (e.g., Davis, 1979).

Nowhere are the differences in the discourse systems of the two groups more evident than in narrative events. As argued in Chapter 4, involvement in the discourse per se and involvement with the other interlocutor find their extreme expression in Israeli narrative events at dinner. In the transition from the realm of conversation to the realm of telling, the Israeli story entry process is highly interactive, accomplished through several negotiated turns, focused on aligning recipients to the story, and requiring active listener participation. Involvement in the coconstruction of the narrative in Israeli families is a matter of focusing on the tale rather than the telling; thus, rather than ensuring the telling rights of main teller(s), participants are concerned with contributing to the building of the story world in a polyphonic mode, even to the point of appropriating tales intended to represent the personal experience of a single participant. These features of narrative discourse led me first to think of the Israeli style as highly involved interpersonally and as echoing in this way the Eastern European participatory listenership learning styles of the Yeshiva (Spolsky & Walters, 1985) as well as the conversational style of Jewish New Yorkers of similar background (Tannen, 1984).

In contrast, the Jewish American narrative events bring to the fore an accent on performance. Jewish American story entry negotiations focus on explicit allocation of floor space, drawing clearer lines of demarcation between the realm of conversation and the realm of telling. As in all genres of Jewish American discourse at dinner, participants show a high concern (though it is not necessarily realized in actual disourse) for the orderly management of floor space and speaker rights through explicit bids for turn and turn allocators. In the process of narrative co-construction, the focus of participants is on supporting the telling rather than on aiding in the construction of the tale. One of the by-products of this concern is the celebration of monologic performances; another is the ritualistic enactment of stories about the recent experiences of family members, namely the *today rituals*. As a key metaphor for the narrative discourse of these families, the today rituals evoke two facets of American culture in general. First, they can be interpreted as yet another enactment of the concern with egalitarianism and individualism—principles grounded in the utilitarian philosophy that shaped modern American discourse systems (Scollon & Scollon, 1995)[9]—as each member of the family, especially the children, is allocated his or her right to tell. Second, the

---

[9]Scollon and Scollon (1995) argued that the current American discourse system is in essence utilitarian, deriving its origins from the 18th century utilitarian theories of Locke, Smith, Montesquieu, and Kant, and that its predominating ideology therefore is one of individualism and egalitarianism.

formally recurring mode of their performance ties them to other routinized interaction rituals in American society at large (Goffman, 1967), highlighting the role of social convention in regulating interpersonal communication in this society. Certainly, social convention is a major factor in shaping verbal interaction in all societies; the point is the degree to which such conventions are expected to regulate the sequence, content, and form of specific encounters. In this respect, American discourse systems, Jewish American included, appear more highly scripted by far, or in Janney and Arndt's (1992) terms, more social-politeness oriented, than their Israeli correlates.

As Chapter 3 and 4 demonstrate, participation in narrative events, as indeed in all dinner talk, is distributed in the two groups in ways that further reflect underlying cultural differences. By according non-family members full participatory rights and by allocating mainly to women the responsibility of keeping the conversation going, Israeli families highlight the intimacy and informality of family dinners in this culture. By extending interpersonal involvement to all guests at dinner, research observers included, they downplay differences in real closeness between the adults present, construing all adult relations as if they are close and symmetrical. This is in line with the ethos of solidarity politeness that one finds in Israel from family dinners to television talk shows.

In principle, the American discourse system is motivated by similar beliefs. Scollon and Scollon (1995) attributed to American public discourse systems "a reinforced emphasis on direct talk, on avoiding elaboration and extravagance, and on promoting close, egalitarian social relationships" (p. 115). Yet in actual practice, at least in the private sphere and as enacted by our Jewish American families, talk is not universally direct. There are islands of ceremonial elaboration (as in today rituals), and relations with outsiders are construed as egalitarian but definitely not as close. Thus we saw that non-family members are accorded (or feel entitled to) only limited participatory rights and that they take special care not to be personally too involved. Furthermore, because the dinner event with a guest is perceived as not quite an intimate affair, the responsibility for sociability rests mainly with the men, who take it upon themselves to represent the family to the guest.

Throughout this book, and especially in this chapter, I have referred to the notions of socialization and sociability as two separate analytical concepts. In depicting the dynamics of dinner talk, I have argued that the tensions between socialization goals and sociability goals provides the key for understanding the flow of dinner talk and for following the inner logic of its constant shifts between different thematic frames and conversational genres. In this chapter I argued for commonalities in the premises and practices of socialization, combined with diversity in styles of sociability. In conclusion, I turn again to these concepts to suggest that in the actual practice of dinner talk these two dimensions are in fact complementary and overlapping.

The view advocated throughout this book is that the intergenerational encounter of family dinners is a prime site of discursive socialization, yet the way in which children learn about and gain access to cultural discourse worlds at dinner is not limited to adult–child interactions. A major contribution of this approach is that it looks at the ways in which children become members of their culture by considering their participation in a naturally occurring, multiparty, and intergenerational speech event not specifically designed for their needs. It is important that adult sociable talk at dinner acts just as much as an agent of socialization when there is little or no child participation at all. Because talk and culture are inseparable, through listening to adults exchange views and stories about a rich variety of topics in the sociable mode, children learn distinctly cultural (and perhaps familial) notions of tellability, norms for turn-taking, and rhetorical skills for story construction. On the other hand, talk framed as socializing is no less sociable. Regardless of the degree of child participation, in all talk at dinner, whether related to the instrumental needs of serving food or concerned with family news or elaborating topics of non-immediate concern, speakers negotiate their personal, familial, and cultural identities and promote personal relations in ways particular to their own culture. Thus, on one level family dinners need to reconcile pressing needs of socialization (such as teaching table manners) with those of sociability (conversing for the sake of conversation). On another level they successfully practice socialization by being sociable and achieve sociability through the idiom of socialization.

CONCLUSION

The book tells the story of different modes of reconciliation between sociability and socialization at dinner. It is a story grounded in examining the discursive practices of three small groups of families at one speech event. The families are all middle-class, and the event is defined by all as a family meal. Such a small number of families is certainly not representative of all middle-class families in either Israel or the United States. Nor are the patterns of dinner talk depicted necessarily the same as those found in other familial encounters. Furthermore, the presence of a semi-official guest for dinner certainly affected the proceedings; no doubt there is a stronger element of family self-representation in the talk than would have emerged otherwise. However, only specific cases can be portrayed in such detail. Due to the descriptive detail of discursive practices each group of families emerges as having a clear distinctive voice of its own, a voice that is probably very close to its ways of speaking on other familial occasions. This distinctive voice may even be seen to have been sharpened by the presence of a guest, whose relation with the families became the litmus paper for testing cultural attitudes to outsiders. For all the families, dinner talk is contextually bound in many ways. Because the situation is shared by all the families, the specific outlines of the speech event surface clearly, showing the centrality of dinner talk as a primary site for socialization and sociability.

Although I have extended the analysis in several directions, at its base this book presents a discourse-analytical study of naturally occurring talk, a study grounded in sociolinguistic and pragmatic traditions. Though most current approaches to discourse are committed to the study of language in context—to the need to consider texts with and within their social and cultural contexts—there is little agreement on how this is to be achieved empirically (Schiffrin, 1994). This study of family dinner talk meets the challenge in two ways: first, by unveiling the complexities of one type of spatiotemporally bounded speech event across different cultural groups of similar social backgrounds and second, by teasing out the distinctively cultural voice of each group of families participating in such an event. On the first account, the findings reinforce the need to take speech events seriously in studies of discourse; they show the degree to which the nature of talk is contexted situationally, bounded and defined through underlying context-bound parameters that its participants rely on and invoke in negotiating social meanings. On the second account, a different level of context is called into play. Only by relating the discursive practices observed to wider cultural contexts, a process necessitating the crossing of disciplinary boundaries in search for understanding, can the meaning of dinner talk (or for that matter, any other speech activity) be fully appreciated as a form of cultural behavior.

REFERENCES

Andersen Slosberg, E. (1990). *Speaking with style: The sociolinguistic skills of children*. London: Routledge & Kegan Paul.

Aries, P. (1962). *Centuries of childhood: A social history of family life*. New York: Vintage Books.

Aronsson, K., & Rundstrom, B. (1988). Child discourse and parental control in pediatric consultations. *Text, 8*, 159–189.

Aston, G. (1988). *Learning comity: An approach to description and pedagogy of interactional speech*. Bologna: Cooperativa Libraria, Universitari Editrice Bologna.

Auer, J. C. P. (1988). A conversation analytic approach to code-switching and transfer. In M. Heller (Ed.), *Codeswitching: Anthropological and sociolinguistic perspectives* (pp. 187–215). Berlin: Mouton de Gruyter.

Austin, J. (1962). *How to do things with words*. Oxford: Oxford University Press.

Avineri, S. (1985). *The historical roots of Israeli democracy*. Second Annual Guest Lecture, Kaplan Centre, Jewish Studies & Research, University of Cape Town. March 31, 1985.

Avruch, K. (1981). *American immigrants in Israel: Social identities and change*. Chicago: University of Chicago Press.

Bakhtin, M. (1981). *The dialogic imagination: Four essays* (edited by M. Holquist). Austin: University of Texas Press.

Bar Yosef, R., & Shamgar Hendelman, L. (1991). Introduction. In R. Bar Yosef & L. Shamgar Hendelman (Eds.), *Families in Israel* (p. 9). Jerusalem: Academon.

Bates, E. (1976). *Language and context: The acquisition of pragmatics*. New York: Academic Press.

Bateson, G. (1972). *Steps to an ecology of mind*. New York: Ballantine.

Bauman, R. (1986). *Story, performance and event*. Cambridge: Cambridge University Press.

Becker, J. A. (1988). The success of parent's indirect techniques for teaching preschoolers pragmatic skills. *First Language, 8*, 173–181.

Becker, J. A. (1990). Processes in the acquisition of pragmatic competence. In G. Conti-Ramsden & C. Snow (Eds.), *Children's language* (Vol. 7, pp. 7–24). Hillsdale, NJ: Lawrence Erlbaum Associates.

Beebe, L. M., & Takahashi, T. (1989). Do you have a bag? Social status and patterned variation in second language acquisition. In S. Gass, C. Madden, D. Preston, & L. Selinker (Eds.),

Variation in second language acquisition: Discourse and pragmatics (pp. 103–125). Clevedon, England: Multilingual Matters.

Bellah, R. H., Madsen, R., Sullivan, W. M., Swidler, A., & Tipton, S. M. (1985). *Habits of the heart*. New York: Harper & Row.

Ben Ari, E. (1989). Masks and soldiering: the Israeli army and the Palestinian uprising. *Cultural Anthropology, 4*, 372–389.

Ben Rafael, E. (1982). *The emergence of ethnicity: Cultural groups and social conflict in Israel*. London: Greenwood.

Ben Rafael, E. (1994). *Language, identity and social division*. Oxford: Clavedon Press.

Ben-Shachar, R. (1994). Translating literary dialogue: A problem and its implications for translation into Hebrew. *Target, 6*, 195–221.

Berger, P., & Luckman, T. (1966). *The social construction of reality*. New York: Doubleday.

Berk-Seligson, S. (1986). Linguistic contraints on intrasentential code-switching: a study of Spanish/Hebrew bilingualism. *Language in Society, 15*, 313–348.

Berman, R., & Armon-Lotem, S. (1990). *Transcription and coding conventions; Language acquisition project*. Working paper No. 6, Tel Aviv University.

Bernstein, B. (1971). *Class, codes & control* (Vol. 1). London: Routledge & Kegan Paul.

Bernstein, B. (1990). *The structure of pedagogic discourse. Volume 4, Class, codes and control*. London: Routledge & Kegan Paul.

Biale, D. (1986). *Power and powerlessness in Jewish history*. New York: Schoken.

Blum-Kulka, S. (1983). The dynamics of political interviews. *Text, 3*, 131–153.

Blum-Kulka, S. (1987). Indirectness and politeness: Same or different. *Journal of Pragmatics, 11*, 147–160.

Blum-Kulka, S. (1992). The metapragmatics of politeness in Israeli society. In R. Watts, R. J. Ide, & S. Ehlich (Eds.), *Politeness in language: Studies in its history, theory and practice* (pp. 255–281). Berlin: Mouton de Gruyter.

Blum-Kulka, S. (1994). The dynamics of family dinner-talk: Cultural contexts for children's passages to adult discourse. *Research on Language and Social Interaction, 27*, 1–51.

Blum-Kulka, S., Danet, B., & Gerson, R. (1985). The language of requesting in Israeli society. In J. Forgas (Ed.), *Language and social situation* (pp. 113–141). New York: Springer-Verlag.

Blum-Kulka, S., & House, J. (1989). Cross-cultural and situational variation in requesting behavior. In S. Blum-Kulka, J. House, & G. Kasper (Eds.), *Cross-cultural pragmatics: Requests and apologies* (pp. 123–155). Norwood, NJ: Ablex.

Blum-Kulka, S., House, J., & Kasper, G. (Eds.). (1989). *Cross-cultural pragmatics: Requests and apologies. Advances in discourse processes* (Vol. 31). Norwood, NJ: Ablex.

Blum-Kulka, S., & Katriel, T. (1991). Nicknaming practices in families: A cross-cultural perspective. In S. Ting-Toomey & F. Korseny (Eds.), *Cross-cultural interpersonal communication: International and intercultural communication manual* (Vol. 15, pp. 58–77). London: Sage.

Blum-Kulka, S., & Sheffer, H. (1993). The metapragmatic discourse of American-Israeli families at dinner. In G. Kasper & S. Blum-Kulka (Eds.), *Interlanguage pragmatics* (pp. 196–224). New York: Oxford University Press.

Blum-Kulka, S., & Snow, C. (1992). Developing autonomy for tellers, tales and telling in family narrative-events. *Journal of Narrative and Life History, 2*, 187–217.

Bratt-Paulston, C. (1986). Linguistic consequences of ethnicity and nationalism in multilingual settings. In B. Spolsky (Ed.), *Language and education in multilingual settings* (pp. 117–152). Clevedon, Avon: Multilingual Matters.

Briggs, C. (1988). *Competence in performance: The creativity of tradition in Mexicano verbal art*. Philadelphia: University of Pennsylvania Press.

Brown, G., & Yule, G. (1983). *Discourse analysis*. Cambridge: Cambridge University Press.

Brown, P., & Levinson, S. (1987). *Politeness: Some universals in language usage*. Cambridge: Cambridge University Press.

Brown, R. (1991, September). *Language and the relational self.* Paper delivered at the 4th International Conference on Language and Social Psychology, Santa Barbara, California.

Brown, R., & Gilman, A. (1960). The pronouns of power and solidarity. *American Anthropologist, 4,* 24–29.

Brown, R., & Gilman, A. (1989). Politeness theory and Shakespeare's four major tragedies. *Language in Society, 18,* 159–212.

Bruner, E., & Gorfain, P. (1984). Dialogic narration and the paradoxes of Masada. In E. Bruner (Ed.), *Text, play and story: The construction and reconstruction of self and society* (pp. 56–80). Washington, DC: The American Ethnological Society.

Bruner, J. (1983). *Child's talk.* New York: Norton.

Bruner, J. (1986). *Actual minds, possible words.* Cambridge, MA: Harvard University Press.

Bublitz, W. (1988). *Supportive fellow-speakers and cooperative conversations.* Amsterdam: John Benjamins.

Burton, D. (1980). *Dialogue and discourse: A sociolinguistic approach to modern drama dialogue and naturally occurring conversation.* London: Routledge & Kegan Paul.

Calhoun, D. (1973). *The intelligence of a people.* Princeton, NJ: Princeton University Press.

Carbaugh, D. (1988). *Talking American: Cultural discourses on Donahue.* Norwood, NJ: Ablex.

Cazden, C. B. (1988). *Classroom discourse: The language of teaching and learning.* Portsmouth, NH: Heineman.

Cazden, C. B., John, V. P., & Hymes, D. (Eds.). (1972). *Functions of language in the classroom.* New York: Teachers College Press.

Chafe, W. E. (1985). Linguistic differences produced between speaking and writing. In R. D. Olson, N. Torrance, & A. Hildyard (Eds.), *Literacy, language, and writing* (pp. 105–124). Cambridge: Cambridge University Press.

Cicourel, A. (1992). The interpretation of communicative contexts: Examples from medical encounters. In A. Duranti & C. Goodwin (Eds.), *Rethinking context* (pp. 291–311). Cambridge: Cambridge University Press.

Clancy, P. (1986). The acquisition of communicative style in Japanese. In B. B. Schieffelin & E. Ochs (Eds.), *Language socialization across cultures* (pp. 213–251). Cambridge, England: Cambridge University Press.

Clark, H. (1987). Four dimensions of language use. In J. Verschueren & M. Bertuccelli-Papi (Eds.), *The pragmatic perspective* (pp. 9–29). Amsterdam: John Benjamins.

Clifford, J. (1988). *The predicament of culture: Twentieth century ethnography, literature and art.* Cambridge, MA: Harvard University Press.

Clyne, M. (1982). *Multilingual Australia: Resources, needs, policies.* Melbourne: River Seine.

Clyne, M. (1985). Language maintenance and shift—some data from Australia. In N. Wolfson & J. Manes (Eds.), *Language of inequality* (pp. 195–206). The Hague: Mouton.

Cohen, S. (1989). *Two worlds of Judaism: Israeli and American.* New Haven: Yale University Press.

Corsaro, W. (1979). "We're friends, right?": Children's use of access rituals in a nursery school. *Language in Society, 8,* 315–336.

Craig, R. T., & Tracy, K. (Eds.). (1983). *Conversational coherence.* Beverly Hills: Sage Publications.

Crow, K. B. (1983). Topic shifts in couples conversations. In R. T. Craig & K. Tracy (Eds.), *Conversational coherence* (pp. 136–157). Beverly Hills: Sage.

Dascal, M. (1983). *Pragmatics and the philosophy of mind.* Amsterdam: John Benjamins.

Dascal, M., & Idan, A. (1989). From individual to collective action. In F. Vandamme & R. Pinxten (Eds.), *The philosophy of Leo Apostel* (pp. 133–148). Ghent: Communication and Cognition.

Dascal, M., & Katriel, T. (1979). Digression: A study in conversational coherence. *PTL: A Journal for Descriptive Poetics and Theory of Literature, 4,* 203–232.

Davis, D. B. (1979). American family: Historical perspective. In D. Reiss & H. A. Hoffman (Eds.), *The American family* (pp. 35–69). New York: Plenum.

De Ber, Z. (1995). *Children's stories at dinner: American–Israeli families.* Unpublished Master's thesis, Hebrew University. [In Hebrew] van Dijk, T. (1977). *Text and context: Explorations in the semantics and pragmatics of discourse*. London: Longman.

van Dijk, T. (1981). *Studies in the pragmatics of discourse*. The Hague: Mouton.

Doleve-Gondelman, T. (1989). *Ethiopian Jews in Israel. Family portraits: A multi-faceted view*. The NCJW Research Institute for Innovation in Education, School of Education, The Hebrew University, Jerusalem. [in Hebrew]

Dominguez, V. (1989). *People as subject, people as object: Selfhood and peoplehood in contemporary Israel*. Madison, WI: University of Wisconsin Press.

Dorval, B., & Eckerman, C. O. (1984). Developmental trends in the quality of conversation achieved by small groups of acquainted peers. *Monographs of the Society for Research in Child Development, 49*(Serial No. 206).

Duranti, A., & Goodwin, C. (Eds.). (1992). *Rethinking context: Language as an interactive phenomenon*. Cambridge: Cambridge University Press.

Eakins, B., & Eakins, R. G. (1976). Verbal turn-taking and exchanges in faculty dialogue. In B. L. Dubois & I. Crouch (Eds.), *The sociology of the language of American women* (pp. 53–62). San Antonio: Trinity University.

Edelsky, C. (1981). Who's got the floor? *Language in Society, 10*, 383–423.

Edmondson, W. (1981). *Spoken discourse: A model for analysis*. London: Longman.

Edmondson, W., & House, J. (1981). *Let's talk and talk about it. A pedagogic interactional grammar of English*. Munchen: Urban & Schwarzenberg.

Eisenstadt, S. N. (1985). *The transformation of Israeli society*. London: Weidenfeld & Nicolson.

El Or, T. (1990). *Educated and ignorant: On ultra Orthodox women and their world*. Tel-Aviv: Am Oved. [in Hebrew]

Erickson, F. (1982). Money tree, lasagna bush, salt and pepper: Social construction of topical cohesion in a conversation among Italian-Americans. In D. Tannen (Ed.), *Analyzing discourse: Text and talk* (pp. 43–71). Washington, DC: Georgetown University Press.

Erickson, F. (1988). Discourse coherence, participation structure, and personal display in family dinner table conversation. *Working Papers in Educational Linguistics, 4*, 1–26.

Erickson, F. (1990). The social construction of discourse coherence in a family dinner table conversation. In B. Dorval (Ed.), *Conversation organization and its development* (pp. 207–239). Norwood, NJ: Ablex.

Erickson, F., & Mohatt, G. (1982). Cultural organization of participant structure in two class-rooms of Indian students. In G. Spindler (Ed.), *Doing the ethnography of schooling* (pp. 132–174). New York: Holt, Rinehart & Winston.

Ervin-Tripp, S. (1979). Children's verbal turn-taking. In E. Ochs & B. Schieffelin (Eds.), *Developmental pragmatics* (pp. 391–414). New York: Academic Press.

Ervin-Tripp, S. (1982). Ask and it shall be given you: Children's requests. In H. Byrnes (Ed.), *Georgetown University roundtable in language and linguistics* (pp. 235–245). Washington, DC: Georgetown University Press.

Ervin-Tripp, S., & Gordon, D. P. (1986). The development of children's requests. In R. E. Schiefelbusch (Ed.), *Communicative competence: Assessment and intervention* (pp. 61–96). San Diego, CA: College Hill Press.

Ervin-Tripp, S., Guo, J., & Lampert, M. (1990). Politeness and persuasion in children's requests. *Journal of Pragmatics, 14*, 307–333.

Even-Zohar, I. (1990a). Aspects of the Hebrew-Yiddish polysystem: A case of multilingual polysystem. *Poetics Today, 11*, 152–174.

Even-Zohar, I. (1990b). The emergence of native Hebrew culture in Palestine: 1882–1948. *Poetics Today, 11*, 175–195.

Even-Zohar, I. (1990c). The role of Russian and Yiddish in the making of Modern Hebrew. *Poetics Today, 11*, 111–121.

Even-Zohar, I. (1990d). Void pragmatic connectives. *Poetics Today, 11*, 219–247.

Faerch, C., & Kasper, G. (1989). Internal and external modification in interlanguage request realization. In S. Blum-Kulka, J. House, & G. Kasper (Eds.), *Cross cultural pragmatics: Requests and apologies* (pp. 221–248). Norwood, NJ: Ablex.

Fairclaugh, N. (1993). Critical discourse analysis and the marketization of public discourse. *Discourse and Society, 4*, 133–169.

Feiring, C., & Lewis, M. (1987). The ecology of some middle-class families at dinner. *International Journal of Behavioral Development, 10*, 377–390.

Fisher, W. (1987). *Human communication as narration*. Columbia, South Carolina: University of South Carolina Press.

Fishman, J. (1985). *The rise and fall of the ethnic revival: Perspectives on language and ethnicity*. Berlin: Mouton.

Fishman, J., Cooper, R. L., & Conrad, A. D. (1977). *The spread of English*. Rowley, MA: Newbury House.

Fishman, P. (1978). Interaction: The work women do. *Social Problems, 25*, 397–406.

Foucault, M. (1972). *The archeology of knowledge* (A. M. Sheridan Smith, trans.). New York: Harper & Row.

Fraser, B. (1980). Conversational mitigation. *Journal of Pragmatics, 4*, 341–350.

Fraser, B., & Nolen, W. (1981). The association of deference with linguistic form. *International Journal of the Sociology of Language, 27*, 93–111.

Fraser, N. (1990). Rethinking the public sphere: A contribution to the critique of actually existing democracy. *Social Text, 25*, 56–80.

Gal, S. (1979). *Language shift: Social determinants of linguistic change in bilingual Australia*. New York: Academic Press.

Gal, S. (1989). Between speech and silence: The problematics of research on language and gender. *Papers in Pragmatics, 3*, 1–39.

Garfinkel, H. (1984). *Studies in ethnomethodology*. Cambridge: Polity Press. (Original work published 1967).

Garvey, C. (1984). *Children's talk*. London: Fontana Paperbacks.

Geertz, C. (1973). *The interpretation of cultures*. New York: Basic Books.

Genette, G. (1980). *Narrative discourse* ([trans. from French (Original work, Figures 3, published 1972)]). Ithaca, NY: Cornell University Press.

Giles, H. (1979). Ethnicity markers in speech. In K. R. Scherer & H. Giles (Eds.), *Social markers in speech* (pp. 251–280). Cambridge: Cambridge University Press.

Gleason, J. B. (1987). Sex differences in parent–child interactions. In S. Phillips, S. Steele, & C. Tanz (Eds.), *Language, gender and sex in comparative perspective* (pp. 189–199). Cambridge: Cambridge University Press.

Gleason, J. B., Perlman, R., & Grief, E. (1984). What's the magic word: Learning language through politeness routines. *Discourse Processes, 7*, 493–502.

Gleason, J. B., & Weintraub, S. (1976). The acquisition of routines in child language: "Trick or Treat." *Language in Society, 5*, 129–136.

Goffman, E. (1959). *The presentation of self in everyday life*. New York: Doubleday.

Goffman, E. (1961). *Encounters: Two studies in the sociology of interaction*. Indianapolis: Bobbs Merrill.

Goffman, E. (1963). *Stigma: Notes on the management of spoiled identity*. New York: Penguin.

Goffman, E. (1967). *Interaction ritual: Essays on face to face behavior*. New York: Doubleday.

Goffman, E. (1974). *Frame analysis*. New York: Penguin.

Goffman, E. (1981). *Forms of talk*. Philadelphia: University of Pennsylvania Press.

Gold, D. L. (1989). A sketch of the linguistic situation in Israel today. *Language in Society, 18*, 361–389.

Goodenough, W. H. (1981). *Culture, language and society* (2nd ed.). Menlo Park: Benjamin Cummings.

Goodwin, C. (1981). *Conversational organization: Interaction between speakers and hearers*. New York: Academic Press.

Goodwin, C. (1984). Notes on story structure and the organization of participation. In M. Atkinson & J. Heritage (Eds.), *Structures of social action* (pp. 225–246). Cambridge: Cambridge University Press.

Goodwin, M. (1990). *He-said-she-said: Talk as social organization among Black children*. Bloomington, IN: Indiana University Press.

Goody, E. (1978). Towards a theory of questions. In E. Goody (Ed.), *Questions and politeness* (pp. 17–43). Cambridge: Cambridge University Press.

Goodz Singerman, N. (1989). Parental language mixing in bilingual families. *Infant Mental Health Journal, 10*, 25–44.

Grice, H. P. (1975). Logic and conversation. In P. Cole & J. Morgan (Eds.), *Syntax and semantics 3: Speech acts* (pp. 41–58). New York: Academic Press.

Grief, E., & Gleason, J. B. (1980). Hi, thanks, and goodbye: More routine information. *Language in Society, 9*, 159–167.

Gu, Y. (1990). Politeness phenomena in Modern Chinese. *Journal of Pragmatics, 14*, 237–257.

Guiora, R. (1985). A text-based analysis of non-narrative texts. *Theoretical Linguistics, 12*, 115–135.

Gumperz, J. J. (1986). Introduction. In J. J. Gumperz & D. Hymes (Eds.), *Directions in sociolinguistics: The ethnography of communication* (pp. 1–26). New York: Basil Blackwell. (Original work published 1972)

Gumperz, J. (1982). *Discourse strategies*. Cambridge: Cambridge University Press.

Habermas, J. (1987a). *The philosophical discourse of modernity: Twelve lectures*. Cambridge: Polity Press.

Habermas, J. (1987b). *The theory of communicative action, Vol. 2. Lifeworld and system: A critique of functionalist reason*. Boston: Beacon.

Halmari, H., & Smith, W. (1994). Code-switching and register shift: Evidence from Finnish–English child bilingual conversation. *Journal of Pragmatics, 21*, 427–445.

Halpern, B. (1983). America is different. In M. Sklare (Ed.), *American Jews: A reader*. New York: Berman House.

Hamers, J. F., & Blanc, M. H. (1989). *Bilinguality and bilingualism*. Cambridge: Cambridge University Press.

Handelman, D. (1990). *Models and mirrors: Towards an anthropology of public events*. Cambridge: Cambridge University Press.

Handelman, D., & Shamgar-Handelman, L. (1990). Holiday celebrations in Israeli kindergartens. In D. Handelman, *Models and mirrors: Towards an anthropology of public events* (pp. 162–189). Cambridge: Cambridge University Press.

Harding-Riley, E. P. (1986). *The bilingual family: A handbook for parents*. Cambridge: Cambridge University Press.

Harshav, B. (1990). The miracle of Hebrew revival. *Alpayim, 2*, 1–24. [In Hebrew]

Harshav, B. (1993). *Language in time of revolution*. Berkeley: University of California Press.

Hasan, R. (1992). Meaning in sociolinguistic theory. In K. Bolton & H. Kwok (Eds.), *Sociolinguistics today: International perspectives* (pp. 81–119). New York: Routledge & Kegan Paul.

Heath, S. B. (1982). Questioning at home and at school: A comparative study. In G. Spindler (Ed.), *Doing the ethnography of schooling: Educational anthropology in action* (pp. 103–131). New York: Holt, Rinehart & Winston.

Heath, S. B. (1983). *Ways with words: Language, life and work in communities and classrooms*. Cambridge: Cambridge University Press.

Helfrich, H. (1979). Age markers in speech. In K. R. Scherer & H. Giles (Eds.), *Social markers in speech* (pp. 63–96). Cambridge: Cambridge University Press.

Heredia-Deprez, C. (1990). Comment est-on bilingue en famille? Elements de methodologie. *La Linguistique, 26*, 95–105.

Herman, S. N. (1977). *Jewish identity: A social psychological perspective*. London: Sage.

Horowitz, D. (1993). *The heavens and the earth: a self portrait of the 1948 generation.* Jerusalem: Keter. [in Hebrew]

Horowitz, D., & Lissak, M. (1989). *Trouble in utopia: The overburdened polity of Israel.* Albany: State University of New York Press.

Howe, I. (1976). *World of our fathers.* New York: Harcourt Brace Jovanovitch.

Huerta-Macias, A. (1981). Codeswitching: All in the family. In R. Duran (Ed.), *Latino language and communicative behavior* (pp. 153–168). Norwood, NJ: Ablex.

Hymes, D. (1974). *Foundations of sociolinguistics: An ethnographic approach.* Philadelphia: University of Pennsylvania Press.

Hymes, D. (1981). *"In vain I tried to tell you": Essays of Native American ethnopoetics.* Philadelphia: University of Pennsylvania Press.

Hymes, D. (1989). Models of the interaction of language and social life. In J. Gumperz & D. Hymes (Eds.), *Directions in sociolinguistics: The ethnography of communication* (pp. 35–72). Oxford: Basil Blackwell. (Original work published 1972).

Ide, S. (1989). Formal forms and discernment: Two neglected aspects of linguistic politeness. *Mulitlingua, 8,* 223–248.

Inbar, M., & Adler, C. (1977). *Ethnic integration in Israel.* New Brunswick, NJ: Transaction Books.

Irvine, J. (1979). Formality and informality in communicative events. *American Anthropologist, 81,* 772–791.

Janney, R. W., & Arndt, H. (1992). Intracultural tact versus intercultural tact. In R. J. Watts, S. Ide, & K. Ehlich (Eds.), *Politeness in language* (pp. 21–43). Berlin: Mouton.

Jefferson, G. (1972). Side sequences. In D. Sudnow (Ed.), *Studies in social interaction* (pp. 294–338). New York: Free Press.

Jefferson, G. (1978). Sequential aspects of storytelling in conversation. In J. Schenkein (Ed.), *Studies in the organization of conversational interaction* (pp. 219–248). New York: Academic Press.

Kahane, R., & Kopstein, S. (Eds.). (1980). *Problems of collective identity and legitimation in Israeli society: A reader.* Jerusalem: Academon. [In Hebrew]

Kasper, G. (1990). Linguistic politeness: Current research issues. *Journal of Pragmatics, 14,* 193–219.

Kasper, G., & Blum-Kulka, S. (Eds.). (1993). *Interlanguage pragmatics.* New York: Oxford University Press.

Katriel, T. (1986). *Talking straight: Dugri speech in Israeli sabra culture.* Cambridge: Cambridge University Press.

Katriel, T. (1991). *Communal webs: Communication and culture in contemporary Israel.* Albany, NY: State University of New York Press.

Katriel, T., & Philipsen, G. (1990). What we need is communication: Communication as a cultural notion in some American speech. In D. Carbaugh (Ed.), *Cultural communication and intercultural contact* (pp. 77–95). Hillsdale, NJ: Lawrence Erlbaum Associates. (Original work published 1981).

Keenan, E., & Schieffelin, B. (1976). Topic as a discourse notion: A study of topic in the conversations of children and adults. In C. N. Li (Ed.), *Subject and topic* (pp. 335–385). New York: Academic Press.

Keppler, A., & Luckman, T. (1991). "Teaching": Conversational transmission of knowledge. In I. Markova & K. Foppa (Eds.), *Asymmetries in dialogue* (pp. 143–166). Savage, Maryland: Barnes & Noble.

Kirshenblatt-Gimblett, B. (1989). The concept and varieties of narrative performance in East-European Jewish culture. In R. Bauman & J. Sherzer (Eds.), *Explorations in the ethnography of speaking* (pp. 263–283). Cambridge: Cambridge University Press. (Original work published 1974).

Kirshenblatt-Gimblett, B. (1975). A parable in context: A social-interactional analysis of story telling performance. In D. Ben Amos & K. S. Goldstein (Eds.), *Folklore: Performance and communication* (pp. 106–130). The Hague: Mouton.

Kitagawa, C. (1980). Saying "yes" in Japanese. *Journal of Pragmatics, 4,* 105–120.

Kochman, T. (1981). *Black and White styles in conflict.* Chicago: University of Chicago Press.

Kurland, B. (1992). *The role of language choice and language mixing in language socialization.* Unpublished Master's Thesis, Department of Psychology, Harvard University.

Labov, W. (1972a). *Language in the inner city: Studies in the Black English vernacular.* Philadelphia: University of Pennsylvania Press.

Labov, W. (1972b). *Sociolinguistic patterns.* Oxford: Basil Blackwell.

Labov, W., & Fanshel, D. (1977). *Therapeutic discourse: Psychotherapy in conversation.* New York: Academic Press.

Labov, W., & Waletzki, J. (1967). Narrative analysis. In J. Helm (Ed.), *Essays on the verbal and visual arts: Proceedings of the 1966 meeting of the American Ethnological Society* (pp. 12–44). Seattle: American Ethnological Society.

Lakoff, R. (1975). *Language and woman's place.* New York: Harper & Row.

Lakoff, R. T. (1990). *Talking power: The politics of language in our lives.* New York: Basic Books.

Lanza, E. (1990, July). *Can bilingual two-year-olds code-switch?* Paper presented at the Fifth International Congress for the Study of Child Language, Budapest, Hungary.

Leech, G. (1983). *Principles of pragmatics.* New York: Longman.

LeVine, R. (1990). Infant environments in psychoanalysis: A cross-cultural view. In J. W. Stigler, R. A. Shweder, & G. Herdt (Eds.), *Cultural psychology* (pp. 454–477). Cambridge: Cambridge University Press.

Levinson, S. (1988). Putting linguistics on a proper footing: Exploration in Goffman's concepts of participation. In P. Drew & A. Woolton (Eds.), *Goffman: An interdisciplinary appreciation* (pp. 161–227). Oxford: Polity Press.

Liebes, T., & Grissak, R. (1995). Television news and the politization of women. In D. Peletz (Ed.), *Political communication in action.* Cresskill, NJ: Hampton Press.

Liebes, T., & Katz, E. (1990). *The export of meaning.* New York: Oxford University Press.

Liebman, C. S., & Cohen, S. (1990). *Two worlds of Judaism: The Israeli and American experience.* New Haven: Yale University Press.

Liebman, C. S., & Don-Yehiya, E. (1981). *Civil religion in Israel.* Berkeley: University of California Press.

MacWhinney, B. (1991). *The CHILDES project: Tools for analyzing talk.* Hillsdale, NJ: Lawrence Erlbaum Associates.

Malinowsky, B. (1923). The problem of meaning in primitive languages. In C. K. Ogden & I. A. Richards (Eds.), *The meaning of meaning* (pp. 296–336). New York: Harcourt Brace.

Maltz, D., & Borker, A. (1982). A cultural approach to male–female communication. In J. Gumperz (Ed.), *Language and social identity* (pp. 195–217). Cambridge: Cambridge University Press.

Mashler, Y. (1994). Metalanguaging and discourse markers in bilingual conversations. *Language in Society, 23,* 325–367.

Matsumoto, Y. (1989). Politeness and conversational universals: Observations from Japanese. *Multilingua, 8,* 207–221.

Maynard, D. (1980). Placement of topic changes in conversation. *Semiotica, 30,* 263–290.

McCabe, A., & Peterson, C. (1991). Getting the story: A longitudinal study of parental styles in eliciting narratives and developing narrative skill. In A. McCabe & C. Peterson (Eds.), *Developing narrative structure* (pp. 217–255). Hillsdale, NJ: Lawrence Erlbaum Associates.

Mead, G. H. (1973). The art and technology of field work. In R. Narroll & R. Cohen (Eds.), *A handbook of method in cultural anthropology* (pp. 246–265). New York: Columbia University Press.

Mead, M. (1959). *Four Families* [Film with commentary by Margaret Mead; 60 mn, sound, black & white]. National Film Board of Canada.

Miller, P. J., & Byhouwer Moore, B. (1989). Narrative conjunctions of caregiver and child: A comparative perspective on socialization through stories. *Ethos, 17,* 428–449.

Miller, P., Potts, R., Fung, H., Hoogstra, L., & Mintz, J. (1990). Narrative practices and the social construction of self in childhood. *American Ethnologist, 17*, 292–309.

Mochnik, M. (1995, October). *A small suffix that did well.* Paper delivered at the Israeli 21st Annual Applied Linguistics Conference, Levinsky College.

Myerhoff, B. (1978). *Number our days.* New York: Dutton.

Ninio, A. (1988). The roots of narrative: discussing recent events with very young children. *Language Science, 10*, 35–52.

Ninio, A., & Snow, C. (1996). *Pragmatic development.* Boulder, CO: Westview.

O'Barr, W. M. (1982). *Linguistic evidence: Language, power and strategy in the courtroom.* New York: Academic Press.

Ochs, E. (1986). Introduction. In B. Schieffelin & E. Ochs (Eds.), *Language socialization across cultures* (pp. 1–17). Cambridge: Cambridge University Press.

Ochs, E. (1988). *Culture and language development: Language acquisition and language socialization in a Samoan village.* Cambridge: Cambridge University Press.

Ochs, E. (1992). Indexing gender. In A. Duranti & C. Goodwin (Eds.), *Rethinking Context: Language as an interactive phenomenon* (pp. 335–359). Cambridge: Cambridge University Press.

Ochs, E. (1993). Constructing social identity: A language socialization perspective. *Research on Language and Social Interaction, 26*, 287–306.

Ochs, E., & Schieffelin, B. (1984). Language acquisition and socialization: Three developmental stories and their application. In R. Shweder & R. A. Levine (Eds.), *Culture theory* (pp. 276–323). Cambridge: Cambridge University Press.

Ochs, E., Smith, R., & Taylor, C. (1989). Detective stories at dinnertime: Problem solving through co-narration. *Cultural Dynamics, 2*, 238–257.

Ochs, E., Taylor, C., Rudolph, D., & Smith, R. (1992). Storytelling as a theory-building activity. *Discourse Processes, 15*, 37–72.

Olshtain, E., & Blum-Kulka, S. (1985). Degree of approximation: Non-native reactions to native speech act behavior. In S. Gass (Ed.), *Input in second language acquisition* (pp. 303–329). Rowley, MA: Newbury.

Olshtain, E., & Blum-Kulka, S. (1989). Happy Hebrish: Mixing and switching in American-Israeli family interaction. In S. Gass, C. Madden, D. Preston, & L. Selinker (Eds.), *Variation in second language acquisition, Volume 1. Discourse and pragmatics* (pp. 59–84). Philadelphia: Multilingual Matters.

Olshtain, E., & Weinbach, L. (1987). Complaints: A study of speech act behavior among native and nonnative speakers of Hebrew. In J. Verschueren & P. Bertalucci (Eds.), *The pragmatics perspective* (pp. 195–211). Amsterdam: John Benjamins.

Olson, D. (1977). From utterance to text: The bias of language in speech and writing. *Harvard Educational Review, 47*, 257–281.

Pellegrini, A. D., Brody, G., & Stoneman, Z. (1987). Children's conversational competence with their parents. *Discourse Processes, 10*, 95–106.

Peres, J., & Katz, R. (1981). Stability and centrality: The nuclear family in modern Israel. *Social Forces, 59*, 687–704.

Perlman, R. (1984). *Variations in socialization styles: Family talk at the dinner table.* Unpublished doctoral dissertation, Boston University.

Pfaff, C. (1979). Constraints on language mixing. *Language, 55*, 291–318.

Polanyi, L. (1989). *Telling the American story.* Cambridge, MA: MIT Press.

Polkinghorne, D. (1983). *Methodology for the human sciences.* Albany: State University of New York Press.

Polss, L. (1990). *Starting the story: A cross-cultural analysis of conversational story entrance talk.* Unpublished Master's Thesis, Hebrew University, Jerusalem.

Pomerantz, A. (1984). Agreeing and disagreeing with assessments: Some features of pre-ferred/dispreferred turn shapes. In J. M. Atkinson & J. Heritage (Eds.), *Structures of social action* (pp. 57–101). Cambridge: Cambridge University Press.

Pontecorvo, C., & Fasulo, A. (in press). Learning to argue in family shared discourse: The reconstruction of past events. In L. Resnick, R. Saljo, & C. Pontecorvo (Eds.), *Discourse, tools, and reasoning: Essays in situated cognition*. New York: Springer Verlag.

Poplack, S. (1980). "Sometimes I'll start a sentence in English Y TERMINO EN ESPANOL"; towards a typology of code-switching. *Linguistics, 18*, 581–618.

Poplack, S. (1988). Contrasting patterns of codeswitching in two communities. In M. Heller (Ed.), *Codeswitching: Anthropological and sociolinguistic perspectives* (pp. 215–245). Berlin: Mouton de Gruyter.

Queen, A. S., Habenstein, W. R., & Quadagno, S. J. (1985). *The family in various cultures*. New York: Harper & Row.

Rabin, C. (1976). Acceptability in a revived language. In S. Greenbaum (Ed.), *Acceptability in language* (pp. 149–167). The Hague: Mouton.

Reger, Z., & Gleason, B. J. (1991). Romani child directed speech and children's language. *Language in Society, 20*, 601–619.

Reichman, R. (1978). Conversational coherency. *Cognitive Science, 2*, 283–327.

Reisman, K. (1974). Contrapuntal conversation in an Antiguan village. In R. Bauman & J. Sherzer (Eds.), *Explorations in the ethnography of speaking* (pp. 110–125). Cambridge: Cambridge University Press.

Ricoeur, P. (1983). *Hermeneutics and the human sciences*. New York: Cambridge University Press.

Rimmon-Keenan, S. (1983). *Narrative fiction: Contemporary poetics*. New York: Methuen.

Rintell, E., & Mitchell, C. J. (1989). Studying request and apologies: An inquiry into method. In S. Blum-Kulka, J. House, & G. Kasper (Eds.), *Cross-cultural pragmatics: Requests and apologies* (pp. 248–273). Norwood, NJ: Ablex.

Rodriguez, R. (1980). Aria: A memoir of a bilingual childhood. *The American Scholar, 33*, 25–42.

Rogoff, B. (1990). *Apprenticeship in thinking: Cognitive development in social context*. New York: Oxford University Press.

Rogoff, B., Mistry, J., Goncu, A., & Mosier, C. (1993). *Guided participation in cultural activity by toddlers and caregivers*. Monographs of the Society for Research in Child Development, Serial No. 236, Vol. 58, No. 8.

Romaine, S. (1984). *The language of children and adolescents: The acquisition of communicative competence*. Oxford: Basil Blackwell.

Romaine, S. (1989). *Bilingualism*. Oxford: Basil Blackwell.

Rubinstein, A. (1977). *To be a free people*. Tel Aviv: Schoken. [In Hebrew]

Sachs, J. (1979). Topic selection in parent-child discourse. *Discourse Processes, 2*, 145–153.

Sacks, H. (1973). *A preference for agreement in natural conversation*. Paper presented at the Linguistic Institute, Ann Arbor, Michigan.

Sacks, H. (1974). An analysis of course of a joke's telling in conversation. In R. Bauman & J. Sherzer (Eds.), *Explorations in the ethnography of speaking* (pp. 337–353). Cambridge: Cambridge University Press.

Sacks, H. (1978). Some technical considerations of a dirty joke. In J. Schenkein (Ed.), *Studies in the organization of conversational interaction* ([edited by Gail Jefferson from unpublished lectures: fall 1971, lectures 9–12], pp. 249–270). New York: Academic Press.

Sacks, H., Schegloff, E., & Jefferson, G. (1974). A simplest systematics for the organization of turn taking in conversation. *Language, 50*, 696–735.

Sacks, J. (1982). "Don't interrupt!": Preschoolers' entry into ongoing conversations. In C. E. J. Johnson & C. L. Thew (Eds.), *Proceedings of the Second International Congress for Child Language, 1* (pp. 344–356). Washington, DC: University Press of America.

Saunders, G. (1988). *Bilingual children: From birth to teens*. Clevedon: Multilingual Matters.

Saville-Troike, M. (1994, June). *Language maintenance/shift in immigrant speech communities*. Plenary Presentation at the International Conference on Immigration, Language Acquisition and Patterns of Social Integration, The Hebrew University of Jerusalem.

Saville-Troike, M., & Kleigfen, J. (1986). Scripts for school: Cross-cultural communication in elementary classrooms. *Text, 6,* 207–221.

Schegloff, E. A. (1968). Sequencing in conversational openings. *American Anthropologist, 70,* 1075–1095.

Schegloff, E. A. (1992). In another context. In A. Duranti & C. Goodwin (Eds.), *Rethinking context* (pp. 191–229). Cambridge: Cambridge University Press.

Schegloff, E. A., & Sacks, H. (1973). Opening up closings. *Semiotica, 8,* 289–327.

Schieffelbush, J., & Pickar, J. (Eds.). (1984). *Communicative competence: Acquisition and intervention.* Baltimore: University Park Press.

Schieffelin, B. (1990). *The give and take of everyday life: Language socialization of Kaluli children.* Cambridge: Cambridge University Press.

Schieffelin, B., & Eisenberg, A. (1984). Cultural variation in children's conversation. In R. L. Schiefelbush & J. Pickar (Eds.), *Communicative competence: Acquisition and intervention* (pp. 377–423). Baltimore: University Park Press.

Schieffelin, B., & Ochs, E. (Eds.). (1986). *Language socialization across cultures.* Cambridge: Cambridge University Press.

Schiffrin, D. (1984a). How a story says what it means and does. *Text, 4,* 313–346.

Schiffrin, D. (1984b). Jewish argument as sociability. *Language in Society, 13,* 311–335.

Schiffrin, D. (1987). *Discourse markers.* Cambridge: Cambridge University Press.

Schiffrin, D. (1994). *Approaches to discourse.* Oxford: Basil Blackwell.

Schley, S., & Snow, C. (1992). The conversational skills of school-aged children. *Social Development, 1,* 119–133.

Schneider, D. M. (1976). Notes toward a theory of culture. In K. H. Basso & H. A. Selby (Eds.), *Meaning in anthropology* (pp. 197–220). Albuquerque, NM: University of New Mexico Press.

Schumann, J. H. (1978). The acculturation model for second-language acquisition. In R. C. Gingas (Ed.), *Second language acquisition and foreign language teaching* (pp. 27–50). Arlington, VA: Center for Applied Linguistics.

Scollon, R., & Scollon, S. (1981). *Narrative, literacy and face in interethnic communication.* Norwood, NJ: Ablex.

Scollon, R., & Scollon, S. (1995). *Intercultural communication: A discourse approach.* Oxford: Basil Blackwell.

Scotton, C. M. (1988). Self-enhancing codeswitching as interactional power. *Language and Communication, 8,* 199–211.

Scotton, C. M. (1990). Codeswitching and borrowing: Interpersonal and macrolevel meaning. In R. Jacobson (Ed.), *Codeswitching as a worldwide phenomenon* (pp. 85–110). New York: Peter Lang.

Searle, J. (1969). *Speech acts.* Cambridge: Cambridge University Press.

Searle, J. (1979). *Expression and meaning: Studies in the theory of speech acts.* Cambridge: Cambridge University Press.

Searle, J. (1981). The intentionality of intention and action. *Manuscrito, 4,* 77–102.

Shapira, A. (1989). *Visions in conflict.* Tel Aviv: Am Oved. [in Hebrew]

Shavit, Y. (1987). *The new Hebrew nation: An Israeli heresy and fantasy.* London: Frank Cass.

Sharwood-Smith. (1983). On first language in the second language acquirer. In S. Gass & L. Selinker (Eds.), *Language transfer in language learning* (pp. 222–231). Rowley, MA: Newbury.

Shuman, A. (1986). *Story telling rights: The uses of oral and written texts by urban adolescents.* Cambridge: Cambridge University Press.

Shutz, A. (1970). *Reflections on the problem of relevance.* New Haven: Yale University Press.

Silverstein, M. (1976). Shifters, linguistic categories and cultural description. In K. Basso & H. Selby (Eds.), *Meaning in anthropology* (pp. 11–55). Albuquerque: University of New Mexico Press.

Simmel, G. (1961). The sociology of sociability. In T. Parsons, E. Shils, K. D. Naegele, & J. R. Pitts (Eds.), *Theories of society: Foundations of modern sociological theory* (pp. 157–163). New York: The Free Press. (Original work published 1977).

Sinclair, J., & Coulthard, R. M. (1975). *Towards an analysis of discourse: The English used by teachers and pupils*. Oxford: Oxford University Press.

Smith-Rosenberg, C. (1985). *Disorderly conduct: Visions of gender in Victorian America*. New York: Oxford University Press.

Snow, C. (1977). The development of conversation between mothers and babies. *Journal of Child Language, 11*, 423–452.

Snow, C. (1984). Parent–child interaction and the development of communicative ability. In R. Schiefelbush & J. Pickar (Eds.), *Communicative competence: Acquisition and intervention* (pp. 69–107). Baltimore: University Park Press.

Snow, C. (1989). Understanding social interaction and language development: Sentences are not enough. In M. Bornstein & J. Bruner (Eds.), *Interaction in human development* (pp. 83–103). Hillsdale, NJ: Lawrence Erlbaum Associates.

Snow, C. E. (1991). Building memories: The ontogeny of autobiography. In D. Cicchetti & M. Beeghly (Eds.), *The self in transition: Infancy to childhood* (pp. 213–242). Chicago: University of Chicago Press.

Snow, C. E., & Dickinson, D. K. (1991). Skills that aren't basic in a new conception of literacy. In A. Purves & E. Jennings (Eds.), *Literate systems and individual lives: Perspectives on literacy and schooling* (pp. 175–273). Albany, NY: State University of New York Press.

Snow, C., & Ferguson, C. (Eds.). (1977). *Talking to children*. New York: Cambridge University Press.

Snow, C. E., & Goldfield, B. A. (1982). Building stories: The emergence of information structures from conversation. In D. Tannen (Ed.), *Analyzing discourse: Text and talk* (pp. 127–141). Washington, DC: Georgetown University Press.

Snow, C. E., Perlman, R., Gleason, J. B., & Hooshyar, N. (1990). Developmental perspectives on politeness: Sources of children's knowledge. *Journal of Pragmatics, 14*, 289–307.

Spolsky, B., & Walters, J. (1985). Jewish styles of worship: A conversational analysis. *International Journal of the Sociology of Language, 56*, 51–65.

Spradly, J. (1979). *The ethnographic interview*. New York: Holt, Rinehart & Winston.

Stahl, A. (1993). *Family and child-rearing in Oriental Jewry*. Jerusalem: Academon. [in Hebrew]

Steiner, G. (1975). *After babel: Aspects of language and translation*. Oxford: Oxford University Press.

Strauss, A. L. (1987). *Qualitative analysis for social scientists*. Cambridge: Cambridge University Press.

Swacker, M. (1976). Women's verbal behavior at learned and professional conferences. In B. L. Dubois & I. Crouch (Eds.), *The sociology of the language of American women* (pp. 155–160). San Antonio: Trinity University Press.

Tannen, D. (1980). A comparative analysis of oral narrative strategies. In W. Chafe (Ed.), *The pear stories* (pp. 51–87). Norwood, NJ: Ablex.

Tannen, D. (1981a). Indirectness in discourse: Ethnicity as conversational style. *Discourse Processes, 3*, 221–238.

Tannen, D. (1981b). New York Jewish conversational style. *International Journal of the Sociology of Language, 30*, 133–149.

Tannen, D. (1984). *Conversational style: Analyzing talk among friends*. Norwood, NJ: Ablex.

Tannen, D. (1985). Relative focus on involvement in oral and written discourse. In D. R. Olson, N. Torrance, & A. Hildyard (Eds.), *Literacy, language and learning* (pp. 125–147). Cambridge: Cambridge University Press.

Tannen, D. (1986). *That's not what I meant*. New York: Ballantine Books.

Tannen, D. (1989). *Talking voices: Repetition, dialogue and imagery in conversational discourse*. Cambridge: Cambridge University Press.

Tannen, D. (1990). *You just don't understand*. New York: William Morrow.

Toolan, M. J. (1988). *Narrative: A critical linguistic introduction*. London: Routledge & Kegan Paul.

Toury, G. (1977). *Translational norms and literary translation into Hebrew 1930–1945*. Tel Aviv: The Porter Institute for Poetics and Semiotics. [in Hebrew]

Varenne, H. (1977). *Americans together*. New York: Teachers College Press, Columbia University.

Varenne, H. (1992). *Ambiguous harmony: Family talk in America*. Norwood, NJ: Ablex.

Verschueren, J. (1985). *What people say they do with words*. Norwood, NJ: Ablex.

Vuchinich, S. (1984). Sequencing and social structure in family context. *Social Psychology Quarterly, 47*, 217–234.

Vuchinich, S. (1990). The sequential organization of closing in verbal family conflict. In A. D. Grimshaw (Ed.), *Conflict talk: Sociolinguistic investigations of arguments in conversation* (pp. 118–139). Cambridge: Cambridge University Press.

Vygotsky, L. S. (1978). *Mind in society: The development of higher psychological processes*. Cambridge, MA: Harvard University Press.

Watts, R. J. (1989). Relevance and relational work: Linguistic politeness as politic behavior. *Multilingua, 8*, 131–166.

Watts, R. J. (1991). *Power in family discourse*. Berlin: Mouton.

Weiler, J. (1991). Between a heroine and a whore. *Politica, 39*, 57–62.

Weinreich, U. (1953). *Languages in contact*. The Hague: Mouton.

Weirzbicka, A. (1991). *Cross-cultural pragmatics: The semantics of human interaction*. Berlin: Mouton de Gruyter.

Weitman, S. (1988). Personal names as cultural indicators: Trends in the national identity of Israelis 1882–1980. In N. Gertz (Ed.), *Perspectives on culture and society in Israel* (pp. 141–151). Tel-Aviv: Open University.

Weizman, E. (1989). Requestive hints. In S. Blum-Kulka, J. House, & G. Kasper (Eds.), *Cross-cultural pragmatics: Requests and apologies* (pp. 71–96). Norwood, NJ: Ablex.

Weizman, E., & Blum-Kulka, S. (1992). Ordinary misunderstandings. In M. Stamenov (Ed.), *Current advances in semantic theory* (pp. 417–433). Amsterdam: John Benjamins.

Wells, G. (1981). *Learning through interaction*. London: Cambridge University Press.

Wells, G. (1985). *Language development in the pre-school years*. Cambridge: Cambridge University Press.

Weltens, B. (1987). The attrition of foreign language skills: A literature review. *Applied Linguistics, 8*, 2–39.

Wertsch, J. (1985). *Vygotski and the social formation of mind*. Cambridge, MA: Harvard University Press.

Wilson, A. J., & Zeitlyn, D. (1995). The distribution of person-referring expressions in natural conversation. *Research on Language and Social Interaction, 28*, 61–92.

Wittgenstein, L. (1968). *Philosophical investigations* (3rd ed., G. E. M. Anscombe, Trans.). New York: Macmillan.

Wolfson, N. (1976). Speech events and natural speech: Some implications for sociolinguistic methodology. *Language in Society, 5*, 189–205.

Wolfson, N. (1983). An empirically based analysis of complimenting in American English. In N. Wolfson (Ed.), *Sociolinguistics and Language Composition* (pp. 82–96). Rowley, MA: Newberry.

Wolfson, N., D'Amico-Reisner, L., & Huber, L. (1983). How to arrange for social commitments in American English: The invitation. In N. Wolfson (Ed.), *Sociolinguistics and language acquisition* (pp. 116–131). Rowley, MA: Newbury.

Wootton, A. J. (1981). The management of grantings and rejections by parents in request sequences. *Semiotica, 37*(1/2), 59–89.

Young, K. (1987). *Taleworlds and storyrealms: The phenomenology of narrative*. Dodrecht: Martinus Nijhoff Publishers.

Zborowski, M., & Herzog, E. (1952). *Life is with people: The culture of the shtetl*. New York: Shoken Books.

APPENDIXES

Family Origin of Subjects' Parents and Grandparents

	Israelis		Jewish Americans		American Israelis	
	pa**	gr	pa	gr	pa	gr
Native*	4	5	17	7	20	7
Russia and Poland	30	51	12	32	22	51
Romania, Czechoslovakia, & Yugoslavia	4	12	—	2	—	2
Germany	2	5	3	6	2	2
England and the United States	2	1	—	—	—	—
Lebanon	1	2	—	—	—	—
Total***	44	76	32	47	44	62

*Native means Palestine for the Israeli families and the United States for Jewish American and American Israelis families.

**pa = parents, gr = grandparents. Information on parents is presented individually; information on grandparents is presented per couple.

***The numbers represent families for whom detailed information was available. Totals in the three Appendixes vary by availability of information. All families not included are of European background (see note 17, Chap. 1).

APPENDIX B
History of Languages Spoken*

Language	Israelis				American Israelis				Jewish Americans			
	Parents		Grandparents		Parents		Grandparents		Parents		Grandparents	
Hebrew	6	15.3%	3	3.9%	8	25%	22	39.3%	–	–	14	26.4%
Yiddish	1	2.5%	6	7.9%	–	–	4	7.1%	17	56.6%	6	11.3%
English	1	2.5%	–	–	11	34.4%	–	–	–	–	–	–
French	1	2.5%	2	2.6%	–	–	–	–	–	–	–	–
German	3	7.7%	7	9.2%	–	–	2	3.5%	1	3.3%	4	7.5%
French & German	–	–	–	–	–	–	–	–	1	3.3%	–	–
Yiddish + 1 language**	21	53.8%	38	50%	12	37.5%	28	50%	10	33.3%	28	52.8%
Yiddish + 2 languages***	1	2.5%	10	13.1%	4	3.1%	–	–	1	3.3%	1	1.8%
Russian & Hebrew	1	2.5%	2	2.6%								
French, Hebrew & Arabic	1	2.5%										
Hebrew, Arabic & Ladino	1	2.5%	2	2.6%								
English, French & Hebrew			2	2.6%								
Serbo-Croatian	2	5%	4	5.2%								
Total (subjects)	39	100%	76	100%	32	100%	56	100%	30	100%	53	100%

*Based on responses to the question, "What languages were spoken at home by your parents/grandparents?"

**Included in this category are: Hebrew, Russian, Polish, Romanian, English, and Hungarian.

***Included in this category are: Russian & Polish, Hungarian & Romanian, Polish & German, Romanian & French, English & Russian.

APPENDIX C

Patterns of Immigration—Subjects' Grandparents*

Born	Israelis					American Israelis					Jewish Americans		
	Emigrated to			Did not emigrate	Died in Holocaust**	Emigrated to			Did not emigrate	Died in Holocaust	Emigrated to		Did not emigrate
	Israel	England	Canada			USA	Canada	Israel			USA	France	
Poland	3	2		6	12	12			2	4	6		4
USSR	9	2	2	6	6	27	1	2	3		20		2
USA								1	6				6
Germany	1			3							2	2	
Austria						2					2		
Romania	5										4		
Czechoslovakia	2			5									
Yugoslavia				4									
Israel				5									
Lebanon				2									
Hungary						1							
Europe***						1			5				
TOTAL	20	4	2	31	18	43	1	3	16	4	34	2	12

*Represents families for whom information was provided.
**We asked specifically about immigration but not what happened to those who did not emigrate. Hence, there might be more who died in the Holocaust.
***Country not specified.

297

Author Index

SUBJECT INDEX